和食

WASHOKU

WASHOKU
Recipes from the Japanese Home Kitchen

Elizabeth Andoh

Photography by Leigh Beisch

TEN SPEED PRESS
Berkeley

The publisher and author wish to thank ceramic artists
Catherine White, Warren Frederick, and Romig Streeter for
the generous loan of their work.

Frontispiece: tying bundles of komatsuna *(left)*
and spinach (right) for blanching

Library of Congress Cataloging-in-Publication Data
Andoh, Elizabeth.
    Washoku : recipes from the Japanese home kitchen /
    Elizabeth Andoh; photography by Leigh Beisch.
        p. cm.
    Includes index.
    1. Cookery, Japanese. I. Title.
    TX724.5.J3A53 2005
    641.5952--dc22
                                        2005013640

ISBN-13: 978-1-58008-519-9

Printed in Singapore

Cover and text design by Toni Tajima
Food styling by Karen Shinto
Prop styling by Sara Slavin
Photography assistance by Angelica Cao
Styling assistance by Katie Christ

12 11 10 9 8 7 6

First Edition

CONTENTS

ACKNOWLEDGMENTS

The collective observations, opinions, and creative energy of many people enabled me to complete this book.

I embarked upon *Washoku* by seeking an advocate who would champion my cause and help me find the right editorial home. Rebecca Staffel (then at the Doe Coover Agency) and later Doe, herself, undertook my project with enthusiasm, helping me hone my ideas and suggesting I speak with Aaron Wehner at Ten Speed Press. Terrific advice! A master at streamlining text, Aaron embraced the challenges of making the foreign seem familiar, and proved to be the exacting yet patient editor I sought to travel with me over rough writing terrain.

Along the way, Aaron assembled an amazing team of professionals to work with us: Asking astute questions with dogged thoroughness, Sharon Silva worked copy-editing miracles on my tangle of cross-references. The expertise of Ken DellaPenta (gifted indexer) and Karen Levy (meticulous proofreader) is gratefully acknowledged. Toni Tajima, undaunted by my information-dense manuscript, applied her abundant design talents to making it visually exciting, yet easy to read. Photographer Leigh Beisch, ably assisted by Angelica Cao, worked entirely with natural light in her San Francisco studio to create the vibrant images you see here. Karen Shinto, deftly assisted by Katie Christ, drew inspiration from the traditions of *washoku* and applied her own modern, American sensibility to styling the food. I am particularly pleased that the work of my talented ceramicist friends Warren Frederick, Romig Streeter, and Catherine White could be incorporated into many of the photographs.

Friends and colleagues Cynthia Glover, Gary Goldberg, Dana Jacobi, Joan Jacobs, and Alice and Halsey North patiently listened to me agonize over the best way to use my acquired knowledge and accumulated experience to enable and inspire others to explore the pleasures of *washoku*.

Early on, I decided to recruit volunteers living outside Japan who would reflect my readership. In December of 2002, I sent out a call for help through my e-newsletter looking for those who wanted to try their hand at preparing meals to satisfy their aesthetic appetite, as well as physical hunger. My electronic missive reached perhaps a thousand people, many of whom had attended classes at A Taste of Culture, the culinary arts program I run out of my Tokyo home. Expecting no more than a few replies, I was overwhelmed by more than two hundred enthusiastic offers of assistance! Eventually, a smaller, geographically diverse group of *washoku* volunteers emerged, and a core of dedicated aides (living in Tokyo at the time)—Laurie Bannister, Claire Baram, Lori Steinbrunner, Yukari Pratt, Christopher Raab, and Jessica Wickham—helped me organize and manage the project.

Abundant thanks to my earnest *washoku* recipe testers, constructive critics, and those who generously shared their kitchens and cooking experiences with me: Janice Matsumoto Cha, Marilyn Chohaney, Nora and Brian Compton, Randi Danforth, Ann Duncan, Stella Fong, Bob and Mary Lou Heiss, Jana Horii, Jeri Jackson, Holly Kawakami, Lesley Koch, Jeff and Eva Koehler, Adam Kowit, Karen Krueger, Heidi Latsko, Simon Leake, Sunhee Lee, Steve and Michiko Levine, Bruce Matheson, Carol Negiar, Tammy Nickel, Amanda Robinson, Bina Sasenaraine, Connie Sathre, Tara Shioya, Beverly Sing, Sandy Sterner, Madeleine Vedel, Carolyn Beth Weil, Catherine White, Pat Wickham, Cynthia and Luke Wimer, Suzanne Yamamoto, Judith L. Yanis, Amanda Zimlich, and Ruth Znotins. Your feedback and support has been invaluable.

Most of my adult life has been spent in Japan, where I have had the good fortune to participate in warm friendships and receive valuable mentoring. Members of the Ohta family (in particular Eiko and her now fully grown daughter, Masumi), with whom I stayed shortly after I settled in Tokyo, have remained steadfast friends and kitchen cohorts throughout the years. The Yanagihara family, at first Master Toshio and later his son, Kazunari, and daughter-in-law, Noriko, patiently educated and nurtured me in Japan's classical culinary arts. The Andoh women—Teruko, Yohko (Yokoi), and Nobuko (Okashita)—continue to share their *washoku* wisdom with me. And Kiyoko Andoh, whose spirit keeps me constant kitchen company, inspired in me a lasting curiosity and enduring respect for traditional home cooking.

The love and encouragement of my husband, Atsunori, and our daughter, Rena, nourish me daily. And had it not been for my mother, Caroline Saxe, who mustered the courage to let me go half a world away, I could not have found such pleasure and fulfillment. Thank you each and all.

INTRODUCTION

Washoku, literally the "harmony of food," is a way of thinking about what we eat and how it can nourish us. The term describes both a culinary philosophy and the simple, nutritionally balanced food prepared in that spirit.

My first encounter with *washoku* was nearly forty years ago when I suddenly, and serendipitously, found myself staying with the Andoh family on the Japanese island of Shikoku. My urban American sensibilities were challenged by more than the rural plumbing that first summer. Hunger forced me to be adventurous at table, where my curiosity grew, along with my appetite, for things Japanese.

I was particularly impressed by the rhythm and flow of activity in the Andoh kitchen. This was the cherished, domestic domain of Kiyoko Andoh, the woman who was to become my mother-in-law. From the start, she encouraged me to call her Okaasan (literally "mother," it is also a term of endearment and respect for women who care for others).

Okaasan moved about her daily routine with determination and grace, feeding the Andoh household—children (and their friends), grandchildren (and their friends), workers at

Clockwise from top left: my husband, Atsunori, and I, c. 1969; my mother-in-law and my daughter, Rena, c. 1989; and the original Andoh home (no longer standing) in Shikoku, with rice field in foreground, c. 1967

the family-owned factory (and some of their family members), and foreign visitors (me) alike. Running such a large, busy home required not only consummate culinary skill, but also an understanding of the value of nutritious, wholesome food and a knack for balancing the budget.

Okaasan's ability to integrate smoothly such practical considerations as getting meals on the table in several shifts (early risers, after-school lessons, and factory overtime needed to be accommodated) with a deep artistic sensibility (fashioning a flower from a carrot, or reflecting on the texture and shape of tableware) was remarkable. A fine cook for whom the ways of *washoku* were deeply ingrained and practiced daily, Okaasan never had occasion to doubt the wisdom of this time-honored approach.

Because I had no language skills at first with which to question or challenge, I merely watched the activity around me and tried to follow suit. I desperately sought to grasp the logic of it all, or at least discern some predictable patterns. Later, as I acquired fluency in Japanese and broadened my experience to include formal culinary training at the Yanagihara School of Classical Japanese Cooking, I fine-tuned my understanding of the principles and practice of *washoku.* It is those ideas and skills that I am sharing with you in this book.

Washoku: The Five Principles

The calligraphy for *wa* is used to refer to things indigenous to Japanese culture. In the realm of food, *washoku* distinguishes Japanese food from foreign-inspired cuisines, such as *yōshoku*, or Western-style food.

The philosophy and practice of *washoku* can best be summarized by a set of five principles that describe how to achieve nutritional balance and aesthetic harmony at mealtime. The first three principles—one each concerning color, flavor palate, and choice of cooking method—deal with the practical considerations of food preparation. The fourth principle defines the sensual nature of food—that is, the need for food to appeal to all the five senses, not just taste and smell. The final principle, which is more spiritual and philosophic, compels us to appreciate both human endeavor and the natural forces that provide for us.

The five principles of *washoku* are as follows:

Five colors, or *go shiki,* suggests that every meal include foods that are red, yellow, green, black, and white. (Often very dark colors, particularly deep purple—eggplant, grapes—and sometimes brown—shiitaké mushrooms—are counted as black.) Vitamins and minerals naturally come into balance with a colorful range of foods.

Five tastes, or *go mi,* describes what the Japanese call *anbai,* a harmonious balance of flavors—salty, sour, sweet, bitter, and spicy—that ensures our palates are pleasantly stimulated, but not overwhelmed.

Five ways, or *go hō,* urges cooks to prepare food by a variety of methods, simmering, broiling, and steaming being some of the most basic. By combining various methods at every meal, it is easy to limit the total amount of sugar, salt, and oil consumed, thereby avoiding excessive calories.

Five senses, or *go kan,* advises cooks to be mindful not only of taste, but also of sight, sound, smell, and touch (in this case, the texture of food as we eat it).

Five outlooks, or *go kan mon,* are rules concerned with the partaking of food and have a strong basis in Buddhism. Indeed, many Buddhist temples in Japan that serve vegetarian fare (*shōjin ryōri*) will have these rules written on their menus. They instruct us, first, to respect the efforts of all those who contributed their toil to cultivating and preparing our food; second, to do good deeds worthy of receiving such nourishment; third, to come to the table without ire; fourth, to eat for spiritual as well as temporal well-being; and fifth, to be serious in our struggle to attain enlightenment.

The five principles are not unique to Japanese foodways. Many Asian cultures share similar beliefs. Indeed, the ideas arrived from China by way of the Korean peninsula about a thousand years ago. In Japan, the five principles intertwined with indigenous Shinto beliefs, such as humanity's oneness with nature, and evolved into a broadly encompassing, deeply integrated culinary philosophy. A vocabulary emerged to describe various aspects of this distinctive Japanese food culture. *Kisetsukan* is what the Japanese call their keen appreciation for seasonal cycles and other rhythms of nature. The word *shun* is used to describe a point in time when a particular food is at its peak of flavor. *Shun* can last for several weeks or even months—or it can be as fleeting as a few hours or days. The notion of *meisanbutsu,* or "regional specialties," holds locally produced foodstuffs in especially high regard. In Japan, where lakes, rivers, and the ocean provide abundant food to complement the harvest of the land, the phrase *umi no sachi, yama no sachi* (the bounty of the sea, the bounty of the mountains) describes the harmonious union of foods from both land and water sources.

As with other aspects of culture, such as language and dress, foodways settle in and are eventually taken for granted by the society that gave rise to them. Most Japanese today would have a hard time articulating *washoku* notions, and would not usually discuss among themselves the guidelines for assembling a nutritionally balanced, aesthetically pleasing meal. Yet when choosing items from an à la carte restaurant menu, selecting prepared dishes to take home from a department-store food hall, or purchasing packaged food from a convenience store or supermarket, most Japanese will, by instinct, employ the five principles on some level to create culinary harmony.

Despite the pervasiveness of *washoku* in Japanese food culture, the word itself and the concepts associated with it are relatively unknown outside the country, even among aficionados of Japanese cooking. And although its origins are deeply rooted in Japanese culinary history and habits, *washoku* can be practiced and enjoyed outside Japan, by Japanese and non-Japanese alike. Selecting ingredients at their peak of seasonal flavor, choosing locally available foods from both the land and the sea, appealing to and engaging all the senses, using a collage of color, employing a variety of food preparations, and assembling an assortment of flavors—a *washoku* approach to cooking gives the creative and contemplative cook an opportunity to satisfy his or her own aesthetic hunger while providing sustenance and sensory pleasure to others.

Putting Theory into Practice

To demonstrate how *washoku* principles are applied to ordinary meals, I will guide you, step by step, through the planning, preparation, and presentation of three complete menus. Simple preparations, such as those in the first menu, are often set up on a tray and served together. Not every dish needs to fulfill all the considerations of five colors, cooking methods, flavors, and so forth. Rather, these elements can cumulatively meet the guidelines for a balanced *washoku* meal or, if served in progression, unfold over the course of a lunch or dinner.

The first menu follows a common meal plan known as *ichi-ju san-sai.* Literally, "one broth, three dishes," the meal is actually composed of five dishes, not four as you might expect (rice is assumed to be part of every meal; indeed, the word *gohan* means both "cooked rice" and "meal"). Our nourishing *ichi-ju san-sai* menu (illustrated on page 4) is made up of a soup (Miso Soup with Enoki Mushrooms, page 117), a featured dish (Miso-Marinated Broiled Fish, page 229), two side dishes (Soy-Braised Hijiki and Carrots, page 187, and Citron-Pickled Chinese Cabbage, page 218), and rice (Rice with Mixed Grains, page 139).

This sample *washoku* menu incorporates vibrant and soft hues, textured and smooth foods, and delicate and assertive flavors. Fulfilling the five-colors principle, we have green (*mitsuba,* floating in the soup, and pickled Chinese cabbage), red (salmon, carrots, and chile pepper threads), yellow (lemon with the fish), white (rice, tōfu, and enoki mushrooms in the soup), and black (*hijiki*). In addition to providing visual interest, the color range ensures nutritional balance: green vegetables are rich in vitamin A, carrots are packed with carotene, citrus are rich in vitamin C, white rice mixed with various seeds and grains provide many B vitamins, and black *hijiki* is an excellent source of calcium.

Each of these dishes employs a different cooking method: the fish is seared with heat (broiling, grilling, skillet braising, and pan searing all fall within the realm of Japanese *yaki mono,* or seared foods), the *hijiki* is briefly sautéed in oil before being simmered with carrots in seasoned sea stock, the lightly pickled cabbage is considered "raw" because it has not been treated with heat, and the miso-enriched soup is simmered. Steamed rice completes the menu. Intake of fats and oils, salt, and sugar is limited by varying the preparation methods.

When you begin to eat, you appreciate that the rich, salty flavor of the miso-marinated fish is nicely balanced with the tartness of the juice from the lemon that garnishes it. The *hijiki* and carrot dish, cooked in a sweetened soy sauce and finished with a nutty, faintly bitter accent of toasted sesame seeds, provides a welcome counterpoint to an otherwise savory meal. Textures and shapes are varied, too: silky cubes of tōfu in the soup, slender stalks of enoki mushrooms, crisp and succulent slices of pickled cabbage, which are spiced with fiery threads of *tōgarashi* chile pepper.

Not all food prepared in the *washoku* manner needs to be a multidish menu. Many simple single-dish meals benefit from the five-principles approach to preparing food. My second example, Rice Bowl with Three-Colored Topping (page 153), is a *domburi,* or a casual meal-in-a-bowl. The word *domburi* refers to both the bowl itself and the foods served in it. Typically, *domburi* are large, deep bowls filled halfway with cooked rice and then topped with a variety of foods.

When plated and viewed from above, this *domburi* appears to be a circle divided into three wedges. One is bright yellow with corn kernels, another green with small peas, and the third a rich auburn brown with braised chicken. Where these wedges converge at the center is a garnish of shredded red pickled ginger, or perhaps a cherry tomato, and a few squares of spicy, soy-simmered jet black kelp. As you eat, the white rice beneath the toppings becomes visible. Yellow, green, red, black, and white—a five-colored meal-in-a-bowl.

Steamed rice, skillet-braised chicken, blanched vegetables, pickled ginger, and simmered kelp demonstrate the multimethod approach to food preparation. The combination of soy sauce and sugar, used to braise the chicken and simmer the kelp, balances salty and sweet flavors. Though not as sour as some pickles found in the Japanese pantry (Red-and-White Pickled Radishes, page 221, for example), the red pickled ginger here hints at tartness, as would a cherry tomato. The kelp condiment is blanched in a vinegar-water solution before it is braised in the sweetened soy. Finally, touches of ginger and *sanshō* pepper provide spicy accents that help bring harmony to the meal.

I offer a third example here: a soup-and-sandwich lunch. This menu shows that *washoku* meals can be assembled with entirely non-Japanese foods. Imagine the following: pale and creamy potato-leek soup, nutritionally and aesthetically enhanced by a garnish of snipped chives and minced parsley,

A "one broth, three dishes" menu (clockwise from top left): Citron-Pickled Chinese Cabbage (page 218), Soy-Braised Hijiki and Carrots (page 187), Miso Soup with Enoki Mushrooms (page 117), Miso-Marinated Broiled Fish (page 229), and Rice with Mixed Grains (page 139)

alongside tuna salad spread on triangles of whole-grain toast, accompanied by a lemon wedge, several cherry tomatoes, crisp radish sprouts, and pitted black olives. As with the purely Japanese sample menus, this American lunch follows the color, flavor palate, and multi-preparation guidelines of a *washoku* meal. Because it adheres to the five principles, this soup-and-sandwich lunch also achieves nutritional balance and visual interest.

. . .

Far from a rigid set of rules that constrict the creative process, the underlying principles of *washoku* provide a convenient framework for considering the many practical issues and aesthetic possibilities inherent in meal preparation. If you enjoy lavishing time and creative energy on preparing food for yourself and others, the *washoku* planning process will excite and energize you. When you feel pressed for time, a well-stocked *washoku* kitchen lets you throw together balanced meals—they do not have to be Japanese ones—in short order. The *Washoku* Pantry (page 10) will help you assemble a basic larder and answer questions you might have regarding unfamiliar ingredients called for in the recipes. A companion section, In the *Washoku* Kitchen (page 66), catalogs the techniques and tools you will need to transform foodstuffs into harmonious meals.

Although the *washoku* approach can be applied to any cuisine, specific *washoku* recipes emerged from a rich Japanese food tradition. The stories and legends associated with these dishes are acquired quite naturally by anyone brought up in a Japanese household. They are experienced, not taught, and are rarely shared across the cultural culinary divide. In recipe headnotes and sidebars, I have included historical notes to illuminate, and entice you to try, classic *washoku* fare. I was not concerned with being clever, trendy, or original when choosing recipes. Quite the opposite: from a huge *washoku* repertoire, I chose practical, typical dishes that would tempt you while I taught you, and build your confidence while I nourished you. Suggestions on how to coordinate dishes to create *washoku* meals are offered in Kitchen Harmony notes that accompany many of the recipes.

Washoku as a notion, and in practice, compels those who prepare it to consider the total dining environment. After care has been taken in choosing foods that nourish both body and mind, preparing the *washoku* table excites the aesthetic appetite. Setting the Table, Setting the Stage (opposite) offers you ideas and inspiration, while smaller shards of practical advice on food presentation—organized as Harmony at Table notes—are scattered throughout the chapters. By being attentive to the impact of color, shape, texture, and motif at table, you can create an infinite variety of moods, thus satisfying your aesthetic, as well as physical, hunger.

Omakasé and Kaiseki Cuisines

I am often asked whether *washoku* applies only to home cooking, and what relationship exists between *washoku* and *omakasé* ("leave it to the chef" tasting menus served at high-end restaurants), or between *washoku* and *kaiseki* (both the *kaiseki* cuisine that traces its origins to the Japanese tea ceremony and the banquet-style *kaiseki* meals offered at elegant establishments). Although I have chosen domestic kitchens as the focus of this book, *washoku* should not be equated solely with home cooking. It would be misleading to ignore the principles of *washoku* as practiced by Japanese food professionals. They are as essential, and applicable, to the world of restaurant dining as they are to home-cooked meals.

Tasting menus that showcase the creativity of a chef are not unique to Japanese dining traditions. *Omakasé*, however, is more than just a meal: it is a relationship of mutual trust and appreciation between customer and establishment, guided by the principles of *washoku*. Those who plan and prepare the meal (the chef and other food professionals) take pleasure in considering the needs of those who will partake of it, and diners (guests, customers), in turn, agree to abandon themselves to the dining drama that unfolds at table. Rather than focus on

exotic foods flown in from faraway places, the *washoku* professional will seek out local products to showcase and celebrate *shun*, aware of the balance that needs to be struck between marine and terrestrial sources, color, cooking method, and flavor.

Two rather esoteric phrases, both coined by Sen no Rikyu, the sixteenth-century philosopher and aesthete credited with refining the world of tea and *kaiseki* cuisine served at the tea ceremony, express sentiments inherent in a *washoku* outlook. The first of these, *ichi go, ichi é* (one moment, one meeting), demonstrates the importance of creating a specific sense of time and place with each meal—a fleeting but magic moment of shared cooking and dining pleasure that can be fondly remembered but never re-created. In planning and preparing *kaiseki* meals, it is the *washoku* host who coordinates foodstuffs that highlight *shun* with culinary motifs and tableware that enhance *kisetsukan*. The goal is to create a unique dining experience for their guests, one that is mindful of seasonal and ceremonial considerations, while accommodating individual preferences.

The second phrase, *wabi sabi* (subdued elegance, charm of the ordinary), admires humility and values understatement. In the world of Japanese culinary endeavor, particular respect is afforded those who transform humble foodstuffs into simple, yet stunning meals.

A Note about Language

For more than thirty years, I have been writing about Japan and various aspects of its food and culture, hoping to inform and entertain my readers. Because I write for English-language publications, I struggle with how best to convey habits and notions that may be foreign to my readers, how to make seemingly alien procedures feel comfortable to them. What key bits of information should I offer to help them make sense of it all?

And what words should I use?

In taking on the challenge of communicating ideas, language becomes many things: a precious tool with which to

Setting the Table, Setting the Stage

Much of the exhilaration I feel when practicing *washoku* is the unabashed pleasure of matching food to vessel. At a *washoku* table, there is no concern for uniformity of tableware throughout the meal. Rather, the cook is encouraged to use containers fashioned from a variety of materials—lacquer, glass, paper, stoneware, and porcelain are a few of the possibilities—and of various shapes and sizes to enhance the food. He or she might even borrow bits of nature, such as wood, leaves, and shells, and incorporate the hints they provide into the display of food. By melding disparate flavors, aromas, textures, sounds, and images, the thoughtful cook engages all of the senses, achieving harmony at table.

Creating a sense of time and place is important as well. The season and occasion suggest certain color schemes and motifs borrowed from nature or folklore. After a long, blisteringly hot summer, I awake one morning late in September to an unexpected chill in the air. I happily reset my breakfast tray, replacing the delicate, blue-streaked porcelain plate that had suggested a refreshing stream during the heat and humidity of summer with a rustic dish shaped like a maple leaf. Savoring the air-dried, mirin-glazed mackerel on my autumnal plate, I anticipate crisp days ahead.

Pottery suits the Japanese temperament and table particularly well, I think, because it is a melding of natural forces with human endeavor. Clay is a wholly organic product of the earth that is taken and shaped by human skill and ingenuity. The process of glazing and firing is again a blend of nature and man-made technology. A dramatic range of styles emerges: the crackled blue glaze of *seiji* ware, the rough-hewn bronze tones of the Shino kilns, the delicate and colorful *iro-é* patterns of which Kutani ware is perhaps the most famous, and the popular *somé-tsuké* blue and white underglaze typified by Imari ware.

Bamboo, in its natural form, is a hollow yet sturdy receptacle that is easily adapted to the needs of food storage and service. The Japanese preserve this natural capability and both increase its usefulness and enhance its beauty by shaping segments of bamboo into bowls, platters, baskets, and utensils. *Sasa,* the smooth leaves of bamboo saplings, are gracefully tapered, making them both lovely and useful: extended to display a grilled fish, or curved to enclose a soft rice-flour pastry. Long before plastic wrap or cooking parchment was invented, *také no kawa* (dried, mature bamboo bark) made excellent wrappers for cooking and transporting food.

Standing in my kitchen before the cupboard crammed with dishes, cups, trays, chopsticks, and other tabletop accessories, I feel a surge of creative power. This evening, I choose a Bizen ware platter from the shelf. It is deceptively simple: a dark slab of unglazed, unpainted clay no bigger than a sheet of paper. Yet its surface glows with soft russet and amber markings, some shiny and round as a full moon, others muted with blurred edges. On this wildly unique canvas, I paint a mental image: a random convergence of pearly white chunks of steaming daikon interspersed with glistening bits of soy-simmered cod. Golden needles of fresh *yuzu* (citron peel) are scattered across the fish-and-vegetable stew, mimicking the platter's tawny freckles.

A closer look at the same platter reveals a mottled dab of ashen blue in one corner, and a showering of ocher flecks nearby. I now conjure up a deeply green tuft of parsley set at an angle against a haystack of pale cucumber shreds—the backdrop for firm but lushly ripe wedges of tomato at the center of the platter. To complete this imagined *otsukuri,* or "creative arrangement" of fresh foods, I mentally place a small russet-colored, rough-hewn saké cup to the side. I pour some pale, creamy mustard miso sauce into it to use as salad dressing.

At the back of the cupboard, I glimpse a boldly beautiful plate from Tottori Prefecture's Ushinoto kiln—half black, half aqua green—that sets me off on my next culinary daydream. I picture Rice Curry (page 155) on the plate, a mound of snowy white, steamed rice at its center, partially covered by a tumeric-tinted, curry-flavored chicken stew. Several sweet-and-sour *rakkyō* bulbs (imagine sweet pickled pearl onions) and shreds of spicy, red *beni shōga* ginger nestle against the rice where it is met by the thick, golden sauce. In my mind's eye, this dish is paired with a salad of soft lettuces and crisp, sliced cucumbers, mounded in a frosted glass bowl. Form and function are brought into harmony at table.

fashion images; a mirror in which culture can be both magnified and reflected; and, because so many words cannot be easily transliterated and translated, a source of frustration. Since no single, functional standard that everyone agrees on for transliterating and translating Japanese to English exists, I must devise my own system. Here, as in the past, I have given great thought to this problem.

Since the start of work on this book several years ago, many volunteer recipe testers and assistants scattered around the globe have shared their valuable opinions and offered helpful suggestions to me. My current system incorporates their collective experience and reflects their endeavor to integrate *washoku* into their non-Japanese households.

For the most part, spelling in this book follows the basic pattern of my previous books: my goal is to get speakers of English to pronounce the words as close to the original Japanese as possible. To that end, I use a modified Hepburn system, keeping the important macron, or "long mark," that alerts speakers to an extended vowel sound. The difference between long and short vowel sounds are critically important in Japanese: *Ōba* is a broad-leafed herb (also known as *shiso*), but *oba* is my auntie.

I have borrowed a familiar accent mark from French to help you pronounce final *e* sounds as "ay." *Agé* is pronounced "ah-gay," not "age" (*g* sounds are hard, like good and great; soft *g* sounds are written with a *j*). The letters *r* and *l* and *m* and *n* are often used interchangeably, and there is no consensus among academics or editors. I have chosen *ramen* not *larmen* for Chinese-style noodles, and *kombu* not *konbu* for kelp, but not everyone will agree with me.

Whether to provide English translations of Japanese words is similarly fraught. I am delighted the Japanese word *nori* has finally entered the lexicon because I can now use that word, rather than the unappetizing and inaccurate "seaweed" (it is a cultivated aquatic plant, not a weed) or the puzzling "laver," both of which still commonly appear on package labels. And thank goodness I no longer need to call *tōfu* "bean curd" (it is really the solidified whey, not the curd of soybean milk), because it, too, has become entrenched in the lexicon. (Note, though, that I have modified the commonly encountered spelling, to include the important macron mark.) But what to do about the many different kinds of nori and tōfu, such as *yaki nori* and *ajitsuké nori,* or *abura agé* and *yaki-dōfu?* I decided to use a combination of English modifier and Japanese name. *Yaki nori* becomes toasted nori and *ajitsuké nori* becomes seasoned nori. *Abura agé* are fried tōfu slices, *yaki-dōfu* is a block of grilled tōfu, and so forth. In the case of some compounds, it is the Japanese word that modifies an English one: shiitaké mushrooms, soba noodles, and *kabocha* squash. My goal in all cases is to help you understand the relationship of these ingredients to one another, while providing a simple way of managing the words in the body of the recipe.

When dealing with more obscure foodstuffs like *konnyaku,* the cryptic translations "yam cake" and "devil's tongue jelly" do not help you know, or come to love, this homely, funny-smelling, but quite marvelous ingredient. I wanted to wipe the slate clean and start again with the original, *konnyaku,* and try to build a new and positive image of the food. When I wasn't sure whether readers would know enough about an ingredient to purchase the correct thing and use it properly, I provided a page reference to the discussion of it in The *Washoku* Pantry (page 10).

Some foods are so well known by their English names— sesame oil, soy sauce, vinegar—that to introduce the Japanese word in the text seemed burdensome. Should you want to know what the item is called in Japanese, refer to the pantry, where I have included the full and proper Japanese name in roman letters.

THE WASHOKU PANTRY

THE CLASSIC JAPANESE LARDER brims with an incredible diversity of shelf-stable marine and terrestrial items, dried, salted, fermented, and other preserved foodstuffs that augment fresh produce, meat, poultry, tōfu products, eggs, and fish. What the Japanese refer to as *umi no sachi,* or "bounty of the ocean," includes both cultivated and wild plants and animals (and their by-products) obtained from ponds, rivers, streams, and the open sea. Similarly, *yama no sachi,* or "bounty of the mountain," typically encompasses both farmed and found-in-nature foods, such as roots and shoots, herbs and sprouts, shrubs, fungi, fruits, leafy and flowering plants, beans, grains, seeds, and nuts. These are harvested and gathered in flat and terraced fields, in dense forests, and in hilly terrain.

Here, you will find detailed information on ingredients called for throughout this book. Whenever possible, I have clustered items together into categories. Because often it is the subtle difference between kinds of miso or vinegar that is confusing, grouping them will make it easier to compare them. Alternative ingredients, should you not be able to find the item described, are indicated where possible, with more specific substitution information provided in the recipes. When a pantry ingredient is discussed further in the techniques and equipment chapter, In the *Washoku* Kitchen, I have provided a cross-reference to the relevent page or pages.

Taking Stock

Look in your cupboard, refrigerator, and freezer. What, if any of the items listed in this section, do you already have on hand? Check expiration dates; some of what you have may need to be tossed out. Spoilage, of course, is the biggest issue, but the quality level of flavor, texture, and aroma is also important.

Most pantry items are shelf stable and best stored at room temperature. That means avoiding extremes of heat and cold and keeping the foodstuff dry and away from direct light. Some pantry items, such as soy sauce, sesame paste, miso, and mirin, will maintain superior flavor and aroma if refrigerated after opening, though these items will not spoil if stored on a cool, dry shelf. Several Japanese condiments and pickles, however, such as soy-simmered kelp and pink pickled ginger, should be refrigerated from the start and consumed fairly quickly. This is especially true for the homemade varieties, for which I provide recipes.

Although the premodern Japanese home did not have artificial refrigeration, cold storage from October through May was easily achieved by placing items on verandas or in other protected outdoor locations, or in unheated auxiliary kitchens. During the summer, slatted bamboo mats, called *sudaré,* angled against tubs of pickles or vats of miso paste, would block sunlight, providing shady storage space in well-ventilated rooms. Water sprinkled directly on the mats and on the earthen or stone floors helped cool the space, too. It is certainly not necessary for you to re-create such a rustic setting in your modern kitchen. However, if you struggle with limited space, know that many items can be kept in drawers or on shelves.

Essentials of the Washoku Pantry

There are ten foodstuffs that comprise a basic *washoku* pantry, ingredients I would like you to have on hand all the time. Four of these are shelf-stable, dried items used primarily to make stock: *kombu* (kelp), *katsuo-bushi* (bonito flakes), *iriko* (dried sardines), and dried shiitaké mushrooms. None is particularly attractive, and some may smell odd to the uninitiated. Yet these homely foodstuffs are powerhouses of flavor-enhancing glutamates that will elevate ordinary ingredients to highly flavorful cuisine.

Five fermented products are constantly used as seasonings: miso, soy sauce, rice vinegar, saké, and mirin. The fermentation process introduces healthful organisms that aid in digestion, improve nutrition, and add complexity and depth of flavor.

The final foodstuff is rice, for which the Japanese language has many words. *Okomé* is rice that has been harvested, dried, and threshed; it is the uncooked raw ingredient called for in rice recipes.

In the pantry listings that follow, essential items are noted with an asterisk.

Expanding Your Culinary Repertoire

A second group of foodstuffs will expand your culinary repertoire considerably. Most of them are *kambutsu* (dried items) and other relatively shelf-stable foods, so they can be mail ordered if you cannot find them locally (see Resources on page 309). Properly stored, they will keep for quite some time.

Wakamé, hijiki buds and stems, sheets of toasted nori, a marine herb called *ao nori,* and *kanten* (gelatin) are some of the sea items that can enrich your pantry and daily diet. Recommended fresh items from fields, forests, and mountains include ginger and a related rhizome called *myōga,* and *ki no mé,* the leaves of the *sanshō* pepper plant. Although it is rare to find whole, fresh wasabi roots outside Japan, tubes of paste containing grated root have become more readily available. Several herbs can be grown from seed in your garden or in a deep windowsill pot: *mitsuba, shiso* leaves and seeds, and radish sprouts called *kaiwaré.*

Dried and preserved items from the land include *kampyō* (gourd ribbons), *kiriboshi* daikon (shredded radish), sesame seeds, *tōgarashi* (dried red chile pepper), *shichimi tōgarashi* (seven-spice blend), mustard, *sanshō* (peppercorns; most readily available dried and pulverized), and dried *yuzu* (citron) peel. *Uméboshi* (pickled plums) are eaten as a condiment, while the deep purple-red shiso leaves that tint the plums are dried and pulverized to make a delightful herb called *yukari. Panko,* coarse, light bread crumbs, are used in several recipes.

Sugar and salt are common ingredients in *washoku* dishes, and descriptions of the best types to buy are provided below. Also cataloged below are many of the other shelf-stable ingredients called for in this book, as well as fresh ingredients, with an emphasis on produce, fish, and seafood.

BEANS

Dried beans, which are an excellent source of protein, calcium, iron, and fiber, have long played an important role in the traditional Japanese diet. When stored in a dark, cool, dry place, they will usually keep for a year or more. Although not particularly difficult, dried-bean cookery does require time and an action plan. Recipes in this book guide you through several distinct preparation stages, starting with the dried pantry item and ending with a richly seasoned and fully cooked food.

The ten essentials of The Washoku *Pantry (clockwise from top left): soy sauce, mirin, dried shiitaké mushrooms, saké, iriko (dried sardines), Hidaka kombu (kelp), katsuo-bushi (bonito flakes), rice, brown rice vinegar, and Saikyo shiro miso*

Adzuki Beans

These dried red beans are used as both a savory element, such as in Soy-Simmered Kabocha Squash with Red Beans (page 206), and a sweet element, such as in Chunky Red Bean Jam (page 108). All adzuki beans will bleed a deep maroon, but the variety known as *sasagé mamé* yields a particularly appetizing shade and, despite their delicate appearance, the beans hold their shape well during cooking. They may be slightly more expensive than ordinary adzuki but, when available, are the dried red bean of choice.

Dried Soybeans (daizu)

The most nutritious, important, and versatile dried bean is the *daizu,* and indeed it is written with a pair of ideograms for "big" or "important" and "bean." It is the source for such soy foods as tōfu, soy sauce, miso, and *kinako* (toasted soy flour), and is also cooked as a vegetable, as in Slow-Simmered Daizu with Assorted Vegetables (page 189).

DUMPLING WRAPPERS, FLOUR, KATAKURIKO, AND PANKO

In the *washoku* kitchen, foods are often coated with bread crumbs, dipped in a batter, dredged in potato starch, or enclosed in a wrapper made of wheat dough. Although none of these ways of preparing foods is unique to Japan, or requires the purchase of highly unusual ingredients, the Japanese products and techniques warrant a brief mention.

Dumpling Wrappers (gyōza no kawa)

Sold in Asian groceries as *gyōza no kawa* in packages of 18, 24, or more, these thin dumpling wrappers are made from wheat flour. Although they can be frozen for long-term storage, the sheets are difficult to separate without ripping them once thawed. It is better to make the dumplings within a day or two of purchasing the wrappers fresh, and then freeze any extra formed, uncooked dumplings. When ready to cook, place frozen dumplings in the skillet, sear until brown, and then proceed to add water and steam them. Allow an extra minute of cooking time to ensure the frozen meat cooks thoroughly.

Flour

When making tempura batter, I prefer using a low-gluten wheat flour for the tender, light texture it gives the coating. Available in many American markets, self-rising flour (which has salt and baking soda already mixed in) works well. Or you can make your own by adding 1/2 teaspoon baking soda and 1/4 teaspoon salt for every cup of low-gluten wheat flour you use.

Kinako (toasted soy flour): Whole dried soybeans are roasted and crushed to make *kinako,* a silky-textured, nutty-flavored, highly nutritious powder. Sold in small plastic bags, it should be stored on a dark, dry shelf until opened. The flour's natural oils can cause it to go rancid quickly once it is exposed, so to preserve its rich, toasted flavor, refrigerate any opened packages and consume within a few weeks.

The recipe for Wafū Waffle (page 302) mixes *kinako* with cinnamon. This same mixture either on its own or with a pinch of brown sugar added is delightful sprinkled on buttered toast in place of cinnamon sugar. Plain *kinako* is also wonderful sprinkled over yogurt.

Katakuriko (potato starch)

Originally processed from the root of *Erythronium japonicum* (*katakuri,* or dogtooth violet), *katakuriko* is a silky, white powder extracted from potatoes that is used to thicken sauces and dredge food before frying. In Asian markets, *katakuriko* is labeled as potato starch; regular cornstarch is a fine substitute.

Panko (bread crumbs)

The Japanese first learned to make bread from the Portuguese and adapted their word—*páo*—for it, combining it with *ko,* which means "flour," "crumb," or "powder." The shardlike, irregular shapes of Japanese bread crumbs deliver an unusually crunchy surface when deep-fried. The crumb coating tastes good even after the fried food has cooled, an important consideration in Japan where most breaded and fried foods are eaten at room temperature.

Some *panko* brands are made with egg- and/or honey-enriched bread. Both tend to color more quickly when fried and add a sweetness that I do not always want. I prefer to buy crumbs made from plain bread. All varieties are sold in clear plastic bags. Store in an airtight container on a dark, dry shelf. Even with proper storage, they begin to taste stale after a few months.

FISH (dried, semidried, processed)

In addition to an abundance of freshly caught fish and seafood, Japanese regularly consume dried, semidried, and processed fish. This is nothing new; long before artificial refrigeration was possible, salting and air-drying helped preserve, or at least significantly retard spoilage of, fish. And mashing and seasoning the meat that clung to the bones after fish were filleted expanded the food value of the day's catch. Though no longer a necessity, these foods remain appreciated by today's Japanese for their flavor and convenience.

Chirimen-Jako (semidried minuscule sardines) and Shirasu-Boshi (blanched minuscule sardines)

Chirimen-jako are minuscule sardines that have been briefly blanched in seawater and then set out to air-dry. Sometimes called simply *chirimen* (crumpled), they turn pearl gray if allowed to dry for several days and become a bit chewy and delightfully briny. These fully dried *chirimen* are not as perishable as the softer, whiter *shirasu-boshi*. Both types of tiny sardines are typically imported from Japan in frozen form. Keep frozen, or if they begin to defrost between the store and your kitchen, do not refreeze, rather, refrigerate them immediately and consume within four or five days. If the fish remain frozen, they have a shelf life of several months.

Both *chirimen* and *shirasu-boshi* are excellent sources of calcium (a heaping tablespoon has the calcium equivalent, but half the calories, of a glass of milk) and are eaten as is as a topping for porridge, salads, or lightly simmered vegetables. They can also be tossed into rice (tartly seasoned sushi rice or plain cooked rice) to make pilaflike dishes. Sometimes these tiny fish are marked as dried anchovies on English-language labels in Asian groceries.

Ichiya-Boshi (air-dried fish)

Literally, "dried overnight," *ichiya-boshi* should have a pleasant seashore aroma and never be sticky, with the exception of *mirin-boshi*, which are marinated in syrupy wine and sprinkled with sesame seeds. The fish are split and gutted (but not usually filleted; typically the backbone remains, as does the head and tail), salted to leach out unwanted odors and for preservation, and then set out in the fresh air to dry. Depending on the variety, air-dried fish will either be belly split (*hara-biraki*), in which case the head is also butterflied, or back split (*sei-biraki*), in which case the head is kept whole and pushed to one side. Greenling and horse mackerel are belly split, while pike are back split.

Greenlings are fairly large fish and often come to market with their heads removed. The center bones separate easily from the meat after cooking, making them easy to eat. Because greenlings can be up to a foot or more in length, a single air-dried fish is often cut in half to make two portions. If you have long, narrow plates and prefer that each portion include equal amounts of head and tail meat, cut the fish horizontally along the backbone. If you have round or square plates, cut the fish slightly on the diagonal to yield two pieces, one with mostly head meat (which has a richer flavor and oilier texture) and the other primarily with tail meat (which is drier and flakier).

Horse mackerel, which is pictured on the bottom right in the photo on page 16, is the most readily available variety of air-dried fish and comes in various sizes. Choose a 6- or 7-ounce fish to serve as a main course for each person. Pike is delightfully briny but mild, and is a bit more challenging to eat because of its many fine bones.

In Asian grocery stores, air-dried and salt-cured fish will be in the refrigerated or frozen foods section. Refrigerate your purchase immediately (in its original wrapping is fine) on returning home and eat within 2 days. No matter what variety of air-dried fish you buy, if it is frozen, allow it to thaw fully in the refrigerator before cooking it.

Iriko, Niboshi (dried sardines)*

Both *iriko* (the word I first learned in Shikoku) and *niboshi* (the more commonly used name elsewhere in Japan for the same thing) are dried sardines used primarily to make stock. They contain naturally occurring glutamates that unlock the flavor potential of other foods with which they are cooked. Unlike chemical monosodium glutamate, the flavor-enhancing essence stored in *iriko* does not cause unpleasant side effects when consumed. In many areas of Japan, *iriko* are favored over *katsuo-bushi* (dried bonito flakes) in making home-style stocks. In the Sanuki region of Shikoku, they are used in making broth for *udon* and for *sōmen* noodles, as well as for miso soups, especially those that use barley miso.

Iriko range in size from quite small (no more than an inch or so long) to 2¹/₂ or 3 inches long. As the fish dry, they shrivel, often in such a contorted manner that the backbones are curved or twisted. The fresher the fish when brought on land, the more twisted they become when dried. Look for bent fish—the Japanese describe them as *hé no ji,* referring to *hé,* one of fifty-six syllables in the writing system that looks like a crooked, upside-down "V" (*ji* is a "letter," or symbol, in Japanese). Like all dried staples, *iriko* should be stored in a dark, dry spot. After opening the original cellophane package, transfer the contents, including the packet of drying agent, to a lidded jar or canister.

To maximize the flavor-enhancing ability of the dried sardines and to keep potential bitterness to a minimum, you must trim away the gills and the contents of the belly cavity. First, snap off and discard the heads. Then, pinch each fish at the midpoint along its abdomen to split open the belly cavity.

Because the fish are dried, this is not a messy procedure. With your fingertips, pull away and discard the crumbly, blackened material in the belly. However, to ensure that the mineral-rich dried sardines will boost the nutrient level of the stock you are making with them, keep all the skeletal material as well as the meaty parts, discarding only the entrails.

To release the full flavor of the dried fish, soak them for a short while in whatever liquid a recipe calls for—water in most instances, soy sauce and/or saké on occasion—before heating.

Kamaboko (steamed fish sausage), Chikuwa (grilled fish sausage), Hanpen (fluffy fish cake)

The Japanese consume an amazing variety of fish sausages, dumplings, and pâtélike products made from different types of fish ground to a paste. Collectively, these foods are referred to as *neri seihin,* or ground-to-a-paste products. Typically, bits and pieces left over from filleting large, mild white-fleshed fish are mixed with less marketable, stronger-flavored species to make *surimi,* or "ground fish." This paste is then molded into a loaflike shape and steamed to make *kamaboko,* or molded around bamboo poles and grilled to make *chikuwa.* The latter, a cylindrical sausage with distinctive grill marks on the exterior, reveals an empty center when sliced. Most *surimi* products arrive from Japan frozen and should be consumed within 24 hours of thawing them.

Kamaboko rimmed in pink is often served with pure white slices. The color combination of red (or pink) and white is considered felicitous. Traditionally, the color was a natural, tasteless plant-based dye; nowadays it is usually artificial. Most *kamaboko* comes packaged on a wooden plank. Keep the sausage on the plank when slicing it. To release the slices, run your knife parallel to the plank.

In Shikoku, two regional *kamaboko* varieties are regularly used to top noodle dishes or eaten as beer snacks: swirl-patterned Naruto, named after the whirlpool off the Shikoku coast of Tokushima Prefecture, and a pure white, rib-ridged type. Both are cylindrical and not mounded on planks. The

Dried, semidried, and processed fish (clockwise from top left): iriko, chirimen-jako, ichiya-boshi, *and two kinds of* chikuwa

*essential pantry item

ridged type has plastic straws sticking to the outside that are pulled off before slicing. As the fish paste cools down after steaming, the pressure from the straws creates the ridges. Before plastic, bamboo strips or other twigs were used.

Chikuwa sausages are made by molding a seasoned paste made of mild white fish (usually in the cod or snapper family) around lightly oiled sticks of bamboo (traditional, artisanal way) or stainless steel pipes (modern, commercial way) and grilled. In days past, the sticks were stuck vertically around a wood-burning hearth and the fish was slowly roasted, a technique that is still used in some artisanal production plants today. When the grilling or roasting is done, the outer layer is golden brown and slightly blistered. After the sausage cools, it is twisted and slipped off the stick, resulting in a cylindrical sausage with a hollow center. Occasionally, *chikuwa* sausages are stuffed with other ingredients, such as cucumber strips, and then sliced into chunks and eaten as a beer snack with either mustard or wasabi on the side. More commonly, though, they are thinly sliced and mixed with vegetables in stir-fried dishes or pilaflike dishes.

Previously frozen sausages should not be refrozen. Packages will have a sell-by date stamped on them. Refrigerate from time of purchase until eating; any leftovers should be used within 2 days of opening the package.

Airy and soufflélike, *hanpen* is fish cake made from mild-flavored fish in the cod family, beaten egg whites, and *yama imo* (mountain yam). It is typically a 3- or 4-inch square and fairly flat, though soft and spongy when pinched. Sold in most Asian grocery stores in America (look in the freezer section or refrigerated case), it can be used to prepare a simple clear broth (see page 124). It is also a common ingredient in the fish sausage stew called *oden. Hanpen* can be sliced in half on the diagonal, slit, and stuffed with other ingredients in a manner similar to stuffed tōfu pouches (Treasure Boats, page 278).

This delicate fish sausage is highly perishable. Keep refrigerated and be sure to use by the date indicated on the package. Do not refreeze.

Katsuo-Bushi (dried bonito flakes)*

A tunalike fish, called bonito in English and *katsuo* in Japanese, swims in fairly temperate waters. In Japan, Tosa, on the Pacific coast of the island of Shikoku, is famous for its *katsuo*—so much so that dishes using it as an ingredient often have Tosa as part of their name. Fresh bonito is an early summer and fall delicacy. The Japanese also eat flakes of dried bonito, or *katsuo-bushi,* throughout the year. These smoky flakes, made by scraping rock-hard dried bonito fillets against a sharp blade, are used as a garnish, as a condiment, and when making stocks, broths, and sauces.

In Japanese grocery stores, most packages of dried fish flakes combine bonito with other less-expensive fish, such as sardines and mackerel. The price will tell you. In the traditional *washoku* kitchen, whole dried fillets were rubbed over a sharp blade to produce curly flakes. The box holding the blade had a drawer into which the shavings fell. When full, the drawer was removed. Just as freshly ground coffee beans are far superior to beans ground weeks before, so too is freshly shaved bonito to preshaved flakes.

Today, it is hard to find a cook using one of these boxes in a home or even in a restaurant. Instead, it is more common to see scissors cutting open individual 3- or 5-gram packets of preshaved fish flakes (about $1/4$ cup tightly packed). If you will be using *katsuo-bushi* only occasionally, buy these small packets, affectionately labeled "fresh pack." Five or six of them are sold as a unit in either a cardboard box or a large plastic bag. Large bags of flakes go rancid rather quickly once they are opened. Even when stored on a dark, dry shelf, optimal flavor and aroma lasts for only 4 to 6 weeks. If, however, you will be making dashi two or three times a week, you will finish these larger 100-gram (a little less than 4-ounce) bags in less than a month, and I suggest you purchase them instead. They will be more economical, and the quality of the flakes in larger bags tends to be higher.

Three kinds of katsuo-bushi *(clockwise from top):* katsuo-bushi, ito kezuri *(thin curls), and* atsu kezuri *(thicker chunks)*

*essential pantry item

Katsuo-bushi is also sold in two additional forms, *ito kezuri*, or thin curls, and *atsu kezuri*, or thicker chunks, both packaged in plastic bags. The *ito kezuri* (literally, "thread shavings;" illustrated on page 19), which look like slender bits of pinkish beige curling ribbon, are used to garnish other foods, most commonly *ohitashi* (Spinach Steeped in Broth, page 190), *yaki nasu* (Chilled Roasted Eggplant, page 193), and *tamago-dōfu* (Chilled Egg Custard, page 285), or blocks of plain chilled silky tōfu, drizzled with soy sauce.

The thick pieces are ideal for making *bannō-jōyu* (the generic name for seasoned soy concentrate) and other recipes that favor intensely smoky overtones. In the days when every home had its own box, these chunks were the bits left after tissue-thin flakes had been scraped off. When I first began cooking in a *washoku* kitchen nearly forty years ago, I was fearful of injuring my fingertips, even with a guard in place. My leftover chunks were thick and plentiful and my seasoned soy concentrate full of flavor.

▒ IN THE WASHOKU KITCHEN: **dry-roasting, 85**.

Unagi no Kabayaki (glazed grilled eel)

Prebroiled eel is shipped overseas frozen, in vacuum-sealed pouches. Most often, a small packet of sauce, called *taré*, and a smaller packet of *sanshō* pepper (page 47) are packaged with the eel. Although the eel is fully cooked, it is best to reheat it until it is warmed through and aromatic. Instructions should be on the package you purchase, and I suggest you follow them when provided. However, if instructions are unavailable, you can do one of the following: reheat the eel in its sealed pouch by placing it in a pot of boiling water for 1 or 2 minutes, or remove the eel from its pouch and use either a microwave (medium setting for 90 seconds) or a broiler (medium heat for 2 to 3 minutes, checking often to avoid scorching). You can brush some of the sauce on the eel as you reheat it and then finish with a pinch of the *sanshō* pepper. However, too much sauce or pepper can overwhelm the eel.

A Guide to Buying and Storing Fish

Fresh Whole Fish

Buying: The eyes should be clear and full with no traces of blood or cloudiness. The gills should be bright red or pink with no sour odor. The skin and scales should be firm, not bruised, and moist, but not slimy.

Storing at home: Rinse in cold water, pat dry with paper towels, and wrap loosely in parchment or waxed paper before refrigerating. Use within 24 hours.

Fresh Fillets or Steaks

Buying: The flesh should be firm and moist and have a translucent sheen. The odor should be fresh and never ammonia-like. Be alert to so-called belly burn, caused by the caustic digestive enzymes of the fish that continue to "burn" through the gut wall and leak into the body cavity. This happens if a fish is caught while feeding and is not gutted immediately. Gaps between segments of the flesh and brownish and scarred flesh are signs of belly burn.

Storing at home: Rinse under cold water and pat dry. Cook immediately, or refrigerate for up to 24 hours wrapped in parchment or waxed paper, plastic bags, or plastic wrap.

Frozen Fish

Buying: Be alert to freezer burn, which is caused by loss of moisture (through the crystallization) of the fish's natural water content. This dehydration process typically causes the fish to appear chalky. After cooking fish with freezer burn, the texture turns fibrous and tough.

Storing at home: Thaw in the refrigerator, or in a sealed plastic bag under running cold water. Thawed fish should never be refrozen.

If you need to hold thawed fish an extra day, rinse under cold water, pat dry, place on a clean plate, wrap snugly with plastic wrap, and refrigerate immediately.

Smoked or Cured Fish

Buying: The flesh of smoked fish should be firm but silky with a bright, glossy sheen and no traces of salt or blood. If bought whole, such as smoked trout or chub, the flesh should flake away easily from the skin and bones. The skin should be moist but not sticky to the touch.

Salt-cured fish often comes to Asian grocery stores frozen (look in the refrigerated or frozen foods section), and usually as half steaks (pieces are rimmed with skin, often with the center bone still intact). The degree of salt curing varies, and *ama-jio,* or mild (literally, "sweet salt"), salt-cured fish is the most versatile item.

Storing at home: Wrap smoked fish snugly in clear plastic wrap, refrigerate, and use within 36 hours of purchase for optimal flavor and texture. To freeze sliced smoked salmon (first make sure it hasn't been previously frozen for shipment), lay slices on a sheet of parchment or waxed paper and cover with a second sheet. Roll up the sheets jelly-roll fashion and enclose the roll snugly in plastic wrap.

Wrap salt-cured fish loosely in moist paper towels, especially if purchased frozen, to absorb any drips (do not refreeze). Keep previously frozen, thawed fish refrigerated until cooking and use within 2 or 3 days.

Bivalves (clams, mussels, oysters)

Buying: Clams, mussels, and oysters are often displayed in their shells on beds of shaved ice. Their shells should be shut or ever so slightly ajar—never gaping, never chipped.

Fresh shucked meats should be plump, sitting in their own clear liquor on their own half shell. If sold in containers, check for clarity of packing liquid (no cloudiness or foam) and freshness of odor (no ammonia and/or overly fishy smell).

Shucked oyster and clam meats are often sold in pasteurized vacuum-sealed packages or in cans. (Lump crabmeat is sold the same way.) The packing liquid should be entirely clear, with no foam visible. Keep these foods refrigerated at all times. Once opened, use immediately, or transfer any leftovers to a clean glass jar and refrigerate in the packaging liquid for up to 12 hours.

Storing at home: Place bivalves in cool, salty water to cover. This helps them purge sand and sediment. The exception is *shijimi,* tiny freshwater clams with jet black shells. They should be placed in plain water, not salty. Leave for 30 minutes and change the water. When purged, drain and use immediately, or store in a bowl or pan in the refrigerator for up to 6 hours.

Fresh-Caught Fish

Most people who fish for sport are well aware of local regulations and the rules of proper storage, but here are two reminders: Ice the fish right away, and keep it packed in plenty of ice until you get home. If using a holding tank, change the water often to ensure a steady supply of oxygen and to keep the water temperature cool.

Note: Filleting and handling fish that will be consumed raw requires special training; purchase from a knowledgeable source, or enjoy at a reliable restaurant.

FISH (fresh)

I have organized this catalog of fish by flavor profile, beginning with mild-flavored *shiromi-zakana* ("white-fleshed fish") and progressing to the more assertive, oily *ao-zakana* ("blue-fleshed fish"), some of which are referred to as *hikari mono*, or the "shiny ones," because of their sleek, steely appearance. By grouping them in this manner, I hope to prepare you to make informed choices when shopping and cooking with whatever may be available to you in your local markets.

▨ IN THE WASHOKU KITCHEN: **decorative slashing, 68; blanching (shimo furi), 75.**

Mild-Flavored Shiromi-Zakana

Flounder, Sole, Turbot, Plaice, Fluke, Halibut: These are flatfishes with mild flavor and white flesh and are excellent for steaming and poaching. Japanese names include *karei* (flounder family), *hiramé* (type of halibut), and *ohyō* (type of halibut). Different types have different seasons, so that some sort of flatfish is likely to be in your market throughout the year. Halibut and fluke are large sea creatures and typically come to market already cut into steaks. Flounder and sole sold in American markets are most often stripped of skin and bone; the fillets are usually less than $1/2$ inch thick and rarely weigh more than a pound. Plaice and turbot are less readily available in America, but their delicate texture makes them worth seeking out.

Snapper, Sea Bream, Grouper, Porgy: Meaty and with white or ivory flesh, these highly versatile fish can be salt broiled or poached and served in their own broth, both whole and in steaks or fillets. Fillets are also braised in soy, or marinated in miso and then broiled. Japanese names include *tai* (sea bream, snapper family), *amadai* (porgy family), *kinmedai* (snapper family), and *hata* (grouper family). In Japan, these fish are also served as sushi and sashimi.

In American markets, I have been able to buy these fish cleaned (scaled and gutted) but whole (1 to $1^1/_2$ pounds each), cut into steaks (about 6 ounces each with skin and bone), and also filleted with skin attached (about 4 ounces each).

Bass: Bass (*suzuki*) are mild and are good candidates for grilling, simmering, or braising with a distinctive sauce. Firm flesh makes fillets easy to handle, but attention to cooking time is needed to prevent bass from becoming tough and dry.

Rockfish, Perch: Rockfish (*meibaru*) and perch are best when simmered, braised, or steamed. In Japan, they are most often served whole, in a presentation style known as *sugata ni*, with the head facing to the left, tail to the right, belly forward, and back away from the diner.

Richer, Meatier Shiromi-Zakana

Cod, Haddock, Whiting, Hake, Pollack: Cod (*tara*) and related fish, including haddock, whiting, hake, and pollack, are meaty and fairly mild and have flesh that is usually firm and snowy white (indeed, the calligraphy for cod is a combination of "fish" and "snow"). These varieties are typically breaded or dipped in batter and fried. They can also be steamed, though care should be taken not to overcook them.

Sablefish, Black Cod, Lingcod, Greenling: Sablefish, black cod, lingcod (*gindara*), and greenling (*hokké*) are richer, oilier members of the cod family and are particularly tasty when broiled, braised with flavored miso, or pan seared. Both fresh and salted half steaks of cod are sold throughout Japan (see page 21). Grilled or steamed plain and served with either grated daikon or lemon wedges and a drizzle of soy sauce, they make a quick meal on a busy day.

Smelts: Smelts (*wakasagi*) are plentiful in most parts of Japan, where they are sometimes fished through the ice. In the American midwest, the Pacific Northwest, and parts of Alaska, smelts are available toward the end of winter. In Japan, smelts and similar small fish such as *kisu* are batter-fried, stewed in a sweetened soy sauce, or fried and then marinated in a spicy sweet-and-sour sauce.

Mild-Flavored Ao-Zakana

This group of fish boast a meaty texture and rich, though not overly "fishy" flavor. They fare well with both moist (poaching, braising, steaming) and dry (grilling, pan searing) cooking methods.

Salmon: *Beni-jaké,* or sockeye salmon, and *gin-jaké,* or coho salmon, are sold as both fresh and salted half steaks; all pieces include a strip of skin and some include the center bone. Because the life cycle of salmon includes time spent in freshwater, the fish is vulnerable to parasite infestation and should not be consumed raw.

The degree of salt curing varies, and in Japan, *ama-jio* (mild) salt-cured salmon is the most popular item. It is often grilled plain and served with either grated daikon or a wedge of lemon and a drizzle of soy sauce. It is kept in the refrigerated or frozen fooods section of Asian groceries. In this book, recipes calling for salted salmon also provide suggestions for using fresh salmon, which is regularly available in fish stores.

Saberfish, Swordfish, Bonito: Readily available in most North American markets, saberfish, also known as cutlass (*tachiuo*), swordfish (*kajiki maguro*), and bonito (*katsuo*), are suitable for pan searing, skillet braising, and outdoor grilling. In Japan, most bonito are preserved as *katsuo-bushi,* dried flakes used for making stocks and broths (page 18). The fish has two seasons: early-summer fish, called *hashiri-gatsuo* (literally, "running out to feed"), are lean; fall fish, called *modori-gatsuo* (literally, "returning home"), are fatty. In Japan, both are enjoyed as sushi and sashimi; the fall catch is typically flash seared and marinated as well.

Japanese Bluefish: Known as *ginmutsu,* this fish comes to market during winter. It is buttery and delicious braised in a sweetened soy sauce or marinated in miso and then broiled.

Full-Flavored Ao-Zakana

Yellowtail: *Buri,* most often called yellowtail in American markets, is a favorite wintertime fish in Japan, where it is enjoyed grilled, pan seared, simmered, and as sushi and sashimi. Like several other species, yellowtail comes to market at various stages in its life cycle. *Buri* is the mature adult, while *hamachi* is the younger adolescent.

Amberjack: Similar to yellowtail in flavor and texture, amberjack tastes best when grilled, pan seared, or prepared as sushi and sashimi. Two varieties of amberjack are commonly available in Japan, *kampachi* and *hiramasa.*

Tuna: Many Americans associate fresh tuna, or *maguro,* with Japanese food. In Japan, it is served primarily as sushi or sashimi, though occasionally it will be marinated in either soy sauce or miso before flash broiling.

Assertively Flavored Ao-Zakana

Mackerel, Kingfish, Horse Mackerel: Mackerel (*saba*), with dark blue, wavy stripes on a deep silver ground, and kingfish or king mackerel (*sawara*), with steely gray speckles on a pale silver ground, are readily found in North American fish markets during the winter and into the spring. In Japan, horse mackerel (*aji*), typically 7 to 8 inches long and sporting a distinctive bony S curve of scales on both sides of the lower body, are plentiful and inexpensive, with an extended spring and summer season. Mackerel and kingfish fillets are delicious when salt grilled (*shio yaki*), marinated in miso and broiled (*Saikyō yaki*), braised in a miso-thickened broth (*miso ni*), or glaze grilled (*teri yaki, yuuan yaki*). In Japan, salt grilling horse mackerel whole after gutting them, known as *sugata yaki,* is the most common method of cooking. Very small fish are sometimes prepared *nanban-zuké* style, fried whole and then marinated in a tart and spicy sauce. *Aji tataki,* a minced tartare of fresh mackerel, ginger, and herbs, is also popular.

Sardines: Fresh whole sardines (*iwashi*) are readily available and inexpensive in Japan, where they are grilled, pan seared, fried, and simmered, and they are increasingly available in the United States, especially on the west coast. Because their flesh is soft and easily bruised (the calligraphy for sardine is a combination of "fish" and "weak"), they are typically filleted with deft fingers, rather than knives. In Japan, sushi bars will serve both raw and cooked sardines, demonstrating their prowess in sourcing top quality fish and the skill of their staff.

• • •

Cephalopods

Octopus, Squid: Several varieties of octopus (*tako*) and squid (*ika*) are available in Japan, many of them sourced from foreign waters to meet the high demand. Octopus typically comes to market already blanched (the white flesh will be opaque, the dark areas purple-pink) and can usually be eaten as is (your market will tell you whether it requires further cooking). When buying squid, choose whole creatures with their purplish skin intact, since it lends a lovely rosy tint to stewed squid dishes.

FRESH HERBS AND RHIZOMES

Although the Japanese pantry is stocked primarily with dried and preserved foods that boast an extended shelf life, several fresh herbs and rhizomes enliven daily *washoku* fare.

Many commercially grown Japanese herbs are cultivated hydroponically so that they come to market with roots embedded in spongy material. Several kinds of fresh Japanese herbs can be grown in pots on a sunny windowsill. I encourage you to try your hand at growing your own herbs from seeds.

To keep hydroponically grown herbs fresh for several days, wrap the sponge (root end) in moist paper towels, and then place in an open plastic bag in the refrigerator. If you have the space, store them in an upright position. Prune away any yellowing or darkened leaves and stalks before using.

Fresh herbs (from left to right): mitsuba, myōga, *and shiso*

Ginger (shōga)

A rhizome, rather than a root, ginger grows in knobby clusters. When it is mature, its fairly thick skin and flesh are deep gold, in contrast to the pale ivory or champagne skin and flesh of new ginger. Fresh ginger is increasingly available in supermarkets and grocery stores throughout North America. Most of it is grown in Hawaii, and because of the volcanic soil there, it sometimes has a slightly blue or blue-gray tint just below the skin. Powdered ginger is not an acceptable substitute for fresh.

Over the years, different people have taught me different ways of storing fresh ginger. I usually find that keeping unpeeled knobs in an open plastic bag in the refrigerator is best. If you do not mind having to wash away dirt each time you use ginger, and you have a small pot of moist earth in which to bury it, that is fine, too.

▦ IN THE WASHOKU KITCHEN: **grating and juicing,** 71.

New Ginger (shin shōga): Bulbous new ginger, or *shin shōga*, has a gossamer thin peel and pale yellow flesh tipped with blushing pink. In Tokyo, new ginger comes to market in June and July during the rainy season, just when dampened spirits—and metabolisms—most appreciate its juicy fire tempered with a hint of sweetness. If you are able to find new ginger at Asian or specialty markets in your community, it will transform a good dish into something nearly sublime! Try making Rice Cooked with New Ginger (page 141) or Blushing Pink Ginger (page 223).

Most new ginger is juicy and tends to be a bit stringy when grated. It is best cut into thin slices or fine shreds or grated for its juice. To obtain juice, squeeze the gratings.

Stem Ginger (yanaka shōga): Tender, young stem ginger arrives in Tokyo markets in late spring and can be found, sporadically, throughout the summer. I have seen it on occasion in Asian food markets in North America, too. Sold in bunches of 2 or 3 stalks, each 5- to 6-inch "ginger stem" is made up of a green stalk to which several bulblike knobs of ginger are attached. Choose thin-skinned knobs with a dull sheen and pale gold tones tinged with pink. Those with slender green stalks and intensely pink coloring at the base of the stem are particularly well suited to pickling whole (page 223).

Mitsuba

Mitsuba (illustrated on page 24) has a crisp texture and mild taste somewhere between celery and watercress. Both the leaves (bright green) and stalk (pale celadon) are edible. The leaves are clustered in bunches of three, hence this herb is sometimes called trefoil in English. Most commonly used to garnish soups, coarsely chopped *mitsuba* is typically placed in the bottom of a bowl. Pouring hot soup over leaves and stalks is usually sufficient to "cook" the herb.

Commercial *mitsuba* is often grown hydroponically and thus comes to market with roots embedded in a sponge. Just before using, cut the stalks away from the sponge about 1/8 inch from the bottom, keeping the stems aligned. Depending on the recipe, you will be asked to cut the stalks in short or longer lengths.

Myōga

A bulb-shaped rhizome with a taste similar to ginger, *myōga* (illustrated on page 24) is used to season broths and pickles and as a condiment for tōfu, noodles, and fresh fish. Choose firm, tightly layered bulbs that are smooth, dry, and blushing pink tipped in dark green. Store them in a plastic bag in the refrigerator for up to 1 week. When black spots appear between the layers of the bulb, or the bulb becomes limp and spongey, *myōga* is past its prime.

Radish Sprouts (kaiwaré)

Kaiwaré means "split seashell"; the cleft, cloverlike leaf of the sprout visually reminds the Japanese of an open seashell. A second name, *tsumamina*, comes from *tsumamu*, which means "to pinch" or "to pluck," and *na*, which refers to edible greens. These deliciously sharp and nutritious (packed with vitamin C) sprouts are highly perishable and should be eaten within a day or two of purchase. Look for intensely green leaves and crisp, clean, pale stalks with the roots still attached to a moist sponge. Package sizes vary a bit, but most contain 2 or 3 ounces. Seeds for sprouting at home are also available from many seed catalogs.

Store the sprouts as originally wrapped, or wrap loosely in slightly damp paper toweling, slip into a plastic bag, and place in the vegetable bin of your refrigerator. Before using the sprouts, you will need to rinse and trim them. Hold them by the spongy end and swish them in a deep bowl of cold water. Brown seedpods will float to the surface and be easy to discard. If any of the leaves are yellowed, blackened, or slippery, remove them by pinching them away from their stalks. Once you have rinsed and pruned the cluster, cut them away from the sponge about 1/8 inch from the bottom, keeping the stems aligned. If a recipe calls for mincing the sprouts, cut 1/4-inch lengths, beginning from the trimmed stem end and keeping the split leaves intact.

Shiso, Shiso no Mi, Aka-jiso, and Yukari

A distant botanical cousin of mint and basil, this herb is vaguely reminiscent of both. It goes by several different names in Japanese and in English. I have chosen to call it by its most common Japanese name, *shiso*. When you seek it out at Asian groceries, you may find it is called *ōba*, perilla, or beefsteak plant. And, just as basil has an opal version with purplish leaves, so *shiso*, too, has a red-leafed variety called *aka-jiso*, or *yukari*.

The mature leaves of *shiso* (illustrated on page 24) are flat and dark green, have sharply defined sawtooth edges that look like fine pinking shears, and are about 3 inches long and 2 inches wide at the thickest part of the base. They are usually sold in stacks of 10 leaves that have been plucked from the stalk. Wrap leaves in a moistened paper towel and then place in a zippered plastic bag, pressing out excess air as you seal it. Refrigerated leaves usually keep for 4 to 5 days. Black spots and/or disintegrating edges are signs of spoilage.

Shiso is fairly easy to grow on a sunny window ledge (in seed catalogs it is sometimes called perilla). Growing it means you can enjoy both the leaves and the seedpods, called *shiso no mi.* As the plant matures, bell-shaped seeds appear at the top of the stalks. These are the edible seedpods.

Pluck the seedpods from their stalks and toss them with an equal quantity of coarse salt. Continue to toss, squeezing gently to extract the *aku* ("bitterness" inherent in many foods, in this case a darkish liquid). Rinse away this *aku* and pat the seedpods dry. Coarsely chop them with a sharp knife before tossing into freshly cooked rice or a salad of mixed greens.

The red or opal variety of *shiso,* called *aka-jiso,* is used primarily for making *uméboshi* and other pickled vegetables, such as *shiba-zuké* (page 38). Salted and squeezed, the leaves "bleed" to produce a purple-pink liquid. In the process of pickling, this brine becomes a tart vinegar (*umé-zu,* page 49). Once the plums are pickled, the same leaves can be used to tint (and flavor) slices of sweet-and-sour lotus root. Salt-cured *aka-jiso* leaves, packaged with their purple brine in vacuum-sealed, clear plastic pouches, are also for sale at some stores.

Salt-cured *aka-jiso* can be dried to make a delightful herb called *yukari* (this word is used to describe both the leaf and the herb made from the dried and crushed leaf; the herb is illustrated on page 48), which is sprinkled on cooked rice and fried foods. Most commercially packaged dried *yukari* has additives; I have provided a recipe for drying your own on page 112.

FRUITS

Several of the fruits suggested in the dessert chapter may not be immediately familiar to you. In addition to the descriptions and suggestions found in the recipes, here is a bit more information about them.

In general, look for unblemished fruit that is heavy in the hand (heft usually indicates juicy ripeness). Depending upon the kind of fruit, shapes will vary, and fully ripe, fine-tasting fruit may not always be perfectly formed. Most fruit keeps best stored at cool room temperature. Refrigerate for 30 minutes before eating, if you prefer your fruit chilled.

Asian Pear (nashi)
Crisp and juicy, like many varieties of apples, this fruit is often called a pear-apple by Americans. Green-skinned *kosui nashi* tend to be sweeter than brown-skinned *shinsui nashi,* though both are delicious.

Loquat (biwa)
Japanese loquats are small, like apricots, with orange flesh and skins. They are packed with vitamin A and carotene and boast a wonderful apple-honey-vanilla flavor. The fruit is freestone, with multiple smooth brown pits surrounded by a membrane that clings to the fruit's flesh. It is worth taking the time to peel away the membranes, which are often astringent.

Rub the fuzz from the whole fruit to ease peeling. Then, start at the stem end (where the fruit was attached to the tree) and peel back the skin with your fingers, as though you are peeling a banana. Trim off the flowering (puckered) end.

Persimmon (kaki)
Most varieties of Japanese persimmon are bright orange with glossy skins and turn fully ripe before becoming soft. They are ideally eaten when still very firm and at cool room temperature.

Two varieties of persimmon that are popular in Japan are also available in North America: the plump, oblate, intensely orange Fuyu, and the larger, squarish Jiro. Both are nonastringent types (as opposed to the Hachiya, an astringent cultivar), and in the United States the Jiro is often sold as Fuyu. Dark brown streaks, visible in some peeled persimmons, are due to a concentration of natural sugars, not a sign of bruising.

The Japanese also enjoy *hoshi-gaki,* or dried persimmons. Both the soft, somewhat sticky *anpo-gaki,* which have a honey-like sweetness, and the stiffer *Ichida-gaki* and *koro-gaki,* which appear to be dusted with powdered sugar, are eaten as a snack with green tea and are used in making confections and saladlike dishes. The white coating on the stiffer varieties is formed from the peeled fruits' own sugars as they dry. In the autumn, peeled persimmons are strung on long ropes and hung to dry under the thatched eves of farmhouses in many parts of Japan.

Soft *anpo-gaki* persimmons are more perishable than the stiffer varieties and are best kept refrigerated. Other kinds of *hoshi-gaki* should be kept in a plastic bag on a cool, dry shelf.

Persimmons are rich in vitamin C and fiber. As with other fruits that are dried, the sweetness intensifies and nutritional values are more concentrated in the dried fruits.

White Peach (hakutō)

Large and freestone or cling, Japanese peaches have cream-colored or extremely pale yellow flesh and skins. Typically, there are mottled areas of blushing pink as well.

Yuzu (Japanese citron)

Available fresh in Japan from late summer (when the fruit is still green) through winter (the peel is bright yellow), the peel of the *yuzu*, or citron, is prized for its aroma (the juice is used on occasion, though it is quite bitter and cloudy). Thin strips of peel are floated in broths, added to pickling mediums, and tossed with various saladlike ingredients. The zest is grated and added to sauces and used to garnish grilled fish and poultry and sauced or pickled vegetables.

In Japan, *yuzu-buro* (the practice of floating fresh whole fruits in deep tubs of steaming bath water) is enjoyed on *tōji*, the winter solstice. Throughout the winter, I make *yuzu-buro* from fruit that remains after I have used the peel and zest in cooking. The aromatic oils of the citrus perfume the bath water and make a terrific skin softener, too.

Freeze-dried *yuzu* peel (illustrated on page 48) is available year-round in Asian groceries outside Japan. It is typically packaged in foil-lined pouches that can be resealed. The bits can be floated, as is, in a clear broth or crushed to a powder and used as a spice to add lemony zip to sauces.

▦ IN THE WASHOKU KITCHEN: **grating, 71.**

KONNYAKU AND SHIRATAKI NOODLES

Processed from *konnyaku imo,* a tuber of the large yam family, *konnyaku* is usually sold in block or loaf form, suspended in a bit of liquid in vacuum-sealed, clear plastic packages. The size and shape can vary from small pieces (about 4 ounces) to larger blocks (about 12 ounces). Packages of *konnyaku* often include confusing labeling, bearing rather cryptic names such as yam cake, devil's tongue jelly, and tuber aspic, to name a few. Most blocks range in color from speckled gray (bits of *hijiki,* page 41, have been added) to mottled beige (usually a sign that fresh *konnyaku imo* has been used) to nearly white (made from refined *konnyaku imo* powder). The speckled gray type will work well for any recipe in this book that calls for *konnyaku.* For added visual interest, use a combination of light and dark types in the same recipe.

Konnyaku is an inexpensive filler-food that provides volume and chewing satisfaction with no extra calories. Rich in fiber, it has been touted as a "cleanser" of the digestive track. "Flavored" varieties that can be eaten as is (no cooking is required) are often available at Asian groceries. Drain and serve them chilled with dipping sauces. Green-speckled *ao nori* (page 41) is good with Tart Miso-Mustard Sauce (page 99) or Smoky Citrus-Soy Sauce (page 97). Spicy, pinkish *tōgarashi* (page 47) is good with Pungent Red Miso Sauce (page 101).

Shirataki (literally, "white waterfall") is the poetic name for thin noodles processed from *konnyaku.* They absorb the flavors of foods cooked with them and are often added to one-pot dishes such as sukiyaki and to braised dishes. In this book, they are used in two recipes, Soy-Stewed Bits of Beef (page 266) and Treasure Boats (page 278).

When you open a package of *konnyaku* or *shirataki* noodles, you will immediately notice a distinctive (and somewhat unpleasant) smell. It is not a sign of spoilage. If you do not need the entire package for the recipe at hand, transfer the balance to a lidded container, cover with fresh cold water, and

Speckled gray konnyaku *and light* konnyaku *in loaf form and as braid-cut pieces, a cluster of* shirataki *noodles in a bowl of water, and an all-purpose Japanese knife (*santoku-bōchō, *page 69)*

refrigerate. Change the water daily to maintain freshness for up to 5 days. The container in which you store *konnyaku* may become discolored with a chalky-gray residue of *sekkai,* a lime-based coagulant used to solidify the loaf. This residue is not a sign of spoilage.

To eliminate unwanted moisture and make *konnyaku* or *shirataki* noodles more porous—and to remove *aku* (bitterness), in this case residual *sekkai*—the Japanese use one of several methods: dry-roasting, blanching, or salt-rubbing. Each recipe calling for *konnyaku* or *shirataki* will specify the best method. Despite their gelatinous appearance, both *konnyaku* and *shirataki* noodles become firmer with cooking.

▦ IN THE WASHOKU KITCHEN: **braid cutting,** 70; **blanching,** 75; **salt-rubbing,** 76; **dry-roasting,** 85.

MISO*

There are hundreds—possibly thousands—of different types of miso (fermented soybean pastes) that the Japanese regularly enjoy. Sometimes *komé kōji,* a cultured rice spore medium, is added to the soybean mash to enhance the fermentation process. Other miso pastes are made with cultured wheat or millet, or combinations of grains and beans. Still others are made just with soybeans. The variety of raw materials and the length of fermentation time produce a wide range of flavors, from mild to pungent, and textures, from smooth to chunky, in the final product.

Generally, miso is classified as either dark or light when listed in recipes, though there are medium shades (and flavors), too. When the choice is important to achieve a certain outcome, the recipe will specify what is needed. For recipes that call for dark miso, you can use any kind of *aka* (literally, "red") miso. Sendai miso is usually a good choice, as it complements a wide range of foods, including tomatoes and olive oil that are not part of the traditional Japanese palate. Similarly, for recipes that call for light miso, any *shiro* (literally, "white") miso will do. I usually recommend a combination of

*essential pantry item

Saikyō miso and *genmai miso,* to tone down the sweetness of Saikyō miso alone. Blending different kinds of miso is known as *awasé miso* and is common practice. Creating blends allows you to customize the flavor, hue, and texture.

In Japan, preferences for one type of miso or another are typically linked to regional identity. The phrase *témaé miso* means "to toot your own horn," a sentiment not often voiced in Japanese society, where humility is admired. But when it came to pride in your own homemade miso, modesty was abandoned in the traditional kitchen. Today, it would be hard to find a household where miso is made, let alone a homemade version worth bragging about.

I always have five or six varieties of miso on hand. I recommend starting your own collection with Saikyō miso, Sendai miso, and *mugi miso,* and then adding Hatchō miso and *genmai miso* once you become more at ease with cooking with miso. Below is a detailed description of each of these types.

Most commercial miso pastes come packaged in plastic tubs or bags. After opening the container, reseal and store in the refrigerator for up to 2 months for optimal aroma, though spoilage is rare even after 6 months or more. A white and/or green, moldy growth around the edges or across the surface of the bean paste is a sign of unwanted bacteria. Scrape these molds off and use the remaining bean paste within a week or so. Pinkish molds are a more serious matter, and you will need to scrape very deeply and use the remaining untainted miso in a day or two, or throw out the entire package.

▦ IN THE WASHOKU KITCHEN: **straining,** 78; **marinating,** 78.

Genmai Miso

What distinguishes this miso from the others is that it is made with whole-grain rice (*genmai*). The amount of salt used to make miso from any whole grain is slightly greater than the amount used to make miso from hulled grains, which means that people needing to monitor the sodium levels of the food they eat should probably avoid whole-grain miso.

Four kinds of miso (clockwise from top left):
Hatchō miso, Sendai miso, Saikyō shiro miso, *and* mugi miso

Hatchō Miso

Those born and raised in Aiichi Prefecture (Nagoya is the capital of the region) favor the deep burnished brown, thick-as-fudge Hatchō miso in soups and sauces. The name refers to an area, Hatchōmé, or eighth district, in Okazaki City where the first commercially produced fermented bean paste was made. Beans alone (other grains such as rice or barley are not blended into the fermenting mash) are used to make the miso, a smooth but stiff bean paste that is vaguely reminiscent of Chinese hoisin sauce. Indeed, miso making was probably introduced to Japan from China through the Korean peninsula that juts into the Sea of Japan. Aiichi Prefecture is on the Pacific coast, but at the narrowest part of Japan's main island of Honshu.

Mugi Miso

Made with barley (*mugi*) in addition to soybeans, this miso is winey and usually caramel colored, with bits of barley still visible. Residents of Kyushu and some residents of Shikoku and the southwest provinces of Honshu prefer this barley-enriched miso.

Saikyō Miso

Very sweet with caramel overtones, this creamy *shiro miso* is used in making confectionary and flavored sauces. When used to thicken soup, it is often combined with other miso pastes to balance sweet and salty overtones. Many commercially available brands sold in North America have sweeteners added, so you may need to adjust recipes accordingly. Natives of Shikoku and the Kansai region, particularly those who grew up in Kyoto and Nara, are especially partial to Saikyō miso. The name refers to the "western capital," or Kyoto, formerly the seat of power in Japan.

Sendai Miso

This full-bodied, rice-enriched red miso is pungent without being intensely salty. Some brands are rather chunky, containing bits of crushed beans and rice, while others are quite smooth. It is named for the city of Sendai, north of Tokyo, where this style of miso making originated.

MUSHROOMS

The Japanese cultivate many kinds of mushrooms and also forage for wild ones. The most common types found in the *washoku* kitchen are enoki, *maitaké*, *naméko*, shiitaké (both fresh and dried), *hon shiméji*, and other varieties of *shiméji*.

In the fall, wildly expensive *matsutaké* mushrooms (the equivalent of twenty to fifty dollars for a single mushroom is not uncommon) come to market. In North America, these precious mushrooms grow in the Pacific Northwest. They are found near certain species of pine trees and have a spicy pine-like aroma and almost crunchy texture.

The Japanese do not eat uncooked mushrooms, though they typically cook them for only a brief time. Most mushrooms are cultivated from spores (*matsutaké* is the major exception) and brought to market fresh. Shiitaké mushrooms are also dried. In general, fresh mushrooms are best stored in a paper bag or wrapped in newspaper, then refrigerated in the vegetable bin.

Enoki Mushrooms

Sold in North America as both enoki mushrooms and *enoki-daké*, these slender-stalked, small-capped white fungi have a light floral aroma. Most commercially grown enoki mushrooms come to market packaged in cellophane bags that contain 100 grams, or about 3 ounces. Typically, the bottom half of the bag is opaque, hiding the unattractive clump of moist, sandy organic material on which the mushroom spores are cultivated.

The stalks and caps require only brief cooking. Unless a specific recipe indicates otherwise, just before using, rinse the caps briefly in cold water and then shake the cluster dry. Trim off the bottom third of the stem section and throw it away along with whatever gritty cultivating material may still be clinging to it. Cut the remaining stalks in half, thirds, or even shorter pieces, depending on the recipe in which they will be used. In soup dishes, the caps are typically placed directly in individual bowls and hot soup is poured over them.

Maitaké Mushrooms

Fresh *maitaké* (*mai* means to "dance") mushrooms have ruffled dark tops, thick, snowy white stems, a deep forest aroma, and a meaty texture. In America, I have seen them labeled as hen-of-the-woods mushrooms, I imagine because they resemble cockscombs. Before using them, trim away any grit from the stem portion and break the ruffled tops into bite-sized pieces with your hands. The rough edges that result from tearing, rather than slicing, the caps allow for better flavor absorption when cooking. Slice the thicker, typically smooth white stem portions into thin strips with a knife if you have trouble shredding them with your fingers.

Naméko Mushrooms

These small, round, firm mushrooms have orangey caps and stubby stems. They are naturally coated in a thick, slippery substance and are commonly used in dishes for their unusual texture and earthy, full-bodied flavor.

In Japan, small vacuum-sealed packages, each holding about 1/3 cup of the mushroom caps, are sold in most neighborhood supermarkets on refrigerated shelves. The mushrooms should be firm and have a very thick and viscous coating. They have a short shelf life, about 3 days, and watery packing liquid is a sign of spoilage. If your mushrooms were firm when purchased but have gone limp within a day or two, blanch them in vigorously boiling water for 30 seconds, drain them, and use immediately.

Canned *naméko* mushrooms are also available, though they are not as flavorful as vacuum-packed ones. The canned ones have a shelf life of more than a year, however. Once opened, use them immediately or store refrigerated in a lidded glass jar for up to 3 days.

Fresh and Dried* Shiitaké Mushrooms

Fresh shiitaké mushrooms, called *nama shiitaké*, are prized for their mild, woodsy aroma and pleasantly chewy texture. Only the caps are eaten, though the tough stems can be removed (be sure to trim away any gritty matter) and added to any stock for

*essential pantry item

flavor. Wipe them clean, checkin[g] [re]move any soil or grit that may be clinging [to the] han-nels. Use a cotton-tipped stick (t[he kind sold with cos]metics or medication), if necessa[ry] into narrow wedges, according to rec[ipe] the mushrooms in an open plastic bag [in the veg]etable bin; for maximum flavor and [use within a few d]ays.

Fresh and dried shiitaké mushro[oms are not interch]ange-able (think about the difference between sun-dried and fresh tomatoes, or fresh and dried apricots). The dried mushroom is intensely flavored, is densely textured, and requires extended cooking to become tender. In Japan, the regular consumption of dried shiitaké mushrooms is thought to promote good health. Not surprisingly, they are rich in minerals (especially potassium) and fiber.

Dried shiitaké mushrooms are a staple in the *washoku* pantry. Sold in every Asian grocery in North America, they are imported from many Asian countries. Price is a good indication of quality; the most expensive is usually *donko*, a nubbly-textured, thick-capped variety prized in soy-simmered dishes for its meaty texture and intensely woodsy aroma. Each *donko* mushroom can cost the equivalent of several dollars. For most dishes, however, the flatter, less costly dried shiitaké, either whole caps or presliced bits, will be fine. Store them on a dark shelf in an airtight container with the antimoisture packet from the original cellophane bag.

To **soften dried shiitaké mushrooms,** snap off the stems and set them aside for use in stocks, such as Basic Vegetarian Stock (page 93) or Sanuki Sea Stock (page 95). Soak the caps in warm water to cover (or as directed in recipes) for at least 30 minutes and up to several hours. Adding a pinch of sugar hastens the softening process. Top the mushrooms with an *otoshi-buta* (page 84) or a small, flat plate to submerge them completely in liquid as they soak.

When the mushrooms have softened, strain the soaking liquid to remove gritty bits, reserving the liquid. Rinse the mushroom caps well and resoak them for 5 to 10 minutes in the strained liquid (they must be fully reconstituted before cooking). Strain and save the liquid again. If necessary, you can add water to make up whatever volume is required for a given recipe. This softening procedure can be done days in advance and the mushrooms stored in their strained soaking liquid in the refrigerator.

Shiméji and Hon Shiméji Mushrooms

Sometimes called oyster mushrooms in English, these mushrooms have pearly gray caps and white, stubby stems. Large clusters measure several inches across. Before using, trim away any grit from the stem portion and discard. Break apart the darker-capped pieces with your fingers. Any large clusters should be torn into bite-sized pieces. The rough edges from tearing, rather than slicing, allow for a better transfer of flavors between mushrooms and soup or sauce.

NOODLES

A wide variety of noodle dishes, served both hot and chilled, in broth or with dipping sauces, are enjoyed throughout Japan. Regional preferences, however, are strong and obvious: Most people in the Sanuki region of Shikoku (prefectures of Kagawa and Ehime, on the Inland Sea) eat thick, white wheat noodles called *udon* at least once a day, while residents of the Shinshu District (Nagano Prefecture, in the center of the main island of Honshu) consume soba, or buckwheat noodles, daily. Those living in and around Nagoya prefer *kishimen,* a flat, white wheat noodle, to *udon,* using them in both hot and cold noodle dishes. Ramen, also called *chūka soba* or *shina soba* (Chinese-style noodles), are popular in many parts of Japan, but the northernmost island, Hokkaido, and the southern island of Kyushu are two strongholds of ramen-eating culture. *Sōmen,* thin, white wheat noodles, are eaten chilled everywhere in Japan during the hot months, as are *hiya mugi,* which are similar to *udon* but usually thinner and squarish. Sanuki natives enjoy *nyūmen,* or hot *sōmen* noodles, in miso soup year-round.

Suggestions regarding the purchase of various noodles are included with the descriptions that follow. Store all dried noodles as you would any pasta.

Harusamé (mung bean noodles)

Harusamé (literally, "spring rain") are noodles made from mung bean flour. Sold in dried form, *harusamé* are either soaked in hot water and used to make a salad or broken into bits to coat food for deep-frying. When soaked, the noodles turn translucent, looking somewhat like a sudden spring shower. When deep-fried, the noodles puff up, looking more like mists or clouds than rain.

Ramen (thin Chinese-style noodles)

These Chinese-style noodles are sold regularly in all Asian groceries under a variety of names, with ramen, *chūka soba,* and *shina soba* the most frequently encountered. Recipes in this book can be made with either regular dried (not "instant" dried) or fresh noodles, as long as they have not been seasoned in any way. I do not recommend precooked noodles. They are disappointing in flavor and texture and are usually loaded with chemical additives.

Soba (buckwheat noodles)

Packages of dried soba noodles are sold at every Asian grocery and at many ordinary supermarkets and health-foods stores in North America. Many packages are subdivided into bundles of between 80 and 100 grams (roughly $2^1/_2$ and 3 ounces); one bundle makes a generous single portion.

Some soba noodles are made from ground buckwheat only, though they tend to break easily after cooking. Buckwheat, though nutritious, has no gluten (the "glue" in wheat flour that makes bread chewy). Most soba noodles are made from a combination of wheat flour and milled buckwheat grain; *hachi wari soba* (literally, "80 percent buckwheat") is the most commonly consumed combination.

Instead of wheat flour, or sometimes in addition to it, a glutinous yam called *yama imo* is grated and added to the

A variety of noodles (clockwise from top): sōmen *(banded in black),* kishimen, soba, fresh *udon,* harusamé, *and ramen*

noodle dough. When making Buckwheat Noodle Roll (page 174), I recommend this type with the yam binder.

Sōmen (thin, white wheat noodles)

Sōmen noodles are the exception to several standard practices regarding the making, cooking, and eating of Japanese noodles. Unlike other Japanese noodles that are available both fresh and dried, *sōmen* noodles are always sold in dried form. The dough is made from high-gluten wheat flour, salt, and water and then stretched by hand with the aid of chopsticks and a thin coating of vegetable oil before being hung out to dry on racks. Residents of the Sanuki region claim that *sōmen* noodles improve somewhat with the passage of time and will store them for a year or two before cooking them.

Udon (thick, white wheat noodles)

Wheat flour and salted water (traditionally sea water) combine to make a noodle dough that is a challenge to knead by hand. Modern commercial production uses powerful mixing machines, but in those home kitchens where *udon* is still made from scratch, the dough is kneaded the old-fashioned way—by stomping, rather than hand pressing. The noodlemaker places the dough between pliable plastic sheets and brings his or her full body weight to bear on the stiff mass in a rhythmic tread, gradually making the dough elastic enough to roll out into sheets. These are then cut into strips and set to dry a bit before boiling.

Udon noodles are available fresh, dried, and semidried. All types can be used in the recipes in this book, though cooking instructions differ. See page 168 for guidance.

Hand-kneaded, *hiya mugi* is a white wheat noodle that is rolled out and cut, vermicelli thin. It is served chilled like *sōmen*. In the Nagoya region, between Kyoto and Tokyo, *kishimen*, a flat, linguine-like wheat flour noodle, replaces *udon* in most dishes. It is made by rolling, then folding, noodle dough and cutting it into $1/4$-inch-wide strips. In Asian markets, packages of dried *hiya mugi* and *kishimen* are often sold alongside dried *udon* and *sōmen* noodles.

PICKLES

The category of Japanese foods known as *tsukémono* is usually referred to as pickles in English. However, unlike most pickles in Western cuisines that are preserved foods with an extended shelf life, many Japanese pickles are quite perishable. It would be more accurate, perhaps, to describe *tsukémono* as ingredients that have been "transformed" without cooking.

There are a number of variables in the transformation process: the choice of pickling medium (vinegar, salt, rice bran, and sugar syrup are some of the possibilities), the amount of time required to reach maturity (prime eating time), and the length of time a *tsukémono* remains "fresh" (that is, at optimal flavor, texture, aroma, and so on).

An assortment of *tsukémono* can be arranged attractively and served with rice at any meal. Several of the pickles cataloged here are served with sushi, either as a palate-cleansing condiment or as a filling for plump rolls.

Most pickles are available in vacuum-sealed pouches or other sealed containers. If you buy the pickle in the refrigerated section of the market, then it must be kept refrigerated; if it is on an open shelf, then refrigerate after opening.

Once opened, store the contents of the package with its liquid in a glass jar (or other nonreactive container). Tightly cap and label the package with the name of the food and the date on which you opened the pickles. Consume within 2 weeks, or by the "sell by" date, whichever comes first.

Fukujin-Zuké (chutneylike pickles)

This traditional accompaniment to curry rice is an assortment of crisp, chutneylike pickles tinted deep crimson (traditionally with a natural dye called *beni*, which is also used for red pickled ginger). The name of this pickle refers to the seven Gods of Good Fortune (Shichi Fukujin), and it is made from seven types of vegetables and herbs, usually daikon, turnip, eggplant, two types of gourd, ginger, and *shiso*. It is sold in sealed packages and glass jars. To store, transfer the contents with the pickling liquid to a glass jar. The pickles will keep for 6 to 8 weeks.

Gods of Good Fortune

Like trying to recite the names of all of Snow White's Seven Dwarfs, recalling the names of all seven Gods of Good Fortune can be challenging. For future reference, the seven are: Ebisu, the God of Good Fortune, who carries a fishing rod with a huge sea bream on its hook; pot-bellied, Santalike Hotei, the God of Happiness, who carries a bag filled with gifts; Jurōjin, the God of Longevity, who sports a long white beard and carries a cane; Fukurokuju, the God of Wisdom and Wealth, who in some versions of the legend shares a body with Jurōjin; Daikokuten, the God of Farming and Wealth, who stands on a pair of full rice sacks; Bishamon, both the God of War and the protector of the divine treasure house, who is clad in armor; and Benzaiten, originally known as the Goddess of the River, who became associated with love, music, and the arts, too.

Nozawana-Zuké (pickled green, leafy vegetable)

This brined pickle is named after Nozawa Onsen, a hot-springs resort area in Nagano Prefecture where the green, leafy vegetable is grown and most of the pickles are made. The Nozawana plant is in the turnip family, but it is cultivated for its large, broad green leaves (faintly reminiscent of kale), and not for its white root. In the early fall, after harvest, bunches of leaves are taken to a hot-springs tributary to be washed before being put up in brine. Nozawana pickles are large and, when spread out, can become a tasty wrapper in place of toasted nori for hand-pressed rice.

Nuka-Zuké (rice bran pickles)

See *nuka* (page 39).

Pink Pickled Ginger (amazu shōga, hajikami su-zuké)

Used primarily as a condiment with sushi, thinly sliced pink pickled ginger is referred to as *gari* (an onomatopoetic word suggesting crunchiness) at the sushi bar, where it is served as a palate cleanser and condiment. It is also chopped and added to "scattered" sushi dishes (page 147). It is sold in vacuum-sealed pouches, bottles, or small tubs in most groceries that stock Asian foodstuffs and does not have to be refrigerated until after the package has been opened. It will then keep, well covered, for many months. Most often, the ginger is broadly and thinly sliced, but sometimes it is cut into julienne strips or bottled as whole knobs. It can be labeled *amazu shōga* (literally, "sweet and sour" ginger) or *hajikami su-zuké* (literally, "blushing pickle").

Some brands are more intensely pink than others; the natural color is a pale peach or yellow. Most brands use some food coloring to heighten the natural blushing shade that results from the chemical interaction between very young fresh ginger shoots and rice vinegar. If you have access to fresh young ginger, you can make your own pink pickled ginger (page 223).

Rakkyō Bulbs

Related to scallions, these bulbs are small, white, teardrop shaped, and quite intense in flavor and aroma—tasting more like garlic than scallions. They come to market in the late spring and early summer and are transformed into pickles in many homes. Commercially made pickles are available year round. Pickled first in brine and then in a sweet-and-sour sauce, *rakkyō* can be served with rice at any meal, but most often accompany curry rice or beef stews.

After opening sealed jars, store the bulbs in the refrigerator. If they came in a bag, once the bag is opened, transfer the contents with the pickling liquid to a glass jar. The bulbs will keep for 6 to 8 weeks.

Red Pickled Ginger (beni shōga)

Red pickled ginger is a sharp, lively condiment served with rice and noodle dishes. It is most often sold already sliced into julienne strips in glass jars or sealed plastic tubs with some pickling liquid surrounding it. *Beni* is a natural dye known from ancient days, when it was used for cosmetic as well as culinary purposes (*kuchi beni* means "lipstick"; *kuchi* is "mouth" and *beni* is "red").

Drain just before serving, and use care to avoid staining fingertips, cutting boards, and kitchen towels. Although artificial coloring agents often supplement traditional ones, it is *beni*, the ancient herbal dye, that causes stubborn stains. Once you have opened the package, store it in the refrigerator. It will keep, covered and in its original liquid, for many months.

Shiba-Zuké (eggplant, ginger, and gourd mix)
Historically associated with Kyoto and its environs, this pickle is a mélange of eggplant, ginger (or gingerlike *myōga*), and *uri* gourd that has been pickled in brine and tinted pinkish purple with *aka-jiso* leaves (page 26). *Shiba-zuké* is most often finely minced and served in small mounds on its own or in combination with other pickles as an accompaniment to rice.

Takuan (yellow pickled daikon)
Named after Takuan, an early-seventeenth-century priest, this pickle is made from sun-dried daikon that has been submerged in a paste made from *nuka* (rice bran). Still crunchy, heady in aroma, and pleasantly fermented in taste, it is typically dyed a bright yellow with *kuchinashi no mi* (dried gardenia pods). Many of the commercially produced products include artificial coloring (neon yellow) and unwanted seasonings (sugar, monosodium glutamate), so you will need to read labels carefully.

Uméboshi (pickled plum), Bainiku (plum paste)
You will find two varieties of *uméboshi* on the shelves of Asian grocery stores: soft and plump but wrinkled plums, about 1 inch in diameter, and small, smooth, firm plums that look a bit like olives. The soft plums are of two sorts, those that have been tinted with *aka-jiso* leaves (page 26) and those that have not. Those that have are a very rosy color, and the shriveled,

deep purple leaves that tinted them should be visible through the package. Those that have not been tinted will be a dusty pinkish brown.

Packaged in clear plastic tubs, the homely *uméboshi* seem innocuous. In reality, they possess the most explosively refreshing, mouth-puckering possibilities imaginable! Many Japanese wake up to pickled plums with their breakfast bowl of rice, just as a strong cup of coffee is what many Americans want the first thing in the morning. They are also thought to have medicinal powers to settle and cure intestinal problems.

In this book, I have called for the pulp (*bainiku*) of pickled plums on several occasions. You can make this pulp yourself by pulling the meaty flesh off of the pits, or you can buy the pulp as a thick paste packed in tubes. Check the label to make sure your purchase has no artificial additives.

In the traditional *washoku* pantry, *uméboshi* went unrefrigerated year-round. A cool, dark shelf should be fine in your kitchen, though I would refrigerate opened tubes of paste (to maintain top aroma) and whole plums when the weather is very hot. Most plums "mature" in one year and eating pleasure is normally within a year from that time. Some plums are allowed to pickle for 2 or 3 years before being packaged; these tend to be very intense. Pickled plums do not spoil; if a whitish powder appears on the surface, it is likely crystallized salt.

In gift catalogs in Japan, you occasionally see "historic" *uméboshi* for sale that are one hundred years or older. As with aged wines or brandy, prices are high.

Yama Gobō (wild burdock root)
Pencil-thin wild burdock roots from the mountains are scraped and briefly blanched and then submerged in a tub of miso and allowed to marinate for several months. They remain crunchy but take on a heady aroma, and the color changes to an orangey shade, making them look a bit like carrots. Some *yama gobō* are put up in a slightly sweet, soy sauce–based pickling medium in lieu of the miso; these are usually labeled *shōyu-zuké* and are brown in color.

RICE*

Uncooked Japanese-style rice is short grained and the kernels are plump. Although all Japanese varieties seem sticky (they cling together, making eating with chopsticks easier), there are two distinctly different types: glutinous rice (*mochi-gomé*) and nonglutinous rice (*uruchi mai*). I call for only the latter in this book.

California is growing excellent nonglutinous Japanese-style rice. It is being marketed throughout the United States under a number of different labels (Kokuho Rose and Tamaki are widely available). Most stores sell 2- or 5-pound packages, in addition to the 25-pound bags bought by most Japanese and other Asian households.

Transfer your rice from the original paper bag to an airtight container. Store the rice on a cool, dry, dark shelf. It will keep well for at least 1 year.

▦ IN THE WASHOKU KITCHEN: **rice cookers, 84; shaping and molding, 86; equipment for making sushi, 88.**

Nuka (rice bran)

The *nuka*, or rice bran, removed in the polishing process has traditionally been used in *washoku* households to make a pickling paste. Eating vegetables pickled in *nuka* reintroduces many of the vitamins and minerals that would otherwise be lost in polishing. Because pickles and white rice are served together, nutrients are balanced at table.

Although I personally keep a *nuka toko* (rice-bran pickle pot) in my Tokyo apartment, taking pleasure in monitoring it, not many households do so any longer. Making and maintaining the *nuka* pickling medium requires a high level of care and devotion. If you want to enjoy *nuka-zuké* pickles, ask about them at your local Asian grocery. Often the owner, or some employee, sells homemade pickles, usually cucumbers, turnips, or radishes. Rinse off the paste clinging to the pickled vegetables just before slicing and serving. Despite being called pickles, these transformed vegetables are quite perishable and should be refrigerated until consumed, within 24 hours of purchase.

*essential pantry item

Omochi (pounded rice taffy)

Pounded from steamed glutinous rice, this sticky rice taffy is eaten on special occasions such as the New Year holiday. Snacks and sweets made from *omochi* are also eaten throughout the year. In certain regions of Japan known for rice cultivation, such as the Tohoku area in the northwestern region of the main island of Honshū, small dumplings made from this pounded rice are topped with crushed fresh soybeans (*zunda aé*) to make a summertime treat. See the Kitchen Harmony notes on page 203 for details on how to make these dumplings.

Shin Mai (newly harvested rice)

Shin mai, or newly harvested rice, is often labeled as such; look for it in stores in the fall. Storage procedures are the same for all varieties of raw rice, but cooking varies; see directions for cooking new crop rice on page 138.

Togi-Jiru (water drained from washing rice)

The cloudy water that results from washing rice is called *togi-jiru,* and it can be used later the same day to cook corn on the cob; fresh peas and beans; or root vegetables such as daikon, lotus root, and burdock root. The vegetables will taste sweeter because their natural sugars are enhanced by the starchy water. The water is also used in the garden, especially for watering flowering plants such as geraniums.

Zakkoku Mai (millet, buckwheat, whole grains, and seeds mix)

A number of products have come on the market to enrich plain white rice. Some of these are fancy vitamin-pill-like tablets, capsules, or powders that are added to raw rice just before it is cooked. As the rice cooks, these supplements coat the grains of polished rice with nutrients, such as calcium and vitamin-B complex. Other products come in premeasured packets of mixed grains. I like a blend of buckwheat, *keshi no mi* (white poppy seeds), *kuro mai* (black rice, an heirloom strain that tints the cooked rice pink), *awa* (a sticky millet that adds a pleasantly chewy texture), and *hato mugi* (flat barley) that is available in

Tokyo supermarkets. It is packaged in many small, separately sealed pouches, each ready to be mixed with 1^1/$_2$ cups raw rice just before cooking.

Store as you would any grain, in a lidded container on a dark, dry, cool shelf.

Several kinds of multigrain mixtures are also for sale in Asian groceries outside Japan. Or you can make your own mixture using a combination of flat barley, quinoa, amaranth, sesame seeds, flaxseeds, oatmeal, and/or poppy seeds. Figure on 2 tablespoons mixed grains and seeds for every 1^1/$_2$ cups raw rice; adjust the level of cooking water by adding 1 teaspoon more water for every 2 tablespoons mixed grains and seeds.

SEA VEGETABLES

The Japanese consume a wide variety of marine vegetation. Among the many sea vegetables cataloged below, *kombu* (kelp) is of particular importance; not only is it the foundation of an array of stocks (the leftovers of which are made into a condiment), but it is also used when simmering, poaching, or steaming fish to keep it from sticking to the pot and to add flavor.

Ao Nori (sea herb flakes)

This marine alga (illustrated on page 48) is harvested from shallow ocean beds and then dried. It comes to stores packed in glass jars alone or combined with terrestrial herbs and spices. I have called for sea herb flakes as a garnish in a few rice recipes where their fresh seashore aroma encourages hearty appetites. The Japanese use the flakes as a seasoning for potato chips!

Store the flakes on a dry shelf, away from direct sunlight or heat. They will not spoil, but their delicate sea-air aroma fades after several months. The full aromatic power of the herb can best be brought out by rubbing it between your fingertips or palms just before using.

Dried sea vegetables (clockwise from top): sheet of toasted nori, naga hijiki, *sticks of* kanten, *and long strips of* hoshi wakamé

Hijiki

A calcium-rich sea vegetable commonly eaten in Japan, *hijiki* is widely available in Asian groceries worldwide. Even in Japan, it is sold primarily as a dried shelf-stable item. I have included a recipe in this book for the most commonly prepared *hijiki* dish, a soy-braised preparation (page 187). I prefer the tender, short buds labeled *mé hijiki*, but the longer pieces, *naga hijiki*, can also be used. Both come packaged in cellophane bags and appear to be a mass of crinkly, brittle, jet black strands. When softened and cooked, they have a slight anise flavor.

Stored in its original bag on a dark, dry shelf, it will keep indefinitely. Flavor, aroma, and nutrition (exposure to light will compromise its vitamin levels), however, are best within the first year of purchase.

Kanten (Japanese agar-agar), Tengusa

The Japanese have used aquatic plants to make both savory aspics and sweet confections for more than a thousand years. And it is likely that the gelling properties of certain marine algae, such as red *tengusa*, was understood, and used, in cooking on the Asian continent long before that.

Traditionally, *tengusa* had been (and still is) dried and boiled to make *tokoroten*, a nearly colorless, very stiff aspic. Sometime in the late seventeenth century, *kanten*, a new and easy-to-use form of the sea gelatin, appeared in Japanese pantries and at table. Its discovery is credited to serendipity. It seems that one day a frugal (or perhaps very hungry) servant salvaged *tokoroten* that had been left over from some wintertime feast. Lying in the snow where it had been subjected to subzero temperatures at night, but sunny and cold daytime conditions, the *tokoroten* had freeze-dried naturally.

The resulting spongy but brittle white mass was dubbed *kanten*, literally "cold sky," by the monks at Manpukuji Temple, near Kyoto. Known as agar-agar in most English-speaking countries, *kanten* is shelf-stable, unlike its perishable predecessor, *tokoroten*.

The frigid mountainous terrain of Nagano Prefecture, where the 1998 Winter Olympics were held, has an ideal climate for making *kanten,* and today nearly all commercially produced *kanten* is made there. Traditionally sold in sticks that were softened and shredded just before using, it is now sold in a convenient powdered form, too.

Kombu (kelp)*

Aware of the natural flavor-enhancing properties of certain sea vegetables, the Japanese have both gathered wild and cultivated many varieties of *kombu* for centuries. Most *kombu* is harvested in the chilly waters around and near the coastline of Hokkaido, Japan's large northern island. Depending on the time of year and the location of the seabeds, the shape and color of *kombu* can vary from thick and stony gray to thin and green with a reddish cast.

All varieties of *kombu* are long—several yards long. Depending upon the specific variety, however, and the way in which it has been packaged, *kombu* is sold in precut segments as short as 2 or 3 inches or in folded pieces a foot or more in length. With all varieties of *kombu,* let price be your guide, knowing the superior product is more expensive. Many kinds of *kombu* appear chalky, but this whitish powder is not an indication of mold or spoilage. Rather, the substance contains natural glutamates and should not be wiped away. Unlike artificially produced monosodium glutamate, the naturally occurring glutamates in *kombu* have never been known to cause unpleasant or dangerous reactions when consumed. Store in an airtight container on a dark shelf, where it will keep indefinitely. Although *kombu* does not spoil, its subtle sea-sweet aroma does fade after a year or so, sometimes taking on musty overtones.

Since dried *kombu* is so light, it is more practical to indicate a recipe amount by length or surface area than it is to weigh it. When making stocks, take the required surface space as a single piece whenever possible, breaking it only if necessary to fit into your pot. After making stock, examine the piece of kelp you used. You will notice that it is the exposed and cut

*essential pantry item

or broken edges that become viscous (especially true of higher-glutamate varieties), while the broad surfaces are smooth but not slippery.

Get in the habit of saving *kombu* after stock making. It can be recycled into Kelp and Mushroom Relish (page 110) and also be used as a flavor enhancer when pickling vegetables. Store it in a closed glass container or plastic bag in the refrigerator for up to a week.

There are several kinds of *kombu,* most named for their region of origin and each with its own distinctive characteristics. I want to acquaint you with four varieties:

Hidaka Kombu, Dashi Kombu: If a package of *kombu* is labeled *dashi kombu* (literally, "kelp for stock making"), it will probably be of the Hidaka variety, a fine, reasonably priced all-purpose kelp. It has a lower concentration of glutamates than some other varieties, but still contributes a mild, flavor-enhancing brininess to the stocks and sauces in which it is used. Packages typically contain pieces 3 to 4 inches long. Each piece is sufficient to flavor a scant quart of stock.

Ma Kombu: The flavor of *ma kombu* (botanically *Laminaria japonica*), a kelp particularly rich in naturally occurring glutamates, is best unlocked by soaking the *kombu* first in cold water for at least 20 minutes and up to several hours and then slowly drawing out its flavor over low heat until the water has barely reached a boil. Although it makes a rich, deeply flavored broth, the broth is typically cloudy and not suited to making clear soups. Broad-leafed and gray-green, often with chalky white streaks, *ma kombu* is favored by residents of the Kansai area (Osaka and Kyoto), where it is used to make stock and to line skillets in which fish and vegetables are simmered.

Rausu Kombu: Thick and sturdy, this high-glutamate *kombu* is often the choice of anyone sticking to a truly vegetarian diet because broth made from it has a meaty flavor. It is also a good choice for lining the pan in which fish will be poached; it keeps

Varieties of kombu: *large, broad* Rausu kombu *(center), a strip of* Rishiri kombu *(right), smaller strips of* Hidaka kombu *(bottom left), and two pieces (a fairly broad strip and a narrow-tipped piece) of* ma kombu *(top left)*

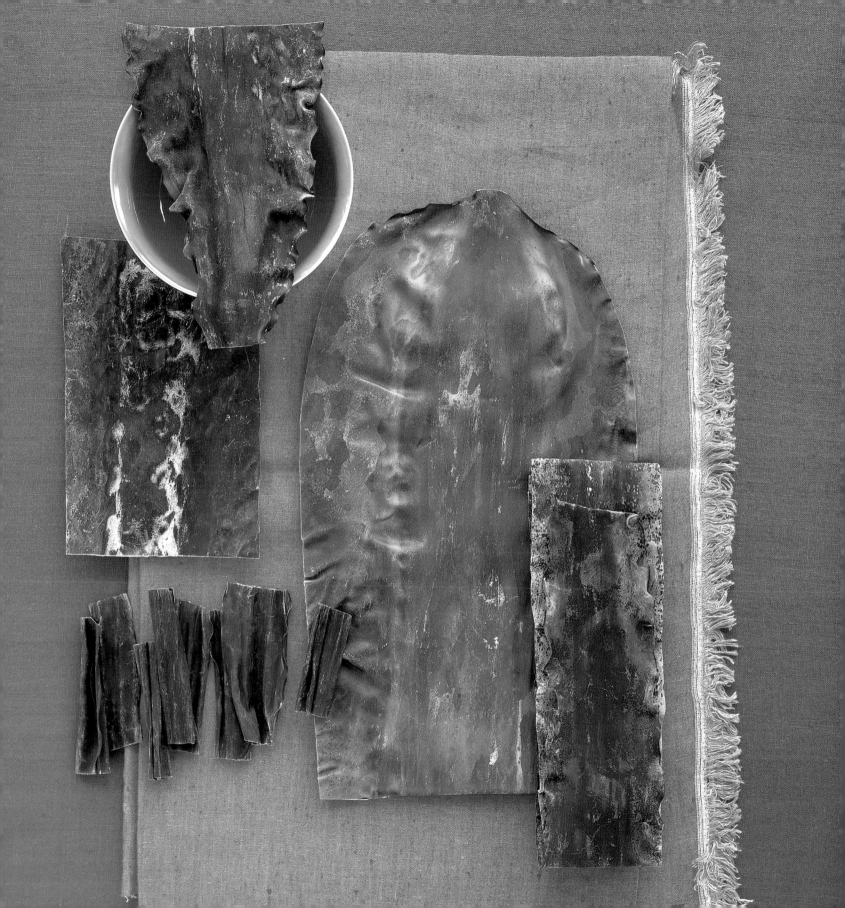

the fish from sticking to the pan, adds flavor to the sauce, and becomes tender and delicious.

Rishiri Kombu: This sturdy, dark *kombu* (botanically *L. ochotenis*) makes crystal clear stock with a delicate, herbal flavor. It is the *kombu* of choice when making clear soups. As with other high-glutamate varieties, *Rishiri kombu* yields the most flavor when it is soaked in cold water before heating. A cold-water infusion can be made and kept refrigerated for several days until needed. Slowly release its flavor over very low heat until a few bubbles appear at the rim of the pot.

Nori

The Japanese word *nori* is often translated as "seaweed," which is unfortunate and inaccurate. It is actually a generic term for a variety of marine vegetables that are both gathered in the wild and cultivated.

The Japanese have cultivated sea vegetables for centuries. Among those kinds regularly consumed in Japan, *Asakusa nori* (named for the place near Tokyo Bay where historically most of this product was grown) is the most popular in the United States. For most sushi dishes, and for the soba noodles rolled in nori to look like sushi (page 174), I recommend the purchase of *yaki nori,* or "toasted nori," which is high-quality *Asakusa nori* that has been toasted.

Most full-sized sheets of nori sold in Asian groceries are toasted and unseasoned. Precut sheets, used primarily as a garnish for rice, are sometimes seasoned with a sweet soy sauce (see seasoned nori, below).

Seasoned Nori (aji nori, aji tsuké nori): Buy seasoned nori, known as both *aji nori* and *aji tsuké nori,* in individually wrapped small packets, typically 5 sheets to a packet. Each sheet measures 2^1/$_2$ or 3 inches long and about 1^1/$_2$ inches wide. The packets are either packaged (in multiples of 10) in a cellophane bag, or stacked in a tin cylinder (in Japan, this tends to be a gift package).The sheets become quite sticky when exposed to air, so open and eat at the table. A packet is often included on a breakfast tray, for eating with rice.

Store seasoned nori sheets with their antimoisture packets from the original package in a cool, dark, dry spot. If they become soggy, turn them into Nori Sauce (page 108); use a light hand on seasoning because the sheets have already been seasoned with soy sauce and sugar.

Toasted Nori (yaki nori): Look for flat, unfolded full-sized sheets (about 7^1/$_2$ by 8^1/$_4$ inches) of toasted nori (illustrated on page 40). They typically come in 10-sheet and 50-sheet packages. Store them with their antimoisture packets from the original package in a cool, dark, dry spot. Toasted nori can be stored in a tightly closed bag or tin in the freezer; the sheets will thaw instantaneously and may be refrozen any number of times. Care needs to be taken, though, to keep moisture in the surrounding air from being trapped (and frozen, crystallizing) in the bag before refreezing.

Wakamé (sea tangle)

This mineral-rich, brown sea alga is used in many Japanese dishes, especially soups and salads. You will find it at all Asian groceries in either fresh-salted (*nama wakamé*) or dried form (*hoshi wakamé;* illustrated on page 40); peeking inside the cellophane package, *wakamé* appears to be very dark green, nearly black. When softened, the sea vegetable is a tangle of deep, jade-colored fronds.

Although most recipes do not specify one form or the other, the fresh-salted variety is usually more suitable for salads, while the dried bits are better suited to mixing with ground meat or floating in soups.

A springtime delicacy harvested from early March through mid-April, *nama wakamé* has actually been blanched (reddish brown fronds turn emerald green as they emerge from the cauldron) and heavily salted, despite its name. The word *nama* (literally, "fresh") is used here to distinguish it from *hoshi* (literally, "dried"), and alerts consumers to the relatively short shelf life of the product and the need to keep it refrigerated, or at least in a very cool spot in the kitchen.

Look for *nama wakamé* in the refrigerated section of Asian groceries. Because there are many seabeds throughout Asia where this vegetable is commercially cultivated, and because the salting helps extend its shelf life, fresh *wakamé* is often available in stores through the summer and early autumn.

A staple of the Japanese (and Korean) pantry, dried *wakamé* is sold in both small bits and longer strips, packaged in cellophane. If necessary, longer strips can be cut with scissors to make small bits. Dried *wakamé* appears to be crinkly and looks almost black; when softened, it reverts to smooth, green fronds. Look for *hoshi wakamé* on the shelves of any Asian grocery.

To prepare dried *wakamé* for cooking, soak in cold water to cover for about 3 to 5 minutes. It will expand to many times its original dried volume, so choose the size of your bowl accordingly. To prepare fresh *wakamé* for cooking, rinse it in cold water to remove residual salt and sand and then soak it in freshly drawn cold water for just 1 or 2 minutes. Do not soak *wakamé* longer than suggested here; the flavor, texture, aroma, and nutritional value suffer with extended soaking. Drain the softened fronds, squeezing out excess liquid. Trim off any tough ribs.

SEEDS AND NUTS

Seeds and nuts, such as sesame seeds, poppy seeds, chestnuts, pine nuts, and walnuts, play an important though supporting role in the making of many *washoku* dishes.

▦ IN THE WASHOKU KITCHEN: **grinding, crushing, and mashing, 73; dry-roasting, 85.**

Sesame Seeds (goma)

Sesame is an enormously versatile ingredient in constructing *washoku* menus and is used whole, cracked, and crushed as a garnish for noodles and vegetable dishes; cracked or ground to a paste for sauces and dips; and as an aromatic cooking oil (see page 50). The nutty richness of sesame blends well with sweet, sour, and salty flavors. Because sesame seeds are a fine source of calcium, iron, and vitamin B_1, they can provide a nutritional boost to your meals.

Two varieties of sesame seeds are regularly used in Japanese cooking: white (*shiro goma*) and black (*kuro goma*). Both are the seeds of the slender, flowering stalks of sesame plants. The stalks grow to an average of 3 feet high, and a single plant will produce either white or black seeds. Mature plants that have gone to seed are cut down and allowed to dry before the seeds are thrashed from them.

Both white and black sesame come to market as raw whole seeds called *arai goma* and as dry-roasted whole seeds called *iri goma*. Dry-roasted seeds, both white and black, are available crushed (*suri goma*), cracked (*kiri goma*), or ground to a smooth paste (*neri goma*). For convenience in preparation, some recipes call for a prepared paste. In some recipes, the choice of white or black sesame may be an aesthetic one.

Black sesame has both medicinal and culinary uses in Japan. Traditionally, the seeds have been used in making skin salves and ointments. In the kitchen, they are often used in combination with salt (the mixture is called *goma shio*) for sprinkling on rice and mixed with sugar in confectionary.

Whole white sesame seeds come to market both hulled (*muki goma* or *migaki goma*) and unhulled (*goma*). Unhulled white seeds tend to have a nuttier flavor than the hulled ones. The cream-colored hulled seeds, however, crush more easily to make a smooth paste.

If you decide to purchase just one kind of sesame, it should be raw whole white seeds, or *arai shiro goma*, for optimal flavor and aroma. Then dry-roast the seeds yourself just before using them (see page 85). Depending on the recipe, you will leave the seeds whole, or crack, crush, or grind them.

Once sesame seeds have been dry-roasted, their oils come to the surface, which is what makes them so wonderfully aromatic. However, once the oils surface and are exposed to the air, they can go rancid quickly. Store your untoasted sesame seeds in a closed container on a dry, cool shelf in your cupboard. All opened packages of pretoasted sesame should be stored in the refrigerator or other very cool, dry spot in your kitchen, if you want to keep them fresh for more than a few weeks. Crushed or cracked seeds and paste go stale quickly.

Black Sesame Paste (kuro neri goma) and White Sesame Paste (shiro neri goma): Both black sesame paste, which is jet black, and white sesame paste, which is beige, are used to make savory and sweet foods. In this book, I have called for black sesame paste to make an intensely flavored sorbet (page 298) and white sesame paste to make Creamy Sesame-Miso Sauce (page 100). Both pastes are illustrated on page 48.

Sesame paste is usually sold in glass jars. Check the label to make sure you are buying unadulterated sesame paste (some brands have sweeteners and starch fillers added). Unlike tahini and other sesame pastes found in markets that carry Near Eastern foodstuffs, Japanese sesame paste is made from roasted seeds. The oil in sesame paste will separate out, floating to the top of the jar. This is not a sign of spoilage. Either stir to recombine or pour off excess oil for a less oily, stiffer, denser paste.

Until opening, jars of sesame paste can be stored on any dark, cool shelf. Once you have opened a jar, it is best to refrigerate it. For maximum flavor and aroma, consume within 1 month of opening.

White Poppy Seeds (keshi no mi)

Japanese poppy seeds are pale ivory in color, rather than bluish black, and are appreciated for their mild, nutty flavor and unique texture. *Keshi no mi* are used as a garnish for slow-simmered dishes such as Ginger-Stewed Eggplant (page 192), and in combination with other more incendiary spices in a blend called *shichimi tōgarashi* (page 47). For optimal flavor and aroma, keep the seeds in a sealed container on a cool, dark, dry shelf.

• • •

Almonds

The Japanese frequently use almonds in Western and Chinese-style confections. Unsalted nuts, whether whole and toasted or slivered, will work best in the recipe for Green Tea Chocolate-Almond Clusters (page 300).

Kuri no Kanrō Ni (chestnuts in syrup)

Peeled, beveled, and bright yellow, sweet-stewed chestnuts bottled in syrup are available at most Asian groceries in North America. The vivid color is natural—the result of stewing the chestnuts with cracked *kuchinashi no mi* (dried gardenia pods)—and the syrup is gently sweet (*mizu amé*, or barley malt, is used with, or instead of, regular sugar). Small bottles hold about a dozen chestnuts. After opening, refrigerate in their syrup and use within 1 month.

Pine Nuts (matsu no mi)

Although most North Americans will associate pine nuts with Mediterranean cusines, Japan has an abundance of pine trees that yield flavorful *matsu no mi*. In addition to their use in making sauces, *matsu no mi* are also pressed into ground meat and fish to form a coating and then deep-fried.

Walnuts (kurumi)

Japanese walnuts tend to be smaller and more intensely flavored than their American counterparts. They can be crushed until smooth and creamy to enrich sauces, or coarsely chopped to add texture to salads.

SPICES AND SEASONINGS

A variety of spices and seasonings are used when preparing *washoku* menus, at times to provide an accent, but most often to achieve harmony by bringing disparate flavors into balance. I begin with spices and spicy pastes and then discuss condiments such as vinegar and soy sauce.

Japanese Curry Powder (karé)

Nowadays, a wide variety of authentic Indian spice blends are available in Japanese markets. In my early years in Japan, however, consumers had a choice of only two products: a bright yellow, mildly spicy curry powder and a sweet-and-spicy block of curry roux. Old-fashioned curry powder (illustrated on page 48), packaged in small tins, is what I call for in this book. If you wish to capture the retro flavor of mid-twentieth-century Japan, without introducing additional animal fats (most packaged roux contains large amounts of beef suet and lard), this is the product you want. Curry powder (and packaged roux) is still enormously popular, and you will see many brands at any Asian grocery store.

Although the powder does not easily spoil, it does get musty within a month or two of opening the tin. Store it on a cool, dry shelf, sealing it snugly after each use.

Japanese Mustard (karashi)

The Japanese favor an intensely yellow, sharply flavored, hot mustard. It is available in powdered form (reconstitute with cold water, a few drops at a time, stirring to make a thick, smooth paste) and also in tubes in two types, smooth (illustrated on page 48) and rough textured. The tubes are certainly convenient, but check the labels for additives. After opening a tube, keep it refrigerated to maintain optimal aroma and full punch.

Salt (shio)

The salt used in the traditional Japanese kitchen is moist and fairly coarse and is processed from seawater. In Japanese markets, the best sea salt—round and sweet, never harsh and sharp—comes from Okinawa and the Inland Sea region. Kosher salt makes a good substitute, though it takes longer to wilt vegetables when pickling them.

Sanshō

The berry of the prickly ash plant is dried and crushed to make a tip-of-the-tongue-numbing, but delicately aromatic spice called *sanshō* (illustrated on page 48), also known as *kona-zanshō* (literally, "powdered" *sanshō*). It is sold in small jars, tins, or plastic containers and, once opened, should be stored in the refrigerator or freezer to protect its delicate scent.

Sanshō, in the form of small packets of the powdered spice, often accompanies *unagi no kabayaki* (glaze-grilled butterflied eel) and *yakitori* (glaze-grilled skewered chicken). Occasionally, whole preserved berries are available salted and partially dried, or simmered in soy sauce. These are wonderful added to simmered vegetable, meat, or fish dishes. Store the preserved berries in a closed freezer-safe container in the freezer. Recently, dried berries have become available in mill-topped containers that enable you to crack the berries just before using. I suggest seeking these out.

In the springtime, fresh leaves, called *ki no mé,* are plucked from the prickly ash plant and used to garnish soups, sauces, and salads, and to crush into miso-based sauces. The delicate-looking leaves are highly aromatic (lay them on the open palm of your hand and slap them just before floating in a broth or placing on food) and pack a surprising tongue-tingling punch when you bite into one.

The leaves are harvested from both male and female plants; the berries (peppercorns) are from the female only.

Shichimi Tōgarashi (7-spice pepper blend)

The Japanese use dried chile peppers, usually in powdered form, to season several dishes. Here, the powdered pods have been blended with six others herbs and spices (sesame seeds, flaxseeds, white poppy seeds, *ao nori,* dried *yuzu* peel, and *sanshō* pepper is the most commonly found combination). Sold in small glass jars or tins, the blend (illustrated on page 48) should be stored tightly closed, on a dark, dry shelf.

Tōgarashi (dried whole red chile pepper)

The Japanese dry a variety of red chile peppers, which they call *tōgarashi* (illustrated on page 48), and use them to spice up a number of rice, noodle, vegetable, fish, and meat dishes. The dried whole peppers are also called *taka no tsumé,* or "hawk claws," probably because of their shape.

When dried whole *tōgarashi* is crushed, it becomes *ichimi tōgarashi* (literally, "one flavor chile"). It is used on its own or in a blend of spices known as *shichimi tōgarashi* (page 47).

The seeds of the chile are incendiary and should be used with caution. After handling the dried pods, be sure to wash your hands with warm, soapy water. The natural oils of the chiles can be particularly irritating to your eyes if you should accidentally rub them.

Store the chiles as you would any spice, in a closed jar or other container, on a dark, dry shelf.

Wasabi (Japanese horseradish)

The gnarled wasabi root, indigenous to Japan, has been enjoyed for centuries—prized for its herbaceous aroma and nose-tingling fire—primarily with fresh fish and tōfu.

Fresh wasabi roots are hard to find outside Japan, but if your local Japanese food store has them in its refrigerated case, by all means treat yourself. Choose pale green roots with even coloration, preferably with their dark, ruffled leaves still attached. Black speckling on the root can be an early sign of spoilage. But look carefully, because it is sometimes just cling-ing soil. When you are ready to grate the root, whittle away the leaves and stem. Scrape away the outer peel, exposing just as much of the root as you need at that time. Use a *samékawa* grater (page 71) if possible. After grating, cover whatever is left of the root with plastic wrap and refrigerate. It should keep well for at least a week.

Most often, wasabi is sold as a powder in tins or as a paste in tubes. The powder is usually a mix of ordinary horseradish (not *Wasabia japonica*) and green food coloring. Stir together equal amounts of the powder and cold water to create a spicy paste for perking up bland foods. Although the powder does not spoil, it often develops a dusty, stale aftertaste within a few months of opening the tin. Close tightly after each use and store on a dark, dry shelf in your cupboard.

Spices, seasonings, and herbs (clockwise from top left): freeze-dried yuzu peel (page 28), wasabi paste, Japanese mustard, a trio of spices (shichimi tōgarashi, sanshō, and ichimi tōgarashi), black sesame paste (page 46), Japanese curry powder, tōgarashi, ao nori (page 41), white sesame paste (page 46), and yukari (page 26)

Most tubes of wasabi contain some *W. japonica*, albeit mixed with sorbitol and other seasonings and emulsifiers. Check the label. I keep opened tubes refrigerated to preserve the aroma, although the paste will not spoil.

In Japan, the leaves and bruised roots are chopped and pickled in *kasu*, the lees from saké making. Sometimes small jars of *wasabi-zuké* are available at Asian grocery stores. A spicy, heady spread for sandwiches can be made by blending a bit of this pickle with mayonnaise.

IN THE WASHOKU KITCHEN: **grating, 71.**

• • •

Mirin (sweet, syrupy rice wine)*

This syrupy rice wine has a low-alcohol content and so is often sold in ordinary supermarkets in Japan. It is not a drinking wine, but is instead used as a seasoning and glazing agent in cooking. The best-quality mirin is made in a process similar to that of saké making, though the variety of rice used is *mochi-gomé*, a sweet glutinous rice, instead of *uruchi mai*, the more commonly eaten rice. Most commercially available brands have sugar added, however.

Mirin does not spoil easily, though its aroma fades quickly. Store on a dark, dry shelf until opening; refrigerate after opening for optimal aroma. The cap and rim need to be wiped well after each use or they will stick badly, just as they do with maple or other syrups.

Plum Vinegar (umé-zu)

This intense, rose-colored, salty-and-sour by-product of pick-ling *uméboshi* (page 38) is used to tint and flavor a number of foods in the *washoku* kitchen. Because it is so concentrated, it is often diluted with water, plain rice vinegar, or dashi.

Plum vinegar is sold in bottles in most Asian groceries and many health-foods stores. Store it on a dark, cool cupboard shelf. Although the vinegar does not spoil easily, its fruity aroma fades within a few weeks of opening; refrigerating open bottles helps extend this time.

*essential pantry item

Rice Vinegar (junmai su, komé-zu)*

Unless otherwise indicated, vinegar in the *washoku* kitchen refers to ordinary rice vinegar, which is mild and fragrant, processed from a variety of grains, primarily, but not exclusively, rice. Many Americans become instant fans of its subtle verve and never return to harsh distilled white vinegar or fruit-based vinegars.

Because there are so many brands available, and each manufacturer produces several products and grades of product, you will need to read labels carefully. In general, price is a good indication of quality. Rice vinegar is graded in a manner similar to that of olive oils (extra virgin is from the first pressing, virgin is from successive pressings). The highest-quality rice vinegar made from polished (white) rice is *junmai su* ("pure" rice vinegar; that is, made only from rice and not seasoned with sugar and salt), made from the first pressing of fermented rice mash. The next in order of quality and purity is *komé-zu* (literally, "rice vinegar"). Products labeled *su* (vinegar) typically include additives such as alcohol and are made from mixed grains, not just rice.

Store all vinegars tightly capped on a cool, dark, dry shelf in the kitchen. Vinegar typically darkens with age and/or exposure to light and/or heat.

Brown Rice Vinegar (kuro-zu): The most expensive whole-grain rice vinegar is *kuro-zu* (literally, "black vinegar"), which is distilled from brown rice without the addition of alcohol. Most of the top brands are made in Kagoshima Prefecture on the southern island of Kyushu. Pleasantly tart with malted overtones, *kuro-zu* has a clean finish on the palate and is what I use when making salad dressings and sauces, especially my Smoky Vinaigrette (page 99).

Less costly *jun genmai su* (pure unpolished rice vinegar) and *genmai su* (unpolished rice vinegar) are also fine choices. All vinegars made from whole-grain rice are darker and richer in nutrients than vinegars made from polished rice.

*essential pantry item

Seasoned Rice Vinegar (sushi su, awasé-zu): A flavored rice vinegar, specifically for seasoning rice that will be used in sushi dishes, is called *sushi su* or *awasé-zu*. These products have sugar, salt, and sometimes monosodium glutamate added to them. I have included a recipe to make your own (page 145).

Saké (rice wine)*

Distilled from steamed rice, saké is also known as *nihon shu*, or "Japanese wine." At table, the choice of *kara kuchi* (dry) or *ama kuchi* (sweet) is primarily one of personal taste and, to a lesser degree, an issue of pairing specific foods with sweet or dry saké.

In the kitchen, saké performs many tasks: It is used in marinades, to deglaze skillets, to rinse away fishiness or animal odors (what the Japanese refer to as *nama kusai*, "reeking raw"), and to balance sweet (sugar, mirin) and salty (soy sauce, miso) flavors. Because of such multitasking, I find that a dry saké tends to be the most versatile. Avoid products labeled "cooking wine," which is typically a mixture of inferior rice wines with the addition of sugar or other additives. Price is a good indication of quality. Store saké tightly capped, on a cool, dark shelf.

Sesame Oil (goma abura)

Sesame oil comes in two varieties, dark aromatic sesame oil that is used as a flavor accent, and light-colored sesame oil that is used as any other vegetable oil might be, to dress salads, sauté, and fry foods. Both are extracted from white sesame seeds, which are slightly richer in oil than the black seeds. Unless otherwise indicated, sesame oil in this book refers to the dark variety.

Soy Sauce (shōyu)*

A few different types of soy sauce are used in the *washoku* kitchen, each for a slightly different purpose. In most cases, you will find that regular, or dark, soy sauce, what the Japanese call *koikuchi shōyu*, is suitable. Throughout this book, I have referred to this all-purpose item—made from *daizu* (dried soy beans), wheat, water, and salt—as soy sauce.

Reduced-sodium soy sauces are products developed in response to the American consumer concerned about the high-sodium content of certain foods. I find them of limited use and questionable flavor and prefer to choose recipes that use little or no soy sauce or dilute regular soy sauce with *dashi* and/or saké to reduce the sodium content of my food. Read the labels carefully, and calculate your own dietary needs.

Available in glass and unbreakable clear plastic bottles, soy sauce is best kept tightly capped on a dark pantry shelf. Although it does not spoil easily, its subtle, full-bodied bean aroma does fade after several weeks. If you have space in the refrigerator, keep it there.

Light-Colored Soy Sauce (usukuchi shōyu): When making some dishes, the intense color of regular soy sauce would make the food look stained and unappetizing. In those instances, a full-strength light-colored soy sauce is used. Typically, it is paired with mirin instead of sugar and saké to balance its intense saltiness.

Tamari Soy Sauce (tamari-jōyu): In addition to the all-purpose and light-colored soy sauces, there is a very dark and intense soy sauce known as tamari, used mainly as a dip for sashimi. Derived from the verb *tamaru,* which means "to accumulate," *tamari-jōyu* traditonally refers to the thicker, intense concentrate that settles at the bottom of large vats of soy sauce. Today, especially in America, some products labelled *tamari* are made with little, or sometime no, roasted wheat; indeed, health-foods stores will often sell tamari soy sauce as a wheat-free, nutritionally richer sauce than ordinary soy sauce. Check the label carefully to make sure the product you buy has the specific nutritional profile you seek.

Tonkatsu Sōsu
(thick, fruity Worcestershire-like sauce)

This sauce, made from soybeans, tomatoes, and fruit, has an intriguing sweet, yet mildly spicy flavor that is intended to perk up the bland taste of breaded and fried foods. In fact, its name derives from the breaded pork cutlet (*tonkatsu*) that it was originally created to accompany.

Buy a small bottle unless you have a large crowd to feed regularly. Although the sauce doesn't spoil, its fruity aroma fades after several months, even when kept on a dark, dry shelf. You'll also find this sauce useful alone or in combination with your favorite barbecue sauce as a last-minute glaze on broiled or grilled foods. It is fine for glazing the top of a meat loaf, too.

SUGAR AND OTHER SWEETENERS

In contemporary Japanese cooking, cane sugar is the most common sweetner, though it is not usually sold in granulated form. Instead, ordinary Japanese sugar is moist, packs down readily, and dissolves easily when stirred into room-temperature liquids or mixed with other foods. Since this sugar is rarely for sale outside Japan, I have adjusted all recipes that call for sugar to utilize the kind of granulated product sold in America.

Other sweeteners are also used in many recipes, and they are briefly described here.

Ama-Zaké

Rice begins its transformation to saké with the addition of cultured spores called *kōji.* In the earliest stages of fermentation, starches change to sugar. The resulting mash, *ama-zaké,* is intensely sweet, with alcohol levels so low that no special labeling is required.

Ama-zaké is sipped on ceremonial occasions in Japan such as Oshōgatsu (New Year's holidays) and Hina Matsuri (Dolls' Day, celebrated on March 3). *Ama-zaké* is also the "magic" ingredient in many of the frozen desserts in this book.

Most packages of *ama-zaké* contain about 250 grams, just short of one standard American dry measuring cup (some packages are subdivided into five packets of 50 grams each). Buy only naturally sweet *ama-zaké;* read labels carefully to make sure no sweeteners or starchy fillers have been added. Store in the freezer or refrigerator, and bring to room temperature just before using.

Kuro-Zatō

Mineral rich and with a mellow, but deeply malted flavor, Okinawan *kuro-zatō* (literally, "black sugar") is sold in various forms, with textures ranging from loose and rather moist to stiff and rock-hard. Since the recipes in this book melt the sugar to make a syrup, any variety can be used, though the moist, softer type is easier to measure. *Kuro-zatō* is also known as *kokutō*.

Mizu Amé

Just as corn syrup is extracted from corn, *mizu amé* is made from barley and similar grains and is often labeled "barley malt" on packages. It is a clear, thick, and sticky syrup and provides a gentle sweetness. If you wish to "thin" either the Chunky Red Bean Jam (page 108) or the Brown Sugar Syrup (page 110) to make it pour more freely without adding much in the way of extra sweetness, try adding a spoonful of *mizu amé*. Store as you would any syrup.

Wasanbon

Pale beige and powdery, *wasanbon* is a highly refined form of cane sugar. Pressed into wooden molds to make *higashi* ("dried sweets" served at the tea ceremony), it dissolves when placed on the tongue, infusing the mouth with malted sweetness. The process of pressing and polishing the sugar most likely originated in China but has been practiced in Japan since the eighteenth century. Shikoku, in particular the prefectures of Tokushima and Kagawa (the Sanuki region), is known for its production of *wasanbon*. Try using it in lieu of powdered sugar, or mix it with *kinako* (page 14) for sprinkling on ice cream, yogurt, or buttered toast. Store as you would powdered sugar.

TEA

Ocha means "tea" and nearly always refers to *ryokucha*, or "green tea," in Japan, where it is sipped regularly both with and between meals. Green tea leaves are plucked from *Camellia sinensis* bushes during several harvests from spring through early fall. Before being dried, the leaves are steamed to heighten color and aroma and to prevent unwanted fermentation (it is this fermentation that turns tea leaves brown, giving English teas their characteristic color and flavor).

Health-promoting benefits have traditionally been associated with the regular consumption of green tea. Its antibacterial, anticarcinogenic, and age-retarding properties have been touted in particular, along with its ability to reduce cholesterol levels and lower hypertension. Green tea is rich in vitamins A, C, and E.

There are many varieties of Japanese teas available in Asian groceries and specialty-foods shops. Price is a good indication of quality.

Bancha

Composed of lesser-quality leaves, stems, and twigs, typically from late-season harvests, *bancha* produces a mild beverage, often with slightly smoky overtones. It is drunk everywhere throughout the day.

Genmaicha

A confetti-like mixture of roasted whole rice grains (some are brown, others have puffed into white popcornlike kernels) and *bancha* leaves, *genmaicha* has a distinctive whole-grain flavor and aroma. It goes particularly well with rice crackers and other salty snacks.

Some varieties of *genmaicha* are mixed with lesser-quality *matcha* (page 54), the jade-colored powdered tea used in the tea ceremony. These teas will look slightly dusty in the package, and when brewed will have a pale green, cloudy appearance. The *matcha* adds a hint of both sweetness and astringency to an otherwise toasty-toned tea.

Gyokurō

Gathered during the first spring harvest, *gyokurō* (literally, "dewy jewel") is the highest-quality leaf tea. It is often paired with traditional Japanese confections because its slightly vegetal overtones provide a welcome foil against what would otherwise be cloying sweetness.

Brewing and Storing Tea

It is best to brew green tea in small quantities, repeating the procedure if necessary to serve more than 4 or 5 people at one time. The temperature of the water and the length of time the leaves steep vary with the different teas. For each variety, though, the goal is the same: to activate the glutamates (these provide a sweet, herbal nuance) but hold the tannins in check (to prevent bitter, astringent overtones). In general, the higher-quality teas should be brewed for a short time at low temperatures.

The Japanese typically drink green tea from small cups, each holding about two-thirds of a standard American measuring cup. For every 4 or 5 portions, measure out 2 teaspoons of loose tea. If you wish to make tea bags to simplify cleanup, use the convenient *ocha pakku* sold in many Asian groceries. Typically each package, priced at just a few dollars, holds 40 or more 2- to 3-inch square paper pouches. Do not overstuff the bags (fill each with no more than 2 teaspoons). The hot water needs room to circulate around the tea, and the leaves need room to expand. Place the loose tea, tea bag, or tea ball in a small, dry pot.

To enjoy tea as a warm beverage, pour $^2/_3$ cup freshly boiled water into each drinking cup. Allow the boiling water to stand in the cups for about 30 seconds. This warms the cups while cooling the water. The Japanese often use a separate open pot that looks somewhat like a gravy boat and is called a *yu-zamashi* (literally, "hot-water cooler"). By exposing the boiled water to cool air, the water temperature drops rapidly. Pour cooled water from the cups, or the *yu-zamashi* pot, into the teapot filled with tea leaves.

Allow the tea to steep *undisturbed* (do not swirl the pot about) before pouring small quantities into each cup, in turn. Repeat until all cups have been filled. Subsequent infusions can use slightly hotter water, and the hot water can be gently swirled in the pot. With each infusion, however, the brewed tea should be poured entirely from the pot; allowing the leaves to steep at length in large amounts of water yields a bitter beverage.

Sencha, kukicha, and *genmaicha* should be infused with hot water (about 175°F) and allowed to steep for about 1 minute before pouring. Subsequent infusions can be made with slightly hotter water (about 195°F) and allowed to steep for less than 1 minute.

Gyokurō should be infused with very warm water (about 140°F) and allowed to steep for about 1$^1/_2$ minutes before pouring. Subsequent infusions can be made with slightly hotter water (about 175°F) and allowed to steep for about 1 minute.

Very hot water (about 195°F) should be poured over *konacha* and allowed to stand, undisturbed, for about 1 minute before pouring. Subsequent portions can be made with nearly boiling water (200°F) and allowed to steep for about 1 minute. Remember that this beverage will be a cloudy suspension, not a clear infusion.

Hōjicha should be infused with boiling water (212°F) and allowed to steep for about only 30 seconds before pouring. Subsequent infusions can be made with additional boiling water and allowed to steep for no more than 1 minute.

To enjoy tea as as a cold beverage, first brew as though you were making hot tea and allow the beverage to cool naturally before covering it and chilling it in the refrigerator. If you wish to serve the tea on ice, brew a concentrate with twice the amount of tea, but do not allow it to steep for longer periods of time.

Storing tea: Tea is ideally stored in a dry, dark place away from heat. It does not require refrigeration, although some people prefer to refrigerate or freeze it. The greatest danger in that practice is moisture, so be sure to make your packages as airtight as possible.

Traditionally, tea has been stored in ceramic jars (*cha tsubo*), metal-lined wooden boxes (*cha-bako*), or paper-covered metal canisters (*cha-zutsu*). Tea is also sold, and stored, in metal cans called *kan*.

Hōjicha

Hōjicha is made of roasted green tea leaves. It has a smoky flavor and is often served with fried foods, such as tempura or *tonkatsu* (breaded pork cultlets), because it is thought to aid in the digestion of fats and oils.

Konacha

Konacha is powdered tea, which means that, unlike an infused tea, you consume the pulverized leaves when you drink the tea. It is typically paired with sushi because its intense grassiness acts as a palate cleanser, allowing each variety of fish to be savored in its turn. And no doubt the antibacterial properties of green tea enhance the hygienic image of sushi bars.

Kukicha

Made from the twigs of the tea plant, or a mixture of twigs and leaves, *kukicha* can be of several grades. It is often less costly and less astringent than *sencha*.

Matcha

This jade-colored powder, pulverized from newly plucked tea buds, is whisked (with a special bamboo tool) into hot water to make ceremonial tea. *Matcha* also provides the distinctive color and flavor of green tea ice cream and is used in making many traditional confections. Only the first-harvest buds of tea plants shaded from direct sunlight are used for *matcha*, making it costly. It should be kept in a cool, dry place (it is often refrigerated in shops). Consume it within a month of purchase to enjoy the full meadowlike aroma and subtle sweetness that lies just below the astringent surface flavor.

Sencha

This high-quality leaf tea typically has delicate, grassy overtones. It is served in better restaurants and to guests in homes or offices.

Other Teas: Mugicha, Kombucha

Other beverages that are called tea, such as *mugicha* brewed from roasted barley and served chilled in the summer, or *kombucha*, made by dissolving pulverized salted *kombu* (page 42) in very hot water, are not true teas because they do not include parts of the *Camellia sinensis* bush.

TŌFU*

Tōfu is made by soaking dried soybeans, usually overnight, until swollen to many times their original size. The beans are then crushed and boiled to produce a foamy, thick, snowy white liquid known as *go*. The *go* is cooked over low heat for 10 to 15 minutes and then strained to yield *tōnyu*, or soy milk, and *okara*, the lees. The soy milk is solidified into puddinglike blocks or loaves widely known in Japan and elsewhere as tōfu.

The addition of *nigari* (calcium chloride) is what curdles the soy milk, transforming it into tōfu. This process is ancient and, like many bits of culinary technology found in Japan today, most likely originated in China. A number of different soy products can result from these basic steps, depending on such variables as the pressure exerted on the curdled soy milk, the timing, the amount and quality of the coagulating agent (fine tōfu is made with *nigari* extracted from seawater, rather

*essential pantry item

than artificially produced calcium chloride), and the lining of the container used for forming the tōfu.

Because English-language labels on packages sold outside Japan are confusing and inconsistent, I have decided to call all such products tōfu, adding English descriptive modifiers, such as "firm" or "fried," as needed.

Below are descriptions of each of the kinds of tōfu called for in this book, listed alphabetically by their combined English and Japanese names. I have done my best to describe the characteristics of each type, so that no matter what a product is called, you can decide whether or not it is suitable for the particular recipe you want to make. In selecting recipes for this book, I was influenced by the quality of tōfu products that my team of recipe testers found available to them in North America, Asia, and Europe. A few of my devoted volunteers actually make their own tōfu from scratch, but I decided that for most readers this would be neither practical nor possible.

▦ IN THE WASHOKU KITCHEN: **dicing, 70; mashing, 73; draining and pressing, 77.**

Firm Tōfu (momen-dōfu)

This tōfu, known as *momen-dōfu* (literally, "cotton-wrapped" tōfu), is firmer and more roughly textured than the silken variety and has noticeable cross-hatching on the surface. The pattern is an imprint left from the muslin (*sarashi*, page 77) used to line the containers in which the tōfu is made.

Firm tōfu is the most versatile of the many kinds available and is especially recommended when adding cubes to miso-thickened soups. In Asian markets outside Japan, a product labeled "extra-firm" tōfu is also available. In Japan, something similar to this would be sold as Chinese-style bean curd, and used in stir-fried dishes and stews of Chinese and Southeast Asian origin.

Fried Tōfu Dumplings (ganmodoki)

Ganmodoki, also known as *ganmo,* are balls made from mashed tōfu mixed with minced vegetables and black sesame seeds.

Storing Tōfu

All types of fresh tōfu are highly perishable and should be kept refrigerated. Submerge blocks of firm, silken, and grilled tōfu in fresh water in a deep container (lidded plastic containers used to store leftovers are fine) or in a covered bowl. Change the water daily and consume the tōfu within 2 or 3 days. Cloudy water or a thin, sticky film on the surface of tōfu indicates spoilage; so does an off odor. In both cases, discard the tōfu immediately. I do not recommend freezing fresh tōfu, because it changes the texture from creamy to grainy and spongy.

Sealed containers of tōfu should be refrigerated in their original packaging. Observe the sell-by date, adding no more than a few days to it before opening the package, and once the package has been opened, store as you would fresh tōfu, described above.

Sheets of fried tōfu and fried tōfu dumplings should be stored in their original packaging or transferred to a closed plastic bag; blanch or blot away excess oil just before using. As with other forms of fresh tōfu described above, fried tōfu products need to remain refrigerated until use and should be consumed within 2 days of the sell-by date listed on the package. Varieties imported from Japan are often frozen, resulting in a slightly chewy texture, but that is not a problem when making Treasure Boats (page 278) or Sushi Pillows (page 152).

Most often these dumplings are simmered with vegetables in a slightly sweet, soy-seasoned broth (Soy-Simmered Deep-fried Tōfu Dumplings, page 274).

In Kyoto and the Kansai District (southwest provinces), dumplings such as these are sometimes called *hiryōzu*. If the Asian grocery where you shop imports products from Kansai vendors, you may find that name instead of *ganmo* or *ganmodoki* on the package. (The etymology of *hiryōzu* is interesting: The calligraphy translates as "flying dragon's head," which suggests Chinese roots, but it is also possible that the ideograms were chosen for their sounds, rather than their intrinsic meaning. The inspiration for this Kyoto term may have been *filhó*, the Portuguese word for a fried dumpling or fritter, which, when spoken by Portuguese missionaries of the seventeenth century, the Japanese heard as *hi-ryō-zu*.)

If you want to try making *ganmodoki* from scratch, see the recipe for Handmade Deep-fried Tōfu Dumplings (page 276).

Fried Tōfu Slices (abura agé), Fried Tōfu Blocks (atsu agé)

To make these fried tōfu products, blocks of fresh firm bean curd are drained and weighted to press out excess liquid. When making *abura agé*, the drained block is cut into thin slices; when making *atsu agé*, the block is left whole for deep-frying. The size of fried tōfu slices varies with the proportions of the block of tōfu from which they are made. Most slices are 6 by 3¹/₂ inches.

When frying *abura agé*, a pocket of air forms in the center of each slice. These pockets can be pried open and stuffed with a variety of other ingredients, such as sushi rice (Sushi Pillows, page 152), thinly sliced vegetables (Treasure Boats, page 278), ground meat, or eggs to be poached. You can also cut fried tōfu slices into strips and use them in soups and stir-fried dishes.

Blocks of fried tōfu are commonly cut into cubes (each will be snowy white at the center, rimmed with a browned crust) and used in place of meat in stir-fried dishes.

A recipe may suggest that you briefly blanch the fried tōfu just before using, to remove the thin layer of oil that clings to the slices. Or a recipe may advise blotting up the excess oil with paper towels. Although the image of fried foods as undesirable persists, a single slice of blanched or blotted *abura agé*, typically weighing less than an ounce, has only 80 calories, the same amount as a small glass of low-fat milk. One-third of a block of fried tōfu, just under 2 ounces, has about 85 calories and the calcium equivalent of a small glass of whole milk.

Fried tōfu slices and blocks are readily available in tōfu shops and supermarkets throughout Japan. In America, locally made fried tōfu can be found in communities with a large Asian population, and imported fried tōfu can be found frozen in many Asian grocery stores.

Prying open slices of fried tōfu: In most Japanese households, where long cooking chopsticks (page 83) are standard kitchen equipment, a single chopstick is used to open the slices, rolling pin style. Start from the closed end and roll the chopstick toward the cut edge. Alternatively, lay a slice of fried tōfu on the open palm of one hand and slap down on it with the other palm. This allows the air trapped inside the slice to escape from the cut edge. Gently pry the pouch open with your fingertips.

▦ IN THE WASHOKU KITCHEN: **blanching, 75.**

Grilled Tōfu (yaki-dōfu)

Yaki-dōfu is firm tōfu that has been drained and weighted slightly to remove excess liquid and then grilled. It has obvious grill markings on both the top and the bottom surfaces of the blocks. The grilling adds pleasant toasty overtones that enhance the natural beanlike flavor. *Yaki-dōfu* is the tōfu of choice in Broiled Tōfu with Flavored Miso (page 281) and in many one-pot dishes, including sukiyaki.

You can make home-grilled tōfu from firm or extra-firm tōfu by placing it under the broiler or on a grill; typically, home-grilled tōfu takes on a yellow cast and has less pronounced grill marks than the commercially made product.

Varieties of tōfu (clockwise from top left): slices of fried tōfu, strips of home-grilled tōfu, block of fried tōfu, firm tōfu, and silken tōfu

Silken Tōfu (kinugoshi-dōfu)

Kinugoshi-dōfu (literally, "silk-strained tōfu") is soft and delicate, with a glassy-smooth surface. It is the primary ingredient in Sesame-Crusted Tōfu (page 272) and is also used in soups and Creamy Tōfu Sauce (page 107). However, it is too fragile for broiling with flavored miso sauces.

When freshly made, silken tōfu recalls warm, creamy custard with a delightfully nutty aftertaste. If you can find a source of high-quality, artisanally made silken tōfu in your community, enjoy it piping hot, or chill it and serve it icy cold. The former is a dish known as *yu-dōfu*, while the latter is called *hiya yakko*. Both are served with only a drizzle of soy sauce and are accompanied by grated ginger, snipped chives, and other assorted condiments. I have a passion for fine tōfu, and when apartment hunting in Tokyo, chose my current location because of its proximity to two excellent tōfu shops.

VEGETABLES

Information about the purchase, storage, or usage of various vegetables is helpful as reference, but can be disruptive of the flow of action, or needlessly repetitive, if placed within the recipes themselves. Instead, I created this mini-catalog, arranged in alphabetical order, by the primary name—sometimes Japanese, sometimes English, often a mixture of both—as it appears in the ingredient list of recipes in this book.

Bean Sprouts (moyashi)

An inexpensive vegetable that adds volume and texture to Chinese-style stir-fried and noodle dishes, *moyashi* can be sprouted from either mung beans or soybeans. Some markets sell already trimmed sprouts (their long, thread-thin ends have been snapped off), though untrimmed ones are fine for the ramen soup recipe in this book. Bean sprouts are highly perishable, so store them in the refrigerator and use within a day or two of purchase.

Bitter Melon (goya, also niga uri)

Eaten in many Asian and Polynesian cultures, bitter melon, which resembles a fat, bumpy cucumber, is a common ingredient in the markets and at table in Okinawa. In tropical and semitropical climates, eating it is thought to restore energy sapped by the heat. It is named for its distinctive bitter aftertaste, an astringency that can be kept partially under control by salting (and draining off the accumulated liquid) the melons or by cooking them with sour foods (vinegar, citrus fruit). In some Japanese markets, bitter melon is sold under the name *niga uri* (literally, "bitter melon").

When shopping, look for bright green, bumpy-skinned, firm melons free of dark spots and light-colored splotches, two signs of spoilage. They should also feel fairly heavy in your hand. Lightweight bitter melons are usually beyond their prime, with loose seeds surrounded by dry and crumbly material down their center channel. Fresh bitter melon has a moist, spongy-soft center with seeds firmly embedded in it. Wrap loosely in a plastic storage bag; it will keep in the vegetable bin of your refrigerator for up to 5 days.

Burdock Root (gobō)

Fresh burdock root (illustrated on page 60), sold at many Asian grocery stores outside Japan, is the only form worth buying, as the canned root is tasteless and the texture is often stringy. The best are beige, under a thin layer of dark soil left clinging to the exterior, and no thicker than the average felt-tipped marker. Avoid roots with a diameter of more than 1 inch; they are usually spongy at the core. The roots can be as short as 8 or 9 inches, but most are about 1 foot long. The vegetable should be sold with the dirt still clinging to it and then stored, with the dirt intact, in a paper bag in your refrigerator. It will remain fresh for weeks.

Rinse and scrape a burdock root just before using to retain as much aroma and nutrients as possible. Hold it under running cold water, lightly scratching away the soil with the back of your knife. The root's woodsy aroma is concentrated in its outer layers, so avoid heavy scraping that would remove too much of the peel. Do not be alarmed to see the surface turning brown even as you scrape. Some Japanese soak burdock root in cold water to minimize the earthiness of its flavor; others abhor the practice. If you prefer a mild flavor, soak the burdock strips in plain cold water for about 2 minutes (do not be alarmed to see the water turn brown), then drain and cook immediately to preserve the nutrients.

IN THE WASHOKU KITCHEN: **soaking, 76.**

Chinese Cabbage (hakusai)

This leafy, pale, elliptically shaped cabbage is popular throughout the Orient. Its English name shows that its popularity in the West is due to its use in Chinese cooking. Some varieties are similar to napa cabbage. The *hakusai* grown and harvested in America is sweeter than its Japanese counterpart and quite delicious used raw in salads.

When buying, look for compact heads that feel fairly heavy for their size. Ribs should be a pearly white (though speckling on the outer ribs of the vegetable is quite common) and the leaves a pale to medium shade of green. Most produce markets will cut a large head in half or into quarters, lengthwise, for you if you need less than the average 2-pound head. Store wrapped in a clean kitchen towel in the vegetable bin of your refrigerator. It will stay fresh for about 1 week.

Daikon

Many daikon varieties are grown in Japan year-round. Some are plump and bulbous, and others are slender and tapered. Some are sharp, spicy, and crisp, making them perfect for grating as a condiment or for shredding into salads; others are mild and have a dense texture, making them more suitable for simmering and steaming. Several varieties harvested in the fall are dried in preparation for pickling (*takuan*, page 38) or for making *kiriboshi daikon* ribbons (below). A good daikon is firm and white, has a luminous cast (some varieties have a green "neck"), and feels hefty when held. Most varieties have a tuft of stiff, pale green stems with short, dark green ruffled leaves.

The entire vegetable is edible: stems and leaves can be pickled in brine (see Kitchen Harmony notes for Impatient Pickles, page 218) or blanched and tossed into soups (Miso Soup with Fried Tōfu, Leafy Greens, and Scallions, page 118); the peel can be shredded and sautéed (see Kitchen Harmony notes for Fiery Parsnips, page 215); the bottom of the root can be steamed (Steaming Radish Swathed in Citrusy Miso Sauce, page 214), cut into chunks and simmered in soups (Miso-Thickened Pork and Vegetable Soup, page 119; Temple Garden Chowder, page 126; Mushroom, Lotus Root, and Tōfu Chowder, page 130); or shredded (New Year's Salad, page 220), and the top of the root (near the tufts of green leaves) can be grated and used as a condiment (Tempura Pancakes, Temple Vegetarian Style, page 210; Chilled Udon Noodle Salad, page 173; Flash-Seared Steak with Two Sauces, page 267; and Salt-Broiled Kingfish, page 231).

Store daikon wrapped in newspaper or paper towels in the vegetable bin of your refrigerator. It will remain crisp for 2 to 3 days (best for grating and shredding for salads) and then get a bit limp (it is still fine for steaming and braising). It is still good for pickling from 1 to 2 weeks after purchase. Peels can be accumulated and saved for the Fiery Parsnips for a week in a closed plastic bag.

Special note on grating daikon: Grated daikon is rich in vitamin C, which is thought to counteract the possible carcinogenic effects of charcoal-grilled foods. To preserve this air-sensitive nutrient, grate the radish just before eating. If you will be serving grated daikon with broiled fish, peel and grate it (preferably on a ceramic grater to avoid a metallic taste) while the fish cooks. Transfer the grated radish to a fine-mesh strainer lined with *sarashi* (page 77), lift up the corners of the cloth in a baglike shape, enclosing the grated radish, and squeeze gently to drain off excess liquid.

IN THE WASHOKU KITCHEN: **peeling, 68; beveling, 69; grating, 71.**

Kiriboshi Daikon: Packages of *kiriboshi daikon*, or dried shredded daikon (illustrated on page 65), are readily available outside Japan in Asian groceries. The shreds are straw or hay colored and somewhat pliable, and are packed in cellophane and stocked on shelves with other shelf-stable products. As with other dried foods, such as dried shiitaké mushrooms or dried apricots, flavor is concentrated, especially the sweeter tones.

Dandelion Greens (shungiku)

Shungiku, known as dandelion greens throughout most of North America, are the edible stalks and leaves of a variety of chrysanthemum. Occasionally available in local farmers' markets in the fall and winter months in North America, these greens have a fresh herbal bite that perks up soups and casseroles. Seeds for growing your own dandelion greens are available from many seed catalogs.

When buying, look for deep green leaves; the smaller ones are usually more tender and less bitter than broad-leaved kinds. Any budding tips should be discarded before using. Wrap bunches of leafy greens in moist paper towels in an open plastic bag in the vegetable bin of your refrigerator; standing them upright, if space permits, will keep the stalks straight and crisp. They will stay fresh for 4 or 5 days. In Japan, dandelion greens are always blanched or cooked before eating.

IN THE WASHOKU KITCHEN: **blanching, 74**.

Édamamé (fresh green soybeans)

If you can find fresh soybeans in the pod at your local farmers' market, you will be well rewarded for the extra effort it takes to pull the pods from the branches. Several stiff branches, usually with roots attached and earth still clinging to them, are bundled together to make a bunch; the green, slightly hairy bean pods dangle from the branches. After putting on kitchen or gardening gloves to protect your hands from being scratched, pluck the pods from the branches. To remove the fuzz from the pods, place them in a *suribachi* (page 73), the

Fresh vegetables (clockwise from top left): Japanese-style sweet potato, Japanese eggplant, lotus root, burdock root (horizontal), kabocha squash, Japanese cucumbers, and Japanese leeks

ideal tool for the job, with 1 tablespoon of coarse sea salt or kosher salt for every pound of pods. (You can also use a heavy-duty plastic bag.) Toss the beans in the salt, then gently rub them against the grooved surface of the mortar (or massage through the bag) to remove as much "fuzz" from the pods as possible. Transfer the pods to a strainer and shake to remove excess matter. Follow this procedure for all recipes in which fresh bean pods are specified.

With the growing interest in the nutritional power of soy foods, briefly blanched and flash-frozen soybeans in their pods are increasingly available in North American supermarkets. In the recipes in this book, I provide instructions for preparing both fresh and frozen soybeans.

Japanese Cucumber (kyūri)

Tender and nearly seedless, Japanese cucumbers are fabulous. They average 8 inches in length and about 3/4 inch in diameter, but like zucchini, cucumbers left on the vine for even a few extra days can become quite bulbous. Choose slender cucumbers with thornlike stubble on their skins, an indication that they have been recently picked. The stubble is easily rubbed off with a damp cloth or coarse salt; this technique is also done to remove *aku* (astringent bitterness). The salt often turns green in your hand as you rub, so don't be alarmed.

Japanese cucumbers are fairly easy to grow and seeds are readily available. Kirby cucumbers, or other varieties that have edible skins and relatively few seeds, can be used when Japanese cucumbers are not available.

IN THE WASHOKU KITCHEN: **peeling, 68; shredding, 70; rubbing, 76**.

Japanese Eggplant (nasu)

Many varieties of eggplant are available in Japan, all of them summer and fall crops. Some are large and bulbous (*Kamo nasu* from Kyoto), others are long and slender (*naga nasu*; illustrated opposite), and still others are no larger than my thumb (*ko nasu*). All are sleek and very dark purple (nearly black). True Japanese eggplants have dark stamens (petals), not green ones as I have seen at farmers' markets in North America. The skins of all Japanese eggplants are tender and the flesh is nearly seedless.

Eggplants are best stored at cool room temperature. If you must refrigerate them because of space considerations, wrap them in newspaper or paper towels and place in an open plastic bag. Japanese eggplants are not that difficult to grow and seeds are available from many seed catalogs. Freshly picked eggplants will keep for up to a week.

Japanese Leek (naga negi)

The Japanese eat two kinds of *negi*, or onion: *naga negi*, or "long" onions, known in North America as Japanese leeks, and *tama negi*, or "round" onions, known in most American markets as yellow onions.

Japanese leeks (illustrated on page 60) are naturally sweet, mild flavored, and highly aromatic when pan seared or grilled. They tend to be slender, rather than stubby, and sandy soil is rarely trapped between their layers, making them easier to clean. They are increasingly available at Asian groceries outside Japan and are worth tracking down in your community. Seeds are available from many catalog companies, and *naga negi* are fairly easy to grow.

House-grown varieties are available year-round, though *naga negi* was traditionally a cold-weather crop. Look for long, slender, smooth, pearly white stalks with short, bristly tufts (roots) still attached. Use the tough portions of the green tops for enriching stocks and soups.

Wrap in newspaper (dampened slightly if you live in a very dry climate) and keep on a cool, dark shelf in the pantry, or refrigerate. Japanese leeks will keep well for up to 10 days.

Japanese-Style Sweet Potato (Satsuma imo)

This tuber (illustrated on page 60) hails from Satsuma, the historical name for Kagoshima Prefecture on the island of Kyushu. It probably originated in South America and traveled to Japan by way of Okinawa sometime early in the Edo period (seventeenth century). Until the early twentieth century, it is likely that most Japanese derived at least 10 percent of their nutrients from this potato (only the nobility could afford rice).

Today, sweet potatoes are eaten both as a snack and as a side dish. When the cold weather arrives, vendors selling stone-baked sweet potatoes from carts appear on streets in every city and village in Japan. In this book, you will find recipes for soups (Dark Miso Soup with Sweet Potato, page 122; Temple Garden Chowder, page 126) and side dishes (Sweet Potato Simmered with Kelp, page 209; Tempura Pancakes, Temple Vegetarian Style, page 210). Both the skin and the flesh are eaten. Japanese-style golden-fleshed, red-skinned sweet potatoes sold in North America are delicious in all of these recipes.

IN THE WASHOKU KITCHEN: **soaking, 76.**

Japanese White Turnip (kokabu)

Turnips sold in America usually have a tough skin (sometimes coated with inedible wax) and a reddish area near where the leaves grow, and it is rare to see the leaves attached. In contrast, Japanese turnips are small, white, sweet, and tender. They appear in markets, with their bushy tufts of green leaves attached, from early autumn through early summer, and they are extremely versatile. In the *washoku* kitchen, they are enjoyed thinly sliced and lightly salted to wilt in salads, lightly pickled in a sweet-and-sour brine, pickled in rice-bran mash, briefly simmered, and even grated and steamed. The leaves can be prepared as you would spinach, either *ohitashi* style (blanched and then "marinated" in smoky broth) or dressed with soy-seasoned, toasted, and crushed sesame. These tender turnips cook in less than a minute in broth to make either a puréed or miso-thickened soup. Garnish either soup with turnip leaves that have been blanched in salted water and finely chopped.

Kokabu are fairly easy to grow in temperate climates from mid-March through November; seeds are available from many catalogs. You will be well rewarded for growing your own. Store as you would any root vegetable; for extended storage, cut off the leaves, wrap in moist paper towels, and place in a plastic bag in the refrigerator.

Kabocha Squash

In Japan, most varieties of *kabocha* squash (illustrated on page 60) come to market in the summer and early fall. Heirloom varieties such as *kurokawa* (black skinned), *Edo* (after the former name for Tokyo), and *kikuza* (chrysanthemum seat) have very dark, deeply grooved skins and pale yellow flesh. Recent hybrids, such as *Ebisu* (named after one of the seven Gods of Good Fortune) and *kuri* (as its name "chestnut" suggests, this squash has a sweet and nutty flavor), have mottled green skins and deep, orangey gold flesh. All varieties of *kabocha* squash are packed with carotene and the edible skin boasts large amounts of vitamin A.

Cooking time will vary widely depending on the variety and where it is grown. Squashes from New Zealand, Mexico, and Africa find their way to Japanese markets and some North American markets, too. With the exception of most African-grown squashes, these non-Japanese varieties tend to crumble more easily than the Japanese-grown crops.

Although some grocery stores sell segments or chunks, most markets sell the vegetable whole. It is highly versatile, suitable for both sweet and savory dishes, and stores well for weeks, so do not hesitate to buy a whole *kabocha*.

Store whole squashes at room temperature. After cutting, loosely wrap any pieces in plastic wrap and place in the vegetable bin of your refrigerator for up to 2 weeks.

You will need a sharp, heavy-bladed knife to cut through the tough outer layers of a *kabocha*. Ask your grocer to cut it in half for you when you buy it. To cut it into smaller wedges or chunks, always place the cut edge face down on your cutting board, so that the squash half remains steady as you apply pressure to your knife when cutting into smaller pieces.

IN THE WASHOKU KITCHEN: **beveling, 69.**

Kampyō (dried gourd ribbons)

Large, pale pumpkinlike gourds called *fukubé* are spiral cut into long, 1/2-inch-wide ribbons, which are then dried for several days. The ribbons (illustrated on page 65) remain pliable, despite the drying. They are sold in cellophane bags, each bag containing either uncut ribbons (about a yard long) or very short ones (about 6 inches long). I suggest you buy the uncut ribbons, which are easier to use when tying up edible packages such as the Treasure Boats on page 278. Store the gourd ribbons in a closed plastic bag on a cool, dark shelf; they will keep for months.

Komatsuna (leafy green)

In Japan, this calcium-rich leafy green (illustrated on page ii, at left) appears in markets nearly year-round, although early autumn through the New Year holiday is considered *shun*, the peak of flavor. It can be cooked as you cook spinach. In the *washoku* kitchen, *ohitashi* style (blanched and then "marinated" in smoky broth) is the most common preparation, with *goma aé* (blanched leaves tossed in soy-seasoned crushed sesame) a close second. *Komatsuna* is also good dressed in a creamy sesame and miso sauce or a creamy tōfu sauce.

IN THE WASHOKU KITCHEN: **blanching, 74.**

Kyoto Red Carrot (Kyō ninjin)

During the cold winter months, especially at New Year's time, *Kyō ninjin* come to markets throughout Japan. Grown around Kyoto from heirloom seeds, the long, intensely red carrots are incredibly sweet when cooked, though they are not especially suitable for eating raw.

Seeds for growing your own red carrots are available from several seed catalogs in the United States. Store the red carrots as you would any carrots. The tops are edible, although often quite bitter. Blanch briefly and squeeze out excess moisture before eating.

Lotus Root (renkon, hasu)

Called both *renkon* and *hasu* in Japanese, lotus root (illustrated on page 60) is often found fresh in Asian markets and groceries in the spring and fall. Typically harvested from muddy marshes as a string, or chain, of oblong roots, the vegetable frequently comes to market cut into small segments of a few ounces each.

Buy firm, unscarred segments with clean canals. You can check the latter two ways: if a cut surface permits, peek inside to see the many hollow channels, or tap the roots to make sure they sound hollow.

When peeling and slicing lotus root, use a stainless-steel or ceramic blade to prevent discoloration. Immediately soak the cut pieces in acidulated water (1 tablespoon vinegar for every cup of cold water) to prevent further discoloration.

To blanch lotus root, mix a fresh batch of vinegar and water in a nonreactive pot and bring to a boil. Drain the soaking slices and blanch them in the boiling water for 1 minute. Drain but do not refresh under cold water.

IN THE WASHOKU KITCHEN: **soaking, 76.**

Mountain Yam (yama imo)

This is one of several tuber vegetables the Japanese enjoy for its mild flavor and slippery, crunchy texture. It is eaten raw, crudité style, accompanied by flavored dips and sauces; grated to make a creamy sauce for fresh tuna; used as a binder when making soba noodles or tōfu dumplings; and steamed and mashed to make dumplings or croquettes.

You need to peel the yam before using it. Work with caution, because the exposed surface is very slippery. I recommend you wear thin, disposable latex gloves or hold the peeled tuber by one end wrapped with paper towels. This will ensure a firm grip and also eliminate the chance that your hands may begin to itch. An enzyme in the freshly peeled tuber sometimes causes temporary irritation to the skin. Should this happen to you, rinse your hands in vinegar or lemon juice.

When using grated yam as a binder, a single tablespoon (about 1 ounce raw) will bind about 8 ounces of densely pressed tōfu.

IN THE WASHOKU KITCHEN: **grinding, 73.**

Snow Pea (endomamé)

Many Asian cuisines use snow peas. The snow peas available in Japanese markets have tender pods encasing very small, rather sweet peas. The Japanese trim the pea pods before blanching them briefly. To trim, strip each pod of its "string" by snapping back the base (this is where the snow pea was attached to the vine) and pulling along the top. The Japanese like to keep the opposite end, the tuft end, intact. Most American markets, however, sell snow peas with these hairlike extensions removed.

Snow peas require only brief cooking. Bring water to a rolling boil in a small saucepan and blanch the peas for just 1 minute. To preserve their full flavor and crisp texture, drain them and let cool naturally, rather than shocking them with cold water. Since the pea pods cannot easily be squeezed after soaking them in cold water, the peas become waterlogged, losing flavor and nutrients.

Dried vegetables (clockwise from top left): kampyō *and* kiriboshi daikon

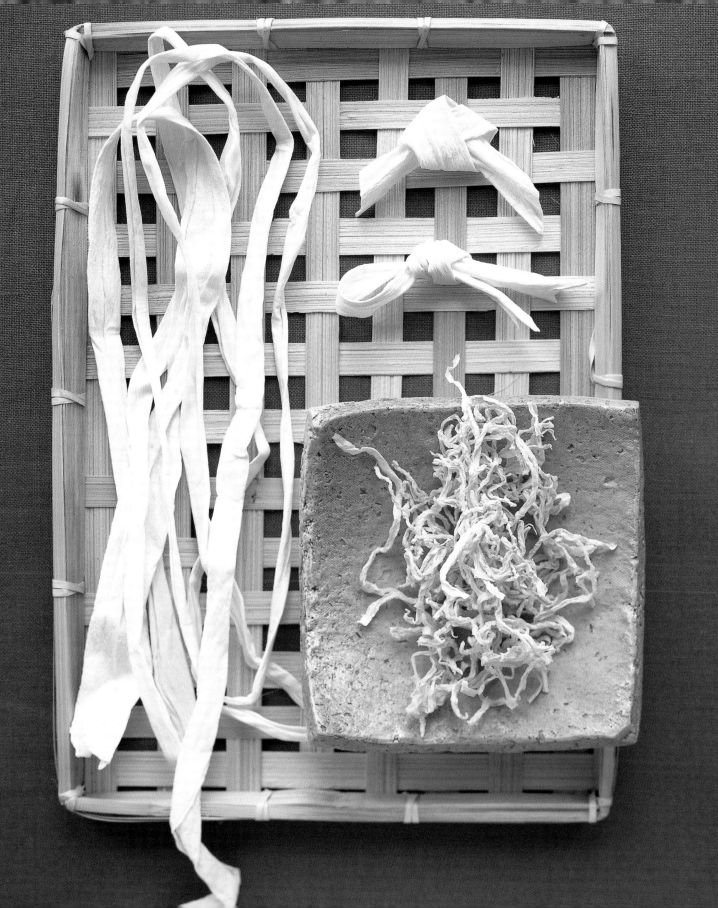

IN THE WASHOKU KITCHEN

THE FIRST *WASHOKU* KITCHEN I had a chance to observe and participate in belonged to my future mother-in-law, Kiyoko Andoh, aka Okaasan, a woman of incredible energy who, even when she slipped on two-inch-high *geta* clogs, barely reached my shoulder.

It was the mid-1960s and the Andoh household had two kitchens, both fully functional. The one nearest the service entrance was an old-fashioned, turn-of-the-twentieth-century affair with a *doma* (dirt floor), an *ido* (well for water), an *okama* (wood-burning stove for cooking rice), and a *haéirazu* ("no flies allowed" cupboard) for storing dried and preserved foods. The newer kitchen, closer to the main entrance, provided easy access to both the tatami-outfitted room where the family gathered to eat, gossip, and watch television and to the room where guests were ushered on formal occasions. The modern kitchen boasted a raised wooden floor, a temperamental hot-water heater, an electric rice cooker, and a refrigerator affectionately known as Mr. Penguin, for the ice that formed thickly around the rim of the door.

Depending on the occasion, both hastily assembled meals and formal multicourse banquets were prepared from these kitchens. Okaasan, who balanced nutritional needs and nurturing instincts with the demands of managing a large household, was not adverse to shortcuts or using modern equipment in lieu of, or in tandem with, traditional tools. When time permitted, rice was cooked with well water in the slow, old-fashioned way, the aroma filling the household with anticipation. But for convenience sake it would often be transferred to the rice cooker-warmer so it could be enjoyed later in the day. Okaasan used a high-speed blender (a gift from one of her daughters who had traveled overseas) and a *suribachi* (mortar) in equal measure to mash and grind. She deftly handled *saibashi* (long cooking chopsticks), using them to flip, poke, and stir foods with ease, but was never shy about using metal tongs, rubber spatulas, and stainless-steel ladles, too.

Okaasan's ability to incorporate new tips and tricks into her traditional habits was marvelous. She picked up ideas from chatting with local vendors, reading ladies magazines, and watching television cooking shows. She proved an excellent role model, demonstrating that *washoku* was not a rigid set of rules, but rather a flexible framework in which to collect and consider new ideas.

To help you understand the pace and flow of activity in the *washoku* kitchen, I focused this discussion on the practical considerations of food preparation, cataloging various tasks and the tools and gadgets—both the old and the new—that can assist you in performing them. Not all of my suggestions follow classic procedure, and I alert you when I have departed wildly from the norm, giving you the chance to choose between time-honored and innovative ways.

The discussion begins with techniques used to ready ingredients for preparing a meal, such as cutting, grating, and marinating. Then it proceeds to the basics of applying heat, whether by broiling, frying, steaming, or other means. When a special tool is required or recommended, I have provided a description of it. In some cases a single item, such as *sarashi* cloth, can be used to perform several different tasks (wrapping fish for marinating, straining stocks) and will appear in several entries. Sources for obtaining traditional Japanese equipment are listed on page 309.

CUTTING

Professionals in a classic Japanese kitchen use many different cutting techniques; most require a great deal of patience and practice to master. In this book, I have purposely limited the number of specialized techniques you need to make the recipes. Slicing, shredding, peeling, dicing, and scoring, however, are frequently required procedures in any kitchen. In order to cut well, you need a sharp, well-maintained knife. An ALL-PURPOSE KNIFE (*santoku-bōchō*) will help you accomplish many tasks.

Whenever possible, place the ingredient you are cutting flat on the cutting board. That way you will have greater control over unwanted rolling, rocking, and slipping.

Hold your knife firmly to maintain control. Two gripping styles are frequently employed. In the first of these, the index finger is extended along the top of the blade, the thumb is flat against the near side of the blade, and the remaining fingers are curled about the handle. In the alternate grip, the thumb is extended along the top of the blade, the index finger placed flat against the far side of the blade, and the remaining fingers are curled about the handle.

For most cutting techniques, you will need to use long strokes and push away from you, lifting and returning the blade to the starting position in as smooth a manner as possible. In those instances, slicing is accomplished on the forward-moving stroke, not on the return. Do not allow your wrist to bounce up and down, as it does in typical French-kitchen technique. With practice, you will pick up speed. Always keep in mind, however, that rhythmic strokes are more important than fast ones.

Cutting a Continuous Peel

Cutting a broad, thin continuous peel, or *katsura muki*, can be a challenge and will probably require some practice before you feel comfortable doing it. A knife called a *na kiri-bōchō* is the usual tool because of its broad, square blade, but an ALL-PURPOSE KNIFE can also be used. Daikon is a good choice for practicing this technique. Cucumbers work well, too, while carrots are difficult until you get the knack.

Your right and left hands are simultaneously engaged in rather different motions (somewhat like rubbing your belly and patting your head at the same time): The hand holding the knife will make up-and-down sawing motions. At the same time, the hand holding the daikon needs to roll slowly, rotating the daikon into the knife blade.

Decorative Slashing

To ensure even and thorough cooking, and to prevent the skin on fish from tearing and shrinking in an unattractive manner as the fish cooks, the Japanese use a technique called *kazari-bōchō*, or "decorative slashing."

When preparing a small, whole flatfish, the *kazari-bōchō* is usually a single slit down the center of the top side of the fish along the center bone. Unlike round fish that have one eye on each side of their head, flatfish have both eyes on the top side. Depending on the species, the eyes can be facing right or left.

When preparing a small, whole round fish, the *kazari-bōchō* is usually a pair of shallow, diagonal slashes running from upper left to lower right on one side of the fish. If the fish is a particularly meaty one, make the slashes on both sides.

When preparing fish fillets, the *kazari-bōchō* is usually shallow cross-hatching or a series of diagonal slashes. Depending on the size of the fillet, these can be a series of 2, 3, 4, or 5 strokes.

Beveling Edges

To keep certain vegetables, such as daikon and *kabocha* squash, from crumbling as they simmer, Japanese home cooks often trim a narrow strip off the edges of each piece to bevel them (*mentori*). This technique promotes even cooking, and the beveled edge provides an additional surface to which sauce can cling.

Rolled Cutting

Using a *ran-giri*, or rolled, style cutting technique with cylindrical vegetables has several advantages. It produces pieces of a similar size and configuration from vegetables, such as carrots or parsnips, which are often bulbous at one end and slender at the other. It is easier to time the cooking process when using uniform pieces. Each multi-surfaced piece of roll-cut

vegetable can easily absorb the flavors of a simmering or braising liquid while retaining its shape nicely.

Begin by slicing your peeled vegetable slightly on the diagonal. Without changing the direction of your knife blade, roll the vegetable toward you, about ¼ turn, and make another slice. Continue rolling and cutting to form many multi-surfaced, triangular-like shapes.

Cutting Strips

Literally, "a thousand cuts," *sen-giri* refers to any thin strip or shred, usually the equivalent of julienne, though sometimes thinner and more threadlike. The strips can be cut on the diagonal (often true of cucumbers and red radishes), straight with the grain (common with daikon and carrots), or against the grain (cabbage, young ginger).

To shred cabbage: Cut a whole head into quarters through the stem end and place one of the flat, cut edges face down on the cutting board. Cut a "V" to remove the white, inner core section (in the frugal *washoku* kitchen, this core is set aside and later cut into gossamer-thin shreds that are quickly pickled; see Impatient Pickles, page 217). The remaining piece of the

ALL-PURPOSE KNIFE
(BUNKA-BŌCHŌ, SANTOKU-BŌCHŌ)

Professional Japanese knives are honed on one side only (requiring special techniques to use them effectively), highly specialized (such as the *sashimi-bōchō* for slicing raw fish only), and very costly, and demand constant maintenance. You do not need them to prepare everyday *washoku* meals at home.

You will find one fairly large, very sharp knife in most Japanese home kitchens. It tends to be a multipurpose knife that incorporates some features of traditional Japanese swordlike blades (heft, and balance of weight between handle and blade) with other features borrowed from Western cutlery (it is honed evenly on both sides of the blade). At the turn of the twentieth century, this multipurpose knife was

dubbed *bunka-bōchō,* a word that at the time alluded to stylish sophistication. More recently, these knives have been called *santoku-bōchō,* or "knives with three features" (illustrated on page 29). These features are a tapered, pointed tip for fine decorative scoring (*kazari-bōchō*); a wide, flat-surfaced body for shredding in a smooth, forward motion (*sen-giri*), broad peeling (*katsura muki*), and beveling edges (*mentori*); and a long, sturdy blade for wide slicing at an angle to the board (*sogi-giri*).

After each use, wash knives by hand with a nonabrasive sponge and mild detergent, rinse thoroughly, and dry carefully with a soft towel. If possible, get your knives sharpened where you purchase them. Most stores selling quality knives offer the service for a reasonable fee.

wedge is a stack, with darker green, outer leaves on top and lighter green, inner leaves on bottom. With fingers tucked into your palm and knuckles straight and perpendicular to where your knife blade will be, press down on the stacked cabbage leaves. As you cut, the hand holding the cabbage stack retreats bit by bit. Lift the blade to realign your knife and repeat in rhythmic strokes. The shredded cabbage will fall to the far side of the blade.

If you do not want to cut the cabbage into quarters, you can peel off the leaves and create bundles by rolling them tightly lengthwise. Cut the roll in half and stack the halves, aligning the cut edges, and then shred as above.

To shred cucumbers into dark-tipped strips: Hold the cucumber firmly to keep it from rolling, and slice it on the diagonal into very thin pieces. Use a forward pushing motion when you cut. Keep the slices aligned.

Press on the row of slices to flatten them slightly, as though you are fanning out a deck of playing cards. Cut lengthwise across these slices so that each strip is tipped in dark green.

Slant Cutting

This slicing technique, known as *sogi-giri*, is used to create pieces of even thickness from a larger chunk of fish or meat of uneven thickness. A lack of uniformity makes it difficult to judge the time and temperature needed to cook an item fully. Cutting on the diagonal through the grain (muscle tissue) of the fish or meat also ensures that the cooked pieces will be tender.

Place the food to be sliced flat on a cutting board in a horizontal position. With the fingers of one hand extended, palm down, press lightly against the food to keep it from slipping. With your other hand, insert the blade of your knife at a 45-degree angle just underneath your extended fingers. Working from left to right on the meat or fish (or right to left,

if left-handed), use smooth, sweeping strokes to take slices of even thickness off the fish or meat. Set each slice aside before beginning the next slice. I find it easier to maintain control of the knife if I hold it with my index finger, rather than my thumb, extended.

Braid Cutting

Although I call this "braid cutting" (that is what it looks like to most North Americans I show it to), the name of this cutting technique, *tazuna-giri*, conjures up an equestrian image to most Japanese—*tazuna* are the twisted reins of a horse bridle. Certain pliable foods, such as *konnyaku* or *kamaboko* fish sausage, can easily be cut this way. You might also try this with bread dough (to make braided rolls) or pastry or cookie dough (to make braided sticks).

To cut konnyaku into a braid: Cut a block of *konnyaku* into $1/4$-inch-thick slices, each about 2 inches long and $3/4$ inch wide. With the tip of a sharp knife held like a pencil, draw a line down the center to make a slit. The slit should be no more than 1 inch long, leaving a $1/2$ inch on top and bottom uncut. Pull one uncut end through the slit to form a braidlike shape, as illustrated on page 29.

Dicing Tōfu

Japanese cooks place firm or silken tōfu on an open palm and use gentle strokes of a sharp-bladed knife to dice it. This is not as dangerous as it sounds. But if you feel uncomfortable following suit, place it on a cutting board.

First, slice the block with horizontal strokes, working from the bottom of the block up. Then, make a series of vertical cuts. Finally, make a second series of vertical cuts perpendicular to the first series. If you are working on a cutting board, use your nonknife hand to keep the horizontally sliced layers in place as you make the vertical cuts, and scoop up the diced tōfu from the board with the flat blade of the knife.

GRATING

A variety of foods are grated regularly in the *washoku* kitchen, with ginger, daikon, wasabi, and mountain yam the most common. In addition, the zest of citrus fruits is often grated. Both traditional tools, such as a METAL GRATER (*oroshi-gané*) and a SHARKSKIN GRATER (*samékawa oroshi ki*) and new gadgets, such as a Microplane grater, are useful. If I were to recommend a single piece of equipment, though, it would be a CERAMIC GRATER.

Extracting ginger juice: To extract juice from a knob of fresh ginger, peel it and rub it in a circular motion over the thornlike projections of a metal or ceramic grater. Using the stub of ginger remaining in your hand, scrape the rough surface of the grater to collect all the gratings in one place. Using a metal grater with a trough at the bottom, the grated pieces easily gather there; the trough of most ceramic graters is around the outer rim. Gently squeeze the gratings to extract the juice; discard the fibrous pulp that remains.

METAL GRATER (OROSHI-GANÉ)

Made from gold- or silver-toned metal, an *oroshi-gané* (illustrated on page 72) sports many thornlike projections. Unlike American graters that must be used over a bowl or plate because the grated food falls through holes, the Japanese grater is a flat surface with a curved trough at one end where the gratings and juice collect, making this grater particularly useful when you want to extract juice from ginger.

SHARKSKIN GRATER (SAMÉKAWA OROSHI KI)

If you are able to find fresh wasabi roots, it is worth seeking out a place to buy a *samékawa* grater. These graters are small (about 1½ inches across), paddle shaped, and covered with what appears to be rough sandpaper, but is, in fact, sharkskin. The surface provides just enough roughness to grate the roots into a creamy, smooth, aromatic paste.

CERAMIC AND PLASTIC GRATERS

Ceramic and plastic graters are easier on the fingers than metal ones (no cuts from trying to grate too hard or too long), though ceramic ones, such as the one illustrated on page 72, chip and crack if not handled with care. Small, decorative graters come in a variety of shapes (vegetables, fruits, and fish are most popular) and are typically brought to the table so that diners can grate their own condiments for dipping sauces. More practical, though, are the round, plate-shaped graters that are about 5 inches across and sport a rubberized rim on the bottom. These are especially useful when grating a large piece of daikon before serving individual portions.

Ceramic graters are good for aromatic foods such as garlic or lemon peel, since odors do not linger, while small (2-inch) plastic graters with removable tops and rubberized bottoms are popular, particularly in small city apartments with limited kitchen-drawer space.

GRINDING, CRUSHING, AND MASHING

In the traditional Japanese kitchen, grinding, crushing, and mashing (*suru, suri tsubusu*) were performed in a SURIBACHI (grooved mortar), though most kitchens today are outfitted with food processors and blenders, as well as GOMA SURI KI (hand-held spice mills). Though efficient tools to mash and pulverize, these contemporary devices do not multitask like an old-fashioned *suribachi*, which performs as both a mixing bowl (foods to be dressed in the crushed sauce are tossed directly in the *suribachi*) and a serving bowl at table.

To crush, mash, and/or grind food in a grooved mortar, place the mortar on a nonslip surface (either a flat, rubber jar opener or a wrung-out dampened towel), or have someone else hold it steady as you grind. Grasp the pestle (*surikogi,* also called a *bō*) near the bulbous bottom with one hand, and cup the palm of your other hand on the narrow top. Using tight, circular motions with your bottom hand, as though drawing the letter O, begin at the center of the bowl and gradually work your way up the sides with wider circles. Repeat several times. The hand on top presses down to steady the stick, while the rotating action of the bottom hand does the real grinding. When your hands tire, alternate between grinding in a clockwise and counterclockwise direction. You can also switch hands for top and bottom positions.

When scraping down the sides of a *suribachi* with a spatula or a wooden paddle or spoon, move in the direction of the grooves to avoid shredding your scraping tool. When you have finished using the mortar, soak it in warm, sudsy water and, using a stiff-bristled brush, scrape in the same direction as the grooves. Rinse, invert, and let dry.

In most instances, food processors work well in place of the traditional mortar, but you may find you need to double a recipe to have enough volume to engage the blades of your machine properly, even in a mini-processor. When using a food processor or blender, it is sometimes best to use the pulse function, stopping often to scrape down the sides of the bowl, to keep the food from being overworked.

SURIBACHI (GROOVED MORTAR)

Traditionally made of clay and with the inside of the bowl unglazed and deeply grooved, the *suribachi* is used with a wooden *surikogi* (pestle) to crush or grind seeds and nuts and to mash or grind fish, tōfu, yam, and meat into pastes. The best pestles are made of *sanshō* wood (bumpy, rough branches of a plant that yields spicy berries, page 47), but most commercial pestles are made from cedar or cypress wood.

Late in the nineteenth century, crushing toasted sesame seeds in a *suribachi* became a metaphor for ingratiating behavior (the oily, pasty seeds that cling to the bowl recalling the fawning behavior of a sycophant). The Japanese expression *goma suri*—literally, "sesame grinding"—is what Americans call "apple polishing."

A smooth marble or ceramic mortar can stand in for a *suribachi* to crush seeds and mash tōfu, but these mortars are not as effective for other operations, such as grinding yams and removing the fuzz from *édamamé*.

GOMA SURI KI (HAND-OPERATED SPICE MILL)

As its name suggests, this convenient gadget cracks and crushes dry-roasted sesame seeds in small quantities. It looks like a pepper mill and functions on the same principle.

Suribachi (grooved mortar) with surikogi *(or bō, pestle), ceramic grater with fresh ginger, and metal grater*

REMOVING BITTERNESS, OIL, AND MOISTURE

The word *aku* is used to describe the unpleasant harshness or bitterness that naturally occurs in many foods. Removing the bitterness, or *aku nuki,* is a common activity in the *washoku* kitchen, as is the removal of excessive oil and moisture from certain foods before cooking them. Sometimes bitterness or oil removal is accomplished by briefly blanching the food; fish, poultry, fried tōfu, *konnyaku* and its noodle derivative, *shirataki,* are good examples. At other times, soaking the food in either plain water or water to which vinegar, *yaki myōban* (alum), or baking soda has been added will leach out bitterness and help keep colors bright. Vegetables such as burdock root, sweet potatoes, and lotus root are often treated to such soaks before they are cooked. *Aku* can also be leached out of certain foods, such as cucumbers and *konnyaku,* by rubbing them vigorously with coarse salt.

When blanching, rubbing, or soaking is necessary to drawn out *aku,* each recipe will guide you to this section.

Blanching

The Japanese frequently blanch foods in boiling water or scalding hot water as the first step in cooking them. Depending on the ingredient, the purpose of blanching varies, as does the vocabulary describing it. When cooking vegetables, especially leafy greens, blanching is usually called *yu-dōshi.* Blanching forces out the *aku,* or natural bitterness, which usually takes the form of froth floating in a pot (or scum clinging to the sides of the pot). Blanching also breaks down tough fibers, allowing the vegetables to pick up the flavors of seasonings added after the blanching step. Some vegetables are plunged in cold water to arrest the blanching process (this is commonly done with leafy greens that can be squeezed later without bruising the vegetable). Most often the blanched vegetables are allowed to cool naturally (and blanching time is shortened accordingly), or fanned cool with an UCHIWA (page 88).

When fried tōfu is blanched, the excess oil is forced out, as is *aku* in the form of a greasy film that rises to the surface. In the case of *konnyaku* and *shirataki,* blanching forces the bitterness out of these foods, leaving a faint ring of chalky residue around the pot that can be scrubbed away.

Shimo furi (literally, "frost falling") is a type of blanching that seals the surface of foods such as chicken or fish, preventing the loss of flavor and nutrients, while forcing out unpleasant *aku* in the form of foamy matter that floats to the top. The name of the technique refers to the subtle change in surface color that results from the brief exposure to heat.

Blanching leafy greens: Fill a large tub with cold water and set leafy greens to soak in the tub. Swish the leaves through the water to clean away dirt caught at the base of the tuft. Pull away and discard any yellowing, blackened, or decaying leaves. Drain off the sandy water from the tub and repeat the procedure.

Have ready several pieces of cotton kitchen string, each 5 or 6 inches long. They are used to tie up clusters of the greens so that the root or tuft ends are aligned (see illustration on page ii). That way, the tougher stems can be held in boiling water to cook longer than the more tender leaves. Having bundles aligned also provides more options for plating the greens.

Shave off a bit of the roots if the greens seem particularly tough and stringy. With a sharp knife, make a shallow X about $1/3$ inch deep through the thickest part of the stem bottoms. This slash is made parallel to the stems, as though you were going to slice lengthwise through them. Rinse the stems again under cold water to remove any remaining grit. Place a small cluster of greens on one of the strings, positioning them perpendicular to it, and tie them up into a bundle about 1 inch in diameter at the base. Repeat to make a few more bundles.

Bring a pot of lightly salted water to a rolling boil. With your fingers, tongs, or chopsticks, hold the bundles of greens by the leaves and dip the stem portion into the boiling water. Hold it partly submerged until the stems are barely wilted, and then carefully release the bundle into the pot. When the water returns to a boil, stir the greens once and drain them. Swiss chard, kale, and carrot and beet tops can be tough and may require 3 to 4 minutes of cooking before draining; test by sampling a piece. Transfer the greens to a bowl of ice water to arrest the cooking; when cool, squeeze out the excess moisture.

Blanching fried tōfu: All fried tōfu products—slices, blocks, and dumplings—are quite greasy when purchased. To remove excess oil from the surface, blanch the fried tōfu briefly in boiling water; 10 to 15 seconds of blanching after the water returns to a full boil should suffice to remove grease and the *aku*. If a recipe, such as Miso Soup with Fried Tōfu, Leafy Greens, and Scallions (page 118), requires you to blanch other foods, too, use the same water, but be sure to blanch the fried tōfu last. Drain the tōfu and, when cool enough to handle, squeeze out all excess liquid.

Blanching *konnyaku* and *shirataki* noodles: Pour off any packaging liquid from the *konnyaku* or *shirataki* noodles. Depending upon the dish in which it will be used, *konnyaku* is sometimes scored, sliced, or diced before blanching. Over high heat, bring several quarts of water to a rolling boil and carefully lower the *konnyaku* or *shirataki* into the pot. After the water returns to a vigorous boil, blanch for just under a minute. Drain and allow the *konnyaku* or *shirataki* noodles to cool naturally, or fan them with an UCHIWA (page 88). (This eliminates moisture and permits them to absorb the flavors of foods with which they are cooked.) Despite their gelatinous appearance, *konnyaku* and *shirataki* become firmer with cooking.

Aku can also be removed from *konnyaku* or *shirataki* noodles by salt-rubbing (page 76) and dry-roasting (page 85).

Shimo furi: When cooking fish, meat, or poultry, blanching is called *shimo furi*, or "frost falling." Briefly exposing fish, meat, or poultry to scalding hot water keeps unwelcome odors at bay and prevents stocks, sauces, and soups from becoming marred with unattractive scum. In the process, the surface turns frosty white, which is how this activity got its name. Because of its delicacy, fish is often wrapped in cloth before being drizzled with or immersed in boiling water.

For fish, the easiest way to perform *shimo furi* (especially if you have a large, deep sink) is to drizzle boiling water over it. Lightly wrap each piece of fish or meat in SARASHI cloth (page 77), or a double thickness of cheesecloth. Arrange the wrapped pieces on a large cutting board and then tilt the board at a gently sloping angle against the inside of the sink; if necessary, invert a small cup or bowl under one end of the board to create the slope. Drizzle a cup or more of boiling water over the cloth-wrapped pieces, letting it drain into the sink. (With fish that has skin on one side, drizzle boiling water over the skin side first.) Flip and repeat. When the cloth is cool enough to handle, remove the fish or meat and blot away any excess moisture. True to its name, the surface of the food will have changed color, now looking frosted.

Similar results can be achieved by dipping cloth-wrapped fish into a pot filled with boiling hot water. Wrap each piece in cloth hammock style, so that you can lower it briefly into a pan of boiling water without scalding your hands. Lay *sarashi* or a double thickness of cheesecloth on your kitchen counter and put the fish pieces in the center. Bring the edges of the cloth together and twist to enclose in a baglike manner. Alternatively, if you have a deep pot with a removable pasta insert, you can set the wrapped fish directly in the insert and briefly submerge it.

Bring a pot of water to a rolling boil and then remove it from the heat. With tongs or cooking chopsticks, carefully dunk the wrapped fish or meat in the pot, swishing it through the hot water. You need to work quickly to keep the food from cooking at this point, which would deprive the finished dish of full flavor and precious nutrients.

Lift the package out of the pot and let it cool on a plate. Unwrap and remove the fish or meat.

When performing *shimo furi* with chicken to make stock, place the chicken pieces in a colander or large strainer in the sink and carefully pour boiling water over them. With long cooking chopsticks or kitchen tongs, turn the chicken and repeat. This cleanses the chicken without sacrificing the flavor potential that standard blanching might.

Rubbing

Cucumbers (as well as zucchini and other squashes and gourds) will taste sweeter if you perform an *aku nuki* procedure on them first. Use either a circular-rubbing technique or a salt-rubbing technique, but do not combine these procedures.

Circular rubbing: Slice off a sliver from the darker green stem end, where the cucumber was attached to the vine. Holding the sliver in one hand and the cucumber in the other, rub the cut ends together in a circular motion. The friction from this action causes a white, pasty substance—this is the *aku*—to appear on the rim of the cucumber. Rinse it away under cold running water and pat the cucumber dry.

Salt-rubbing: This technique uses the abrasive, moisture-leaching power of salt. Place 1 teaspoon of coarse salt in your hand and rub the skin of the cucumber vigorously with it; this same salt can be used to remove *aku* from several cucumbers. Do not be alarmed to see the salt turn bright green. Set the cucumber aside for a minute before rinsing the salt away under cold water. Pat the cucumber dry.

In any recipe that calls for *konnyaku,* salt-rubbing can be used instead of blanching or dry-roasting to remove *aku.* When salt-rubbing *konnyaku,* use 1/2 teaspoon of coarse salt for every 5- or 6-ounce block. Drain the block of *konnyaku* and pat it dry with paper towels. Spread half the salt on one side of the *konnyaku,* rubbing it in thoroughly and as evenly as possible; flip and repeat on the other side. Set the *konnyaku* aside for a few minutes to "sweat." Blot up moisture and proceed to score, slice, or cut the *konnyaku* into whatever shapes you wish.

Soaking Tubers and Roots

Depending on the kind of food being handled, the composition of the soaking water varies.

Soaking Japanese-style sweet potato: To preserve the vivid red coloring of the skin and to prevent the yellow flesh from turning a dingy gray, the Japanese often soak pieces of sweet potato in an alum solution called *myōban sui.* Alum powder is not readily available in American grocery stores, though Asian markets carry it. Baking soda can be substituted.

Rinse the sweet potato under running cold water to remove any dirt clinging to it. Pat it dry and dice it into 1/4-inch pieces if making soup, or into julienne strips if making tempura pancakes.

In a bowl large enough to hold all the pieces, dissolve 1/2 teaspoon *yaki myōban* or 1 teaspoon baking soda in 2 cups tap water. Let the pieces sit in the solution for at least 10 minutes or up to 2 hours. Drain, rinse in fresh cold water, and pat dry.

Soaking burdock root: When it comes to rinsing burdock root, there is a basic agreement in the Japanese kitchen about how to do this: Rinse the burdock root under running cold water, lightly scratching away clinging soil with the back of your knife. Burdock root's woodsy aroma is concentrated in its outer layers, so avoid heavy scraping that would remove too much of the peel.

There is little consensus, however, among Japanese cooks about soaking burdock root after it is has been scraped. Most will soak sliced burdock root briefly in plain water, others will put a few drops of vinegar in the soaking water to further "bleach" it. Those who engage in macrobiotic practices will not soak burdock root at all.

Soaking lotus root: Peel and slice lotus roots using a stainless-steel or ceramic blade to prevent discoloration. Immediately soak pieces in acidulated water (water to which vinegar or citrus juice has been added) to prevent further discoloration. Usually 1 tablespoon vinegar for every cup of cold water will suffice.

If you are frying or sautéing lotus root, you only need to soak it once. If you are blanching the lotus root, you will need a fresh batch of acidulated water to ensure the slices remain snowy white. Drain the slices after a few minutes and pat dry with paper towels.

DRAINING, PRESSING, AND STRAINING

Foods such as tōfu and *konnyaku* are packed in liquid and need to be drained, and sometimes pressed, before using, while miso needs to be strained or thinned in broth before adding to soup. Both techniques employ special equipment—SARASHI cloth in the case of draining tōfu, a MISO KOSHI in the case of straining miso. While best results are achieved with these tools, I provide for alternatives in the discussion that follows.

Draining and Pressing Tōfu

Blocks of tōfu, whether firm, silken, or grilled, need to be drained and pressed before cooking with them. The old-fashioned way calls for wrapping the block of tōfu in SARASHI, sandwiching it between two flat plates or small cutting boards, and then setting it at a 45-degree angle inside a large bowl or

tub, so that the excess liquid drains into the bottom of the container. After an hour, the tōfu is flipped over to encourage even drainage and allowed to sit for another hour or so. At the end of the second hour, the tōfu appears considerably compressed and weighs several ounces less. In the traditional *washoku* kitchen, this draining setup was done at cool room temperature throughout most of the year (it was easy to find such a spot, since most homes had no central heating). Though it still yields the most flavorful and best-textured results, it is admittedly not practical in many modern kitchens. You can, however, create a similar setup in a container that fits on your refrigerator shelf, keeping it there overnight.

Or you can use an ultramodern method: paper towels and the microwave. When you open the package of tōfu, pour off all the liquid and blot the tōfu with plain paper towels. Then wrap it in fresh paper towels, place on a microwave-safe dish,

SARASHI

The Japanese use *sarashi* cloth for many purposes. Its finely woven texture is ideal for wrapping tōfu or grated vegetables that need to be drained of excess liquid, for wrapping fish or tōfu that will be marinated in miso, and for straining *dashi* and other similar stocks made with fish flakes. The cloth will become discolored and pick up odors from these various tasks, but it can be reused. Rinse with warm water only.

In Japan, *sarashi* is sold in 10-meter bolts at restaurant supply shops (the outer stalls at Tsukiji fish market and along Kappabashi Dori avenue in Tokyo) and in the baby wear section of department stores(!). In the 1970s, when my daughter Rena was an infant, diapers were made from *sarashi* as was a special *obi* sash pregnant women would wear as underclothes. The following custom still prevails: On a day late in the first trimester of a woman's pregnancy, and designated as auspicious on the ancient *koyomi* calendar, a mother-to-be is presented with a *sarashi* band by a female relative or close friend.

The expectant mother then asks her physician or midwife to hand-brush the *kotobuki,* a calligraphy used on congratulatory occasions, on the end section of the cloth. When wound about the slowly bulging abdomen, the calligraphy covers and protects the growing life inside.

If you cannot obtain *sarashi,* line a mesh strainer with a paper coffee filter, or use another fine-weave, lint-free cotton cloth, such as a white linen handkerchief. If you use cheesecloth, you will need to layer several pieces to compensate for the open weave.

MISO KOSHI (MISO STRAINER)

A deep-welled, vertical-handled strainer called a *miso koshi* simplifies the task of enriching broth with *miso.* Most *miso koshi* are fitted with a hook at the base of the handle that enables the strainer to rest on the rim of the pot. Many come with a mini-ladle or thick stick that is used to press the miso through the fine mesh of the strainer. The back of an ordinary soup spoon can also be used to stir and press the miso.

and "zap" it for 30 seconds on a high setting. A fair amount of milky liquid will be exuded, which you should pour off. Discard the drenched towels and replace them with fresh, dry towels. Repeat this zap-and-blot procedure once or twice more until the tōfu feels considerably firmer.

Straining Miso

Used in a variety of soups, dips, and sauces, miso can be smooth and creamy or chunky and coarsely textured, depending on the type and brand. If you use a MISO KOSHI (page 77), a specialized long-handled, deep-welled strainer, when adding miso to a soup, you will be able to keep the bits of rice, bean, or barley present in the miso paste from entering the finished soup. This straining step is especially appreciated if the soups will be drunk directly from the bowl, in typical Japanese fashion.

To strain miso, place it in the *miso koshi* and immerse in the pot. Stir the miso in the strainer to force it through the mesh. If you do not have a *miso koshi,* place the miso paste in a bowl, add several spoonfuls of stock from the pot, and whisk to dissolve the bean paste. Ladle in some additional stock and stir to mix well before adding the thinned miso to the pot. If highly textured, the miso broth can be strained with a fine-mesh strainer to remove bits of beans and rice.

SOFTENING AND REHYDRATING DRIED FOODS

Drawers and shelves in the traditional *washoku* pantry were filled with *kambutsu* (dried foods), providing cooks with flavor-enhancing stocks and nutritious side dishes throughout the year. Items such as dried shiitaké mushrooms, *kampyō* (gourd ribbons), *kiriboshi daikon* (shredded daikon), dried beans, and many varieties of dried sea vegetables and fish have an extended shelf life and are versatile in the kitchen, combining well with an array of fresh ingredients and seasonings. These foods can be ordered from catalogs and online if Asian groceries in your community do not carry them (see Resources, page 309)

To extract the most flavor from items such as *kombu* (kelp) and *iriko* (dried sardines) when making stocks or sauces, soak them in a cold or room-temperature liquid before slowly heating. This is especially true of high-glutamate varieties of kelp. Other dried foods, such as *adzuki* beans, are soaked and then simmered for a long period of time to make them tender. In some cases, the addition of sugar (when softening dried shiitaké mushrooms, for example) or salt (when softening *kampyō*) helps break down tough fibers in dried foods.

MARINATING

Many traditional Japanese recipes call for marinating an ingredient in a seasoned liquid or paste before it is cooked, such as in Citrus-and-Soy-Glazed Swordfish (page 227), Miso-Marinated Broiled Fish (page 229), and Tender-Stewed Curried Chicken (page 252). Other foods are marinated after they have been treated with heat, as in Crisp Fried Smelts in Spicy Vinaigrette (page 245) and Spinach Steeped in Broth (page 190). Since the method varies, I have provided specific marinating instructions in the individual recipes. In the case of marinating in miso, ingredients are wrapped in SARASHI (page 77) before being placed in the paste to prevent too-rapid absorption and protect delicate items, facilitating their removal later.

Other foods are transformed by a combination of brining and applying pressure, a pickling process employed in dishes such as Impatient Pickles (page 217). A special device called a SHOKUTAKU TSUKÉMONO KI (tabletop pickle pot; pictured opposite and described on page 80) is useful when making these preparations. Other pickled dishes, such as Sweet-and-Sour Lotus Root (page 222), use vinegar-based liquids, and in these instances nonreactive containers are best.

When marinating or pickling foods, a nonreactive container, such as a glass baking pan or dish, prevents any unpleasant chemical interactions from taking place. The

Shokutaku tsukémono ki (tabletop pickle pot), pictured with cabbage, myōga, and a small mound of Impatient Pickles (page 217)

Japanese use porcelain and glass as well as a type of enamel-lined metal container called *horo*, an ancient technology that is thought to have first traveled the Silk Road from Egypt to Japan in the sixth century.

———————————— ✸ ————————————

SHOKUTAKU TSUKÉMONO KI
(TABLETOP PICKLE POT)

Traditionally, large, flat stones were used in brine-pickling vegetables. More recently, the Japanese have developed a special pot called a *shokutaku tsukémono ki* (illustrated on page 79). It is small, made of sturdy, clear plastic, and has a screw-top device that applies pressure in lieu of heavy stones. The pot can sit on a kitchen counter or refrigerator shelf.

Recipes that suggest the use of this device provide specific instructions for salting, seasoning, and layering the vegetable. If you cannot find this pickle pot, you can devise your own brine-pickling setup with a deep bowl and some heavy objects. Choose books, bricks, or heavy canned goods that weigh a total of 10 pounds and are slightly smaller than the diameter of the bowl you will be using. You will also need a flat plate that is an inch or so less in diameter than the bottom of your bowl. It will become the lid, sitting directly on the vegetable. Because your weights will sink down below the level of brine, they must be wrapped in waterproof material, such as a plastic bag.

——————————————

• • •

A *washoku* meal combines foods prepared by various methods, nearly all of which include the application of heat (*nama*, or raw saladlike foods, and on occasion raw fish and seafood, being the major exception). Simmering in shallow liquid (what the Japanese refer to as *niru*) and searing with heat (*yaku*) are the two most frequently employed cooking methods. In addition, frying, steaming, and dry-roasting are important ways in which ingredients get transformed into finished dishes in the *washoku* kitchen.

BROILING, GRILLING, AND PAN SEARING

On a Japanese menu, *yakimono* refers to foods that have been seared with heat, either by broiling or grilling. In North America, grilled foods are cooked over or on a grill, while broiling suggests an overhead source of heat. The Japanese use a single word—*yaku*—to describe the application of direct, searing heat, whether the source is above or below. In recipes that appear in this book, I have followed American conventions in my choice of vocabulary, but have been mindful of describing where the food is placed in relation to the source of heat being used.

Oil is used sparingly, if at all, in *yakimono* preparations; the naturally occurring fish oils and animal fats lubricate the food as it cooks. Before being broiled, a piece of fish might be air-dried, marinated in miso, or simply sprinkled with salt. *Yakimono* vegetable preparations include eggplant seared with heat (Chilled Roasted Eggplant, page 193); the charred skin, which keeps the eggplant juicy as it cooks, is peeled away before eating. When tōfu is seared, it is typically slathered in a sauce, as in Broiled Tōfu with Flavored Miso (page 281).

The category *yakimono* also includes pan-seared dishes (*nabé yaki*), which typically use a bit of oil to brown, crust, caramelize, or glaze the food being seared. Stir-fried or sautéed foods, however, are categorized as fried or deep-fried foods.

Broiling

Japanese household broilers are small and fitted with a tray in which a rack rests. The source of heat is a double row of flames or coils located above the rack. Fish or meat is placed on the rack and the drippings collect in the tray. If you have a similar broiler setup in your kitchen, place some water in the tray to prevent flare-ups from the fish oils. Add a few drops of vinegar, some used green tea leaves (leftover leaves from infused tea earlier in the day), or a scrap of lemon, lime, or orange peel to the water to help tame unwanted odors. Some disposable foil broiler trays are lined with a substance that absorbs excess fat and odors. If you use these, do not use water or the suggested deodorizing substances.

Increasingly, Japanese urban families have closed, electric-fired, countertop grills they call "fish roasters" for broiling fish indoors. Most are fashioned in a clamshell design, opening on top to reveal electric coils on the bottom, a rack in the middle, and more electric coils on the inner surface of the lid. Similar cooking units are sold in America under various names.

Grilling

Placed on earthen or stone floors outside the kitchen, Japanese hibachi (literally, "pots of fire") and similar units called *shichirin* and *konrō* were traditionally fueled by *binchō,* a long-burning charcoal that provides intense heat with no discernable—that is, unwanted—aroma. Because of its superior attributes, *binchō* is still used today in many professional kitchens. In some old-fashioned rural homes, or inns built in the traditional *minka* farmhouse style, you may still find a hearth, or *irori.* Whole skewered fish, stuck vertically (head down, tail up) in the ash, are rotated once or twice to ensure even cooking.

Nowadays, in most Japanese home kitchens, an *ami* (perforated metal screen) is placed directly over stove-top burners to diffuse and disseminate heat when grilling. Hibachi units remain popular, however. Nearly every urban apartment in Japan boasts a small balcony, which is sometimes used for outdoor cooking in good weather. Typically, a fine-mesh grate is placed over glowing charcoal in the pot, or bowl, of the hibachi. The natural oil in fish and the fat in well-marbled meat provide ample "grease" to prevent sticking. A standard American kettle grill or gas grill will work for all grilling operations in this book.

Pan Searing in Skillets

The decision to pan sear a food, rather than broil or grill it, is usually based on two criteria: the need to introduce some oil to keep the food from sticking (omelet making is a good example) or to keep lean meat or fish, stripped of its protective skin, moist as it is seared (Citrus-and-Soy-Glazed Swordfish, page 227, and Flash-Seared Steak with Two Sauces, page 267, are good examples).

When cooking omelets, a square or rectangular TAMAGO YAKI NABÉ (omelet pan; illustrated on page 82) helps shape and cook Rolled Omelet, Two Ways (page 287). For searing vegetables, meat, fish, and poultry, a standard stainless-steel skillet about 10 inches in diameter is the tool of choice. Pans and skillets with nonstick surfaces are useful for searing and glazing, and for cooking some braised dishes, too. Regardless of whether you are using a nonstick pan, it is best to season it with an oiled wad of paper towel just before each use. I use COOKING CHOPSTICKS (page 83) to grasp the wad and brush the entire surface of the pan with it, paying special attention to the corners of a square or rectangular pan; you may prefer to use a pastry brush dipped in oil.

TAMAGO YAKI NABÉ (OMELET PAN)

Japanese omelets are made in a square or rectangular pan called a *tamago yaki nabé* (illustrated on page 82). The pans come in several sizes and with different surface finishes. A pan measuring about 4 by 7 inches outfitted with a nonstick surface is the easiest to use. Many nonstick pans have a sloped edge on the far side. How this helps you to shape the edges of your omelet will become obvious when you make your final layer in the Tokyo-style (page 287) and Kansai-style (page 289) rolled omelets. If you have a choice in the weight of the pan, choose one with fair heft for its size.

Most Japanese food professionals use a tin-lined copper omelet pan measuring about 6 by 10 inches. These pans are difficult to learn to use, but once you master the technique, the ability to control heat in a professional pan makes it a valuable tool. The copper pans are costly and require care to maintain properly (no harsh detergents or sponges, no plunging into cold water to cool, thorough drying, and patience to reseason with a thin layer of oil before each session).

FRYING AND STIR-FRYING

The technique of cooking foods submerged in oil is called *ageru* ("frying" or "deep-frying"), examples of which are tempura (batter coated) and *tonkatsu* (breaded). The Japanese learned to deep-fry from foreign culinary cultures: the Chinese originally, later the Portuguese and the Dutch. Stir-frying (*itameru*), cooking in a thin layer of oil, probably came from China, too. The Japanese often begin the process by pan searing the ingredients, drizzling in oil around the outer edge of the skillet before tossing and stirring.

For deep-frying and stir-frying, a wok-shaped pan will enable you to use less oil because of its conical shape, though any deep skillet or shallow pot that can withstand high heat and hold oil to a depth of $1^1/_2$ inches with an inch or so of clearance is fine. Other equipment to have on hand includes COOKING CHOPSTICKS, a rack on which to drain the deep-fried foods, and a fine-mesh strainer to clear the oil of batter bits or bread crumbs between batches.

Learning to judge proper oil temperature is critical to success in deep-frying. Since each recipe that calls for deep-frying uses different ingredients, I offer specific guidance each time.

SIMMERING, POACHING, AND BRAISING

Cooking with liquid—simmering, poaching, and braising—is common practice when preparing vegetables, fish, meat, eggs, beans, and grains, including rice, in the *washoku* kitchen.

The best shape and size for a pot or pan varies with the task at hand and portion size. When cooking with relatively little liquid, or when several portions of fish, meat, poultry, tōfu, or vegetables need to be cooked in a single layer, wide and shallow pans (about $1^1/_2$ inches deep) are best. When cooking with more liquid, deeper pots are needed.

When braising foods, the Japanese use an OTOSHI-BUTA (opposite; described on page 84), a special lid that drops down to sit directly on the food, rather than rest on the rim of the pot or pan. The pot or pan must have straight sides to accommodate these lids. If you will be using an *otoshi-buta*, choose pans that are about 1 inch larger in diameter than the dropped lid. I find that 7- to 8-inch-wide pots (holding about 2 quarts liquid) and 9- to 10-inch-wide pans are the most practical sizes for cooking four portions of most dishes.

A very special pan called a DOMBURI NABÉ (opposite; described on page 84) will make poaching the chicken omelet on page 156 a simple matter.

COOKING CHOPSTICKS (SAIBASHI)

Saibashi, distinguished by their length, are incredibly useful for both cooking and arranging food for the table. Once you master the grasp, flipping and poking (especially when making omelets) along with stirring can all be done at a safe distance from the stove (the longer the chopsticks, the farther away). *Saibashi* can also be used in lieu of tongs or a spatula when turning or tossing food.

When blanching foods, *saibashi* permit you to remove just one piece from the hot water to test for doneness. Also, when foods are done, the chopsticks allow you to pluck out all of them, avoiding the need to drain the pot. This means you can use the same pot of boiling water to blanch several foods in succession.

When it comes time to arrange food on a plate, long chopsticks help you place, stack, and coax food into mounds. Finally, these versatile chopsticks are also terrific for getting olives or other foods submerged in liquid out of a jar or other container.

Small and large otoshi-buta *and two kinds of omelet pans (rectangular* tamago yaki nabé *and round* domburi nabé)

OTOSHI-BUTA (DROPPED LID)

Made from a wood, an *otoshi-buta,* or "dropped lid" (illustrated on page 82), rests directly on the food inside a pot, rather than on the rim of the pot. An *otoshi-buta* is particularly useful when simmering or braising with just a bit of liquid, as it keeps the food moist while allowing the liquid to reduce and intensify slowly. The bubbling liquid hits against the underside of the lid during cooking, flavoring and coloring the top surface of the food as well as the bottom, thereby eliminating the need to flip the food. This technique is particularly useful when simmering whole fish, or vegetables such as *kabocha* squash or sweet potatoes, that might otherwise fall apart when flipped.

In Japan, the lids are sold in the *katei yōhin* (housewares) section of department stores. Outside Japan, many Asian groceries sell the lids. The best *otoshi-buta* are made from *hinoki,* a cedarlike wood. Buy a size about 1 inch smaller than the diameter of your pot. Wash the lids with mild soap and warm water and let them dry naturally.

If you do not have an *otoshi-buta,* there are several alternatives. Each recipe that calls for the use of a dropped lid will suggest the best option. You might be able to use a conventional lid, slightly askew, or you may be able to leave the pot uncovered and adjust cooking time and amount of liquid accordingly. In some instances, you may be able to improvise with a double thickness of cooking parchment (cut in a circle, 1 inch smaller in diameter than your pan) weighted down with a small, flat lid from another pot.

DOMBURI NABÉ (CHICKEN-OMELET PAN)

The Japanese use a special pan when making individual servings of a chicken omelet dish known as *oyako domburi* (literally, "parent and child bowl"). The pan is called an *oyako nabé* by some and a *domburi nabé* by others (illustrated on page 82). Typically 6 or 7 inches in diameter, and with a shallow, curved bottom and an upright handle, the pan looks more like a large, sturdy soup ladle than a skillet. I provide instructions for using both this specialized tool and an ordinary 7- or 8-inch skillet in Chicken Omelet over Rice (page 156).

DRIED BAMBOO LEAVES (TAKÉ NO KAWA)

Japanese often wrap food in dried bamboo leaves before poaching or steaming. Indeed, long before aluminum foil and other modern cooking sheets were invented, nature provided these and other leaves that were used as wrappers during cooking and to carry cooked food. *Také no kawa* are beige with speckles, and they are sold with ties for securing them around the food. The *obentō* photograph on page 286 shows the leaves folded into a decorative cone enclosing pickled radishes. Not only do the leaves protect the food enclosed within, but they also impart a subtle aroma to the final dish. If you are unable to find them, cooking parchment can be substituted.

Before using the leaves to wrap food, you will need to wipe them clean. Lay them with their speckled side down and shiny side up on a cutting board or other flat work surface. With a damp cloth, wipe the shiny, inner surface of each leaf to remove any possible dust or soil. These leaves are intended for a single use; when finished, discard them.

RICE COOKERS

Most Japanese rice cookers sold today are electric (rather than gas fueled) and boast sophisticated timers, thermostatically controlled heating mechanisms, and keep-warm features. If you eat rice more than once a week, and the idea of being able to set the cooker to work while you are otherwise occupied sounds attractive, these timer-and-warmer models are terrific and well worth the investment (a 5-cup size runs about $150).

Sizes vary, and you should consider your own lifestyle when you go to purchase one. If it is likely that you will make rice for entertaining (roll-it-yourself sushi parties?), a 5- or 8-cup size is best. If you will cook rice primarily for yourself and perhaps one or two others, then the smaller 2- or 3-cup size may be a better choice. Detailed instructions for preparing rice in a rice cooker, as well as a conventional pot, begin on page 136.

STEAMING

Cooking in a moist heat environment is a fuel-efficient, calorie-limiting method that yields succulent, tender food that can be served piping hot (Steaming Radish Swathed in Citrusy Miso Sauce, page 214) or chilled after steaming is completed (Cold Poached Salmon in Bamboo Leaves, page 238). Several pieces of equipment that will improve the flavor and texture of your steamed foods are described below.

STEAMERS (MUSHI KI)

Steaming requires moist heat to circulate throughout the cooking vessel, and the food being cooked should never touch the liquid. Further, your steamer needs a flat surface on which you can place the food. If you already own a Chinese-style bamboo steamer, it is fine, as is a standard metal stove-top steamer with a flat inset basket or pan. Unfortunately, the popular collapsible steamer baskets are not suitable because their sloping sides and tall, vertical "handle" in the center make it impossible to layer foods properly. Japanese steamers are terrific, especially the square ones, which hold many more items at a time than do ordinary circular steamers. These double-decker affairs have a deep pot on the bottom to hold water and another pot that fits snugly on top; this layer has a flat perforated bottom surface to permit steam to circulate. To ensure even cooking, arrange the items to be steamed in a single layer.

In a pinch, you can improvise a steamer by removing the top and bottom of two empty small cans (tuna fish cans are usually the right size) and place them side by side in the bottom of a deep pot. Place a heat-proof flat plate—one that is about an inch smaller in diameter than your pot—on top. To remove a hot plate from your steamer safely, fashion a sling, placing it under the plate of food being steamed. Fold the end pieces over the food, clipping them in place with a clothespin, if necessary. Use pot holders when lifting the sling.

DRY-ROASTING

Known as *kara iri,* "empty" or dry-roasting is a technique used to enhance the aroma and flavor of seeds, nuts, and *katsuo-bushi* flakes, and to eliminate moisture from *konnyaku* and *shirataki* noodles. Dry-roasting is typically done in a skillet.

Dry-Roasting Seeds and Nuts

Heat a small, heavy skillet over medium-high heat and then add the seeds or nuts. Stir occasionally with a wooden spatula or gently swirl the skillet in a circular motion. In about a minute, white sesame seeds will begin to color, as will pine nuts (black seeds will not darken appreciably). All seeds that still have their hull intact may pop as the warm air trapped between the kernel and hull expands. Dry-roasted seeds and nuts become aromatic as their oils are released; as soon as you begin to smell them, remove the skillet from the heat. The skillet retains heat, so seeds and nuts will continue to toast even after the skillet is taken away from the stove. Continue to stir for another 20 to 30 seconds. If the seeds or nuts look in danger of scorching, transfer them to a dish to cool faster. If you will be crushing the seeds or nuts, do so while they are still warm.

Dry-Roasting Katsuo-Bushi

Warm a small, heavy skillet over medium-high heat. Add the fish flakes evenly across the surface. After a minute or so, warm air currents rising from the pan will cause the tissue-thin fish flakes to flutter and become aromatic. Remove the pan from the stove to prevent scorching and wait a few minutes until the flakes are cool enough to handle comfortably. Transfer the now brittle flakes from the pan before crushing them with your fingertips.

Dry-Roasting Konnyaku and Shirataki Noodles

Dry-roasting *konnyaku* and *shirataki* noodles (a procedure known as *kara iri*) eliminates unwanted liquid—and with it the unpleasant odor that the natural *aku,* or bitterness, imparts—and ensures the *konnyaku* or *shirataki* will absorb the flavors about to be added to the pan. Heat a nonstick skillet over high heat, add the *konnyaku* or *shirataki* pieces, and dry-roast them for about 1 minute, keeping them in constant motion. When the pieces seem dry (you can often hear a squeaking noise as you shuffle them about in the hot skillet), drizzle in oil or add stock, as directed in the recipe, and proceed with cooking.

SHAPING AND MOLDING

Many foods, especially rice and vegetables, are molded or shaped in the *washoku* kitchen. Sometimes the shape reflects seasonal sentiments, such as a carrot being cut like a maple leaf in the fall or a cherry blossom in the spring. At other times, the occasion suggests the form: rice shaped into bite-sized logs (using a *maku no uchi* mold that produces five or seven logs) for a picnic lunch might be configured as an auspicious crane, or a tortoise for a wedding feast. A variety of KATA (rice molds and vegetable cutters) are available to aid with the shaping. SUDARÉ mats assist when rolling sushi (Rolled Sushi, Two Ways, page 149) and shaping several other foods, such as blanched greens (Spinach Steeped in Broth, 190) and soba noodles rolled in toasted nori (Buckwheat Noodle Roll, page 174).

To shape rice using a *maku no uchi* rice mold, separate it into its three component parts: a rectangular frame and two strips, each with either five (or seven) curved and hollowed "valleys." Submerge the parts in a bowl of cold water. Lift out the frame and place it on your work surface. Fit one of the strips into the frame facing up. With hands dipped briefly in cold water, scoop up a scant cup of cooked rice—Cooked White Rice (page 137), Rice with Mixed Grains (page 139), and Rice Tossed with Red Shiso Salt (page 143) can all be shaped into logs—and fill the mold evenly with it. Take the remaining strip and insert it pointing down into the frame. Press down firmly and evenly, while gently lifting the frame up and off the molded rice. Peel off the top strip and invert the rice onto your work surface. With fingers dampened in cold water, peel off the remaining strip, releasing a neat row of rice "logs."

KATA (SHAPE OR MOLD)

The term *kata* is used to describe a variety of molds of different shapes and sizes. Old-fashioned rice molds were made from *hinoki*, a kind of cedar that would impart a mild woodsy aroma to the pressed rice; today, most are made of plastic or aluminum. Well wrung-out, but still damp, *sarashi* cloths (page 77) are also used to mold and shape soft foods such as cooked rice or cooked and mashed root and tuber vegetables. The most readily available tool for shaping and molding rice is your hands. The recipe for Hand-Pressed Rice (page 158) details that process.

The most commonly found molds are used to shape cooked rice into loglike bundles (*maku no uchi*), fans (*ōgi*), flowers (*sakura*, or cherry, *umé*, or plum), or gourds (*hyōtan*). Molds made of wood and plastic should be washed by hand; molds made of metal can be put in the dishwasher.

SUDARÉ (SLATTED BAMBOO MAT) AND ONI SUDARÉ ("MONSTER MAT")

A *sudaré* (illustrated on page 89), also known as a *maki su*, is made by binding many thin, parallel strips of bamboo with twine to form a rectangle, typically 5 by 7 inches in size. An *oni sudaré* has thick slats that create a deeply ridged surface on the foods, such as Rolled Omelet (see illustration on page 286), around which it is rolled. When you have finished using the mat, wash it in warm water by hand, using a soft-bristled brush if necessary to dislodge rice or other bits of food that may be caught between the slats. Set out to dry.

Rice mold (kata) *in the shape of a plum blossom*

Equipment for Making Sushi

Several specialized tools are typically used in sushi making: a large, wide wooden tub in which freshly cooked rice is tossed with seasoned vinegar; a wooden paddle to toss the rice in cutting motions without mashing it; a broad, flat fan to help cool the rice as it absorbs the vinegar; and a slatted mat (page 87) to shape sushi rice into rolls.

Handai (wooden rice tub)

A broad, shallow, flat-bottomed wooden tub called a *handai* (also known as a *sushi oké* or *han-giri*) is used to hold cooked rice that will be seasoned for sushi rice. It is traditionally made from fragrant cedar, which imparts a subtle aroma to the rice. Freshly cooked, still steaming rice makes the best sushi because it is as the rice cools that it is most receptive to acquiring the flavor of the seasoned vinegar with which it is tossed. The main advantage of a *handai* is its ability to absorb excess moisture, thus preventing the rice from becoming mushy.

Well-crafted *handai* are reinforced with a bamboo ring circling the inner rim on the underside of the tub. (The bamboo strip should be obvious, as the grain of bamboo is very different from that of cedar.) A good *handai* is handcrafted and expensive (as much as $70 to $75 for a 6- to 8-cup size). Tubs fitted with bamboo strips are even more costly, but they are of a better quality.

You will need to monitor the condition of any wooden tub at least once a week, checking on moisture levels. If you live in a dry climate, the wood will shrink, causing the metal bands that bind the planks in place to slip down. Store the tub inverted so that the slightly tapered bottom is pointing up; that way, if the bands do loosen, they will fall down to the wider part of the tub. Rinsing the tub in water, or water to which a spoonful of vinegar has been added, is the best way to rehydrate the wood and prevent shrinkage. If you live in a humid climate, or too much moisture accumulates in the closet in which the *handai* is stored, molds will begin to grow on the wood. These can be scrubbed away with plain vinegar or a strong vinegar-and-water solution and a stiff brush. (Folk legends ascribe medicinal qualities to the blue-tinted molds that often grow on cedar tubs in which cooked rice is held; these molds are probably related to penicillin.)

If you do not have a *handai,* use a wide but shallow ceramic or glass bowl (metal retains heat and often imparts a metallic flavor to the rice). A large wooden bowl will work, as long as it hasn't been seasoned with garlic and/or olive oil.

Shamoji (rice paddle)

Usually made from bamboo but occasionally sturdy plastic or ceramic, a *shamoji* is used to scoop up cooked rice from a pot or rice cooker. The paddle comes in three sizes: small, medium, and large. I find them useful tools for kitchen tasks, too, such as sautéing and flipping. If you are using bamboo paddles, hand wash them.

Uchiwa (flat fan)

The Japanese fan away steam from freshly cooked rice waiting to be seasoned for sushi rice. They also choose to fan-cool many blanched vegetables, rather than refresh them in cold water. For these jobs, an *uchiwa* is the perfect—and lovely—tool of choice. Although a flat piece of cardboard serves the same purpose, it is not nearly as attractive a kitchen tool. I do not recommend using a stiff magazine or rolled-up newspaper because the oily ink smell is sometimes transferred to the food. This is especially true if cooling steaming hot rice.

Clockwise from left: handai, uchiwa, shamoji, *and* sudaré

STOCKS, SAUCES, AND OTHER CONDIMENTS

As with any cuisine or style of cooking, *washoku* has its own basic recipes that serve as building blocks in creating other dishes. I have selected those that will provide you with a wide range of possibilities, and have organized them by category, beginning with stocks and moving on to sauces. In the case of the latter, some are based on vinegar and soy sauce, others on sesame and miso, and still others on tōfu and nori. Two sweet sauces—a mineral-rich, dark sugar syrup and a chunky bean jam—are used in assembling desserts. The chapter concludes with a savory relish and five flavored salts.

Many recipes prepared in a *washoku* manner call for dashi, a basic sea stock made from *kombu* (page 42) and *katsuo-bushi* (page 18). I have provided a recipe for stock that is made from *kombu* alone, or in combination with dried shiitaké mushrooms, for anyone on a vegetarian diet.

The Japanese kitchen also makes use of a stock that combines the meaty, familiar taste of chicken with a hint of the briny sea. And because I want to share my early days on Shikoku Island that made such a lasting impression, I include a classic of the Sanuki regional kitchen, *iriko dashi,* which draws on the flavor-enhancing power of dried sardines.

These stocks are neither difficult nor particularly time-consuming to make. The most challenging task will be sourcing high-quality ingredients. Refer to the Washoku Pantry (page 10) to learn more about any ingredients that may be unfamiliar to you.

Most of the sauces store well—some for as long as several months—without losing their verve. Once you have tasted the various sauces, and have begun to use them as components in dozens of dishes throughout this book, you will want to keep many of them on hand to ease and shorten mealtime preparations. I hope, too, that many of these classic recipes will inspire you to create your own salad dressings, sauces, and spice mixtures.

BASIC SEA STOCK

DASHI

Dashi is a subtle broth with the capacity to enhance and intensify the flavor of foods with which it is cooked or blended. That ability is locked within kombu, *a type of kelp, and* katsuo-bushi, *or dried bonito flakes, both of which are rich in water-soluble glutamates.*

Although it takes only a few minutes to make the stock, timing and temperature control are important. To extract the full potential of the kelp's flavor-enhancing properties, you need to start the stock with cold water and slowly heat it until it is barely boiling. Then, to prevent the broth from becoming murky, and to hold possible bitterness at bay, remove the pot from the stove before adding the fish flakes. That way, the smoky, full-bodied flavor of the flakes will gradually seep into the stock.

MAKES ABOUT 1 QUART

15 to 20 square inches kombu (page 42)

4$^1/_4$ cups cold water, preferably filtered or spring water

$^1/_2$ cup loosely packed katsuo-bushi (page 18)

Place the *kombu* in a pot with the water. To draw out maximum flavor, let soak for 10 to 15 minutes before placing the pot over medium heat—this will further infuse the water with the flavor-enhancing properties and nutrients of the kelp.

Remove the pot from the heat as soon as small bubbles begin to break on the surface and at the edge of the pot. Add the *katsuo-bushi,* scattering the flakes across the surface of the water. After several minutes, the fish flakes will begin to sink. The larger the flakes, the longer they will take to sink. To keep the stock from tasting fishy, pour it through a *sarashi* cloth (page 77) or coffee-filter-lined strainer within 3 or 4 minutes of adding the fish flakes. Reserve the *kombu* (see notes) and discard the remaining solids.

This stock loses its delicate aroma and subtle flavors when frozen, so it is best to make it fresh when you need it. Any unused stock will keep well, tightly covered, for 3 to 4 days in the refrigerator. Depending on the type and quality of *kombu* used, sediment sometimes forms at the bottom of the storage container. It alone is not cause for concern. Signs of spoilage include a sweet smell (rather than a smoky one), a film forming on the surface or around the edges of the container, or stickiness when pouring.

——————— ———————

Kitchen Harmony

Store pieces of *kombu* left over from stock making in a jar or closed plastic bag in your refrigerator for up to 1 week to use for making a relish. (If at any point the kelp develops a pasty, sticky whitish substance on the surface, discard it.) Once you have accumulated 3 or 4 pieces, you can make Kelp and Mushroom Relish (page 110).

BASIC VEGETARIAN STOCK

KOMBU-JIRU

In the classic washoku kitchen, vegetarian stock is made from just kombu. Dried shiitaké mushrooms are sometimes added to provide depth and complexity of flavor. Whether you choose to include dried mushrooms or not, using a high-glutamate variety of kelp, such as Rausu kombu, Rishiri kombu, or ma kombu, will greatly enhance the flavor of all foods you cook with stock made from it.

MAKES ABOUT 1 QUART

    15 to 20 square inches kombu (page 42), preferably
        Rausu kombu, Rishiri kombu, or ma kombu
    1 dried shiitaké mushroom or stems from 2 or
        3 mushrooms (optional)
    $4^1/_4$ cups cold water, preferably filtered or spring water

Place the *kombu* and mushroom in a pot with the water. If time permits, let the kelp and mushroom soak for at least 2 hours, or refrigerate for up to 1 day, before placing the pot over medium heat. This will enable the flavor-enhancing glutamates in the kelp and mushroom to infuse the stock gradually with their essence. Bring almost to a boil and then adjust the heat to maintain a bare simmer. Cook for 4 or 5 minutes.

Remove the pot from the heat and let the stock stand for 3 to 4 minutes before removing and reserving the *kombu* (see notes). If you have used mushrooms, strain the stock through a fine-mesh strainer or through a *sarashi* cloth (page 77) to remove any bits of dried mushroom. Reserve mushroom caps (see notes).

As with the standard sea stock, this vegetarian stock also loses its delicate seashore aroma when frozen. It is best to make it fresh when you need it, though unused stock will keep well, tightly covered after it has cooled down, for 2 or 3 days in the refrigerator. The higher the glutamate level of the *kombu* used, the shorter the shelf life. Sediment typically forms at the bottom of the storage container when *Rausu kombu* or *ma kombu* have been used. It alone is not cause for concern. Signs of spoilage include a film forming on the surface or around the edges of the container, or stickiness when pouring.

———— ————

Kitchen Harmony

You can retrieve the shiitaké mushroom along with the *kombu* (see notes for Basic Sea Stock, page 92) to make Kelp and Mushroom Relish (page 110). Though the flavor of the relish will be slightly different than when made with fresh enoki mushrooms, it will still be good.

SMOKY CHICKEN STOCK

TORIGARA DASHI

Although not used often in the traditional washoku *kitchen, this rich chicken stock with smoky overtones may appeal to you more than the "deep sea" flavor of the more classic stocks. If you prefer the familiar taste of chicken stock, you can substitute this stock for Basic Sea Stock (page 92) or Sanuki Sea Stock (page 95) in most recipes.*

MAKES ABOUT 1 QUART

1 pound chicken parts, such as necks, backs, and wings

Boiling water as needed

1 piece kombu (page 42), 3 to 4 inches long and about 2 inches wide

5^1/$_2$ cups cold water, preferably filtered or spring water

1 tablespoon saké

^{1}/$_2$ cup loosely packed katsuo-bushi (page 18)

Place the chicken parts in a colander or large strainer in the sink and carefully pour boiling water over them. With long cooking chopsticks or kitchen tongs, turn the chicken pieces and repeat the boiling-water bath. (This procedure is known as *shimo furi,* or "frost falling"; see page 74.)

Place the cleansed chicken parts and the *kombu* in a pot with the cold water and saké. Bring to a rapid boil over high heat, adjust the heat to maintain a simmer, and skim away froth as it rises. Simmer, uncovered, for 30 minutes, or until the liquid has been reduced by about one-fourth.

Remove the pot from the heat and add the *katsuo-bushi,* scattering the flakes across the surface of the liquid. After 3 or 4 minutes, pour the stock through a *sarashi* cloth (page 77) or coffee-filter-lined strainer. If you want to reserve the *kombu* to make a relish (page 110), see notes for Basic Sea Stock (page 92).

If the stock is not for immediate use, allow it to cool to room temperature, uncovered and naturally, before chilling. Refrigerate in a tightly closed container for up to 5 days, or freeze for up to 2 weeks.

SANUKI SEA STOCK

IRIKO DASHI

My husband was born and raised in the Sanuki region of Shikoku Island, where iriko dashi, *a stock made from dried sardines is the kitchen norm. For most daily dishes, such as miso-thickened soups, tōfu and root-vegetable stews, and steaming bowls of* udon *noodles, my mother-in-law would make a huge pot of the unseasoned stock, adding a pinch of salt or perhaps a splash of rice wine or light-colored soy sauce as needed.*

You can use this dried sardine stock in lieu of the smokier katsuo-*infused Basic Sea Stock (page 92) in any recipe. When making broth or a dipping sauce for* udon, sōmen, *or other wheat noodles, though,* iriko dashi *will definitely yield more flavorful results than stock made with* katsuo-bushi.

MAKES ABOUT 1 QUART

    7 to 8 large or 15 to 20 small iriko (page 17), trimmed
        (about ¹/₂ ounce after trimming)
    4¹/₄ cups cold water, preferably filtered or spring water
    10 to 12 square inches kombu (page 42)
    1 dried shiitaké mushroom or stems from 2 or
        3 mushrooms (optional)

Place the *iriko* in a 3-quart pot with the cold water and *kombu.* For a hearty stock, add the dried mushroom to the pot. If you prefer a milder flavor, it is best not to include it. Let soak for 20 minutes.

Place the pot over medium heat. When small bubbles appear around the edges, adjust the heat to maintain a steady but not vigorous simmer and cook for about 10 minutes, or until the liquid is a pale gold. If large clouds of froth appear, skim them away.

Remove the pot from the heat and allow it to sit, uncovered and undisturbed, for 3 to 5 minutes. Pour the stock through a *sarashi* cloth (page 77) or coffee-filter-lined strainer. Reserve the *kombu* and the mushroom, if used (see notes for Basic Vegetarian Stock, page 93) and discard the remaining solids.

This sardine-enriched stock turns bitter when frozen. It is best to make it fresh when you need it, though unused stock will keep well, tightly covered after it has cooled down, for 2 or 3 days in the refrigerator. A silvery sediment from the fish typically forms at the bottom of the storage container. It alone is not cause for concern. Signs of spoilage include a film forming on the surface or around the edges of the container, or stickiness when pouring.

SEASONED SOY CONCENTRATE

BANNŌ-JŌYU

This multipurpose soy concentrate can enliven a sauce, become a marinade, or add complex flavor to simmered foods. Diluted with water in varying proportions, it can easily become a broth for hot soba noodles or a dipping sauce for chilled sōmen noodles.

Each of the ingredients is packed with naturally occurring glutamates. Unlike chemicals such as monosodium glutamate, typically used in commercial products, the flavor-enhancing properties found naturally in kelp, dried mushrooms, fermented soy, and dried fish do not cause unpleasant side effects. If you do not have any of the higher-glutamate types of kombu on hand, you can use Hidaka kombu.

For those wanting a vegetarian alternative, double the amount of kombu and dried shiitaké mushrooms and eliminate the dried fish and fish flakes.

MAKES ABOUT ²/₃ CUP

- 5 or 6 large iriko (page 17), trimmed
- 8 to 10 square inches kombu (page 42), preferably Rausu kombu, Rishiri kombu, or ma kombu
- 1 dried shiitaké mushroom or stems from 3 or 4 mushrooooms
- ¹/₄ cup atsu kezuri (page 20) or ¹/₂ cup tightly packed katsuo-bushi (page 18)
- ²/₃ cup soy sauce
- ¹/₃ cup saké
- 3 tablespoons sugar
- 3 tablespoons water
- 2 tablespoons mirin

Place the *iriko, kombu,* mushroom, *atsu kezuri,* soy sauce, and saké in a small, deep saucepan and leave to infuse for at least 1 hour or up to 12 hours. (If you are using ordinary *katsuo-bushi,* add the flakes later as directed.)

Add the sugar, water, and mirin to the pan and place over low heat. When the liquid begins to simmer, adjust the heat to keep it from boiling too vigorously. As the sauce simmers, it becomes quite foamy, rising in the saucepan. Watch to make sure it does not overflow. Continue to simmer until the volume has been reduced by about one-fourth and the sauce has become a bit syrupy.

Remove from the heat. (If you are using ordinary *katsuo-bushi,* scatter the flakes across the surface of the liquid. Let stand for 2 to 3 minutes, until the flakes have settled to the bottom.) Pour through a coffee-filter-lined strainer or a *sarashi* cloth (page 77) into a glass jar with a tight-fitting lid. Reserve the solids (see notes). If not using immediately, let cool, cover, and chill before using. Refrigerate for up to 1 month.

Kitchen Harmony

The soy-drenched bits of *kombu,* mushroom, and dried fish that are strained out of the finished liquid concentrate can be made into a light soup broth by returning them to the saucepan, adding 2 or 3 cups fresh cold water, and bringing rapidly to a boil. Strain immediately, this time discarding the solid pieces. This *niban dashi* (literally, "second-time around" stock) is fine in place of the seasoned soup called for in Moon-Viewing Noodles in Broth (page 171), Foxy Soup Noodles (page 172), or Soba Noodles with Tempura in Soup (page 177).

SMOKY CITRUS-SOY SAUCE

PONZU

This mixture of soy sauce and citrus fruit seems to have been inspired by seventeenth-century visitors from Holland (pons means "citrus fruit" in Dutch). To enhance the simple salty, sweet, and tart sauce, it is often made with the addition of katsuo-bushi *or by using a soy sauce previously enriched with dried fish.*

In the classic washoku *kitchen, this sauce is used primarily as a dip for one-pot* nabémono *stews or griddle-seared meat (Flash-Seared Steak with Two Sauces, page 267). In this book, I provide an additional and slightly unusual use: as a dressing for a chilled noodle salad (Chilled Udon Noodle Salad, page 173). In addition, it can be used as is, or mixed with vegetable oil, to dress salads.*

If you have the soy concentrate on hand, the abbreviated version is not only simpler to make, but also has the more complex flavor of the two versions.

MAKES ABOUT $^1/_3$ CUP

Abbreviated Version

3 tablespoons Seasoned Soy Concentrate (page 96)

$^1/_3$ cup Basic Sea Stock (page 92)

2 tablespoons fresh grapefruit, lemon, and/or lime juice

$^1/_4$ teaspoon grated lemon zest (optional)

Traditional Version

2 tablespoons soy sauce

1 teaspoon sugar

$^1/_4$ cup Basic Sea Stock (page 92)

$^1/_4$ cup loosely packed katsuo-bushi (page 18)

2 tablespoons fresh grapefruit, lemon, and/or lime juice

$^1/_4$ teaspoon grated lemon zest (optional)

To make the abbreviated version, combine the soy concentrate, stock, and citrus juice in a glass jar. Add the lemon zest if you want a fruitier aroma. Stir to mix well.

To make the traditional version, combine the soy sauce, sugar, and stock in a small saucepan and bring to a simmer over low heat. Remove from the heat, scatter the *katsuo-bushi* over the surface of the liquid, and let stand for 2 minutes, or until the fish flakes sink. Pour the sauce through a coffee-filter-lined strainer or a *sarashi* cloth (page 77) into a glass jar. Add the citrus juice; for a fruitier aroma, add the lemon zest. Stir to mix well.

Cover and chill the sauce before using. Store any unused sauce in the glass jar in the refrigerator for up to 1 month. Sediment may form on the bottom of the jar, but it is not a sign of spoilage.

SWEET-AND-SOUR SAUCE

AMAZU

This mixture of vinegar and sugar balanced with a bit of salt is used to pickle both spicy and bland foods, helping to bring them into focus and harmony with accompanying dishes. It provides zip to mild lotus root (Sweet-and-Sour Lotus Root, page 222), tames the fire of fresh ginger (Blushing Pink Ginger, page 223), and transforms sharp daikon into a pleasantly tangy side dish (New Year's Salad, page 220).

To make a pink, plum-infused version of this sauce, see notes.

MAKES ¹/₂ CUP

- ¹/₂ cup rice vinegar
- 3 tablespoons sugar
- ¹/₄ teaspoon salt
- 1 piece kombu (page 42), 1 inch square, preferably Rausu kombu, Rishiri kombu, or ma kombu

Combine the vinegar, sugar, salt, and *kombu* in a small saucepan and let the *kombu* soak for at least 20 minutes or overnight; the soaking ensures that the natural glutamates of the kelp will mellow the sharpness of the vinegar and enhance the sweetness of the foods that will be pickled in the sauce.

Place the pan over low heat and, stirring to dissolve the sugar and salt, slowly bring to just below a boil. Cook until the sugar and salt have completely dissolved, then remove from the heat and let the sauce cool in the pan before transferring it, including the *kombu* if you have used it, to a glass jar.

When the sauce is completely cool, cover the top of the jar with plastic wrap and then a tight-fitting lid. Store in the refrigerator for up to 2 months.

Kitchen Harmony

It is best to avoid metal-based pots when cooking with vinegar. Choose an enamel-lined or flameproof glass saucepan, or use a pan coated with a nonstick surface.

A pink version of this sauce can be made by combining ¹/₄ cup plum vinegar with 2 tablespoons each sugar, water, and Basic Sea Stock (page 92). Heat through in a saucepan just until the sugar dissolves.

SMOKY VINAIGRETTE

TOSA-ZU

Many Japanese foods bear regional names. Tosa, the historical name for Kochi Prefecture on the Pacific coast of Shikoku Island, is synonymous with the fish known as katsuo, *or bonito, which explains its use in this recipe name. Twice a year, tidal patterns bring abundant quantities of bonito in and near Tosa Bay. In the spring, lean* hashiri-gatsuo *(literally, "first-run bonito"), caught as they head out to the ocean, are considered a delicacy. And in the fall, when* modori-gatsuo *(literally, "returning bonito") come back fattened up, they are prized for their succulent flesh.*

Here, dried bonito flakes are used to make a smoky-and-tart light salad dressing. I have paired it with aquatic and garden vegetables in Tosa Sea Salad (page 216).

MAKES ¹/₄ CUP

¹/₄ cup brown rice vinegar

1 tablespoon sugar

¹/₄ teaspoon salt

1 piece kombu (page 42), 2 inches square

¹/₃ cup loosely packed katsuo-bushi (page 18)

A few drops of light-colored soy sauce, if needed

A few drops of mirin, if needed

Combine the vinegar, sugar, salt, and *kombu* in a small saucepan. Place over low heat and, stirring to dissolve the sugar and salt, bring to a gentle simmer. Scatter the *katsuo-bushi* over the surface of the liquid, and simmer gently for 30 seconds. Remove from the heat and let the mixture cool completely in the pan. Pour the sauce through a *sarashi* cloth (page 77) or coffee-filter-lined strainer. Discard the solids.

Taste and adjust the seasonings by adding a drizzle of soy sauce if the mixture is too sweet or a few drops of mirin if it is too salty. Use immediately, or store in a tightly covered jar in the refrigerator for up to 2 weeks.

TART MISO-MUSTARD SAUCE

KARASHI SU MISO

As with other recipes calling for seasoned miso, this sauce can be made ahead and stored in the refrigerator for a few weeks. It is particularly good with cooked seafood, and in this book is paired with tender stewed octopus to make an appetizer or a salad (page 249). You can also use this mustard-spiked sauce as an alternative to tomato-based sauces the next time you serve shrimp, lobster, or crabmeat cocktail, or you can use it as a spread in place of mayonnaise when making sandwiches.

MAKES ¹/₃ CUP

2 tablespoons rice vinegar

¹/₄ teaspoon Japanese mustard

3 tablespoons sweet, light miso, preferably Saikyō miso (page 32)

A drop of light-colored soy sauce or salt, if needed

A drop of Basic Sea Stock (page 92) or water, if needed

In a small bowl, stir together the vinegar and mustard until smooth. Whisk in the miso until smooth and well blended.

Taste and adjust with the soy sauce if too sweet or the stock if too thick. Transfer to a glass jar with a tight-fitting lid and store in the refrigerator for up to 4 weeks.

CREAMY SESAME-MISO SAUCE

GOMA MISO

In the traditional Japanese kitchen, briefly cooked vegetables such as green beans or blanched leafy greens such as spinach are often tossed in a creamy mixture of sesame and miso. The finished dish, known as goma miso aé, remains a popular item on home and restaurant menus throughout Japan. The sauce is also good as a dip for cucumber, carrot, and celery sticks.

This recipe provides you with a trio of options: The old-fashioned method of grinding freshly dry-roasted sesame seeds to a smooth paste in a suribachi (page 73) is labor-intensive. The modern food processor simplifies the task tremendously. If you can purchase a jar of shiro neri goma (smooth white sesame paste) in an Asian grocery store, preparing goma miso will be a cinch.

MAKES ABOUT ½ CUP

With Ready-Made Paste

3 tablespoons white sesame paste

3 tablespoons sweet, light miso, preferably Saikyō miso (page 32)

Pinch of salt, if needed

3 tablespoons Basic Sea Stock (page 92)

With Freshly Dry-Roasted Sesame Seeds

¼ cup white sesame seeds, freshly dry-roasted (page 85)

2 tablespoons sweet, light miso, preferably Saikyō miso (page 32)

Scant ¼ cup Basic Sea Stock (page 92)

Pinch of salt, if needed

To make with ready-made sesame paste: In a bowl, mix the sesame paste with the miso. Stir or whisk to blend completely. Taste, and if it seems too sweet, adjust the seasoning with the salt. Blend again until smooth. Thin the mixture with some of the stock, one spoonful at a time. As you add the stock, the sauce will lighten in color.

To make with freshly dry-roasted sesame seeds in a *suribachi:* To release the nutty aroma of the seeds, crush them while still warm (page 85). When they are fully crushed, very aromatic, and look a bit oily, add the miso and continue to grind to combine thoroughly. Drizzle in the stock a bit at a time, grinding further and scraping down to blend after each addition. When the sauce is the consistency of tomato purée, taste it. If it seems too sweet, adjust the seasoning with the salt.

To make with freshly dry-roasted sesame seeds in a food processor: Place the still-warm seeds in the bowl of a food processor fitted with a metal blade. Pulse until the seeds are fully cracked. If necessary, scrape down the sides of the bowl with a spatula, and then pulse again until all the seeds have been evenly crushed. Add half each of the miso and stock and pulse again. Taste and adjust the sweetness with the salt, if necessary. Scrape down the sides of the bowl before adding the remaining miso and stock. Continue to pulse until smooth.

No matter which method you use to make the sauce, transfer it to a glass jar with a tight-fitting lid and refrigerate. It will keep for up to 3 weeks, though the aroma and texture are best within the first week.

———————— ————————

Kitchen Harmony

For specific suggestions on using this basic sauce, see Green Beans Tossed in Creamy Sesame-Miso Sauce (page 198), Flash-Seared Steak with Two Sauces (page 267), and Chilled Chinese Noodle Salad (page 178). Spinach Steeped in Broth (page 190) could also be tossed in the sauce.

PUNGENT RED MISO SAUCE

AKA NERI MISO

Seasoned miso sauces are referred to collectively as neri miso, *or "stirred bean paste." Among the many types commonly used to prepare* washoku *dishes, a pungent red is the most versatile. In this book, I have called for it in Fish Simmered in Pungent Miso Sauce (page 233), Broiled Tōfu with Flavored Miso (page 281), Poached Peaches in Lemon-Ginger Miso Sauce (page 306), and Fall Fruits with Flavored Miso Sauce (page 304).*

This sauce can be made with any aka miso *(literally, "red miso"). However, the consistency and saltiness of miso varies considerably from brand to brand. That's why I have given you a range, rather than exact measurements, for quantities of ingredients such as sugar, saké, and water. Begin with the least amount called for in the recipe, and then adjust for the correct sweet-salty balance and to achieve the proper consistency.*

MAKES ABOUT ¹/₂ CUP

    5 to 6 tablespoons dark miso such as Sendai miso
      (page 32)
    2 to 3 tablespoons sugar
    2 to 3 tablespoons saké
    1 to 2 tablespoons water

Combine the miso, 2 tablespoons each sugar and saké, and 1 tablespoon water in a small saucepan and stir with a wooden spatula until thoroughly mixed.

Place the pan over medium-high heat and cook for 2 to 3 minutes, stirring constantly, until the mixture is glossy and has the consistency of tomato ketchup. It will stiffen and thicken a bit more as it cools. The sauce will bubble and splatter as you cook, so use a long-handled pan and spatula and watch carefully to avoid burning yourself.

Remove the pan from the heat. Use a spoon to take a sample from the pot and let it cool before tasting. Adjust with more sugar if too salty, more saké if too sweet, or more water if too thick. Let cool completely. Transfer to a glass jar with a tight-fitting lid and refrigerate for up to 4 weeks.

Kitchen Harmony

This basic dark miso sauce can be enlivened with various spices added in the cooling-down stage to preserve optimal aroma. Try infusing the sauce with ¹/₄ teaspoon fresh ginger juice or spicy mustard, and pair the resulting sauce with smoked chicken, turkey, or trout.

CITRUSY MISO

YUZU MISO

Make this neri miso *(stirred miso) with the palest-colored and sweetest-tasting white miso you can find. In Japan, Kyoto's Saikyō miso is the best choice. Depending on the specific white miso you are able to find, adjustments may be needed to achieve a good balance between salty and sweet.*

MAKES ABOUT ¹/₂ CUP

3 tablespoons sweet, light miso, preferably Saikyō miso (page 32)

1¹/₂ tablespoons saké

1 teaspoon mirin

¹/₂ teaspoon freeze-dried yuzu peel (page 28), crushed to a powder, or grated fresh lemon zest

¹/₄ teaspoon sugar, if needed

1 to 2 teaspoons water, if needed

Combine the miso, saké, and mirin in a small saucepan and stir with a wooden spatula until thoroughly mixed. Add half of the *yuzu* peel and mix well.

Place the pan over medium-low heat and cook for 2 to 3 minutes, stirring constantly, until the mixture is glossy and has the consistency of tomato ketchup. It will stiffen and thicken a bit more as it cools. The sauce will bubble and splatter as you cook, so use a long-handled pan and spatula and watch carefully to avoid burning yourself.

Remove the pan from the heat. Use a spoon to take a sample from the pot and let it cool before tasting. Adjust with more sugar if too salty, more saké if too sweet, or more water if too thick. Let cool completely. Add the remaining *yuzu* peel and mix well. Transfer to a glass jar with a tight-fitting lid and refrigerate for up to 4 weeks.

和食

Kitchen Harmony

Try adding ¹/₄ teaspoon *sanshō* (page 47) with the final addition of zest to the sauce. The spicy kick it provides is particularly welcome when this sauce is used as a dip for crisp slices of pear or apple.

LEEK MISO

NEGI MISO

In the Japanese kitchen, an assertively seasoned miso such as this one is sometimes nicknamed namé miso, *or "finger lickin' good," which tells you just how addictive the dips and sauces made with it can be. I have called for slathering it on tōfu before broiling until bubbly (Broiled Tōfu with Flavored Miso, page 281) and for spreading it on hand-pressed rice patties before grilling to a crusty and aromatic finish (Toasty Hand-Pressed Rice, page 160). It can also be used as a dip for raw vegetables or a stuffing for celery stalks.*

MAKES ABOUT ¹/₂ CUP

1 small leek, preferably Japanese leek, about 3 ounces, trimmed, white and tender green parts finely minced

1 teaspoon sesame oil

¹/₃ cup mugi miso (page 32)

2 tablespoons mirin

1¹/₂ tablespoons sugar

3 or 4 tablespoons Basic Sea Stock (page 92) or water

Place the leek in a strainer and rinse briefly in cold water to make sure that no dirt is trapped among the pieces. Drain well and pat dry with paper towels.

Heat the oil in a nonstick skillet over medium heat. Add the leek and sauté for 1 minute, or until translucent and aromatic. Add the miso, mirin, and sugar and stir for about 1 minute, or until bubbly. Add the stock and continue to cook, stirring and scraping down the sides with a wooden spoon or spatula, for 2 or 3 minutes, until the sauce becomes glossy and the consistency of tomato paste.

Remove from the heat and let cool completely. Transfer to a glass jar with a tight-fitting lid and store in the refrigerator for up to 6 weeks.

Kitchen Harmony

Try making this same miso using shallot or red onion in place of the leek. A full-bodied and rough-textured miso is usually the best match. When in doubt, *mugi miso* (page 32) or *genmai miso* (page 30) is a good choice.

HERB MISO

SHISO MISO

If you have been growing shiso plants in your summer garden, you will have more than enough leaves, even from a single stalk, to make this sauce. Leaves plucked late in the season tend to be less aromatic, so you will probably opt for the greater quantity listed below.

MAKES ABOUT ¹/₂ CUP

20 to 30 fresh shiso leaves (page 26)

1 teaspoon sesame oil

¹/₃ cup dark miso such as Sendai miso

3 tablespoons mirin

2 tablespoons sugar

3 to 4 tablespoons Basic Sea Stock (page 92) or water

2 tablespoons white sesame seeds, freshly dry-roasted (page 85)

Clockwise from top: Herb Miso, Kelp and Mushroom Relish (page 110), and Chunky Red Bean Jam (page 108)

Rinse the *shiso* leaves under running cold water and shake dry. Trim away the stems and cut the leaves in half lengthwise. Stack the leaf halves, roll up lengthwise, and slice crosswise into shreds.

In a small skillet, warm the sesame oil over low heat and sauté the *shiso* for 1 minute, or until aromatic. Remove from the heat and set aside.

Combine the miso, mirin, sugar, and stock in a small bowl and stir to mix thoroughly. Add to the sautéed *shiso* in the skillet, return the skillet to medium heat, and cook, stirring and scraping down the sides with a wooden spoon or paddle, for about 2 minutes, or until the sauce is glossy and thick and has the consistency of tomato paste.

Remove the pan from the heat, add the sesame seeds, and stir to distribute evenly. Let cool completely. Transfer to a glass jar with a tight-fitting lid and store in the refrigerator for up to 6 weeks.

和食

Kitchen Harmony

Try making flavored dips in the same manner using other fresh herbs. In general, a stronger, more definitive herb, such as parsley, tarragon, or sage, will be better if paired with a pungent dark miso such as Sendai miso. With fresh mint, basil, or dill, you might try using a sweet, light miso such as Saikyō miso (page 32). In lieu of the sesame seeds, you might try a touch of grated lemon zest.

TWO NUTTY MISO SAUCES

MATSU NO MI MISO, KURUMI MISO

These rich, creamy miso-nut sauces make wonderful dips for raw vegetables. Or, thinned with a bit of rice vinegar and dashi, either could be transformed into a delicious dressing for tossing with mixed greens. In a more traditional approach, matsu no mi miso (pine nut miso sauce) is used dengaku-*style, slathered on pan-seared scallops or vegetables that are then placed briefly under the broiler until bubbly. The walnut miso sauce, kurumi miso, is often used to dress briefly blanched vegetables, such as spinach, green beans, or asparagus, that have been prepared* ohitashi-*style, steeped in a soy-tinged broth.*

MAKES ABOUT ⅓ CUP OF EACH SAUCE

Pine Nut Miso Sauce

3 tablespoons pine nuts, freshly dry-roasted (page 85)

1 tablespoon sweet, light miso, preferably Saikyō miso (page 32)

2 tablespoons Basic Sea Stock (page 92)

Pinch of salt, if needed

Walnut Miso Sauce

3 tablespoons walnuts, freshly dry-roasted (page 85)

1 tablespoon dark miso, preferably Hatchō miso (page 32)

3 tablespoons Basic Sea Stock (page 92)

Drop of mirin, if needed

To make the pine nut sauce: Crush the pine nuts, preferably in a *suribachi* (page 73), or in a mini–food processor. If you are using a *suribachi*, grind until the nuts are fully crushed, are very aromatic, and look a bit pasty. If you are using a food processor, use the pulse function. Add the miso and continue to grind or pulse to combine. Drizzle in the stock and continue to grind or pulse, scraping down the sides of the mortar or processor bowl as needed. When the sauce is smooth and the consistency of tomato paste, taste it. If it seems too sweet, adjust the seasoning with the salt. Transfer to a glass jar with a tight-fitting lid.

To make the walnut sauce: After cleaning the *suribachi* or food processor, crush the walnuts to form an aromatic paste. Because Hatchō miso is coarser than Saikyō miso, it should be whisked together with the stock in a separate small bowl to thin it. Add the miso mixture to the crushed walnuts and grind or pulse to combine. Taste the sauce. If it seems too salty, adjust the seasoning with the mirin. Transfer to a glass jar with a tight-fitting lid.

The sauces will keep for up to 3 weeks in the refrigerator, though the aroma and texture are best within the first week.

CREAMY TŌFU SAUCE

SHIRA AÉ

When I took up residence in Tokyo in the late 1960s, I had a tiny refrigerator and shopped for food daily. Like my neighbors, I came to depend on the convenience of local vendors who would bicycle with their wares through the neighborhood, announcing their arrival with distinctive melodies. My local tōfu vendor's high-pitched horn, which could be heard from blocks away, was the signal for me to take a bowl from my kitchen and wait my turn at the corner along with the busy homemakers who lived nearby.

In those days, blocks of tōfu typically weighed a pound or more and could feed a household of four or five easily. They needed to be consumed within a day or two of purchase, and I was always eager to learn new ways to prepare the both highly nutritious and highly perishable food. When I asked the tōfu maker's wife for suggestions, she confessed that her version of shira aé, *a creamy sauce used to dress a wide variety of vegetables, was made with day-old tōfu that she first vigorously boiled. Taking her hint, and my mother-in-law's fine advice, to season the tōfu with sweet, light miso, I developed this recipe.*

Now, whenever I have at least a quarter of a block of tōfu left after making some other dish, such as Mushroom, Lotus Root, and Tōfu Chowder (page 130), I transform it into this creamy sauce.

MAKES ABOUT 1 CUP

1/4 to 1/3 large block silken or firm tōfu, about 4 ounces

2 teaspoons sweet, light miso, preferably Saikyō miso (page 32)

Pinch of salt

Drop of mirin

Fill a saucepan with water and bring to a vigorous boil over high heat. Add the tōfu and cook for 2 minutes. With a slotted spoon, remove the tōfu to a colander lined with a *sarashi* cloth (page 77). When cool enough to handle, gather up the edges of the cloth to enclose the tōfu and twist the top to squeeze out excess moisture. It is fine to mash the tōfu a bit while doing this.

In the old-fashioned Japanese kitchen, the boiled tōfu would then be forced through a fine-mesh strainer called an *uragoshi* and finally mashed in a *suribachi* (page 73). In my modern kitchen (and, I suspect, in other Japanese households today), the boiled and drained tōfu goes into a food processor and is pulsed until smooth. Scrape down the sides of the food processor bowl, add the miso, and pulse the mixture until smooth. Season with the salt and mirin and pulse again until creamy. Scrape down the sides of the bowl as necessary to ensure even mixing.

Transfer to a glass jar, cover with a tight-fitting lid, and store in the refrigerator for up to 3 days.

Kitchen Harmony

This sauce is used most often to dress simmered vegetables, such as Carrots and Konnyaku Tossed in Creamy Tōfu Sauce (page 197), Soy-Braised Hijiki and Carrots (page 187), or Soy-Braised Sun-Dried Radish Ribbons (page 186). It also makes a terrific dip for raw vegetables, especially bell pepper strips.

NORI SAUCE

TSUKUDA NI NORI

High humidity in Japan, especially during the early summer rainy season, makes it a challenge to keep dried foods dry. Despite the antimoisture pellets that are included in most modern packages, rice crackers get sticky and sheets of toasted nori, best known to Americans as wrappers for rolled sushi, go limp. Limp, soggy, or torn toasted nori can be transformed into this thick, yummy sauce, which can be used in place of flavored miso as a dip for vegetables, or spread on hand-pressed rice triangles or blocks of tōfu before broiling.

MAKES ABOUT $^1/_4$ CUP

  2 full-sized sheets toasted nori
  $^1/_4$ cup water
  1 tablespoon saké
  $1^1/_2$ teaspoons soy sauce
  $^1/_2$ teaspoon sugar

Tear the nori sheets into small bits, or cut with kitchen scissors into thin strips. Place these pieces in a small saucepan or skillet and add the water, saké, soy sauce, and sugar. Let the mixture sit for a moment or two until the nori pieces become moist and begin to dissolve. Stir to make a paste.

Place the pan over low heat and heat slowly, stirring until smooth and slightly aromatic. Remove from the heat and let cool completely.

Transfer to a glass jar, cover with a tight-fitting lid, and store in the refrigerator for up to 2 weeks. When spreading this sauce on rice, vegetables, or fish to be toasted or broiled, use low heat, because the sauce tends to scorch easily.

CHUNKY RED BEAN JAM

TSUBU AN

Just as there are Americans who prefer chunky peanut butter over smooth, the Japanese are divided over an, *a thick jam or fudge made from adzuki beans. Some prefer the chunky version,* tsubu an, *and others favor the smooth* koshi an. *Since I am a fan of both peanut bits and chunky sweet beans, I offer the* tsubu an, *which makes a fabulous topping for buttery pound cake or vanilla ice cream. For a more elaborate dessert, try Zensai Parfait (page 301) or Wafū Waffle (page 302).*

Illustrated on pages 104 and 303

MAKES 2 CUPS

  $^3/_4$ cup dried adzuki beans
  About 7 cups cold water
  $^3/_4$ cup white sugar
  2 tablespoons firmly packed brown sugar, preferably kuro-zatō (page 52)
  $^1/_2$ teaspoon coarse salt
  1 teaspoon light-colored soy sauce

Because the adzuki beans in this recipe are used to make a dessert, they are cooked a bit differently than in the Soy-Simmered Kabocha Squash with Red Beans (page 206). Here, it is important to cook them slowly from the dried state, throwing off the first batch of cooking water, to coax out their full flavor and keep any possible mustiness at bay. Fresh cold water is added several times during the cooking process.

As with all dried bean cookery, the beans must be carefully washed to remove straw, pebbles, or other unwanted matter. Place the washed and drained beans in a 3-quart pot with $2^1/_2$ cups of the water and bring to a boil over medium heat. Reduce the heat to maintain a steady but not very vigorous simmer. Cook the beans for about 8 minutes, or until the water turns wine red. Drain the beans, discarding this first batch of cooking liquid (this procedure is referred to as *shibumi kiri,* or "removing astringency"). Rinse the pot to remove any *aku* (froth, scum, or film) that might be clinging to the sides.

Return the beans to the clean pot, add 3 more cups of the water, and place over medium heat. When the liquid comes to a boil, adjust the heat to maintain a steady but gentle simmer. Do not cover the pot. Cook until the water barely covers the beans, about 30 minutes. Add ¹/₂ cup more of the cold water (this is called *bikkuri mizu,* or "surprise water") and continue to cook over medium heat, skimming away froth and loose skins periodically. Repeat the "surprise water" treatment every 15 to 20 minutes for 35 to 40 minutes, or until the beans are tender and give slightly when pinched.

Add the white sugar, stir, and simmer for 20 minutes (after the addition of the sugar, the sauce will darken and appear less cloudy). Add the brown sugar, stir, and simmer for about 5 minutes, or until the sauce becomes glossy and very thick (using a spoon or spatula, you should be able to draw a line that remains visible for several moments along the bottom of the pan). Add the salt and soy sauce (this will mellow the intense sweetness of the sauce and help "set" the consistency) and stir to mix well. Remove from the heat and set aside to cool.

Transfer the cooled sauce to a glass jar, cover with a tight-fitting lid, and store in the refrigerator for up to 2 months.

Kitchen Harmony

Many traditional sweets are made with *tsubu an.* When my daughter was growing up in Tokyo in the 1970s, Tai Yaki Kun was a popular character that appeared in an animated song on television. The prototype for this anthropomorphized creature was a traditional sweet called *tai yaki,* a grilled waffle filled with chunky red bean jam. This sweet snack looks like a fish (*tai* is a sea bream, eaten on happy occasions because of a fortuitous play on the word for *omedetai,* or "congratulations") and is made with a special waffle iron.

A sweet similar to *tai yaki,* but one that requires no special equipment, is *dora yaki* (gong cakes), made by sandwiching *tsubu an* between two silver-dollar-sized pancakes. Use your favorite pancake batter or use the waffle batter on page 302, adding an extra pinch of baking soda to produce "gongs" about ¹/₄ inch thick.

BROWN SUGAR SYRUP

KURO MITSU

Made from kuro-zatō *(unrefined brown sugar), this syrup is used in many traditional sweet dishes. If you can find superior-quality* kuro-zatō, *it has a wonderful malted flavor. The best I have found comes from Okinawa.* Kuro-zatō *tends to lump in the package and may require some effort to break up. For those who do not mind this exercise, smashed sugar can be measured in a conventional measuring cup. (Since the sugar is mixed with water and cooked, the consistency of the final sauce will not be compromised if the lumps are smashed.) Or, if you have a kitchen scale, weigh the sugar lumps. This sauce is used for* Wafū Waffle *(page 302), but it is wonderful spooned over plain yogurt or vanilla ice cream, too.*

MAKES ABOUT $^1/_2$ CUP

$^2/_3$ cup firmly packed brown sugar, preferably kuro-zatō (page 52), about 4 ounces

$^1/_4$ cup boiling water

Pinch of coarse salt

Place the brown sugar and boiling water in a small, deep saucepan. Stir with a wooden spoon or a heat-resistant rubber spatula to dissolve the sugar as fully as possible before placing over the heat.

Place the pan over medium heat and bring to a boil, stirring constantly. Reduce the heat slightly and cook the mixture, continuing to stir, for about 1 minute, or until very foamy. When the foam can no longer be stirred down, the mixture will rapidly thicken and become syrupy. As you lift up your spoon or spatula, the syrup will cling to it, rather than drip from it.

Add the salt to mellow the sweetness and stir it in. Remove from the heat to prevent scorching. Pour the hot syrup into in a heat-proof glass jar and let cool completely.

Cover with a tight-fitting lid and store on a cool, dark shelf for up to 1 month or in the refrigerator for up to 6 months.

KELP AND MUSHROOM RELISH

TSUKUDA NI KOMBU

During the Edo period (1603–1868), the fish market serving the area now known as Tokyo was located in Tsukuda. There, small and bruised fish with little or no commercial value were preserved by simmering them in a mixture of soy sauce and mirin. Huge vats of this seasoned soy were reused, becoming more intense with each new batch of fish simmered in them. When necessary, the soy sauce mixture was thinned with water. In the households of the market workers, kitchen scraps, bits and pieces of kelp, fish flakes, and dried mushrooms left from making stock were recycled in a process that came to be known as Tsukuda ni, or "simmered in the manner of Tsukuda."

In today's frugal washoku *kitchen, pieces of* kombu *that remain after making stock are transformed, Tsukuda ni style, into relish for serving with rice or stuffing into hand-pressed rice triangles. I store my leftover* kombu *in a small, lidded container in the refrigerator. As it fills up, the lid becomes harder to close, signaling that it is time to make a batch of this relish. If at any point the* kombu *develops a sticky, pasty whitish substance on the surface, I discard it.*

Illustrated on page 104

MAKES ABOUT $^1/_2$ CUP

Several pieces kombu (page 42), about 50 square inches total, left over from making stock

2 cups cold water

3 tablespoons rice vinegar

1 teaspoon sugar

1 teaspoon saké

3 tablespoons mirin

4 to 5 tablespoons soy sauce

1 package enoki mushrooms, about 3 ounces, trimmed and cut into 2- to 3-inch lengths

Slice the *kombu* into narrow strips 1¹/₂ inches long. In a nonreactive saucepan, bring the water to a rolling boil over high heat and add the vinegar. The vinegar helps tenderize the *kombu* and eliminate any questionable bacteria if you are recycling the *kombu* from a previous use.

Reduce the heat to maintain a steady, though not vigorous boil and cook the *kombu* for 5 to 6 minutes. The water may become murky and develop a green cast. This is normal. Test for doneness: pinch a strip or two; they should yield easily. If they do not, continue cooking for another 2 to 3 minutes. Drain, rinse in cold water, and drain again.

Rinse and dry the saucepan and add the sugar, saké, mirin, and soy sauce. Place over low heat, bring to a simmer, and add the drained *kombu*. Simmer for 2 to 3 minutes, and then add the mushrooms. Cook over fairly low heat for about 3 minutes, stirring frequently. The liquid will become very foamy as it reduces rapidly; be careful not to let it scorch.

When the *kombu* looks glazed and the liquid is nearly gone, remove the pan from the heat and let the contents cool to room temperature naturally. Serve immediately.

Transfer any leftovers to a glass jar, cover the top with plastic wrap, and then screw the lid in place. Store the relish in the refrigerator for up to 2 weeks. Each time you take some relish from the jar, reseal it with fresh plastic wrap before replacing the lid.

--- 和食 ---

Kitchen Harmony

Dried shiitaké mushrooms left over from making Basic Vegetarian Stock (page 93) can also be used to make this relish. Rinse, remove stems, and slice caps into thin julienne strips or a fine dice. Add instead of, or in addition to, the enoki mushrooms.

Yet another, spicy version of this relish forgoes the mushrooms and seasons the *kombu* with *sanshō* (page 47).

Sometimes, when I can't wait for enough kelp scraps to accumulate, I make this relish with "fresh" *kombu*. I soak several 4- or 5-inch strips of dried *kombu* in cold water for about 20 minutes before cutting them into narrow strips 1¹/₂ inches long. Cook for about 10 minutes in the vinegar-water mixture to tenderize, then continue as above to season and cook the relish.

FIVE FLAVORED SALTS:
Green Tea, Yukari, Fragrant Pepper, Black Sesame, Ocean Herb
GO MI-JIO: MATCHA, YUKARI, SANSHŌ, KURO GOMA, AO NORI

Each of these distinctively flavored mixtures is used as a garnish; none is used to season foods before or during cooking. In the traditional Japanese kitchen, flavored salts perk up plain or multigrain-enriched rice dishes and are also used in place of a dipping sauce for batter-fried foods. In the modern kitchen, flavored salts are often sprinkled on deep-fried vegetable chips (page 212) or croutons that are nibbled on with beer or saké or added to tossed green salads for crunch.

Although flavored salts will not spoil, the aroma of many of them is volatile. Easily assembled, they are best made as needed. Store any leftovers in a tightly sealed glass jar on a cool, dry shelf for no more than a week. Yukari is the exception; it is a bit more trouble to make, but it will keep well for several months. When making these salts, use the best-quality coarse salt you can find. In Japan, I use mineral-rich sea salt from Okinawa.

MAKES 1 GENEROUS TEASPOON GREEN TEA SALT

1 teaspoon coarse salt

$^1/_4$ teaspoon matcha (page 54)

MAKES 1 GENEROUS TABLESPOON YUKARI

1 tablespoon aka-jiso leaves left from pickling plums or
10 flat salt-cured aka-jiso leaves (page 26)

MAKES 1 GENEROUS TEASPOON FRAGRANT PEPPER SALT

1 teaspoon coarse salt

6 or 7 dried sanshō berries or $^1/_4$ teaspoon ground
sanshō (page 47)

MAKES 1 SCANT TABLESPOON BLACK SESAME SALT

$^1/_2$ teaspoon coarse salt

2 teaspoons black sesame seeds, freshly dry-roasted
(page 85)

MAKES 1 GENEROUS TEASPOON OCEAN HERB SALT

$^1/_4$ teaspoon coarse salt

1 teaspoon ao nori (page 41)

To make green tea salt, place the coarse salt in a small dish and sift the *matcha* over it. Stir to mix well. Mound on small plates to be used as a dip for fried foods.

To make *yukari*, no extra salt is needed. Indeed, you must blot away excess brine from salt-cured *aka-jiso* leaves with several layers of paper towels. The magenta color is a natural but intense dye. Be careful with clothing, fingertips, and cutting boards.

If you have a dehydrator, use it to dry the leaves, following the manufacturer's directions. When dry, crush the leaves to a fine powder. If you do not have a dehydrator, you can achieve similar results with a microwave oven. Spread the leaves on a flat glass plate or other nonreactive microwave-safe surface. Microwave the leaves on high for 2 minutes. Flip the leaves over, keeping them spread out, and repeat for 1 minute. Continue to zap in the microwave at 20- to 30-second intervals, flipping the leaves over and spreading them out each time to ensure even exposure of all surfaces. When the leaves are thoroughly dry, crush them. Sift the crushed mass through a strainer to eliminate unwieldy stems and other large pieces.

To make fragrant pepper salt, place the coarse salt in a small dish. If you are able to find whole dried *sanshō* berries, grind them in a spice mill and stir them into the salt. Or stir together already ground *sanshō* into the salt.

To make black sesame salt, combine the salt and the dry-roasted sesame seeds in a small, dry skillet over high heat. Stir with a wooden spoon for about 20 seconds before removing the pan from the heat. Use the mixture warm, or let cool to room temperature before storing.

To make ocean herb salt, place the salt in a small dish. Measure out the *ao nori* separately in a pile next to the salt. Then pinch and rub the *ao nori* between your fingertips as you sift it over the pile of salt. Rubbing the herb releases its wonderful seashore aroma. Stir to mix well.

和食

Kitchen Harmony

Wondering which flavored salt to serve, and with what? There are no hard and fast rules, but the Japanese do recognize what they call *aishō ga ii,* or "good matches."

For example, the slight bitterness of green tea salt will accentuate the sweetness of root vegetables, such as burdock and carrot, and of sweet potatoes. It also makes a wonderful dip for Tempura Pancakes, Temple Vegetarian Style (page 210).

The faintly sour, pleasantly astringent nuances of *yukari* will add a welcome accent to rice dishes, including sushi rice. It is also quite marvelous sprinkled on Italian-style pastas, especially those sauced with cream. Commercially prepared *yukari* is available at many Asian groceries and is ready to use as is. However, some preparations contain chemical preservatives or seasoning agents other than salt. Check the label carefully. Similarly, when making your own *yukari* from the moist leaves in commercially prepared pickled plums, make sure that the plums have not been dipped in honey or other sweeteners.

Soy-glazed eel and deep-fried chicken are beautifully complemented by the fragrant pepper salt, as are vegetable chips made from earthy burdock or crunchy lotus root (Burdock and Lotus Root Chips, page 213) and plump mushrooms stuffed with tōfu (Tōfu-Stuffed Fresh Shiitaké Mushrooms, page 271).

In the classic *washoku* household, the mixture of roasted black sesame and salt known as *goma shio* is used primarily as a garnish for *sekihan,* a festive dish of pink-tinted glutinous rice and adzuki beans. In this book, I have suggested sprinkling this flavored salt on other rice dishes. Commercially prepared *goma shio* is available at many Asian groceries and is ready to use as is. Check the label, because some mixtures contain preservatives and/or anticaking agents.

The marine herb *ao nori,* used extensively to season rice and rice crackers, noodles, potato chips, and seafood, exudes a pleasant seashore aroma. In combination with coarse salt, it becomes a dip for sautéed mushrooms stuffed with tōfu (Tōfu-Stuffed Fresh Shiitaké Mushrooms, page 271). It also makes a delicious topping for plain boiled or mashed potatoes.

SOUPS

SOUP IS AN IMPORTANT PART OF every Japanese meal. In traditional *washoku* meal planning, it complements the menu, helping to create balance through color, flavor, texture, and cooking method. In assembling a soup, imagine what qualities or characteristics each ingredient might contribute to the finished dish. Also, choose flavors (both mild and lively), hues (bright and muted), and textures (crunchy and creamy) that will bring the soup into harmony with the rest of the meal, you are serving.

Miso shiru, or a miso-enriched broth, is an essential component of a traditional Japanese breakfast and appears on lunch and dinner menus as well. There are hundreds, probably thousands, of miso varieties in Japan. The selection of one kind over another typically reflects both regional and personal preferences.

Several miso soups are included in this chapter. Some recipes use sweet, light miso (these tend to be popular in the Kansai region, including Kyoto and Osaka), others call for heady, yeasty *mugi miso* (barley-enriched miso popular in Kyushu and parts of Shikoku), and still others rely on pungent dark miso (favored in Nagoya, Tokyo, and the Kanto Plain regions). Blending different kinds of miso, a practice known as *awasé miso*, is also common and allows you to customize the flavor, hue, and texture of the final dish. Details on the flavor and texture characteristics of various miso pastes can be found in the Washoku Pantry (page 10).

In all cases, miso is suspended in broth, not really dissolved in it. As a result, the miso settles at the bottom of the bowl fairly quickly. The broth that floats above it, known as *uwazumi* (clear above), contains many of the nutrients in the miso, but in less concentrated form. It is often fed to infants and to people on sodium-restricted diets. To enjoy the full flavor and nutrition of miso-enriched broth, stir lightly with chopsticks or a spoon to recombine the miso concentrate with the *uwazumi* just before sipping the soup.

At the *washoku* table, a *suimono*, or clear soup, can be of two sorts: a few morsels floating in a delicate sea of broth, or a chowderlike mélange of seasonal vegetables. The former tends to be served with sushi dishes or as part of a formal multi-course banquet. The latter, clear but studded with chunky vegetables, is more likely to be served as part of a vegetarian meal or in place of a vegetable side dish to complement fish, meat, or eggs.

I conclude the chapter with a recipe for *surinagashi*, a puréed soup that required considerable diligence in the old days when a Japanese homemaker relied on a mortar. In today's kitchen, often equipped with a blender or food processor, this soup is an easily assembled affair.

If the number of options provided in the various soup recipes appears a bit overwhelming, I suggest you start by choosing a single soup that seems appealing or is easy to assemble. As you make the soup, pay particular attention to the timing and method: some ingredients require slow simmering in stock from the start, others begin with braising the ingredients, and still others put the ingredients directly into serving bowls to be "cooked" by pouring hot stock over them. Also note the proportions of miso and other seasonings to stock, and the relative proportion of certain vegetables to one another. Once you grasp these basics, you can mix and match elements as you like.

If possible, serve soup in deep, lidded Japanese bowls. The lids trap heat and aromas, whether the heady fragrance of miso or a delicate garnish in a *suimono,* to provide full enjoyment at table.

MISO SOUP WITH ENOKI MUSHROOMS

ENOKI NO MISO-JIDATÉ

In Japan, wild mushrooms have traditionally been associated with the fall, though for several decades now, slender, white-knobbed enoki mushrooms have been successfully cultivated and are available in supermarkets nearly year-round. My husband, Atsunori, is particularly fond of enoki in soup, and the miso-enriched broth offered here appears on our table several times a week.

Depending on what else is on the menu, I will choose my miso and garnish accordingly. If I am serving the soup with intense, soy-glazed foods, such as Citrus-and-Soy-Glazed Swordfish (page 227) or Tangy Seared Chicken Wings (page 256), I prefer a light barley miso (mugi miso) with yeasty overtones, and I like to garnish the soup with some slightly bitter green, such as mitsuba or watercress. When I am featuring a milder dish, such as Rolled Omelet, Kansai Style (page 289) or Cloud-Steamed Bass (page 242), I use a mixture of full-bodied dark miso pastes, often including brown rice–enriched genmai miso (page 30), and I find that scallions provide a better accent.

Illustrated on page 4

SERVES 4

1 package enoki mushrooms, about 3 ounces, trimmed

4 mitsuba stalks (page 26), 2 watercress sprigs,
    or 2 scallions

3 1/2 cups Basic Sea Stock (page 92)

1/2 block firm tōfu, about 6 1/2 ounces, drained and
    pressed (page 77), then cut into a 1/4-inch dice
    (page 70)

3 tablespoons miso

Cut the trimmed mushrooms into thirds. Place the pieces with the caps directly into individual soup bowls and the remaining stem portions into a pot.

Trim the *mitsuba* or watercress, removing roots and tough stems, then chop the leaves and tender stems coarsely. If using scallions, trim away the root and cut both the white bottoms and the green tops into thin circular slices. Divide the garnish among the bowls.

Add the stock to the pot holding the mushroom stems and bring to a boil over high heat. When the stock begins to boil, skim away any froth and reduce the heat to maintain a steady but not vigorous simmer. Add the tōfu and cook for 1 minute.

Just before serving, place the miso in a *miso koshi* (page 77) and stir directly into the soup. Or place the miso in a bowl, ladle in some of the hot stock from the pot, stir to mix it, and add to the pot.

Ladle the soup into the bowls holding the enoki caps and garnish, dividing it evenly, and serve immediately.

MISO SOUP WITH FRIED TŌFU, LEAFY GREENS, AND SCALLIONS

WAKANA NO OMIOTSUKÉ

In the frugal washoku *kitchen, the tops from daikon and turnips are prepared and eaten as any other leafy green vegetable might be. Briefly blanched and dressed* ohitashi *style (page 190) and blanched and tossed in a creamy sesame sauce (page 100) are two popular preparations. In addition, leafy greens are added to miso-enriched broth. The green tops of root vegetables typically have a hint of bitterness but pair well with slivers of fried tōfu and a mellow miso, either light or dark. If you don't have radish or turnip tops on hand, use broccoli rabe, kale, beet greens, or even flat-leaf parsley.*

SERVES 4

   1 small tuft daikon tops, about 1 ounce
   1 scallion, roots trimmed and white and green parts finely
      minced
   1 slice fried tōfu, about 6 by 3¹/₂ inches
   Pinch of salt
   Splash of saké
   3 cups Basic Sea Stock (page 92)
   2 tablespoons mugi miso (page 32)
   1 tablespoon genmai miso (page 30)

Bring a small pot of water to a rolling boil. Dip the daikon tops into the boiling water for 30 seconds, or just until wilted. Remove the tops with long cooking chopsticks, tongs, or a slotted spoon, reserving the boiling water. When the greens are cool enough to handle, squeeze out the excess liquid, chop them coarsely, and divide them evenly among individual soup bowls. Divide the scallion among the bowls.

Use the reserved boiling water to blanch the fried tōfu (page 75). When the blanched tōfu is cool enough to handle, squeeze out all the excess liquid. Cut the tōfu into a julienne.

Put the fried tōfu strips into a 2-quart pot, preferably one with a nonstick surface. Place the pot over high heat and cook for about 1 minute, or until the strips brown a bit. (There is no need to add oil even after blanching the tōfu; sufficient oil still clings to its surface.) Sprinkle with the salt and then add the saké and jiggle the pot to deglaze any browned bits. Add the stock and adjust the heat so that it barely simmers. Cook for 1 minute.

Just before serving, place the miso in a *miso koshi* (page 77) and stir directly into the soup. Or place the miso in a bowl, ladle in some of the hot stock from the pot, stir to mix it, and add to the pot.

Ladle the soup into the bowls holding the daikon tops and scallions, dividing it evenly, and serve immediately.

MISO-THICKENED PORK AND VEGETABLE SOUP

TON-JIRU

This hearty soup is a jumble of pork bits (ton is written with the calligraphy for "pig"), root vegetables, and diced tōfu in a miso-thickened broth. Standard family fare, especially in large households, ton-jiru is also served in college cafeterias, at rooming-house dining tables, and to volunteers at many community gatherings. The recipe I provide here combines elements from various versions of ton-jiru I have encountered during my years in Japan. The choice of combining mugi miso and Saikyō miso reflects my early experiences in the Sanuki region of Shikoku, while my inclusion of burdock root is typical of Tokyo-made ton-jiru.

SERVES 6 TO 8

1 Japanese leek or small Western leek, about 3 ounces

$^1/_2$ teaspoon vegetable oil

6 ounces boneless pork from loin or shoulder, cut into small, thin strips

1 small carrot, about 3 ounces, peeled and cut into julienne

1-inch chunk daikon, about 2 ounces, peeled and cut into julienne

5 to 6 inches burdock root, about 3 ounces, rinsed and lightly scraped (page 58) and cut on the diagonal into thin slices

Pinch of salt

Splash of saké

2 quarts water

About 12 square inches kombu (page 42)

$^1/_2$ teaspoon soy sauce

1 block firm tōfu, about 14 ounces, drained and pressed (page 77), then cut into $^1/_4$-inch dice (page 70)

1 small bunch mitsuba (page 26), about 15 stalks, trimmed, stems cut into short pieces, and leaves chopped

3 tablespoons mugi miso (page 32)

3 tablespoons sweet, light miso, preferably Saikyō miso (page 32)

Trim away the hairy root and any tough green top of the leek and then cut in half lengthwise. Rinse under cold water to remove any grit or soil. Place the cut edges down on a cutting board and slice on the diagonal into thin strips. Set aside.

Heat the oil in a deep pot over high heat. Stir-fry the pork for 1 minute, or until it begins to color. Then add the leek, carrot, daikon, and burdock root and continue to stir-fry over high heat for 1 minute. Add the salt and saké and stir-fry for 1 to 2 minutes, or until the burdock root emits a woodsy aroma.

Add the water and *kombu*. When the soup begins to boil, skim away any froth and reduce the heat to maintain a steady but not vigorous simmer. Continue to cook, skimming away froth as needed, for 4 to 5 minutes, or until the vegetables are very tender and the pork is thoroughly cooked. Remove and discard the *kombu*. Season with the soy sauce. Add the tōfu to the soup and simmer for 1 minute to heat it through.

Divide the *mitsuba* evenly among individual soup bowls.

Just before serving, place the miso in a *miso koshi* (page 77) and stir directly into the soup. Or place the miso in a bowl, ladle in some of the hot stock from the pot, stir to mix it, and add to the pot.

Ladle the soup into the bowls. The brief exposure to hot soup is sufficient to cook the *mitsuba*. Serve immediately.

Kitchen Harmony

Many versions of *ton-jiru* substitute scallions for leeks and include some kind of mushroom. When I follow suit, departing from the Andoh standard described here, I often choose a pungent dark miso, such as Sendai miso, to balance flavors.

MISO SOUP WITH ONIONS AND POTATOES

HOKKAIDO-FŪ MISO SHIRU

Historically associated with the bounty of the sea, Hokkaido, Japan's northern island, has built a reputation in the past few decades for its superior dairy and agricultural products, too. In particular, Hokkaido is known for its tama negi (round yellow onions) and jyaga imo (white potatoes), ingredients used primarily in Western-style stews and Asian-inspired curries.

Onions and potatoes are also delicious in home-style miso-thickened soup. This version, garnished with wakamé, a mild-flavored sea vegetable, is enjoyed in many Hokkaido households.

SERVES 4

1 small yellow onion, about 2 ounces

1 medium-sized potato, preferably a thin-skinned new
    potato, about 2 ounces

$^1/_2$ teaspoon vegetable oil

Pinch of salt

1 tablespoon saké

$3^1/_2$ cups Basic Sea Stock (page 92)

$1^1/_2$ teaspoons dried bits wakamé (page 44), soaked and
    drained, or $^1/_2$ to 1 ounce fresh-salted wakamé, rinsed,
    soaked, drained, and chopped

3 tablespoons dark miso, preferably Sendai miso
    (page 32)

Halve the onion through the stem. Place the halves, cut side down, on a cutting board and thinly slice with the grain to produce crescent-shaped pieces. If you are using a new potato, scrub it; if you are not, peel it. Slice the potatoes into strips about 1 inch long and $^1/_4$ inch wide and thick.

Heat the vegetable oil in a 2-quart pot over high heat. Add the onion slices and sauté for about 1 minute, or until fragrant and slightly caramelized. Add the potato strips and continue to sauté for about 1 minute, or until browned at the edges. Sprinkle with the salt and then add the saké and jiggle the pot to deglaze any browned bits. Add the stock, bring to a simmer, adjust the heat to maintain a simmer, and cook, skimming away any froth, for 1 to 2 minutes, or until the potatoes are barely tender.

Trim away tough ribs from larger pieces of *wakamé*. Divide the *wakamé* evenly among individual soup bowls.

Just before serving, place the miso in a *miso koshi* (page 77) and stir directly into the soup. Or place the miso in a bowl, ladle in some of the hot stock from the pot, stir to mix it, and add to the pot.

Ladle the soup into the bowls holding the *wakamé*, dividing it evenly. Serve immediately.

DARK MISO SOUP WITH ROASTED EGGPLANT

YAKI NASU NO AKA DASHI

A dark, smoky-flavored miso-thickened broth known as aka dashi *is served at the conclusion of many traditional Japanese meals. In central Japan, particularly in and around the city of Nagoya, fudge-colored, pure-bean Hatchō miso is favored when making this broth. Cooks in other parts of Japan might combine several dark miso pastes, including* genmai miso *(page 30).*

This version with roasted eggplant is a summertime favorite; the sweet potato version that follows is terrific when the weather turns cold.

SERVES 4

 1 quart Basic Sea Stock (page 92)

 1 teaspoon soy sauce

 Splash of saké

 2 Japanese eggplants

 2 tablespoons dark miso, preferably Hatchō miso
  (page 32)

 $^1/_4$ cup tightly packed katsuo-bushi (page 18)

 1 myōga bulb (page 26)

Heat the stock in a 2- to 3-quart pot over medium-high heat, seasoning it with the soy sauce and the saké as small bubbles appear around the rim. Adjust the heat so that it barely simmers.

Grill and peel the eggplants as directed for Chilled Roasted Eggplant (page 193). Cut the roasted eggplants into $^1/_2$-inch lengths and divide evenly among individual soup bowls.

Place the miso in a *miso koshi* (page 77) and stir directly into the simmering broth. Or place the miso in a bowl, ladle in some of the hot broth from the pot, stir to mix it, and add to the pot. Hatchō miso is especially thick and stiff and may take some extra effort to dissolve it in the soup.

Remove the pot from the heat, sprinkle in the *katsuo-bushi* flakes, scattering them across the surface. Let the flakes sit in the miso-thickened broth while you shred the *myōga*; the fish flakes will sink as they become drenched with broth, lending a smoky flavor to the soup.

Cut the *myōga* bulb in half lengthwise. Place the halves, cut side down, on a cutting board and slice into thin shreds. Divide the shreds evenly among the bowls.

Place the pot of miso-thickened broth over low heat to reheat it. To preserve full aroma and fine texture, do not let the soup boil.

Strain the soup through a *sarashi* cloth (page 77) or coffee-filter-lined strainer (or a very fine-mesh strainer) into the bowls holding the eggplant and *myōga*. Discard the fish flakes. Serve the soup immediately.

DARK MISO SOUP WITH SWEET POTATO

SATSUMAIMO NO AKA DASHI

Like the miso soup with eggplant on page 121, this is an aka dashi soup, this time made with the red-skinned, yellow-fleshed Japanese sweet potato called Satsuma imo. *Sweet potatoes often find their way into traditional confectionary, but here the smoky overtone from the* katsuo-bushi *used in the broth brings the natural sweetness into harmony with savory foods. Peeled and seeded* kabocha *squash or sugar pumpkin also works well in place of, or added to, the sweet potato.*

SERVES 4

    1 small Japanese-style sweet potato, about 5 ounces,
        unpeeled, cut into a ¹/₄-inch dice and soaked
        (page 76)
    4 cups Basic Sea Stock (page 92)
    1 teaspoon soy sauce
    Splash of saké
    4 to 6 fresh chives, finely minced
    2 tablespoons miso, preferably Hatchō miso (page 32)
    ¹/₄ cup tightly packed katsuo-bushi (page 18)

Place the potato pieces and stock in a 2- to 3-quart pot and bring slowly to a simmer over low heat. Skim away any froth that appears. Season with the soy sauce and saké and continue to simmer for 3 or 4 minutes, or until the potatoes are barely tender (test with a toothpick; it should meet no resistance).

Using a slotted spoon, transfer the potato pieces to individual soup bowls, dividing them evenly. Garnish each portion with the chives.

Just before serving, place the miso in a *miso koshi* (page 77) and stir directly into the soup. Or place the miso in a bowl, ladle in some of the hot stock from the pot, stir to mix it, and add to the pot. Hatchō miso is especially thick and stiff and may take some extra effort to dissolve it in the soup.

Remove the pot from the heat and sprinkle in the *katsuo-bushi* flakes, scattering them across the surface. The fish flakes will sink as they become drenched with broth. Stir after 30 to 40 seconds. Strain the soup through a *sarashi* cloth (page 77) or coffee-filter-lined strainer (or a very fine-mesh strainer) into the bowls holding the sweet potato pieces and chives, dividing it evenly. Discard the fish flakes. Serve the soup immediately.

FISHERMAN'S BROTH

SENBA-JIRU

The name senba *(literally, "on board boat") suggests that histori-cally this soup was made on board fishing boats, though today it tends to be assembled on the dock after unloading the day's catch. Soups such as this one, made from fish scraps and less marketable sea creatures, can be found in port towns throughout the world.*

My husband enjoys fishing with his buddies (they rent a boat for the day and fish off the Izu Peninsula, south of Tokyo) and often brings home fine fish for dinner. Indeed, in my early days of acquir-ing kitchen knife skills, I looked forward to practice sessions on whatever he caught.

On the days when his catch is sparse, I can easily obtain meaty fish heads in my Tokyo supermarket to compensate. In America, I found that many fish markets were willing to give me heads for free, or very cheaply. Combining several varieties of fish yields a richer broth. Fish in the grouper and snapper families will probably be the most appealing to the uninitiated. Heads (known as kabuto, *or "helmet"), especially those with* kama *(collar meat) attached, make superior broth.*

In Japan, the choice of miso used in this soup usually reflects regional preferences. Although any variety can be used, I suggest a full-bodied genmai miso *or a yeasty* mugi miso.

SERVES 4

    1 or 2 fish heads with collar meat attached, about
      1 pound total weight
    1 teaspoon coarse salt
    4 cups cold water
    About 12 square inches kombu (page 42)
    1 tablespoon saké
    3 tablespoons miso
    1 scallion, roots trimmed and white and green parts finely
      minced (optional)

Have your fishmonger cut the head (or heads) into 4 pieces with a cleaver. Sprinkle the fish pieces on all sides with the salt. Let the salted fish stand for a few minutes to "sweat." This step will remove excessive "fishiness" and yield a more flavor-ful broth.

To prevent unpleasant odors and scum from developing, Japanese cooks blanch fish scraps in boiling water before cooking them, a procedure known as *shimo furi*, or "frost falling." Do this with the fish head pieces, following the direc-tions on page 74.

Place the "frosted" fish in a clean pot with the fresh cold water. Add the *kombu* and saké and slowly bring the soup to a simmer over low heat to encourage a gradual exchange of fla-vors between the fish and the *kombu*-enhanced broth. Skim away any froth that appears.

Just before serving, place the miso in a *miso koshi* (page 77) and stir directly into the soup. Or place the miso in a bowl, ladle in some of the hot stock from the pot, stir to mix it, and add to the pot. Continue to simmer for 1 to 2 minutes.

Typically this soup is served with the whole fish chunks in the bowls. But if you prefer, you can remove the fish from the pot and pull the meat off the bones. Divide the fish chunks or meat evenly among individual soup bowls. To add a bit of color and a nuance of flavor, scatter the scallion over the fish, if desired.

Ladle the soup into the bowls holding the fish. Serve immediately. Japanese drink the soup directly from the bowl, using chopsticks to pluck the meat away from the bones.

CLEAR OCEAN BROTH WITH HERBS AND LEMON PEEL

SUMASHI-JIRU

A clear broth such as this one is often served with sushi dishes. Try serving it with Five-Colored Foods with Sushi Rice (page 147), rolled sushi, either plump rolls or mini inside-out rolls (page 149), or Sushi Pillows (page 152).

SERVES 4

1 slice hanpen (page 17), about 2^1/$_2$ ounces, cut into
^{1}/$_4$-inch dice

1 quart Basic Sea Stock, (page 92), preferably made with
Rishiri kombu (page 42)

1 tablespoon saké

Pinch of salt

^{1}/$_2$ teaspoon light-colored soy sauce

^{1}/$_4$ teaspoon mirin

1 lemon peel strip, about 1^1/$_4$ inches square

^{1}/$_4$ teaspoon sanshō (page 47)

Place the *hanpen* and stock in a deep, 2-quart pot and bring slowly to a boil over low heat to encourage a gradual exchange of flavors between the fish and the stock. The *hanpen* pieces will puff and swell, absorbing the flavor of the stock. At the same time, they will lend a delicate ocean flavor to the stock.

When small bubbles appear at the edges of the pot, add the saké and salt and then adjust the heat so the soup barely simmers. Add the soy sauce and mirin and cook for 1 minute. If any froth appears, skim it away.

Slice the lemon peel into very thin slivers, or cut it into 4 decorative shapes such as flowers or leaves (in Japan, metal cutters in various motifs are available). Place a few slivers or a single decorative piece in each individual soup bowl.

Ladle the hot soup over the lemon peel, distributing the *hanpen* puffs evenly among the bowls. Garnish each serving with a generous pinch of *sanshō* and serve immediately.

EGG DROP SOUP

TAMAGO TOJI

In most home kitchens, egg drop soup is a quickly assembled, last-minute affair, often because a bit of beaten egg remains from another use, such as breading cutlets (Bite-Sized Pork Cutlets, page 263) or fish (Panko-Breaded Fried Cod, page 248), or binding mashed tōfu (Tōfu-Stuffed Fresh Shiitaké Mushrooms, page 271). It typically includes wispy shreds of beaten egg floating cloudlike near the surface. If you would rather have the shreds suspended throughout the broth, follow the instructions for adding a few drops of a cornstarch mixture. Either way, a garnish of mitsuba provides a welcome touch of color and crunch.

SERVES 4

- 1 quart Basic Sea Stock (page 92) or Smoky Chicken Stock (page 94)
- 1 teaspoon saké
- $1/4$ teaspoon salt
- 4 or 5 mitsuba stalks (page 26), trimmed, stems cut into short pieces, and leaves chopped
- $1/2$ to 1 large egg, well beaten
- $1/4$ teaspoon cornstarch mixed with 1 teaspoon cold water (optional)

Pour the stock into a pot and bring to a boil over high heat. Season with the saké and salt and adjust the heat to maintain a steady simmer while you divide the *mitsuba* evenly among individual soup bowls.

Return the soup to a boil. Using long cooking chopsticks or a long-handled spoon, stir the broth vigorously in a clockwise direction to create a whirlpool. Drizzle in the beaten egg in a steady stream. Remove the pot from the stove and stir the soup with a single swirl in a counterclockwise direction.

Or, if you prefer to have your egg shreds suspended in the broth, add the cornstarch paste to the hot soup as you create your whirlpool. Stir once more in the same direction and then drizzle in the beaten egg. Remove the pot from the stove, wait 10 to 15 seconds, and then stir the soup once in a counterclockwise direction.

Ladle the soup into the bowls holding the *mitsuba*, dividing it evenly, and serve immediately.

TEMPLE GARDEN CHOWDER

UNPEN-JIRU

Fucha ryōri, *Buddhist vegetarian cooking that originated in China, was brought to Japan by Ingen, a seventeenth-century philosopher-monk who was also an accomplished cook. This vegetable chowder is one of many courses in a fucha-style banquet. The use of aromatic sesame oil to pan sear some of the vegetables before simmering them is typical of fucha-style cooking.*

Like other Buddhist-inspired culinary practices, using bits and pieces of seasonal produce was a practical solution to limited resources, and also provided a sense of spiritual satisfaction in the avoidance of kitchen waste. Even when the occasion called for a multicourse feast, a frugal philosophy was evident. For the modern cook, this chowder is a perfect way to use up whatever may be languishing in the vegetable bin.

Throughout the year, daikon and carrots appear on washoku menus, and I have included them in all variations of this soup. If you have the leafy tops of either, or both, briefly blanch and mince them and then add them to the soup. In addition, I offer specific suggestions for each of the four seasons, incorporating a few non-Japanese vegetables. Feel free to substitute whatever you find in your local market; the vegetables should total about 12 ounces or 2 cups when sliced or cut. As you choose them, keep in mind the principle of five colors and the possibility of either emphasizing or minimizing textural contrast.

SERVES 4

Year-Round Basic Soup

2-inch piece daikon, about 4 ounces

1 carrot chunk, about 2 ounces

3$^1/_2$ cups Basic Sea Stock (page 92) or Basic Vegetarian
  Stock (page 93)

$^1/_2$ teaspoon salt

1 teaspoon saké

To make the year-round soup, scrub the daikon and carrot, but do not peel, to preserve the integrity of the vegetables. Cut the daikon into 5 or 6 circular slices, stack the slices, and cut the stack into 6 or 8 wedges. If the carrot is slender, slice it into thin rounds. If the carrot is more than 1 inch in diameter, slice it in half lengthwise, place the halves cut side down on a cutting board, and slice on the diagonal into thin, elongated half-moons about 1 inch long. Set the vegetables aside.

Pour the stock into a sturdy 2 quart pot and bring to a rolling boil over high heat. Adjust the heat to maintain a steady but not vigorous simmer. Season with the salt and saké and then add the daikon and carrot. Simmer for 2 minutes, or until the vegetables are barely tender. Skim away any froth that appears. Remove the pot from the heat while you prepare the vegetables for the seasonal soup you are making.

In the Spring

3-inch piece burdock root, about 1 ounce, rinsed and
  lightly scraped (page 58)

$^1/_2$ teaspoon sesame oil

$^1/_3$ cup Basic Sea Stock (page 92) or Basic Vegetarian
  Stock (page 93)

1 tablespoon light-colored soy sauce

1 tablespoon mirin

2 tablespoons cornstarch mixed with 1 tablespoon cold
  water to make a paste

4 or 5 snow peas, trimmed, blanched, and cut in half on
  the diagonal

2 or 3 asparagus spears, trimmed, thinly sliced on the
  diagonal, and briefly blanched

To make the spring soup, slice a slender burdock root into thin rounds. If the burdock root is more than 1 inch in diameter, slice it in half lengthwise, place the halves cut side down on a

Spring chowder (back) and autumn chowder (front)

cutting board, and slice on the diagonal into thin, elongated half-moons about 1 inch long.

Add the sesame oil to a nonstick skillet and place over medium-high heat. Add the burdock root and stir-fry for 2 minutes, or until fragrant and slightly wilted. Blot up any excess oil with paper towels. Add the stock, soy sauce, and mirin, and bring to a simmer. Cook for 1 minute, or until the burdock root is barely tender.

Transfer the burdock root and broth to the pot with the daikon, carrot, and stock. Bring to a simmer and cook for 1 minute, or until the root vegetables are tender and the flavors have married. Skim away any froth.

Raise the heat to high and stir in the cornstarch paste. Continue to stir for about 45 seconds, or until the broth thickens. Add the snow peas and asparagus and heat through. Ladle the soup into individual bowls. Serve immediately.

In the Summer

- $^1/_3$ cup corn kernels, cut from 1 ear of corn
- 1 slender Japanese eggplant, about 3 ounces and 4 or 5 inches long
- 1 small, slender zucchini, about 5 ounces
- 1 teaspoon sesame oil
- $^1/_3$ cup Basic Sea Stock (page 92) or Basic Vegetarian Stock (page 93)
- 1 tablespoon light-colored soy sauce
- 1 tablespoon mirin
- 2 tablespoons cornstarch mixed with 1 tablespoon cold water to make a paste

To make the summer soup, add the corn kernels to the pot holding the daikon, carrot, and stock. Return the pot to very low heat, bring to a gentle simmer, and simmer, skimming away any froth that appears, while preparing the other vegetables.

Trim away the stems and sepals (flaplike pieces at the stem end) from the eggplant and then slice it in half lengthwise. Place the halves cut side down on a cutting board and

slice on the diagonal into elongated half-moons about $^1/_4$ inch thick and 1 inch long.

Zucchini, like cucumbers, will taste sweeter if you follow a procedure known as *aku nuki* or "removing bitterness" (page 76). Once you have completed that step, slice the zucchini in half lengthwise. Place the halves cut side down on a cutting board and slice on the diagonal into elongated half-moons about $^1/_4$ inch thick and 1 inch long.

Add the sesame oil to a nonstick skillet and place over medium-high heat. Add the eggplant and zucchini slices, spreading them out in a single layer if possible. Sear the vegetables for 1 minute, undisturbed. Shake the skillet to flip the pieces over and continue to cook for another minute, pressing down on the vegetables lightly with a spatula so that they color slightly. Blot up any excess oil with paper towels. Add the stock, soy sauce, and mirin, and bring to a simmer for 30 to 40 seconds to allow the flavors to meld. Skim away any froth that appears. Transfer the zucchini, eggplant, and broth to the pot with the daikon, carrot, and stock.

Raise the heat to high and stir in the cornstarch paste. Continue to stir for about 45 seconds, or until the broth thickens. Ladle the soup into individual bowls. Serve immediately.

In the Autumn

- 1 package naméko mushrooms (page 33), about 3$^1/_2$ ounces
- 2 ounces sweet potato, preferably Japanese-style sweet potato, soaked (page 76)
- 1 teaspoon sesame oil
- $^1/_3$ cup Basic Sea Stock (page 92) or Basic Vegetarian Stock (page 93)
- 1$^1/_2$ teaspoons light-colored soy sauce
- 1$^1/_2$ teaspoons mirin
- 2 tablespoons cornstarch mixed with 1 tablespoon cold water to make a paste
- 1 small bunch dandelion greens, trimmed and blanched (page 74), and then cut into $^1/_2$-inch lengths

To make the autumn soup, add the mushrooms with the thick liquid from the package to the pot holding the daikon, carrot, and stock.

Drain the potato and pat dry with paper towels. Cut into $1/4$-inch dice, keeping the skin intact. Add the sesame oil to a nonstick skillet and place over medium-high heat. When the oil is hot, add the potato pieces, spread out in a single layer if possible. Sear the potato for 1 minute, undisturbed. Shake the skillet to flip the pieces over and continue to cook for another minute, shaking the pan occasionally and allowing the potato to color slightly. Blot up any excess oil with paper towels.

Add the stock, soy sauce, and mirin, and bring to a simmer for 30 to 40 seconds to allow the flavors to meld. Skim away any froth that appears. Transfer the potatoes and broth to the pot with the daikon, carrot, and stock.

Raise the heat to high and stir in the cornstarch paste. Continue to stir for about 45 seconds, or until the broth thickens. Add the dandelion greens and heat through. Ladle the soup into individual bowls. Serve immediately.

In the Winter

1 small leek, preferably Japanese leek, about 3 ounces

1 small parsnip, about 4 ounces

1 teaspoon sesame oil

2-inch piece broccoli stalk, about 1 ounce, cut into julienne

$1/3$ cup Basic Sea Stock (page 92) or Basic Vegetarian Stock (page 93)

$1^1/2$ teaspoons light-colored soy sauce

$1^1/2$ teaspoons mirin

2 tablespoons cornstarch mixed with 1 tablespoon cold water to make a paste

To make the winter soup, trim the leek and cut the white portion on the diagonal into $1/8$-inch-thick slices (save the green tops and trimmings for enriching stock). Place the leek slices in a strainer and rinse carefully to remove any sandy soil that might be hidden between the layers.

Scrub the parsnip with the rough side of a kitchen sponge, or scrape with the back of your knife to make sure it is free of dirt and other gritty material. The peel, however, is nutritious and tasty and should not be removed. Slice the parsnip in half lengthwise. Place the halves cut side down on a cutting board and slice on the diagonal into thin, elongated half-moons about $3/4$ inch long.

Add the sesame oil to a nonstick skillet and place over medium-high heat. When the oil is hot, add the leek and parsnip and stir-fry for 1 minute, or until fragrant and slightly wilted. Add the broccoli and stir-fry for another 30 or 40 seconds, or until slightly translucent. Blot up any excess oil with paper towels.

Add the stock, soy sauce, and mirin, and bring to a simmer for 30 to 40 seconds to allow the flavors to meld. Skim away any froth that appears. Transfer the leek, parsnip, and broccoli with the broth to the pot with the daikon, carrot, and stock.

Raise the heat to high and stir in the cornstarch paste. Continue to stir for about 45 seconds, or until the broth thickens. Ladle the soup into individual bowls and serve immediately.

MUSHROOM, LOTUS ROOT, AND TŌFU CHOWDER

KENCHIN-JIRU (SHIITAKÉ, RENKON, MOMEN-DŌFU)

There are hundreds of variations on the basic theme of kenchin-jiru. *What is common to all is the inclusion of some form of tōfu and lots of root vegetables, making the soup into a chowder. This recipe and the one that follows are two simple-to-prepare versions, either of which makes a satisfying brunch or light supper when served with steamed rice and a side dish of pickled vegetables.*

Classic versions of kenchin-jiru *are not enriched with miso, though you could thicken the broth of either, or both, of these chowders with your favorite fermented bean paste. If you do, omit the soy sauce and mirin.*

SERVES 4

    1 carrot, about 2 ounces

    1-inch chunk daikon, about 2 ounces

    2-inch chunk lotus root, about 1^1/$_2$ ounces

    6 fresh shiitaké mushrooms, about 2 ounces total weight

    2 scallions

    3^1/$_2$ cups Basic Sea Stock (page 92)

    1 teaspoon saké

    ^{1}/$_4$ teaspoon salt

    ^{1}/$_2$ block firm tōfu, about 7 ounces, drained and pressed (page 77), then cut into a ^{1}/$_4$-inch dice

    1 tablespoon light-colored soy sauce

    1 tablespoon mirin

Peel the carrot and slice it into thin rounds. Peel the daikon and the lotus root and cut each into quarters lengthwise. Cut each quarter wedge crosswise into thin pie-shaped slices.

Wipe the caps of the mushrooms to remove any soil or grit that may be clinging to them and remove their stems. Cut each cap into eighths, making narrow pie-shaped wedges.

Cut the green tops of the scallions into thin rings and reserve the white portions for enriching the soup, as suggested in the notes. Divide the scallions among individual soup bowls.

Pour the stock into a pot and place over medium-high heat. Season with the saké and salt and bring to a simmer. Adjust the heat to maintain a steady, gentle simmer. Add the carrot, daikon, lotus root, and mushrooms and simmer, skimming away any froth that appears, for about 3 minutes, or until the root vegetables are barely tender (test with a toothpick; it should meet little resistance).

Add the tōfu and then the soy sauce and mirin and stir to blend. Ladle the soup into the bowls holding the scallions and serve immediately.

———————— ————————

Kitchen Harmony

Save the trimmings from the carrot, daikon, scallions, and mushroom stems to enhance the flavor of the soup. Tie them into a bundle with kitchen string (for easy removal later) and add them to the stock at the start of making the soup. Remove and discard the bundle before adding the tōfu.

————————————————————

BURDOCK ROOT AND FRIED TŌFU CHOWDER

KENCHIN-JIRU (GOBŌ, ABURA AGÉ)

This version of kenchin-jiru *makes use of the oil still clinging to blanched fried tōfu to sear woodsy burdock root. As with the mushroom and lotus root chowder on page 130, this is a substantial soup that can be the focus of a meal.*

SERVES 4

1 carrot, about 2 ounces

1 burdock root, about 2 ounces, rinsed and lightly
   scraped (page 58)

1 package enoki mushrooms, about 3 ounces, trimmed

4 or 5 mitsuba stalks (page 26), trimmed and chopped
   into ¹/₃-inch lengths

2 slices fried tōfu, each about 6 by 3¹/₂ inches, blanched
   (page 75) and cut into julienne

¹/₄ teaspoon salt

1 teaspoon saké

3¹/₂ cups Basic Sea Stock (page 92)

1 teaspoon light-colored soy sauce

1 teaspoon mirin

Scrape or peel the carrot and cut it into ¹/₈-inch-thick batons. If the burdock root is more than ¹/₂ inch in diameter, cut it in half lengthwise. Cut into thin strips on the diagonal. Set the vegetables aside.

Cut the trimmed mushrooms into thirds. Place the pieces with the caps directly into individual soup bowls and set aside the remaining stem portions. Divide the *mitsuba* pieces, both pale stalks and green leaves, among the bowls.

Place a deep, 3-quart nonstick pot over medium-high heat. Add the fried tōfu pieces to the pot first. The oil that clings to them, even after blanching and blotting away the excess, is often sufficient to sear the other vegetables. Add the carrot and burdock pieces and cook, stirring occasionally to keep them from sticking, for about 1 minute, or until the vegetables become slightly wilted and the fried tōfu browns a bit at the edges.

Add the salt and saké, and then add the stock and the reserved enoki stem pieces. Adjust the heat to maintain a steady, gentle simmer. Simmer the soup, skimming away any froth that appears, for about 2 minutes, or until the root vegetables are tender (test with a toothpick; it should meet no resistance).

Add the soy sauce and mirin and stir to blend. Ladle the soup into the bowls holding the enoki caps and *mitsuba.* Serve immediately.

GREEN SOYBEAN SOUP

ÉDAMAMÉ NO SURINAGASHI

The Japanese enjoy puréed soups that are intense in both color and flavor. By distilling the essence of whatever vegetable is being featured, such soups assure that shun, *the seasonal peak of flavor, will infuse the meal. Here, green soybeans, most commonly served in their pods as a beer snack in the summertime, make an incredibly nutritious, delightfully nutty puréed soup served either hot or chilled. The small quantity of thin rice gruel (made from leftover cooked rice from a previous meal) added to the purée creates a creamy, full-bodied soup.*

Traditionally, surinagashi *(literally, "grind and pour") soups were made by simmering, mashing, sieving, and straining vegetables to make concentrates. In the modern* washoku *kitchen, a blender simplifies the process immensely.*

SERVES 4

> 1 bunch fresh édamamé, about 1 pound, pods removed and treated (page 61), or 1 bag flash-frozen édamamé in the pod, 12 to 14 ounces
>
> 1¹/₂ cups Basic Sea Stock (page 92)
>
> 3 tablespoons Cooked White Rice (page 137)
>
> 1¹/₂ cups cold water
>
> ¹/₄ teaspoon salt
>
> 1 teaspoon sweet, light miso, preferably Saikyō miso (page 32)

Bring a large pot filled with water to a rolling boil. If cooking fresh *édamamé*, add the beans to the pot and cook for 8 or 9 minutes after the water returns to a boil. When about one-tenth of the pods look as though they are opening at the side seam, the entire batch should be tender. Test by taking an unopened pod from the pot and pressing out a bean. Bite and chew; the bean should be firm but tender, with no crunch.

If cooking frozen beans, toss them into the pot frozen and cook for only 2 minutes after the water returns to a boil. If cooking fully thawed frozen beans, blanch them for only 45 seconds.

Drain and allow the cooked beans to cool naturally, or fan them to hasten the process. Do not refresh the bean pods in cold water, because they will become waterlogged and lose both flavor and nutrients. Shell the beans, discarding the pods and any thin, inner skins. You should have about 1 cup shelled beans. Put them in a blender with the stock and purée until smooth. If you are having trouble getting the blades of your machine to move smoothly, add a bit more stock or water.

Combine the rice, cold water, and salt in a pot and place over medium heat. Bring to a simmer and cook, stirring occasionally, for 10 to 12 minutes, or until the grains of rice swell and begin to lose their shape and a thin gruel has formed. Remove from the heat and let cool slightly.

Add the rice gruel to the soybean purée in the blender and pulse until smooth. Add the miso to the mixture and again pulse until smooth. The soup can be made up to this point 8 hours in advance of serving, covered, and refrigerated. Do not freeze the soup, however, because the texture will suffer.

To serve hot, transfer the soybean purée mixture to a 2-quart pot, warm over low heat to serving temperature, and ladle into individual soup bowls. To serve cold, ladle into individual, chilled bowls.

和食

Kitchen Harmony

If you want to prepare green soybeans for serving as a beer snack, see Green Soybeans Served in the Pod (page 201). Other seasonal vegetables that can be prepared in the *surinagashi* manner include asparagus in the spring and squashes in the summer.

Harmony at Table

At elegant meals, a seafood dumpling, a small block of tōfu, or another ingredient may be artfully nestled at the bottom of a shallow bowl with the *surinagashi* purée ladled carefully around it. Then, just before the bowl is covered, an aromatic garnish or flavor accent— a sprig of peppery *ki no mé* (see *sanshō*, page 47), a strip of *yuzu* (page 28), a dab of fiery mustard or sour *bainiku* plum (page 38)—is placed on top of the item surrounded by the purée.

RICE

IN MY FAMILY'S URBAN AMERICAN HOUSEHOLD of the 1940s and 1950s, rice was something that was hidden in the back of the cupboard. Occasionally, my mother would empty the contents of the small cardboard box into a sturdy pot about 20 minutes before dinnertime. She would immediately pour boiling water from a screaming kettle over the long grains of "converted" rice and then tightly cover the pot. Just before serving, she would "fluff up" the kernels. At the table, the tasteless stuff would be (thankfully) buried under some gravy or sauce.

Imagine my surprise when I tried to prepare rice that way shortly after my arrival in Japan. Now imagine the expression on the faces of those Japanese women who looked on in disbelief as I mumbled, in halting Japanese, something about how the water must be different. That same evening, I received my first lesson in Japanese cooking.

Preparing rice is a basic skill in the *washoku* kitchen. If I had you by my side, I would be talking you through all the variables in the process as we cooked rice together. Instead, I have written in great detail about how to cook rice, hoping to empower you (and spare you the embarrassment and frustration I experienced many years ago).

Before you begin to cook the recipes in this chapter, I urge you to read carefully Washing Rice (page 136) and Measuring Water and Rice (page 136). Once you grasp the basic procedure and understand the proportions of rice to water when cooking, you will be able to prepare a wide range of rice dishes with ease and great success.

The Japanese classify cooked rice dishes according to how they are prepared and served. The recipes in this chapter are clustered in the same way, beginning with polished white rice and a nutritionally enriched variation of multigrain rice. Next, you will find recipes for *takikomi gohan*, or rice dishes cooked with a flavored liquid rather than plain water. *Mazé gohan*, the category that follows, includes pilaflike dishes in which variously flavored foods are tossed into already-cooked plain rice. *Ajitsuké gohan*, rice that is seasoned after cooking, includes *su meshi*, the tart rice used in all sushi dishes.

Domburi are bowls of rice topped with cooked and intensely flavored foods, such as tempura, curried chicken stew, or gingery soy-braised meat. The rice section concludes with several home-style *washoku* classics: hand-pressed, sandwichlike *omusubi*, both plain and toasted; a thick breakfast porridge called *okayu*; and a snack or light meal known as *ocha-zuké* made from toasted rice moistened with tea.

Washing Rice

To cook rice that is tender, full flavored, glossy, and moist but not sticky, you must remove all surface starch from the raw kernels before cooking. And that means washing the rice well. If you are concerned about the possible loss of nutrients during washing, consider making Rice with Mixed Grains (page 139).

Measure the rice into a large bowl and cover it with cold water. Stir and swish the rice vigorously; the water will become cloudy with starch. This *togi-jiru*, or water from washing rice, can be used for cooking vegetables and for watering the garden, though it is often discarded in the modern *washoku* kitchen.

Drain washed rice in a fine-mesh strainer before returning it to the bowl to repeat the procedure with fresh cold water. Continue to rinse, stir, swish, and drain the raw rice until the rinsing water runs clear. This will probably require 3 or 4 washings. Drain the washed rice well after the final rinsing. Notice that the rice becomes slightly more opaque as the kernels absorb moisture from the washing process.

Measuring Water and Rice

When cooking Japanese-style short-grain rice, the amount of cooking water is always slightly more than the amount of raw rice. When measured out over washed rice, the water level should rise about $1/3$ inch above the rice. Measured from the tip of the thumb (when placed on the top of the rice) to just below the first knuckle (this is where the water line should be), this relative-proportion style of measuring prevailed in most homes when I first began to prepare *washoku* meals. My American hands, though fairly small for my overall body size, were never a reliable "tool" for measuring water when I was cooking rice, so I resorted to using measuring cups. That is when I realized that several so-called standard cup sizes were vastly different!

Most Japanese rice cookers are sold with either an *ichi go*–sized plastic cup or a square *ichi go masu* box. Traditionally in Japan, rice was measured in units called *go* that would fill a single, wooden *ichi go masu* box. The modern cups hold approximately 150 grams of raw rice when they are full; these cups are often marked for metric liquid measures with a line drawn near the top at 180 cubic centimeters. Cups that come with modern Japanese rice cookers hold about the same amount as an American $2/3$-cup measure.

To avoid confusion in this chapter, I have used a standard American measuring cup for the rice and water amounts for both the stove-top and the rice-cooker methods, which will simplify the cooking for you. In the case of a rice cooker, this means you need to set aside the cup measure that came with the cooker and you need to ignore the lines indicating water level on the bowl in which the rice cooks. This way, the yield will be the same whether you are cooking on the stove top or in a rice cooker. If you choose to use the cup that came with your rice cooker rather than a standard American measuring cup, be sure to use the equivalent water-level line in the bowl of your cooker rather than the amount listed in recipes in this book. And if you use the enclosed cup, remember that yields will be slightly less.

You will need to use the *same* measuring cup for both the raw rice and the water, even though the rice is a dry measure (typically measured in metal or heavy-duty plastic cups leveled at the rim) and the water is a liquid measure (typically measured in clear glass cups with a spout to a line marked on the vessel). I used a dry measure. For the best results, you should too. Because I initially measured the quantities in Japanese cups before converting to American measures, you will notice that I have listed some quantities as "scant," rather than use an awkward fraction.

COOKED WHITE RICE

GOHAN

When I first arrived in Japan, the old-fashioned way of cooking rice in a pot over a wood-fueled stove was fairly common practice, especially in rural communities. As I learned to cook rice, I also learned this jingle that described the process: Hajimé choro-choro (at first it bubbles) / Naka pa-ppa (and then it hisses) / Akagao ga naite mo (even if the baby is crying from hunger) / Futa toru na (never remove the lid)!

Now, at the beginning of the twenty-first century, nearly every Japanese household boasts a rice cooker, either fueled by gas or by electricity. For purists, and for those who have not yet purchased a rice cooker, I offer a recipe for the traditional stove-top method. And for those who use a rice cooker, I review the steps for cooking rice in a thermostatically controlled appliance.

Cooking small amounts of rice is difficult. For superior results, I suggest you cook 2 or more cups raw rice at a time. If you find you have not eaten all that you have cooked, there are many recipes that make use of leftovers. Consider making Hand-Pressed Rice (page 158) and eating the rice triangles later in the day, or perhaps freeze them to toast several weeks later (Toasty Hand-Pressed Rice, page 160). See page 138 for reheating instructions for leftover rice.

MAKES 2 CUPS COOKED RICE

1 cup Japanese-style white rice, washed (page 136)

1 cup plus 2 tablespoons cold water, preferably filtered or spring water

MAKES 3 CUPS COOKED RICE

$1^1/_2$ cup Japanese-style white rice, washed (page 136)

$1^3/_4$ scant cups cold water, preferably filtered or spring water

MAKES 4 CUPS COOKED RICE

2 cups Japanese-style white rice, washed (page 136)

$2^1/_3$ cups cold water, preferably filtered or spring water

MAKES 5 CUPS COOKED RICE

$2^1/_2$ cups Japanese-style white rice, washed (page 136)

$2^3/_4$ scant cups cold water, preferably filtered or spring water

MAKES 6 CUPS COOKED RICE

3 cups Japanese-style white rice, washed (page 136)

$3^1/_4$ cups cold water, preferably filtered or spring water

To cook the rice on the stove top, place the washed and drained rice in a sturdy, straight-sided pot. A 2-quart pot should suffice for cooking 1 or 2 cups raw rice, but you will need a 3- or 4-quart size for cooking the larger amounts. Add the appropriate amount of water and cover the pot with a tight-fitting lid. Ideally, the rice should sit in its measured water for 10 minutes before cooking; as the rice soaks, the dried grains swell slightly and become opaque, ensuring tender cooked rice. If you are pressed for time, add a few extra drops of water.

Place the pot over high heat and bring the water to a rolling boil. It is best not to remove the lid (remember the rice-cooking jingle) to check on progress. Instead, rely on other clues. You will hear bubbling noises (this is the *choro-choro* stage of the jingle) and see the lid begin to dance. Depending on the strength of your heat source and the amount of rice you are cooking, it should take 3 to 5 minutes to reach this stage.

Reduce the heat to low and continue to cook for about 5 minutes, or until you hear a low hissing sound (this is the *naka pa-ppa* stage) signaling that the water is nearly absorbed. If you must check on progress, peek quickly, replacing the lid immediately. Increase the heat to high again for 30 seconds to dry off the rice.

Remove the pot from the heat, still tightly covered, and let the rice stand for at least 10 minutes. Even if you wish to serve the rice piping hot, these final minutes of self-steaming (called *murasu*) are necessary to achieve the proper texture. The entire process of cooking rice is called *taku*.

To cook the rice in a rice cooker, place the washed and drained rice in the bowl of the appliance. Add the appropriate amount of water, close the lid firmly, and press the button to start the cooker. Depending on the brand of rice cooker, a combination of beeping or clicking sounds and/or lights will alert you to when the active cooking cycle has finished. Allow the rice to self-steam for at least 10 minutes and up to 20 minutes after the active cooking is completed. If your rice cooker has a "keep warm" cycle, you can hold the rice at eating temperature for up to 12 hours.

A light-colored crust, known as *okogé,* sometimes forms on the bottom of the cooked rice, whether cooked on the stove top or in a rice cooker. This is especially likely to happen when using a flavored liquid, rather than water, to cook the rice. The crust can be broken up and folded or tossed to distribute throughout the rice, or kept separate. Many people (including me) who prefer the crusty ends of bread loaves to the soft center cuts have a passion for *okogé* and will set it aside for nibbling later, topped with a sprinkle of salt.

Kitchen Harmony

In Japan, newly harvested rice, called *shin mai,* comes to market from September through November; in America, it is often sold as "new crop rice." You add less water when cooking it than when cooking rice harvested the previous year. If you have access to new crop rice where you live, be stingy when measuring your cooking water. Conversely, if you are cooking with "old" rice (including rice you have had sitting in your cupboard for more than year), be a bit generous with measuring water.

Reheating Leftover Rice

Leftover cooked rice, briefly reheated, can be topped with other foods to make *domburi*-style dishes, such as in Chicken Omelet Over Rice (page 156), Rice Topped with Tempura (page 154), or Rice Bowl with Three-Colored Topping (page 153). Rice Curry (page 155), Gingery Seared Pork (page 258), or Soy-Stewed Bits of Beef (page 266) can also be served over a bed of rice. In addition, leftover rice is perfect for making a soothing porridge (page 164) or a tea-flavored rice soup (page 162).

You can also refrigerate leftover cooked rice for up to 3 days or freeze it for up to 1 month. I often store leftover rice in zippered plastic bags. To reheat frozen cooked rice, use either a microwave oven or a steamer. If you are using a microwave oven, place the frozen rice in its storage bag with the sealed end open on a microwave-safe plate. Heat for 2 to $2^1/_2$ minutes on the highest setting. If the rice is merely cold from having been refrigerated, 1 minute in the microwave should suffice to restore it to just-cooked warmth. Flip the storage bag over, and check to see how warm and pliable the rice has become. Heat for another minute, if necessary. Just before serving, the rice can be heated once more for 30 or 40 seconds on the highest setting.

If you are using a steamer, line it with a *sarashi* cloth (page 77) or a double thickness of cheesecloth that will be large enough to enclose the rice loosely, in a pouchlike manner. First rinse the cloth in cold water and wring it out well before spreading it out in the top layer of a tiered steamer or in a removable steamer basket. Place the rice on the cloth and bring up the outer edges to enclose it loosely. You can hold the edges together with a clip or safety pin. Steam over boiling water for 4 or 5 minutes for frozen rice, or 2 or 3 minutes for cold rice.

RICE WITH MIXED GRAINS

ZAKKOKU MAI

Rice in Japan has historically been both nourishment and wealth. The yield of any field of rice was (and still is) calculated in koku, *which was (but no longer is) a measure of a person's fortune.*

In feudal times, farmers who tilled the fields could not afford to eat the rice they grew, and most of them ate other grains, such as millet and barley. Today's health-conscious Japanese have redis- covered the nutritional value of these grains, and a commercial product known as zakkoku mai, a mixture of millet, buckwheat, and other whole grains and seeds that can be added to short-grain polished rice, has become popular. You can make your own version by using a combination of grains available in groceries and health- foods stores in your community. Directions on figuring the correct ratio of mixed grains to rice are included in the pantry (page 41).

If you are concerned about the loss of nutrients in polished rice, and you enjoy eating nutty-flavored, multitextured rice, you will appreciate this mixed-grain rice. It can be successfully substituted for white rice in nearly every recipe in this book. The major excep- tion, I think, is su meshi, the vinegar-seasoned rice used for sushi. The seasoned vinegar is not easily absorbed by some of the other grains, and the multitextured rice fights for attention with the fla- vor and texture of the fillings in rolled sushi.

Illustrated on page 4

MAKES 3 CUPS COOKED RICE

$1^1/_2$ cups Japanese-style white rice, washed (page 136)

2 tablespoons zakkoku mai (page 39)

$1^3/_4$ cups plus 1 teaspoon cold water

Place the rice in either a pot or a rice cooker, add the *zakkoku mai,* and stir it in for even distribution. Add the water and cook according to the instructions in Cooked White Rice (page 137).

RICE WITH VEGETABLES AND SEAFOOD

KAYAKU GOHAN

This is the sort of dish Japanese home cooks make when bits and pieces of root vegetables begin to clutter their refrigerator or pantry shelves. This pilaf also appears as a side dish with udon *noodles on many restaurant menus, especially in the Sanuki region of Shikoku Island. This is frankly puzzling to many Americans, who seldom consider eating rice and noodles at the same meal. Please do not feel that you must choose between this scrumptious flavored rice and a steaming bowl of thick and slithery wheat noodles (Foxy Soup Noodles, page 172, or Moon-Viewing Noodles in Broth, page 171). Like many Japanese, I enjoy both at the same meal.*

MAKES 3 CUPS COOKED RICE

$1^3/_4$ cups Basic Sea Stock (page 92) or water

1 tablespoon saké

$^1/_4$ teaspoon salt

3 ounces chikuwa (page 17), about $^1/_2$ stick, quartered lengthwise and sliced crosswise into thin pieces

1 very small carrot, about 2 ounces, peeled and thinly sliced or finely diced

1-inch chunk lotus root, about 2 ounces, peeled and thinly sliced or finely diced, or 4-inch piece burdock root, rinsed, lightly scraped (page 58), and thinly sliced or finely diced

2 or 3 fresh shiitaké mushrooms, stems removed and caps thinly sliced

$1^1/_2$ cups Japanese-style white rice, washed (page 136)

1 teaspoon ocean herb salt (see Five Flavored Salts, page 112)

In a small saucepan, season the stock with the saké and salt. Bring to a simmer over high heat and add the *chikuwa,* carrot, lotus root, and mushrooms. Cook for 2 or 3 minutes, or until the vegetables are barely tender. Pour through a strainer, and reserve the *chikuwa* and vegetables and the cooking liquid separately.

To cook the rice on the stove top, place the washed and drained rice in a 2- or 3-quart, straight-sided pot. Measure the reserved cooking liquid and add water, if needed, to bring it up to 1³/₄ cups, and then add the liquid to the pot. Cover, place over high heat, and cook until the liquid begins to bubble, about 5 minutes. Adjust the heat to maintain a steady but not very vigorous boil and continue to cook, covered, until all the liquid has been absorbed, about 5 minutes more.

Remove from the heat and fold in the reserved *chikuwa* and vegetables, distributing them evenly. Re-cover the pot immediately and let it stand to self-steam for another 10 to 15 minutes.

To cook the rice in a rice cooker, place the washed and drained rice in the bowl of the appliance. Measure the reserved cooking liquid and add water, if needed, to bring it up to 1³/₄ cups, and then add it to the rice cooker. Make sure the liquid is cool, or at least room temperature, before pressing the button to start the rice cooker. The cooker's thermostat will malfunction with a hot or very warm liquid. As soon as the active cooking cycle switches off, fold in the reserved *chikuwa* and vegetables, re-cover, and allow the rice to self-steam for at least 10 minutes, or up to several hours if your cooker has a warmer feature.

Just before serving, whether you have cooked the rice on the stove top or in a rice cooker, use a rice paddle to stir the rice and vegetables with light cutting and tossing motions to distribute the bits and pieces evenly. The bottom surface develops a slightly caramelized crust, or *okogé,* that is especially tasty.

Serve the rice hot or at room temperature. Sprinkle each serving with the seasoned salt. Any leftover rice can be frozen for up to 1 month and defrosts well in a microwave (see Reheating Leftover Rice, page 138).

Kitchen Harmony

Should you find *hon shiméji* or *maitaké* mushrooms (page 32) in your market, use these robust, dark-colored mushrooms instead of the more delicate fresh shiitaké. Or, if like my family, you adore mushrooms, use a combination amounting to about ¹/₂ cup total.

If you find some leftover *konnyaku* or *shirataki* noodles (page 28) when looking through your refrigerator, either one can go in with the vegetables and *chikuwa.*

For a purely vegetarian version, substitute finely shredded slices of fried tōfu for the fish sausage, and use dried shiitaké mushrooms instead of fresh. Reserve the soaking liquid from the dried mushrooms to use in place of the Basic Sea Stock.

RICE COOKED WITH NEW GINGER

SHIN SHŌGA GOHAN

This flavored rice, perfumed with aromatic new ginger, makes a lovely accompaniment to simply broiled chicken or fish. Mature ginger can be used, but I urge you to seek out young, tender, sweet-hot new ginger at Asian or specialty-food markets in your community. It will transform a good dish into a sublime one.

MAKES 3¹/₂ CUPS COOKED RICE

1 slice fried tōfu, about 6 by 3¹/₂ inches

Pinch of coarse salt

1 tablespoon saké

2 scant cups Basic Sea Stock (page 92)

2 teaspoons light-colored soy sauce

2 teaspoons mirin

1 small knob ginger, preferably new ginger (page 25), about 1 ounce, peeled and cut into fine threads

1³/₄ cups Japanese-style white rice, washed (page 136)

6 or 7 mitsuba stalks (page 26), trimmed and stems and leaves chopped

Blot the fried tōfu with a paper towel to remove excess oil. If it seems very greasy, blanch briefly in boiling water (page 75), drain, and, when cool enough to handle, squeeze out excess moisture. Slice the fried tōfu into fine strips.

Place a pot, preferably with a nonstick surface, over high heat. Add the tōfu and cook for 1 minute. (There will be ample oil clinging to the surface of the fried tōfu even after blotting or blanching it.) Sprinkle with the salt, stir, and continue to cook for another 30 seconds, and then drizzle in the saké. Add the stock and reduce the heat to maintain a steady but not very vigorous boil. Season with the soy sauce and mirin and continue to cook for another minute. Remove the pot from the heat.

To maximize the aroma of mature ginger, add the threads to the pot now and let cool to room temperature. If you are using new ginger, wait to add it during the rice cooking.

Strain the cooking liquid into a measuring cup, reserving the ginger and tōfu.

To cook the rice on the stove top, place the washed and drained rice in a straight-sided 3-quart pot. Add water, if needed, to the strained cooking liquid to bring it up to 2 scant cups. Add the liquid to the pot and place the reserved tōfu and mature ginger on top of the rice. Cover, place over high heat, and cook until the liquid begins to bubble, about 5 minutes. Adjust the heat to maintain a steady but not very vigorous boil and continue to cook, covered, until all the liquid has been absorbed, about 5 minutes more. Remove the pot from the heat. If you are using new ginger, scatter the threads across the rice now and immediately re-cover the pot. Let the rice stand to self-steam for another 10 to 15 minutes.

To cook the rice in a rice cooker, place the washed and drained rice in the bowl of the appliance. Add water, if needed, to the strained cooking liquid to bring it up to 2 scant cups, and then add it to the rice cooker. Place the reserved tōfu and mature ginger on top of the rice. Make sure the liquid is cool, or at least room temperature, before pressing the button to start the rice cooker. The cooker's thermostat will malfunction with a hot or very warm liquid. Once the active cooking cycle switches off, scatter the new ginger threads across the surface and immediately re-cover. Let the rice stand to allow it to self-steam for at least 10 minutes, or up to several hours if your cooker has a warmer feature.

Just before serving, whether you have prepared the rice on the stove top or in a rice cooker, use a rice paddle to stir the rice, tōfu, and ginger with light cutting and tossing motions to distribute the ingredients evenly. The bottom surface develops a slightly caramelized crust, or *okogé,* that is especially tasty.

Serve the rice hot or at room temperature. Garnish each serving with the *mitsuba.*

RICE COOKED WITH ÉDAMAMÉ

MAMÉ GOHAN

In Japan, fresh green soybeans, true to their Japanese name (édamamé means "branch beans"), come to market on stalklike branches, soil still clinging to their roots, all summer long. To obtain fresh soybeans still on their stalks in America, seek them out at local farmers' markets, or simply substitute the frozen variety. A version of this dish made with fresh fava beans, or sora mamé, is also enjoyed in the summer in Japan. Freshly shelled green peas or baby lima beans, briefly blanched, could be used as well.

MAKES 4 CUPS COOKED RICE

> 1 small bunch fresh édamamé, about 12 ounces, pods removed and treated (page 61), or 8 ounces flash-frozen édamamé in the pod
>
> 2 cups Basic Sea Stock (page 92)
>
> 1 tablespoon mirin
>
> 2 teaspoons light-colored soy sauce
>
> 1 teaspoon soy sauce
>
> 1³/₄ cups Japanese-style white rice, washed (page 136)
>
> 1 teaspoon black sesame salt or ocean herb salt (see Five Flavored Salts, page 112)

Bring a large pot filled with water to a rolling boil.

If cooking fresh *édamamé,* add the beans to the pot and cook for 8 or 9 minutes after the water returns to a boil. When about one-tenth of the pods look as though they are opening at the side seam, the entire batch should be tender. Test by taking an unopened pod from the pot and pressing out a bean. Bite and chew; the bean should be firm but tender, with no crunch.

If cooking frozen beans, toss them into the pot frozen and cook for 2¹/₂ minutes after the water returns to a boil. If cooking fully thawed beans, blanch them for only 45 seconds.

Drain and allow the cooked beans to cool naturally. Do not refresh the bean pods in cold water, because they will become waterlogged and lose both flavor and nutrients. Shell the beans, discarding the pods and any thin, inner skins. You should have about ¹/₂ cup shelled beans.

Combine the stock, mirin, and both soy sauces in a small saucepan and bring the mixture to a simmer. Add the shelled beans and cook for 2 or 3 minutes, preferably with an *otoshi-buta* (page 84) to ensure they fully absorb the flavors of the seasoned stock. Drain the beans, reserving the cooking liquid. Set aside the beans, removing any loose skins.

To cook the rice on the stove top, place the rice in a 3-quart, straight-sided pot. Add water, if needed, to the strained cooking liquid to bring it up to 2 cups, and then add it to the pot. Cover, place over high heat, and cook until the liquid begins to bubble, about 5 minutes. Adjust the heat to maintain a steady but not vigorous boil and continue to cook, covered, until the liquid is absorbed, about 5 minutes more. Remove from the heat, scatter the simmered beans on top of the rice, and re-cover the pot immediately. Let stand to self-steam for 10 to 15 minutes.

To cook the rice in a rice cooker, place the rice in the bowl of the appliance. Add water, if needed, to the cooking liquid to bring it up to 2 cups, and then add it to the rice cooker. Make sure the liquid is cool before pressing the start button. The cooker's thermostat will malfunction with a hot or very warm liquid. As soon as the active cooking cycle switches off, scatter the simmered beans on top of the rice and re-cover the pot immediately. Allow the rice to self-steam for at least 10 minutes, or up to several hours if your cooker has a warmer feature.

Just before serving, whether you have cooked the rice on the stove top or in a rice cooker, use a rice paddle to stir the rice and beans with light cutting and tossing motions to distribute the beans evenly. The bottom surface develops a slightly caramelized crust, or *okogé,* that is especially tasty.

Serve the rice hot or at room temperature. Sprinkle each serving with seasoned salt.

RICE TOSSED WITH RED SHISO SALT

YUKARI GOHAN

In the traditional washoku *home kitchens of the past,* uméboshi *(page 38) were pickled every summer. The red* shiso *leaves (page 26) used to tint and perfume the plums were then sun-dried the following year and crushed before being stored for use as an aromatic herb. Called* yukari, *the dried leaves retain a delightful plumlike aroma.* Yukari *has also been shown to have antibacterial properties, confirming the wisdom of old-fashioned culinary practices. Commercially prepared* yukari *is available at many Asian groceries. Some brands contain chemical preservatives or seasoning agents other than salt, so check the label carefully.*

Long before artificial refrigeration was known, cooked rice was seasoned with yukari *during the late spring and early summer rainy season, when food spoilage was often a problem. The seasoned rice makes wonderful picnic fare, especially when formed into* omusubi *(see Hand-Pressed Rice, page 158).*

SERVES 4

> 3 cups warm, freshly prepared Cooked White Rice
>   (page 137)
> 1 teaspoon yukari (see Five Flavored Salts, page 112)

Turn out the rice into a large bowl, breaking up any lumps using gentle cutting and folding motions. A rice paddle, briefly dipped into cold water, is an excellent tool for this job.

Sprinkle the *yukari* over the rice and toss gently to incorporate well. Serve warm immediately, or let the herbed rice cool to room temperature, fanning away steam as it cools with an *uchiwa* (page 88). Cover and keep away from extreme heat.

Kitchen Harmony

The Japanese enjoy many herb-infused rice dishes. If you have a source for fresh green *shiso* leaves, they make a lovely variation on this recipe. Their herbaceous flavor, vaguely reminiscent of both basil and mint, enhances white rice that could accompany fish, seafood, poultry, or meat. The green leaves, though rich in vitamin A, do not have the antibacterial properties that the red *shiso* leaves have. The green leaves will turn black within 20 minutes of adding to warm or hot rice. To preserve the color of the leaves, lightly salt the warm, *shiso*-flavored rice and serve immediately. Or let lightly salted rice cool completely before adding shredded or minced green *shiso*.

Other fresh Japanese herbs to consider tossing into freshly cooked rice include minced *myōga* (page 26) and *ki no mé* (page 47).

RICE TOSSED WITH SALMON FLAKES

BENI-JAKÉ GOHAN

This is a classic example of mazé gohan *(mixed rice), in which a fully cooked food—in this case, salmon flakes—is tossed together with cooked rice and then accented with minced herbs. Small portions of this pilaflike dish can accompany substantial meat, fish, egg, or vegetable dishes. Mazé gohan dishes such as this one can also be paired with soup and a salad or side dish of vegetables to become the focus of a satisfying meal.*

When planning your menu, be mindful of the five colors, five flavors, and five ways of preparing food. This recipe covers red (the salmon), white (the rice), and green (the herbs), but adding something yellow, either the rolled omelet on page 287 or page 289 or perhaps Lemon-Simmered Kabocha Squash on page 204, and black (or very darkly colored), such as Kelp and Mushroom Relish (page 110) or Ginger-Stewed Eggplant (page 192), will provide nutritional and aesthetic balance.

Salty and sweet flavors predominate here, with the herbs providing a slightly bitter accent; simmering, steaming, and searing with heat are the primary cooking methods. With that in mind, something fried, sour, and spicy, such as Crisp Fried Smelts in Spicy Vinaigrette (page 245) or Sesame-Crusted Tōfu (page 272), would be a welcome addition to the meal.

SERVES 4

3 cups warm, freshly prepared Cooked White Rice (page 137)

$1/2$ cup Seasoned Salmon Flakes (page 246)

1 or 2 teaspoons white sesame seeds, freshly dry-roasted (page 85)

4 or 5 shiso leaves (page 26) or 2 or 3 fresh dill sprigs

Turn out the rice into a large bowl, breaking up any lumps using gentle cutting and folding motions. A rice paddle, briefly dipped into cold water, is an excellent tool for this job.

Sprinkle the salmon flakes and then the sesame seeds over the rice and gently toss, cut, and fold to incorporate well.

Just before serving, trim away the stem portion from the *shiso* leaves. Slice the leaves in half lengthwise, stack them, roll up the stack tightly lengthwise, and cut crosswise to make fine shreds. Cut these shreds in half and scatter them across the rice. Or finely mince the dill and scatter it across the rice. Gently toss, cut, and fold to distribute the herbs evenly.

Serve the rice warm or at room temperature.

SUSHI RICE

SU MESHI

Vinegar-seasoned rice is essential to all sushi recipes. Su meshi (literally, "tart rice") is the word used most often to describe it. At the sushi bar, though, you may hear rice being called shari, *an esoteric reference to the bones of Buddha that reflects the elevated status afforded rice in Japanese society.*

This recipe can be used to make any sushi dish. In this book, it becomes a component of Five-Colored Foods with Sushi Rice (page 147), Sushi Pillows (page 152), and Rolled Sushi, Two Ways (page 149). The quantity given here is enough to make about four portions. To adjust this recipe for other quantities, see my suggestions in the notes. You can halve or double the recipe for the seasoned vinegar (sushi su or awasé-zu). It will keep for 1 month in the refrigerator.

MAKES 4 CUPS COOKED RICE

Seasoned Vinegar

²/₃ cup rice vinegar

2 tablespoons sugar

1 teaspoon salt

1 piece kombu (page 42), 1 inch square (optional)

4 cups warm, freshly prepared Cooked White Rice (page 137)

To make the seasoned vinegar, combine the vinegar, sugar, salt, and *kombu* in a small saucepan. The *kombu* is optional, but it will enhance the overall flavor. Place over medium-high heat and warm, stirring, until the sugar and salt dissolve.

Transfer the warm rice to a *handai* (page 88) or a wide, shallow bowl. Avoid an aluminum vessel, because it will retain heat and can give the rice a metallic taste. Using gentle cutting and folding motions, toss the rice with a rice paddle as you fan it with an *uchiwa* (page 88).

When clouds of steam are no longer rising from the rice, but the rice is still warm, drizzle in some of the seasoned vinegar. Start with just a tablespoonful. Continue to use gentle folding and tossing motions and to fan as you season the rice, steadily adding the remaining seasoned vinegar a few drops at a time. During this cooling-down stage is when the rice is most receptive to absorbing the seasoned vinegar.

Taste occasionally to verify seasoning. If you are making sushi with broiled eel or smoked fish, you will appreciate the extra tartness and most likely use all the seasoned vinegar called for here. If you are making vegetarian scattered-style sushi, however, you may only need ½ cup. Transfer any leftover seasoned vinegar, with the *kombu*, to a tightly lidded jar and refrigerate for up to 1 month. It makes an excellent salad dressing when mixed with a few drops of aromatic sesame oil.

Cover the seasoned rice in the wooden tub or vessel you mixed in with plastic wrap until ready to use.

 和食

Kitchen Harmony

Vinegar-seasoned rice keeps well at cool room temperature for up to 12 hours. Cover it with plastic wrap and place it on a cool, dark shelf. Do not refrigerate or freeze it. Extreme cold makes it tough and crusty, or mushy if frozen and thawed.

If you want to make a smaller quantity, prepare 1½ cups raw rice as directed on page 137. This will produce 3 cups cooked rice ready to be tossed with ⅓ cup seasoned vinegar. To make a larger quantity, prepare 2½ cups raw rice to produce 5 cups cooked rice, for which you will need 1 scant cup seasoned vinegar. Or cook 3 cups raw rice, which will yield 6 cups cooked rice, and toss with 1 generous cup seasoned vinegar.

FIVE-COLORED FOODS WITH SUSHI RICE

GOMOKU CHIRASHI-ZUSHI

A classic preparation from the washoku *home kitchen, this pilaflike rice platter is harmoniously balanced in terms of color, flavor, and cooking method. The five colors are white (rice and lotus root), black (dried mushrooms and hijiki), yellow (egg), green (snow peas), and red (orange-red carrots, pink and red pickled ginger).*

The five flavors—sweet, salty, sour, spicy, and bitter—are all represented, though the focus is clearly on the first three. Soy-simmered mushrooms and hijiki, the sweet-and-sour vinegar used to season the rice and to pickle the lotus root, and ginger all play a major role in defining the character of this scattered-style sushi rice. Spicy overtones from the ginger and hints of mild bitterness from the dry-roasted sesame seeds provide welcome accents.

Slow-simmered foods, such as the rice, mushrooms, and hijiki, and foods seared with heat, such as the omelet and dry-roasted sesame seeds, clearly predominate. They are, however, tempered with bits of fried tōfu (braised with the hijiki) and foods barely treated with heat, such as blanched snow peas, lotus root, and ginger.

SERVES 4 AS A FEATURED DISH, 6 TO 8 IF SERVED WITH OTHER DISHES

4 cups Sushi Rice (page 145)

2 tablespoons white sesame seeds, freshly dry-roasted (page 85)

12 to 15 slices Blushing Pink Ginger (page 223) or purchased pink pickled ginger, blotted dry and finely minced

1/3 cup Soy-Braised Hijiki and Carrots (page 187), drained, blotted dry, and coarsely chopped

Garnish

10 to 12 snow peas, stem ends and strings removed

5 or 6 sheets Thin Omelet (page 290), cut into short, narrow ribbons

10 to 12 slices Sweet-and-Sour Lotus Root (page 222), blotted dry

4 Soy-Simmered Dried Shiitaké Mushrooms (page 188), thinly sliced, squeezed, and blotted dry

1 tablespoon shredded red pickled ginger, drained and blotted dry

With the rice still in the *handai* or bowl in which it was mixed, scatter the sesame seeds and pink pickled ginger evenly over the top and, using gentle cutting and folding motions, toss them with the rice. Add the *hijiki* mixture and toss to distribute the pieces evenly without mashing the rice. The rice paddle you used when cooling the rice is the best tool to use for mixing in these ingredients.

Lightly mound the rice mixture on a large serving platter. The dish can be assembled to this point 3 to 4 hours in advance of serving, covered snugly with plastic wrap, and kept away from extremes of heat or cold. Refrigeration is not recommended, because it makes the rice unpleasantly tough and gluey.

To prepare the garnish, bring water to a rolling boil in a small saucepan. Add the snow peas and blanch for no more than 1 minute. Drain and let them cool naturally, rather than shock them with cold water. When cool enough to handle comfortably, slice them on the diagonal into thin slivers and set aside for garnishing the finished dish just before serving (prolonged contact with the vinegar-seasoned rice will turn the peas from green to brown).

This dish is typically mounded on a large platter from which individual servings are portioned out. It can also be served directly from the *handai* tub in which the rice was seasoned. The five-colored foods—yellow omelet shreds, white pickled lotus root, black simmered shiitaké mushrooms, green snow peas, and red pickled ginger—can be either scattered over the seasoned rice or clustered by color. For suggestions on arranging the five-colored toppings, refer to the notes below. Serve at room temperature.

Harmony at Table

If you choose the at-random arrangement for your sushi platter, scatter the omelet ribbons evenly over the rice mixture to cover the mound completely. Next, scatter the lotus root, then the mushrooms, and snow pea slivers at random, making sure that the yellow ribbons of omelet are still visible here and there. Place the red ginger shreds at the center or in several clusters around the rim of the serving platter.

If you choose to cluster your five-colored toppings, do so either as stripes, wedges, or dots. To make an orderly pattern of stripes, use long cooking chopsticks to guide the placement of the toppings. Lay four chopsticks parallel to each other, diagonally across the mound of rice. Use these as guidelines for filling the space between them with toppings. Alternate colors, beginning with red (pickled ginger), to make a short stripe near the edge of your platter. Next, lay down black shiitaké in a slightly longer stripe. Yellow (egg) will be at the center, and the longest of the stripes. Finish with a stripe of green (snow peas) and of white (lotus root). Remove the chopsticks before serving.

To create four pie-shaped wedges, cross the long chopsticks over the center of the rice. Place yellow omelet ribbons and slices of white lotus root opposite each other, and fill in the other two quadrants with black shiitaké on one side and green snow peas on the other. Remove the chopsticks and place a cluster of red pickled ginger at the center where the colors converge.

Or arrange in neat piles by color, as pictured.

Kitchen Harmony

This dish can be made strictly vegetarian and served as a main course for those who seek to avoid all animal products. When simmering the *hijiki*, use Basic Vegetarian Stock (page 93), and when simmering the dried mushrooms, use vegetarian stock combined with the strained liquid from soaking the mushrooms. In place of the omelet, provide the protein for the meal by using sheets of Soy-Simmered Fried Tōfu (page 283), slicing them into fine shreds, instead of pouches as the recipe indicates.

Conversely, for those who would like to include seafood, consider using *unagi no kabayaki* (page 20), fresh-cooked crabmeat, smoked salmon, or boiled shrimp, either minced and tossed in with the rice or used as a decorative topping.

ROLLED SUSHI, TWO WAYS

FUTOMAKI, URAMAKI

Rolled sushi has become enormously popular throughout the world, and as it travels about, interesting adaptations develop. American contributions to the genre include the now classic avocado-filled California roll (sometimes called merikan-zushi, *or "American sushi," in Japan) and more recently the spicy tuna rolls that expatriate Japanese, such as former Iron Chefs Nobu and Morimoto, created in response to a sophisticated American dining public.*

In this book, I use a combination of cucumber, sprouts, and broiled eel to show how to roll sushi two different ways: futomaki, *the standard plump roll, with the nori sheets on the outside, and* uramaki, *or inside-out roll, with the nori on the inside and rice on the outside.*

Over many years of teaching, I have developed a variation on the classic rolling technique. My version uses half sheets of toasted nori, which I place vertically, with the shorter sides at the top and bottom, on the bamboo mat used for rolling. This method creates what I call mini-rolls, and with a bit of practice, you will soon be making snug, neat rolls, too.

Eel is a tasty and highly nutritious food, and unagi no kabayaki *is fairly easy to find in Asian groceries (look in the freezer section). If you decide to use the* sanshō *pepper, a small packet is often included in the package of eel. If you cannot find the eel, or would prefer to use another food, take a look at the Kitchen Harmony notes for suggestions on alternative fillings, including several vegetarian options.*

MAKES 6 ROLLS, 3 EACH MINI-FUTOMAKI (PLUMP ROLLS)
AND MINI-URAMAKI (INSIDE-OUT ROLLS)

3 full-sized sheets toasted nori

3 cups Sushi Rice (page 145)

1 package unagi no kabayaki (page 20), about 6 ounces

1 small Japanese or other cucumber with edible peel,
   about 2 ounces

1 bunch radish sprouts or other sprouts, about
   2 ounces, rinsed and trimmed

1 tablespoon wasabi paste

2 tablespoons white sesame seeds, freshly dry-roasted
   (page 85)

¹/₄ teaspoon sanshō (page 47) (optional)

Soy sauce for dipping (optional)

Fold and cut the sheets of toasted nori in half to make a total of 6 half sheets, each measuring about 4 by 7¹/₂ inches. With hands moistened in water to keep the rice from sticking to them, divide the sushi rice into 6 equal portions, and coax each portion into a plump cylinder about 3¹/₂ inches long. Each roll will use 1 half sheet of nori and 1 cylinder of rice.

Reheat the eel according to the instructions on the package and cut it into either 6 strips each about ¹/₂ inch wide, or 12 strips each about ¹/₄ inch wide.

The cucumber will taste sweeter if you follow a procedure known as *aku nuki*, or "removing bitterness" (page 76). Once you have completed that step, cut the cucumber on the diagonal into very thin slices. Stack the slices and cut them lengthwise into long shreds, each tipped with dark green peel (page 70). Divide the cucumber shreds into 6 equal piles. Divide the sprouts into 6 bundles, too.

To make *futomaki*: Lay a *sudaré* (page 87) on your work surface so that the slats of the mat run horizontally. If there are string tassels at one end of the mat and not the other, these should be on the far side, away from you. Place a half sheet of nori, rough side up and with the shorter sides at the top and bottom, on the mat. Moisten your fingers with water and then place a cylinder of rice horizontally about one-third up from the bottom edge of the nori. The rice will stick right away, so be sure you position it properly from the start before actually pressing it in place.

(continued)

Flatten the rice, spreading it to cover the lower third of the nori. Slope it as you spread it, so that the far side is slightly higher than the near edge; this will make it easier to shape neat rolls. Moisten your fingers with water to prevent the rice from sticking to them. Leave narrow borders uncovered on both the right and the left edges of the nori to compensate for the rice being pushed outward as you roll.

Spread a thin, horizontal line of wasabi across the center of the rice. Sprinkle 1 teaspoon dry-roasted sesame seeds along this line.

Take a single portion of eel (1 or 2 strips) and lay it just above the line of wasabi and sesame seeds. Take a single portion of shredded cucumber and distribute it evenly just below, and parallel to, the eel. Sprinkle with a pinch of *sanshō*, if desired. Take a single portion of the sprouts and divide the cluster in half. Place the clusters with their stems at the center of the roll and their leaves at the edges, right and left.

Place your thumbs under the near corners of the slatted mat. Hold the edges of the nori in place by pinching with your index fingers. (This will leave three fingers "free" on each hand, to hold fillings in place as you lift and roll away from you.) Lift up the edges of the mat and flip the nori over the rice and fillings, aiming to make contact just beyond the sloped rice. Several inches of uncovered nori should be clearly visible after flipping.

With one hand, hold this nori in place while tugging back slightly on the rolled portion of the mat. This will ensure that your fillings are snugly enclosed. Continue to roll, lifting up the top of the mat and gently pushing the sushi away from you at the same time, creating a bull's-eye pattern.

Let the finished roll sit, seam side down, on a cutting board for a few moments before slicing it. Place the mat loosely over the roll. Then, wiping a sharp knife blade with a damp cloth before each cut, slice the roll crosswise into 3 equal pieces, using the edge of the mat as a guide for each cut. Each piece should be about 1^1/$_2$ inches in diameter and 1 inch thick. Repeat to make 2 more rolls and cut in the same manner.

To make *uramaki*: Lay a *sudaré* on your work surface so that the slats of the mat run horizontally. If there are string tassels at one end of the mat and not the other, these should be on the far side, away from you. Place a half sheet of nori, rough side up and with the shorter sides at the top and bottom, on the mat. Moisten your fingers with water and then place a cylinder of rice horizontally in the center of the nori. Flatten out the rice, spreading it evenly to cover nearly the entire sheet of nori. Leave narrow borders uncovered on all edges, right and left and top and bottom.

Scatter about 1 teaspoon dry-roasted sesame seeds evenly over the rice. Lay a piece of plastic wrap over the rice. Using your open hand to assist, flip the layered plastic wrap, rice, and nori over and replace on the mat, with the plastic wrap side down and the nori on top. Make sure the shorter sides of the nori are still at the top and bottom.

Spread a thin, horizontal line of wasabi across the center of the toasted nori. The wasabi will seem to disappear, as though you are writing with invisible ink, but its fiery flavor will have permeated the nori. Resist the temptation to reapply it, unless you like your sushi at an incendiary level.

Take a single portion of eel (1 or 2 strips) and lay it just above the line of wasabi. Take a single portion of shredded cucumber and distribute evenly just below, and parallel to, the eel. Sprinkle with a pinch of *sanshō*, if desired. Take a single portion of the sprouts and divide the cluster in half. Place the clusters with their stems at the center of the roll and their leaves at the edges, right and left.

Place your thumbs under the near corners of the slatted mat. Hold the edges of the nori in place by pinching with your index fingers. (This will leave three fingers "free" on each hand, to hold fillings in place as you lift and roll away from you.) Lift up the edges of the mat and flip the rice-covered nori over the fillings, aiming to make contact just beyond the eel strip(s). Peel back the plastic wrap and fold it back over the edge of the mat to keep it from being caught and rolled into the center. Continue to roll the sushi away from you, creating a swirl pattern.

Drape the plastic wrap over the finished roll and let it sit, seam side down, on a cutting board for a few moments before slicing it. Place the mat loosely over the roll. Then, wiping a sharp knife blade with a damp cloth before each cut, slice the roll through the plastic wrap, crosswise into 3 equal pieces, using the edge of the mat as a guide for each cut. Each piece should be about 1$^1/_2$ inches in diameter and 1 inch thick.

Repeat to make 2 more rolls and cut in the same manner. Peel off the plastic wrap before serving.

Rolled sushi such as this, made with cooked seafood or vegetables, is fine if left unrefrigerated for up to 3 hours at cool room temperature. Though the toasted nori will lose its crispness if the rolls are not served at once, flavors marry well and the slight chewiness seems to enhance the dish.

Serve at room temperature with soy sauce for dipping, if you like.

和食

Kitchen Harmony

You can use a variety of store-bought pickled vegetables to make an attractive "rainbow" roll. Any one of the following, or several combined in a single roll, will make tasty *futomaki*: *takuan* (page 38), *yama gobō* (page 38), *Nozawana-zuké* (page 36), and *shiba-zuké* (page 38).

Cooked vegetables and egg can also be used to make *futomaki*: Soy-Simmered Dried Shiitaké Mushrooms (page 188), Thin Omelet (page 290), Rolled Omelet, Two Ways (page 287), shredded Blushing Pink Ginger (page 223), and briefly blanched asparagus or green beans.

If you prefer to use seafood other than the eel, try a combination of lump crabmeat, boiled shrimp, or smoked salmon with the shredded cucumber. For the *uramaki*, black caviar or orange-tinted flying fish roe, known as *tobiko*, pairs well with the sesame seeds.

Harmony at Table

If you want to use both types of rolls in a single arrangement, a large brightly colored, monotone platter will make the most dramatic presentation. Many different arrangements are possible, each creating a different pattern. Here is one suggestion:

Arrange the center slices from each roll so that they lean against one another, domino style, alternating a slice of *futomaki* with a slice of *uramaki*. Place this row in the center of your serving dish. Line up the end pieces from both kinds of rolls into two rows. Place one row behind the center row, and the other second row in front of it. The end pieces from both kinds of rolls should be placed with their flat, cut edges to the serving dish and arranged so that the tufts of radish sprouts point upward.

SUSHI PILLOWS

INARI-ZUSHI

A high-volume seller at convenience stores, popular takeout in many department-store food halls, and commonly found on cafeteria menus, Inari-zushi is made by stuffing tartly seasoned rice into fried tōfu pouches that have been simmered in a sweetened soy sauce. The balance of sweet (sugar), sour (vinegar), and salty (soy sauce) flavors appeals to children and grown-ups alike.

The name of the dish is linked to the Inari Shrine near Kyoto, which is associated with foxes. In several Japanese folktales, foxes are portrayed as being fond of fried tōfu. Indeed, the Japanese refer to the golden brown color of the deep-fried tōfu as kitsuné iro, *or "fox colored."*

In Kansai, the area surrounding Kyoto and Osaka, Inari-zushi are typically triangular in configuration, shaped to recall the ears of a fox. In Tokyo, the fried pouches look more like plump pillows.

MAKES 6 OR 8 POUCHES, TO SERVE 3 OR 4

3 or 4 slices Blushing Pink Ginger (page 223) or
    purchased pink pickled ginger, blotted dry

3 or 4 slices Sweet-and-Sour Lotus Root (page 222),
    blotted dry (optional)

2 cups Sushi Rice (page 145)

1¹/₂ teaspoons black or white sesame seeds, freshly
    dry-roasted (page 85)

3 or 4 slices Soy-Simmered Fried Tōfu (page 283),
    drained and blotted dry

Finely mince the pink ginger, making the pieces about the same size as sesame seeds. (You will have about 1 tablespoon.) If you have any slices of the lotus root on hand, especially ones that may not be perfectly shaped, mince these, too, and add them to the pickled ginger.

In a large bowl, toss the rice with the ginger, lotus root, and sesame seeds until all the ingredients are evenly distributed. Divide the rice mixture into 6 or 8 equal portions. Moisten your hands with water and gently shape each portion into a compact ball.

Place a single ball of rice into each pouch of fried tōfu; using your fingers, redistribute the rice to fill the bottom half of each pouch. If you have cut the fried tōfu into triangles, the stuffed portion will be pointed; if you have cut it into squares, the stuffed portion will look like a log. At the open end of each pouch, fold in the sides to look like an envelope flap, and then roll the stuffed tōfu over the flap so that the "seam" is on the bottom.

Your fingers and palms may get a bit greasy from handling the tōfu pouches as you stuff them; use paper towels to wipe your hands when you are finished.

The pillows can be made up to 4 hours in advance of serving, covered snugly with plastic wrap, and kept at room temperature away from extremes of hot or cold. Do not attempt to freeze them; the fried tōfu will be spongy and rather tough when thawed.

If you will be packing the pillows for a picnic, choose an airtight container. The pouches are moist and some liquid may appear after a short time.

RICE BOWL WITH THREE-COLORED TOPPING

SAN SHOKU DOMBURI

When my daughter, Rena, was growing up in Tokyo in the late 1970s, young children were not permitted to use spoons to eat their lunch at school. In those days, lunchtime was as much about learning table manners, appreciation for food (every morsel had to be eaten), and mastering chopstick skills as it was about satisfying hunger.

As a result, eating soboro, *the soy-simmered, fine-crumb ground meat featured in this dish, was beyond her ability when she first entered nursery school. Rena doggedly practiced picking up each cluster of meat, grain of rice, kernel of corn, and small green pea with chopsticks at home during dinnertime. Just before graduating to grade school, she triumphantly packed this rice bowl with three toppings in her lunch box. Beaming with pride, Rena brought home her empty* obentō *(lunch box) and reported on her teacher's praise for her accomplishment!*

San shoku domburi is delicious eaten with a spoon (really easy) or chopsticks (a bit of a challenge).

SERVES 4

Gingery Ground Chicken (page 258)

1 cup fresh or thawed frozen shelled green peas

1 cup fresh or thawed frozen corn kernels

Boiling water, if needed

3 cups Cooked White Rice (page 137), freshly cooked and
    warm or reheated (page 138)

1 tablespoon shredded red pickled ginger or 4 cherry
    tomatoes (optional)

$^1/_2$ sheet toasted nori, crumbled (optional)

If the chicken is freshly prepared, keep it hot. If it has been refrigerated or frozen and thawed, place in a skillet over high heat and stir until hot to break up the bits of meat into small clusters.

If you are using fresh peas and corn, bring a small saucepan filled with water to a rolling boil, add the peas, and cook for about 3 minutes, or until just tender. Drain and set aside. Repeat with the fresh corn. Or, if using frozen vegetables, place the peas and corn in separate small heatproof bowls, pour boiling water over them, let stand for a moment, stir, and drain well.

To assemble the dish, divide the warm rice among 4 *domburi* or other deep bowls. Place a single chopstick on the rim of a bowl, laying it across the center. This becomes your guideline for covering half of the rice neatly with the cooked chicken. With a spoon, spread the hot chicken over half of the rice. Now shift the position of the chopstick so that it is perpendicular to its first position, creating a guideline for dividing the uncovered rice in half. Place $^1/_4$ cup of the green peas over one section, and $^1/_4$ cup of the corn kernels over the other.

If you want to make this meal-in-a-bowl satisfy the five-colors *washoku* principle, and are looking for the aesthetic and nutritional balance of something red and something black, place a cluster of red pickled ginger and bits of nori at the center of the bowl.

Repeat this procedure to complete the remaining 3 bowls. Serve with both spoons and chopsticks.

Harmony at Table

If you do not have *domburi* bowls, you can use wide, shallow soup bowls instead. You will need slightly more ground chicken and vegetables to cover the wider surface space. The recipe here would make 3 portions.

RICE TOPPED WITH TEMPURA

TENDON

Generally, the Japanese prefer to keep their rice separate from the foods they eat with it. Domburi dishes, however, are a delightful departure from this norm. The word refers to both the deep ceramic bowl and the heaping portion of rice topped with sauced meat, fish, or vegetables that is served in it.

Unlike the spare Zen-inspired platters or exquisitely land-scaped presentations so many Americans conjure up when they hear "Japanese food," domburi dishes are the epitome of gener-ously portioned, casually arranged food. Toppings are often left-overs from another meal. In this recipe, leftover batter-fried shredded-vegetable "pancakes" are given a second chance to please.

SERVES 4

> 8 Tempura Pancakes, Temple Vegetarian Style
> (page 210), freshly fried or previously fried and
> refrigerated or frozen
>
> $^1/_3$ cup Basic Sea Stock (page 92)
>
> $1^1/_2$ tablespoons Seasoned Soy Concentrate (page 96)
>
> 3 cups Cooked White Rice (page 137), freshly cooked and
> warm or reheated (page 138)
>
> $^1/_2$ sheet toasted nori, crumbled or cut into narrow
> threads with scissors
>
> 1 scallion, white and green portions finely chopped
> (optional)

To reheat previously made and refrigerated or frozen tempura pancakes, use a toaster oven or a conventional oven. In either case, if using frozen pancakes, take them directly from the freezer, unwrapping them just before placing them in the oven.

If using a conventional oven, preheat to 250°F. Place the refrigerated or frozen pancakes on a rack set over a foil-lined baking pan. To maximize reflective heat from the foil, have the shiny side face up. Bake for 4 or 5 minutes for refrigerated pancakes and 7 or 8 minutes for frozen pancakes, or until warm and dry. If necessary, cover the pancakes lightly with foil, shiny side down, after 2 or 3 minutes, to prevent the edges from scorching.

If using a toaster oven, place the pancakes on a ridged foil pan that fits about 2 inches below the heat coils. "Toast" the pancakes for $1^1/_2$ minutes on a medium-high setting, then flip them over and repeat for another minute. Blot away any mois-ture with paper towels and let the pancakes sit for 3 or 4 min-utes before toasting them again for another minute on each side. If you are reheating refrigerated pancakes, 1 minute of toasting on each side should suffice. If necessary, to prevent the edges from scorching, cover the pancakes lightly with foil after flipping them over.

In a small saucepan, combine the stock and soy concen-trate. Bring to a boil over high heat, stirring constantly. When it becomes foamy, lower the heat and continue to cook for a minute or two, or until it becomes reduced by half and slightly syrupy.

To assemble the *domburi,* divide the warm rice among individual deep bowls and scatter the nori over the top. One at a time, quickly dip each of the pancakes into the warm sauce and place on top of the nori-covered rice. If there is a great deal of liquid left in the saucepan, continue to cook, reducing the amount to about 2 tablespoons. Spoon this remaining "gravy" over the 4 portions of tempura-topped rice and serve immediately.

If there is no other spicy element in your menu, garnish-ing the bowls with the chopped scallion makes a fine accent.

和食

Kitchen Harmony

If you want to make this dish vegetarian, or do not have any Basic Sea Stock or Seasoned Soy Concentrate already on hand, you can make a quick sauce by combining 1 tablespoon each sugar and saké with 2 tablespoons soy sauce in a small saucepan. Cook over medium heat, stirring, for 3 or 4 minutes, or until the sugar dissolves and the sauce is slightly reduced.

Harmony at Table

Traditional *domburi* bowls are ideal for serving this dish, though any large, deep bowls will do. Ordinary rice bowls will be too small, unless you want to make mini-versions of the dish. If you find yourself making soup noodles such as Moon-Viewing Noodles in Broth (page 171) or Foxy Soup Noodles (page 172) often, as well as *domburi* dishes, it will be worth seeking out the proper bowls.

RICE CURRY

KARÉ RAISU

For more than a hundred years, the Japanese have made a dish they call karé raisu, *a stew of onions, potatoes, carrots, and meat (most often chicken) in a thick, turmeric-tinted sauce that they serve with a plate of white rice. Like other dishes the Japanese call* yōshoku *(literally, "Western-style food") it is a hybrid, albeit one that was vaguely inspired by the cuisine of India, or more likely British raj cooking.*

In hotel restaurants in Japan, the thick curry is brought to the table with fanfare, in a silver-plated gravy boat with ladle, and accompanied by chutneylike pickles. Home-style Japanese cooking tends to spoon the curry to the side of a mound of white rice and serve it with pickled ginger and rakkyō. *Either way, the stew and rice are mixed with a large spoon as they are eaten. A green salad, dressed in vinaigrette, is often served in addition.*

For decades now, in various surveys conducted throughout Japan, karé raisu *has remained in the top ten favorite dishes among schoolchildren. Both in home cooking, when it is usually made from a packaged curry roux, and in* yōshoku ya *(Western-style restaurants), when it is typically made from scratch and slowly simmered,* karei raisu *is ubiquitous.*

SERVES 4

$^1/_2$ cup fresh or thawed frozen shelled green peas

4 small, red-skinned potatoes, about 2 ounces each, peeled and quartered

2 carrots, about 3 ounces each, peeled and cut into $^1/_2$-inch chunks

Tender-Stewed Curried Chicken (page 252)

4 to 6 cups Cooked White Rice (page 137), freshly cooked and warm or reheated (page 138)

1 tablespoon shredded red pickled ginger, drained, or $^1/_4$ cup fukujin-zuké (page 36), drained

8 pickled rakkyō bulbs (page 37), drained

Bring a saucepan of water to a rolling boil. If you are using fresh peas, blanch them for 2 minutes. With a slotted spoon, remove the peas and set aside. Add the potatoes and carrots—the water should just barely cover them—and cook until beginning to soften but still firm. Using a slotted spoon, remove the carrots after about $1^1/_2$ minutes and the potatoes after about 3 minutes and add to the pot containing the already cooked curried chicken. Reserve the nutrient-rich blanching water to use, if necessary, to thin the curry sauce later.

Simmer the curried chicken stew with the potatoes and carrots over low heat for 4 or 5 minutes to meld the flavors and soften the vegetables somewhat. If the sauce is very thick, or the stew looks in danger of scorching, add a bit of the reserved blanching water. Ideally, the finished sauce will be the consistency of hot cereal—thick enough to stay put on the plate without seeping under the rice, but thin enough to eat with a spoon.

Just before serving, add the peas to the curry and warm them through. Serve the curry hot over warm rice with the ginger and *rakkyō* bulbs.

Harmony at Table

To serve the curry home style, place the rice, gently mounded, at the back of 4 flat dinner plates. Spoon an equal amount of the curried stew toward the front of each plate. When portioning the stew, make sure that each person has an equal amount of the vegetables. Place the pickled ginger shreds and *rakkyō* bulbs to the side, where the curry and rice meet.

To serve hotel style, spread the rice evenly across 4 flat dinner plates. Bring the warm curried stew to the table in a gravy boat, with a ladle or serving spoon. Spoon a bit of the curried stew onto the rice at the center of the plate, allowing diners to help themselves to more as they eat. Place the pickled ginger and *rakkyō* bulbs each in its own small bowl or in a single divided dish. Set them on the table in much the same way that olives might be served with an antipasto course.

CHICKEN OMELET OVER RICE

OYAKO DOMBURI

Which came first, the chicken or the egg? This meal-in-a-bowl, with the playful name of oyako *(literally, "parent and child"), allows for either possibility.*

The large quantity of stock may seem a bit odd for an omelet recipe, but this style of loose egg cookery is common in Japan. Here, bits of chicken are first poached with onions in a seasoned broth and then bound with beaten eggs before placing the mixture atop a bowl of steaming rice.

The Japanese cook these omelets in a specialized pan called a domburi nabé *(page 84) or* oyako nabé, *though an ordinary skillet can also be used. Directions for both follow.*

SERVES 2 OR 3

    3 jumbo or 4 extra-large eggs
    2 to 3 cups Cooked White Rice (page 137), freshly
        cooked and warm or reheated (page 138)
    1 cup Basic Sea Stock (page 92)
    2 tablespoons light-colored soy sauce
    1 teaspoon sugar
    1 tablespoon saké
    6 ounces skinless, boneless chicken breast meat, sliced
        slant-cut style (page 70)
    1 small yellow onion, about 3 ounces, thinly sliced in
        crescents
    3 or 4 mitsuba stalks (page 26) or watercress sprigs,
        trimmed and stems and leaves chopped into $^{1}/_{2}$-inch
        lengths
    1 full-sized sheet toasted nori, crumbled (optional)

Break the eggs into a bowl and stir lightly to mix the yolks and whites barely. (Japanese like to make this omelet streaked with white.)

If you are making 2 individual omelets successively in a *domburi nabé,* divide the rice ahead of time between 2 bowls. Combine half each of the stock, soy sauce, sugar, and saké in the pan and place over high heat. When small bubbles appear around the edges of the pan, add half of the chicken and onion, stirring to separate the pieces. Skim away any froth that appears and simmer for 1 minute, or until the chicken turns white.

Pour half of the eggs over the simmering chicken and onion and poach for about 45 seconds, or just until barely set. Holding the upright handle firmly, trace circular motions with your arm to swirl the barely set omelet gently in its poaching liquid (there will be very little liquid left at this point).

Sprinkle with the *mitsuba* and, while jiggling the pan, slide the finished omelet onto a bowl of hot rice. Cover this first bowl with aluminum foil to keep it piping hot while you make the second omelet and transfer it to a bowl of hot rice. Garnish each bowl with half of the nori, if desired. Serve at once.

If you are making a single omelet in a skillet, divide the rice among 2 or 3 bowls. Combine all the stock, soy sauce, sugar, and saké in an 8-inch nonstick skillet and place over high heat. When small bubbles appear around the edges of the pan, add the chicken and onion, stirring to separate the pieces. Skim away any froth that appears and simmer for 2 minutes, or until the chicken turns white.

Pour all of the eggs over the simmering chicken and onion and poach for a little more than a minute, or until just set but still quite moist. The omelet should easily come away from the edges of the pan, floating on the little liquid left. Carefully rotate the skillet in a circular motion, gently swirling the omelet.

Sprinkle with the *mitsuba* and then divide the omelet in halves or thirds with a spatula. Jiggling the pan, slide each portion of finished omelet onto a bowl of hot rice. Garnish the bowls with the nori, if desired, dividing evenly. Serve at once.

Kitchen Harmony

If you are looking to add something black to satisfy the five-colors *washoku* guideline and want to boost the nutritional value of this dish, be sure to use the optional nori. If you are looking for something red and spicy, a few shreds of red pickled ginger, minced and scattered across the rice before the omelet tops it, makes a nice variation.

As I have mentioned, the Japanese prefer this dish with loosely set eggs. If you want a firmer omelet, cook it for an additional 30 to 45 seconds after the eggs are added. You may find it easier to eat this dish with a spoon, rather than chopsticks.

HAND-PRESSED RICE

OMUSUBI

My first meal in Japan was an omusubi *stuffed with* uméboshi *that I nibbled, picnic style, on a train-station platform. The startlingly sour pickled plum was a new, exciting taste for me, and the simplicity of the hand-pressed rice, neatly wrapped in nori, struck me as a clever alternative to the American sandwich. Maybe that is why I think of* omusubi *as the Japanese culinary equivalent of a peanut butter and jelly sandwich—the kind of easy meal that a harried Japanese mother quickly shapes from warm rice, just as her American counterpart slaps together a sandwich for her child's lunch box on a busy school morning.*

Although individuals have their own favorite omusubi *fillings (are you a fan of chunky peanut butter or smooth, grape jelly or strawberry jam?) and wrapper preferences (white bread or whole wheat?), this recipe is standard fare in most Japanese households today. I don't know how deep the history of the peanut butter and jelly sandwich runs in America, but* tonjiki, *the compressed rice balls that Japanese culinary historians believe are the predecessor to modern-day* omusubi, *have been happily eaten for at least a thousand years.*

Illustrated on page 286

MAKES 6 FILLED RICE BALLS

> 4 cups Cooked White Rice (page 137), freshly cooked
> and warm or reheated (page 138)

> $^1/_4$ teaspoon salt

Fillings

> 1 tablespoon bainiku (page 38) or flesh pulled from
> 1 soft uméboshi (page 38)

> 2 tablespoons finely minced Kelp and Mushroom Relish
> (page 110), drained

Wrapper

> 2 full-sized sheets toasted nori

Place the rice in a large, shallow bowl and sprinkle the salt evenly over it. Using a rice paddle or broad wooden spatula, toss lightly to mix the salt into the rice. Use light cutting and folding motions to ensure even distribution without mashing the rice. Tossing the rice also helps to cool it so that you can handle it more comfortably. (That being said, most middle-aged Japanese today mist up with nostalgic appreciation as they recall maternal hands glowing pink from morning *omusubi* making with hot rice.) If you are making *omusubi* to eat later in the day, or packing them for a picnic, it's especially important to salt the rice while it is still hot, because the salt acts as a preservative.

Have a bowl of cold water within easy reach. To keep the rice from sticking to your hands as you shape it, you will need to dip your fingers into the water and "paint" your palms with your wet fingers before touching the rice each time.

Have your fillings ready on a plate. To make 3 each of the *bainiku* and the kelp and mushroom filling, divide each filling into 3 equal portions.

Next, divide your salted rice into 6 equal portions and shape each portion into a loose ball with damp hands. (You may want to set aside a small amount of rice that can be used to adjust the size of individual *omusubi* later, or to use as "plugs" to cover up a filling.) In time, practiced hand-eye coordination will guide you in determining proper portion size. In the beginning, though, you might find using a cup (or small bowl) helpful in shaping the rice. Dip the cup into cold water and shake off the excess moisture. Then scoop the warm, salted rice into the cup, pressing it loosely. Now tap out the pressed rice into your damp hands and lightly shape it into a sphere.

Place a single rice ball in the dampened palm of your nondominant hand. With the dampened fingers of your dominant hand, make an indent in the center of the rice ball.

Place a single portion of one of the fillings in the space you have created. As you press the filling in place, cup the hand holding the rice to enclose the filling. (If necessary, you can add an extra spoonful of rice over the filling, using it as a "plug.")

You can form *omusubi* into spheres or oblongs, though triangles are the most popular shape (and the easiest to nibble, I think). To mold a stuffed rice ball into a triangle, place the ball on the flat, open palm of your nondominant hand. Form a V-shaped "roof" by bending the fingers of your other hand over the top of the rice ball. Exert gentle pressure with the top hand to mold the rice—this becomes one of the triangle's pointed tips—using the extended fingers of your bottom hand to flatten the side of the triangle. With your cupped top hand, roll the rice ball toward you, flexing your wrist up. As you do this, the rice ball will flip so that the edge that previously was formed against your top hand now rests on the flat palm of your bottom hand. Exert gentle pressure again to form the second pointed tip on top.

Repeat the roll, press, and flip motion to complete making a triangle. Stuff and shape the remaining *omusubi*. With practice, you will develop your own rhythm and pick up speed. On a busy day, stuffing and shaping several dozen *omusubi* can be a fast way to feed a small crowd.

If you like your toasted nori wrappers to be crisp, cover each triangle in clear plastic wrap until serving. They will keep for up to 6 hours at cool room temperature. When ready to serve, cut each nori sheet lengthwise into 3 equal strips. Use 1 strip to wrap each triangle kimono style: Lay the nori strip horizontally on a dry cutting board. Place a rice triangle on the strip, centering it on the strip and making sure one straight edge of the rice is flush with the bottom edge of the nori. Lift up the left end of the nori strip and lay it over the rice triangle, on the diagonal, and then tuck the edge under the bottom right corner. This will form the left side of a V. Now repeat with the right end of the nori strip to complete draping the triangle.

Serve the *omubushi* at room temperature.

Kitchen Harmony

In addition to the plum and kelp relish fillings listed here, *omusubi* are often stuffed with *katsuo-bushi* (page 18) that have been moistened with a few drops of soy sauce, or with soy-seasoned salmon. In recent years, gingery soy-simmered ground chicken, known as *soboro*, has also become a popular filling. If you want to try some of these variations, use 1½ teaspoons of the Seasoned Salmon Flakes (page 246) or Gingery Ground Chicken (page 258) for each *omusubi* you are stuffing.

Salted, hand-pressed rice will keep well at cool room temperature for 6 hours; those stuffed with pickled plums will keep fresh for up to 8 hours. If you need to store *omusubi* for a longer period, wrap them individually in plastic wrap and refrigerate for up to 24 hours or freeze them for several weeks. Chilled or frozen *omusubi* are perfect for making grilled hand-pressed rice (page 160).

Harmony at Table

Match the shape of the *omusubi* to your mood or to suit the occasion. Although your hands are the best tools for shaping them, a wide variety of plastic, metal, and wooden molds are available to assist you (see Shaping and Molding, page 86).

The way the nori is draped over the rice can vary as well. For example, a child's lunch box might hold *omubushi* wrapped with nori in the shape of a panda's face, a cartoon character, or even a soccer ball. Scissors are the best tool for cutting toasted nori. Many mothers use different patterns of wrapping nori to help their children distinguish one filling from another. In our household, a kimono-style drape usually signals that salmon flakes are inside, while a wide strip placed under the bottom and extending halfway up each side of the triangle most likely means the *omusubi* are stuffed with kelp. Another way of distinguishing fillings is to dab a bit of it on the top of each *omusubi*.

Special Note on Language

I am often asked to explain the difference between *omusubi* and *onigiri*, the other word Japanese use to describe hand-pressed rice. The answer is simple: none. *Musubu*, from which *omusubi* is taken, means to "connect" or "bring together," while *nigiru*, the root of the word *onigiri*, means to "compress or squeeze." Both words are descriptive of the process of making these sandwichlike foods. Neither the generation, nor the gender, nor the geography of the speaker seems to affect the word choice.

Since the word *nigiri* is often used to describe a style of sushi (nuggets of tartly seasoned rice typically covered with a slice of raw fish), I prefer not to use it when speaking of hand-pressed rice. For me, and about half the population of Japan, the word *omusubi* evokes homemade comfort food—what mama used to make (or should have been making, if she was a good homemaker).

TOASTY HAND-PRESSED RICE

YAKI OMUSUBI

Whether brushed with seasoned soy sauce, slathered with a flavored miso paste, or spread with a nori sauce, I find crusty-chewy, salty-sweet yaki omusubi *irresistible. You can grill any triangular* omusubi *(page 158). However, if you know in advance that you will be grilling your hand-pressed rice, you might want to shape them into patties, which affords a broader surface on which to brush your chosen sauce. Using multigrain rice makes a particularly toasty-tasting, nutritious version.*

Illustrated on page 163

MAKES 6 PATTIES

4 cups Rice with Mixed Grains (page 139), freshly prepared and warm or reheated (page 138)

$^1/_4$ teaspoon salt

$1^1/_2$ tablespoons Seasoned Soy Concentrate (page 96)

2 tablespoons Leek Miso (page 103)

$1^1/_2$ tablespoons Nori Sauce (page 108)

$^1/_4$ teaspoon sesame oil (optional)

Place the rice in a large, shallow bowl and sprinkle the salt evenly over it. Using a rice paddle or broad wooden spatula, toss lightly to mix the salt into the rice. Use light cutting and folding motions to ensure even distribution without mashing the rice. Tossing the rice also helps to cool it so that you can handle it more comfortably.

Set up your work space: Within easy reach, have a small bowl of cold water for dipping your fingers to keep rice from sticking to them. Put the soy concentrate, leek, miso, and nori sauce in separate small cups. Set out a pastry brush for applying the soy concentrate and a butter knife for the sauces.

Have your grilling equipment ready, too. Long tongs and/or a heat-proof slatted spatula will make flipping the rice patties easier as they cook. If you will be using a toaster oven, broiler, or salamander (heat source from the top), line the tray of it with aluminum foil, or use a disposable foil tray that will fit in the space. If you will be using a grill or nonstick skillet (heat source from the bottom), preheat it over medium-high heat.

Moisten your fingers and palms with the cold water and shape the salted rice into 6 round, flat patties each about $2^1/_2$ inches in diameter and $^3/_4$ inch thick. If you are concerned about the rice sticking to your grill or foil tray, dab each patty with a wad of paper towel dipped into the sesame oil. This will barely coat the surface of the rice. If you are cooking previously refrigerated or frozen rice patties or triangles, place them cold on the preheated grill or skillet or on the foil-covered tray.

Cook the patties for at least 3 to 4 minutes if made with hot rice, or 7 to 8 minutes if using previously refrigerated or frozen patties, before checking to see whether they will release easily from the cooking surface. Although the patties may seem to stick initially, as they get crusty they will lift away. If there seems to be any resistance, or the patties begin to separate, place them back over the source of heat and cook for another few minutes. When the first surface has crusted nicely, it will be easy to flip the patties and toast or grill the other side.

Paint the top, crusted side, of 2 patties with seasoned soy sauce, spread the tops of 2 more patties with miso sauce, and the remaining 2 patties with nori sauce. When the bottom surface has become nicely crusted, after about 4 minutes, remove the patties from the heat. Serve warm or at room temperature.

Kitchen Harmony

Toasted rice patties brushed with seasoned soy sauce will keep for several hours at room temperature, loosely wrapped in parchment paper. Or refrigerate them for a day. Soy-brushed toasted patties can be successfully reheated in a microwave oven. Place them on a microwave-safe plate, still loosely covered, and heat them on the highest setting for 20 seconds. Remove the parchment paper, flip the patties over, and heat for an additional 20 to 30 seconds. Patties brushed with miso or the nori sauce do not hold up well to reheating.

Toasted rice patties can be prepared ahead of time without any sauce and stored at cool room temperature for several hours, or refrigerated for up to a day. Briefly reheat plain toasted patties in a toaster oven for 1 minute. Spread with sauce and toast for a final 20 seconds, or until aromatic.

TOASTED RICE IN GREEN TEA BROTH

OCHA-ZUKÉ

Ocha-zuké is Japanese comfort food at its most basic—a reliable standby that can be quickly assembled as hunger or mood dictates. It is a favorite snack of college students pulling all-nighters, salaried workers after an evening of barhopping, and housewives after a disappointing restaurant luncheon with friends, and there are hundreds of variations on the theme.

The recipe I have included here is an especially tasty version that calls for pouring a delicately seasoned tea broth over the toasted rice. You have a choice of toasted nori or seasoned salmon for garnish.

SERVES 2 TO 4

1¹/₂ cups Basic Sea Stock (page 92)

1¹/₂ cups freshly brewed green tea (page 53)

¹/₂ teaspoon salt

4 patties Toasty Hand-Pressed Rice (page 160), without
   sauces, still warm or reheated (see note, page 161)

2 tablespoons Seasoned Salmon Flakes (page 246) or
   1 full-sized sheet toasted nori, crumbled or cut into
   narrow strips

4 or 5 mitsuba stalks (page 26), trimmed and stems and
   leaves chopped

1 teaspoon wasabi paste

Combine the stock and tea in a saucepan and place over low heat until small bubbles appear along the edges of the pan. Season with the salt and keep warm over the lowest heat possible. Do not allow the mixture to boil, or it will develop unpleasant, bitter overtones.

Place a warm rice patty in each of 4 deep bowls. Or, to make a more substantial meal, serve 2 patties per person. Pour an equal amount of the hot tea broth over each rice patty. Garnish each serving with an equal amount of the salmon flakes and *mitsuba,* and a dab of wasabi.

To eat, as the rice patty moistens, break it up with a spoon or chopsticks and stir to dissolve the garnish. Most Japanese drink the broth directly from the bowl, using chopsticks in shoveling motions to scrape up rice kernels that cling to the sides.

Kitchen Harmony

Because *ocha-zuké* is such a popular dish, many commercially produced seasoning packets are sold for sprinkling over cooked rice (hot water is then poured on top). I cannot recommend them, however. Like many fast foods, they contain monosodium glutamate and other artificial flavorings and food-coloring agents.

RICE PORRIDGE WITH SOUR PLUM AND HERBS

OKAYU

Shortly after I first arrived in Japan, I acquired the habit of starting my day with a steaming bowl of okayu. This thick rice porridge is the subtle but splendid setting against which sour, rosy-colored, softly wrinkled pickled plums jolt me, and my palate, awake. Some mornings I add the minuscule semidried sardines known as chirimen-jako to my breakfast tray, along with citron-infused cabbage (page 218). I add shredded shiso leaves to my summer porridge, while in the winter I mix in blanched and chopped radish or turnip tops.

I urge you to try this highly agreeable alternative to sugar-coated cereals and doughnuts with coffee. It is one of several dishes that lured me into a lifelong exploration of Japan's traditional food culture and is easily and quickly made with leftover cooked rice.

SERVES 4

- 2 cups Cooked White Rice (page 137) or Rice with Mixed Grains (page 139)
- 4 cups Basic Sea Stock (page 92) or water
- 1/4 teaspoon salt
- 4 uméboshi (page 38), preferably the plump and softly wrinkled variety
- 4 or 5 shiso leaves (page 26) or a handful of green tops from turnips or radishes or other dark, leafy greens such as kale
- 4 tablespoons chirimen-jako (page 15) (optional)
- 2 tablespoons Nori Sauce (page 108) (optional)

If you like your porridge stick-to-your-ribs thick and creamy, place the rice in a 2-quart pot, add 2 cups of the stock, stir with a wooden spoon to break up any lumps, and then begin to cook over low heat.

If you prefer a thinner rice gruel, first place the cooked rice in a strainer and rinse away the surface starch with cold water. Drain, place the rinsed rice in a 2-quart pot with 2 cups of the stock, and begin to cook over low heat.

Continue to cook, stirring frequently, until the grains of rice swell and begin to lose their shape, about 5 minutes. Season with the salt, add the remaining 2 cups stock, and continue to simmer for 1 to 2 minutes over very low heat, stirring occasionally.

Meanwhile, prepare the toppings. To make the *uméboshi* easier to eat with a spoon, pull the fleshy part from the pits and mince the tougher skins with a knife. Discard the pits and divide the plum mash into 4 clusters, each to be used to garnish a single portion of porridge.

If you are using *shiso* leaves, trim away the stem portion, slice the leaves in half lengthwise, stack them, roll up the stack tightly lengthwise, and cut crosswise to make fine shreds. Briefly rinse these shreds under cold water, then drain, pressing out moisture. Divide the shreds into 4 clusters, each to be used to garnish a single portion of porridge.

If you are using leafy greens, bring water to a rolling boil in a small saucepan and briefly dip the greens into the water to wilt them. Lay these wilted greens on your cutting board and chop coarsely. Gather up the pieces with your hands and squeeze out the excess liquid. Add the chopped greens to the simmering rice porridge, stir to distribute, and cook for 1 minute.

The final porridge can be as thick as oatmeal or as thin as a puréed soup. When ready to serve, fill individual deep bowls with the hot porridge. If you have added chopped greens to the porridge, garnish the center of each filled bowl with some plum mash. If you are topping the porridge with shredded *shiso* leaves, place a cluster next to the plum mash in each bowl.

Put the *chirimen-jako* and Nori Sauce in separate small dishes on the table for those who want to add these condiments to their porridge. Serve the porridge with a spoon and/or chopsticks.

Kitchen Harmony

Strictly speaking, the word *okayu* connotes porridge made from raw rice cooked with about three times the amount of water normally used to cook white rice. In most households, though, *okayu* is made from leftover cooked rice. I suspect the appeal of this dish, and the reason it appears on so many family breakfast tables, is in part because Japanese husbands are so rarely home for dinner.

Years ago, I gave up trying to guess whether my husband and I would be sharing the evening meal. When we were first married, I would ask him, "When do you expect to be home?" Depending on whether he knew in advance of some obligatory *otsuki ai*—the insidious custom of entertaining clients and "keeping company" with your boss and colleagues—he would answer either "early," meaning home for dinner by eight o'clock, or "late," meaning he would be eating out with colleagues or business associates and arriving home well past midnight. But on most days, he would not know until the last minute, and I would not have a clue until he walked in the door.

So, like many Japanese housewives, I got into the habit of cooking an extra portion of rice in the evening, and Atsunori and I began eating the leftovers for breakfast—a single portion stretched to two by cooking it with broth or water. This is the unofficial, yet most common household recipe for *okayu*. For the record, though, *ozōsui* is the correct term for cooked rice that is rinsed and then simmered to make a thin porridge.

NOODLES

NOODLES HAVE A SPECIAL PLACE in the hearts, and bellies, of the Japanese. They regularly, and eagerly, consume huge quantities of soba, *udon, sōmen,* and ramen at home and at specialty restaurants throughout the country.

Yet, in this land where rice is venerated, noodles are considered a snack, not a proper meal. No matter the size of their portions, nor whether they are served hot or chilled, in broth, or with a dipping sauce and condiments, noodle dishes lack the status and stature of rice. Often, noodles appear in addition to rice on Japanese menus, a notion that most Americans find frankly bizarre.

When it comes to noodle-eating habits, the Japanese demonstrate strong and obvious regional allegiances. Because I spent my early days in Japan in the Sanuki region, where my husband, Atsunori, was born and raised, I share his passion for good *udon* and *sōmen,* though in fairness to those who have not yet developed a regional noodle identity, I have included recipes for soba and ramen, too.

Good-quality packaged noodles—dried, shelf-stable semidried, and fresh—are readily available outside Japan. Accordingly, I have directed kitchen activity to make use of these premade noodles to create flavor-packed, nutritious dishes.

A brief word about the etiquette of eating noodles in Japan. Slurping, a noisy action called *susuru* in Japanese, is thought to demonstrate appreciation, and is therefore encouraged. So, forget the table manners of your youth (unless it was spent in a Japanese household) and make lots of noise while enjoying your noodles.

Cooking Noodles

The Japanese prefer their noodles to have *koshi,* or "substance," just as the Italians enjoy their pasta al dente. When testing on cooking progress, the simplest and most effective method is to pluck a noodle from the cooking pot, plunge it in cold water, and bite. Ideally, the noodle will be tender with no hard core; the outer surface will be slippery but not overly soft.

Even small quantities of noodles need to be cooked in lots of water. (The water should be plain, not salted.) I find that a large and wide pot, rather than a deep one, allows me to see what is happening and also permits me to scoop up noodles easily with a strainer without having to dump out the cooking water. Timing and strength of the heat source are critical. You will want to keep a clock or kitchen timer on hand so that you can adjust the heat level quickly (if using an electric range, that may mean keeping two burners going at once, one on high, the other on low). Add the noodles when the water comes to a rolling boil, but begin timing only after the water has returned to a boil. Recheck cooking progress as suggested in each recipe.

When done, scoop up noodles into a strainer and lift from the pot to drain, rather than pouring off the cooking liquid. When preparing soba, this nutrient-rich cooking water is used to thin the dipping sauce that typically accompanies cold soba noodles, transforming the intense soy mixture into a warm broth to enjoy at the conclusion of the meal. Saving the hot liquid from cooking any type of noodles makes sense if you plan to serve noodles hot: the recycled cooking water can be used to warm serving bowls and to reheat previously cooked noodles.

Whether serving noodles hot or cold, the Japanese rinse their noodles well under running cold water to remove surface starch and then drain them.

If instructions are provided on the package you purchase, follow the guidelines printed there. If no guidelines are available, follow the basic procedures described here:

For fresh noodles: If cooking ramen, boil them for 45 seconds and then check for doneness. If cooking soba, boil for 1 minute and then check for doneness. If cooking *udon*, boil for 2 minutes and then check for doneness. Recheck cooking progress at 30-second intervals.

For semidried noodles (*han nama*): If cooking ramen, boil for 1 minute and then check for doneness. If cooking soba, boil for 2 1/2 minutes and then check for doneness. If cooking *udon*, boil for 4 to 5 minutes and then check for doneness. Recheck cooking progress at 30-second intervals.

For dried noodles: If cooking ramen, boil for 2 to 3 minutes and then check for doneness. If cooking *kishimen* (page 34) or *hiya mugi* (page 34), boil the noodles for 5 to 6 minutes and then check for doneness. If cooking soba, boil for 6 to 7 minutes and then check for doneness. If cooking *udon*, boil for 7 to 8 minutes and then check for doneness. Recheck cooking progress at 45-second intervals.

The *sashi mizu* technique: This technique is usually recommended when cooking *sōmen* and sometimes soba noodles to ensure that the core of the noodle is cooked without the surface getting too soft. Choose an especially large pot when the recipe requires that *sashi mizu* (added water) be used.

Bring water to a rolling boil in a large, wide pot. Just before adding the noodles, remove the bands that hold them together as bunches. Drop the noodles into the boiling water, scattering them as though you were playing pick-up-sticks. If necessary, stir immediately but only briefly to keep them from sticking to one another.

When the water in the pot returns to a boil, add 1 cup cold water (this is the *sashi mizu*). Continue to cook until the water returns to a boil. Now begin counting the number of minutes listed as the "cooking time" on the package you purchased. If no cooking time is indicated, cook for 1 minute. Test for doneness as described in the general directions, above. Ideally, the noodle will be tender with no hard core. If it is not tender, add a second cup of cold water and again wait for the water to return to a boil. Retest and cook for another 30 to 40 seconds, if necessary.

If serving precooked noodles cold: You can cook *udon, kishimen*, soba, or ramen several hours in advance of serving them cold. You need only rinse them in cold water and drain again before using. This applies to such dishes as Chilled Udon Noodle Salad (page 173) and Chilled Chinese Noodle Salad (page 178). *Sōmen* and *hiya mugi* noodles, however, cannot be successfully precooked, because they become limp and pasty.

If serving precooked noodles hot: The same rules apply as to which noodles can be cooked in advance for hot dishes as for cold. Bring a large pot of water to a rolling boil just before you wish to serve the noodles. When space in my kitchen permits, I set aside the original cooking water in its pot, lidded, and reuse it. This saves me the time and trouble of washing the pot twice, and it preserves the nutrient-rich water, too (later, when cooled down, it can be used to water plants in a garden or windowsill pot). The water will be used both to reheat the noodles and to warm the bowls in which they will be served.

With a ladle, carefully scoop out boiling hot water from the pot and fill each serving bowl halfway. Place a flat plate over the top of each bowl; this "lid" helps retain heat. Place a single serving of cooked noodles in a colander or strainer that can be submerged into the pot of boiling water. The Japanese use a deep-welled, vertical-handled strainer called a *men koshi* (similar to the *miso koshi* described on page 77, only deeper and larger) to facilitate this, but you can use an ordinary colander or strainer in the same manner. Briefly dip the precooked noodles in the boiling water two or three times, submerging

them for 30 seconds each time and jiggling and swishing them to separate any clusters. Lift the colander out of the boiling water and shake and tap the side after the final dip to remove excess water.

To warm the serving bowls one at a time: Ladle some of the boiling hot water into a bowl. Stir and swish the water gently to warm the bowl. Pour the hot water back into the pot, place the noodles in the warmed bowl, and then proceed to top them with whatever the recipe suggests. Ladle in the hot soup broth and serve. This method applies to such dishes as Soba Noodles with Tempura in Soup (page 177), Moon-Viewing Noodles in Broth (page 171), and Foxy Soup Noodles (page 172).

MOON-VIEWING NOODLES IN BROTH

TSUKIMI UDON

As summer turns to fall, the moon wanes in a particularly luminous fashion. Indeed, the harvest moon is celebrated in stories and songs around the world. In Japan, tsukimi, or "moon viewing," also has a place at table. This soup noodle dish with its circular poached egg (the moon) is one way of enjoying the transition of seasons.

Because the Japanese like their eggs loose, with only a hazy film covering the yolk, they tend to poach them directly in the hot soup, making each portion separately. I suspect you will find it simpler to cook all your eggs together (and may prefer your eggs firm), so I have included instructions for preparing noodles both ways.

SERVES 4

    4 cups Sanuki Sea Stock (page 95)
    1 tablespoon Seasoned Soy Concentrate (page 96)
    4 raw large eggs or Impatient Coddled Eggs (page 292)
    12 ounces fresh or 6 ounces dried udon noodles, freshly
        cooked (page 167) or reheated (page 168)
    1 scallion, white and green parts, trimmed and cut into
        thin slivers on the diagonal
    2 teaspoons peeled and grated fresh ginger (optional)

To prepare individual portions, each with a separately poached egg: Season the stock with the soy concentrate and then pour 1 cup of the mixture into a small saucepan and place over medium-high heat. While the stock is heating, crack the eggs open, slipping each one into its own small dish and being careful not to pierce the yolks.

When the stock comes to a full boil, stir it clockwise in a vigorous manner with chopsticks or a long-handled wooden spoon, forming a whirlpool. Remove the saucepan from the stove and carefully slip 1 egg into the pan, aiming for the center of the vortex. Place a lid or flat plate on the saucepan and let the egg poach by retained heat for about 1 minute, or until barely set.

Meanwhile, warm the bowls in which you will be serving the noodles with boiling water (page 169). Place one-fourth of

the noodles in a warmed bowl. Using a flat strainer or a shallow ladle, carefully transfer the lightly poached egg to the bowl, placing it on the center of the noodles. Gently pour the hot stock into the bowl, taking care not to disturb the egg. The noodles should be barely floating in the stock. Cover with a lid. Repeat to make 4 portions in all, covering each fully assembled serving to keep it hot.

To prepare all 4 portions at once with already coddled eggs: Pour the stock into a saucepan, add the soy concentrate, and place over high heat until small bubbles appear along the edges of the pan. While the stock is heating, warm the bowls in which you will be serving the noodles with boiling water (page 169). Place one-fourth of the noodles in each warmed bowl.

Remove the coddled eggs from their shells, carefully scooping out each one with a spoon to avoid piercing the yolk. Place a single egg on the center of the noodles in each bowl. Gently pour the hot stock into the bowls, taking care not to disturb the egg. The noodles should be barely floating in the stock.

Garnish each bowl with the scallion just before serving. In the Sanuki region of Shikoku, small mounds of grated ginger are typically served separately at table.

———————— ————————

Harmony at Table

Chopstick rests and dishes help set the autumnal mood at a *washoku* table. An easy way to create an early fall mood is to incorporate crescents and full circles, suggesting the moon, at each place setting. Or you can use rabbits: according to Japanese legend, when you look at the moon what you see is a rabbit pounding rice taffy, rather than a man's face or a hunk of Swiss cheese, as in Western cultures.

FOXY SOUP NOODLES

KITSUNÉ UDON

In Japanese folklore, foxes, or kitsuné, *are often portrayed as being fond of fried tōfu . This noodle soup is named for the "fox colored" fried tōfu that garnishes it.*

SERVES 3 OR 4

    4 cups Sanuki Sea Stock (page 95)

    2 tablespoons light-colored soy sauce

    2 tablespoons mirin

    1 teaspoon soy sauce

    6 or 8 pieces Soy-Simmered Fried Tōfu (page 283)

    12 ounces fresh or 6 ounces dried udon noodles, freshly cooked (page 167) or reheated (page 168)

    4 ounces spinach or other leafy greens, blanched (page 74) and cut into 1-inch bundles, or prepared as Spinach Steeped in Broth (page 190)

    6 or 8 slices kamaboko (page 17) (optional)

    1 teaspoon peeled and grated fresh ginger

Pour the stock into a saucepan and season with the light-colored soy sauce, the mirin, and the soy sauce. Place over medium-high heat and bring to a simmer. Press out excess cooking liquid from the simmered fried tōfu and place the slices in the hot broth for 30 seconds or so to heat through.

While the stock is heating, warm the bowls in which you will be serving the noodles with boiling water (page 169). Divide the noodles evenly among the warmed bowls. Top each bowl with 2 pieces of fried tōfu and a bundle of spinach. Adding 2 slices of *kamaboko* to each bowl makes this a more filling dish. Pour the piping-hot soup into the bowls, flowing it in near the rim so as not to disturb the toppings.

Serve immediately with a small mound of grated ginger on the side.

和食

Kitchen Harmony

If you have Seasoned Soy Concentrate (page 96) on hand, you can use 2 tablespoons of it in place of the two soy sauces and the mirin.

Rather than discarding the boiling water left over from blanching the spinach, use it to reheat the precooked noodles and warm the serving bowls.

CHILLED UDON NOODLE SALAD

OROSHI KAKÉ UDON

Obon, celebrated in mid-August, is a time for visiting with ancestral spirits, and most Japanese return to their birthplace in a travel ritual known as sato-gaéri. My husband, Atsunori, hails from Kanonji, a small town on the Shikoku coast of the Inland Sea. I spent my first summer in Japan there, so I consider it my adoptive "hometown," even though I am a New Yorker, born and bred.

When our grown daughter, Rena (currently a New Yorker, though Tokyo born), comes back to visit us, sato-gaéri style, we all go together to Kanonji. With each visit we include a stop at Tsuruya, an unpretentious eatery owned by one of Atsunori's childhood buddies. We catch up with local gossip as we slurp bowls of oroshi kaké udon. *Made with thick, slithery wheat noodles, the chilled salad is topped with a heaping mound of grated daikon and a shower of chopped scallions. On the table is a pitcher of citrusy* ponzu *sauce and packets of crisp toasted nori. The sauce is drizzled over the noodles and then the nori is crumbled over the top.*

Here is my nostalgia-driven recipe for Tsuruya's udon salad. I made this for Rena the first summer she joined the adult work world and, because of pressing business, could not join us on our pilgrimage to Shikoku.

SERVES 4

12 ounces fresh or 6 ounces dried udon noodles, cooked (page 167)

3- to 4-inch chunk daikon, 3 to 4 ounces, peeled and grated (page 59) to yield about $1/2$ cup

1 scallion, green tops only, finely chopped

1 full-sized sheet toasted nori, crumbled or cut into narrow threads with scissors

$1/3$ cup Smoky Citrus-Soy Sauce (page 97)

Assemble individual portions of the noodle salad in shallow bowls or deeply flanged plates. You can use the same tableware you might use to serve a chef's or Cobb salad.

If you have cooked the noodles in advance, briefly rinse them under cold water and transfer them to a strainer or colander to drain. Divide the noodles among the plates, placing a portion in the center of each.

Top each serving of noodles with one-fourth of the grated daikon and a scattering of scallion. Add the nori, in a pile at the center of the mound of noodles.

Serve the noodles immediately with the sauce on the side. To eat, drizzle sauce over the grated radish and toss lightly.

BUCKWHEAT NOODLE ROLL

SOBA-ZUSHI

I first encountered soba-zushi, *buckwheat noodles wrapped in toasted nori, at an upscale noodle shop in Tokyo in the early 1990s. Intrigued by the shape—neat bundles looking just like slices of plump rolled sushi—and pleased with the simplicity of eating bite-sized portions of noodles, instead of slurping tangled masses of them, I decided to try making* soba-zushi *myself.*

Although it was possible to form rolls from randomly placed noodles, results improved dramatically when I borrowed a tying technique from classic sōmen *noodle cookery. Be prepared to practice a few times, but once you get the hang of tying and boiling bunches of prealigned noodles and rolling them up,* soba-zushi *becomes a stunning make-ahead, warm-weather lunch. At lunchtime, a single roll would feed one person; in the evening as an appetizer, two or three slices would make a single portion.*

MAKES 2 ROLLS

   About 10 ounces dried soba noodles, preferably made
      with yama imo as a binder (page 34)
   1 Japanese or other cucumber with edible peel, about
      3 ounces
   1 bunch radish sprouts, about 2 ounces, rinsed and
      trimmed
   2 full-sized sheets toasted nori
   $^1/_2$ teaspoon wasabi paste
   1 tablespoon white sesame seeds, freshly dry-roasted
      (page 85) and cracked or ground
   2 tablespoons Seasoned Soy Concentrate (page 96)
   2 tablespoons Basic Sea Stock (page 92)

Many packages of dried soba noodles come already divided into bundles of about $3^1/_2$ ounces, each tied with a band of paper or pliable plastic. If your package is like that, keep the bands intact for the time being. If the package you have purchased is not divided into bundles, split the contents into 4 equal portions of about 3 ounces each.

Cut 4 pieces of kitchen string (the kind used to truss chickens) each about 6 inches long. Lay 1 length of string on a dry cutting board or countertop and place 1 bundle of noodles on top, perpendicular to it. Wind the string twice around one end of the bundle and secure with an ordinary knot. Pull tightly to make sure the string is snug. Stand the noodles up to make sure they are perfectly flush to the board and that the string is as close to the edge as possible without having it slip off. Secure the string with a square knot. If your noodles were prebundled with a band, tie them at one end as just described before carefully slipping off the manufacturer's band from the other end. Repeat to make 3 more bundles of noodles, each tied at one end and open at the other.

Bring several quarts of water to a rolling boil in a deep, wide pot. Holding a single bundle of noodles by the twine with which it is tied, swish the noodles in the boiling water to separate out individual "strands." Then gently release the bundle of noodles into the pot of boiling water. Use long cooking chopsticks to gently poke the bundle and separate the strands.

When the water returns to a boil, adjust the heat to maintain a steady but not particularly vigorous boil and begin counting the number of minutes listed on the package. If there is no indication of time, start with 4 minutes. Test the end of a strand; it should be firm but cooked through. If necessary, cook the bundle for another minute and test again.

(continued)

Buckwheat Noodle Roll served with Sesame-Crusted Tōfu (page 272)

If the noodles are still not tender, cover the pot but remove it from the heat and let the bundle self-steam (what the Japanese call *murasu*) for another 1 or 2 minutes. Retest for doneness, extending the self-steaming time, if necessary, by 30- or 40-second intervals between tests. With a strainer, carefully lift the cooked noodles out of the pot and transfer them to a bowl of ice water. Reserve the *soba yu,* or water in which the noodles were cooked.

Gently "comb out" the tangles from the noodles and then lift the bundle from the cold water. Allow any excess water to drip back into the bowl and fan the noodles out on a flat plate or board. If you want to hold the cooked noodles for several hours or more before rolling, lay plastic wrap on your cutting board and spread the noodles out on it. Fold the wrap to cover the noodles completely and refrigerate until ready to use.

Cook the remaining noodle bundles using the same water. (Often, when serving the noodles *zaru* style on a bamboo tray, the *soba yu* is reserved and served from red lacquer pitchers, to thin the intense dipping sauce. The resulting broth, packed with buckwheat's nutrients, is drunk at the conclusion of the meal.)

The cucumber will taste sweeter if you follow a procedure known as *aku nuki,* or "removing bitterness" (page 76). Once you have completed that step, cut the cucumber on the diagonal into very thin slices. Stack the slices and cut them lengthwise into long shreds, each tipped with dark green peel (page 70). Divide the cucumber shreds into 2 equal piles.

Divide the radish sprouts into 4 equal bundles, keeping the stems aligned.

Lay a *sudaré* (page 87) on your work surface so that the slats of the mat run horizontally. If there are string tassels at one end of the mat and not the other, these should be on the far side, away from you. Place a full sheet of nori, rough side up and with the shorter sides at the top and bottom, on the mat.

Each roll uses 2 bundles of noodles. Place 1 bundle of noodles on the nori with the open, fanned-out end aligned to the right, and the tied end hanging over the left edge of the mat. Next, place the second bundle in the same manner, but farther away and with the open, fanned-out end aligned to the left, and the tied end hanging over the right edge of the mat. The noodles should be spread out in an even layer with just a bit of overlap in the center, and with an uncovered border of nori on top to ensure complete coverage of the contents once the roll is formed. Trim away the tied ends of the noodles on the right and the left.

"Paint" a horizontal stripe of wasabi across the center of the noodles and sprinkle half of the sesame seeds over it. Scatter half of the shredded cucumbers over the sesame seeds and then top with 2 clusters of the sprouts, their stems at the center of the roll and their tufts at the edges, right and left.

Place your thumbs under the near corners of the slatted mat. Hold the edges of the nori in place by pinching with your index fingers. (This will leave three fingers "free" on each hand, to hold fillings in place as you lift and roll away from you.) Lift up the edges of the mat and flip the nori over the noodles and fillings, aiming to make contact just beyond the sloped noodles. An inch or so of uncovered nori should be clearly visible after flipping.

With one hand, hold this nori in place while tugging back slightly on the rolled portion of the mat. This will ensure that your fillings are snugly enclosed. Continue to roll, lifting up the top of the mat and gently pushing the noodle sushi away from you at the same time.

Let the finished roll sit, seam side down, on a cutting board while you make the second one.

Place the mat loosely over the first roll. Wiping a sharp knife blade with a damp cloth before each cut, slice the roll crosswise into 6 equal pieces, using the edge of the mat as a guide for each cut. Repeat with the second roll.

Arrange the slices on a platter. In a small bowl, thin the soy concentrate with the stock and serve as a dipping sauce.

—— 和食 ——

Kitchen Harmony

Toasted nori will lose its crispness if the noodle rolls are not served at once, though, surprisingly, the slight chewiness of the wrapping does not detract from the dish. The rolls are best cut just before serving. If you have cut them in advance, cover with plastic wrap to keep the noodles from drying out at the edges.

Many kinds of fillings can be used in addition to, or instead of, the cucumber and radish sprouts, such as lump crabmeat (or imitation crab), avocado wedges, and/or julienne of smoked turkey or ham. Or, if you wish to keep the rolls vegetarian, try store-bought pickled vegetables, such as *takuan* (page 38), *yama gobō* (page 38), *Nozawana-zuké* (page 37), and *shiba-zuké* (page 38).

If you do not have any Seasoned Soy Concentrate on hand, you can make a dipping sauce: Place a 1-inch square of *kombu* (page 42) in a saucepan with ½ cup soy sauce, 3 tablespoons sugar, and 2 tablespoons saké. Set the saucepan over low heat and cook, stirring occasionally, until the sugar dissolves and the liquid is simmering. Remove from the heat and immediately add 1 or 2 tablespoons *katsuo-bushi* (page 18). Let cool to room temperature and then strain through a fine-mesh strainer. The sauce will keep in a tightly covered container in the refrigerator for up to 1 month.

SOBA NOODLES WITH TEMPURA IN SOUP

TEMPURA SOBA

Soba noodles are ubiquitous in their native Japan, and increasingly popular in America, too. In their homeland, the natural whole-grain, mildly nutty flavor of the noodles is referred to as sobokuna aji, *or "a rustic taste."*

Tempura soba—*combining buckwheat noodles in a piping-hot, smoky soy stock with batter-fried tempura—is a popular menu item. The version I offer here makes use of lacy tempura pancakes.*

SERVES 4

8 Tempura Pancakes, Temple Vegetarian Style
    (page 210), freshly fried or previously fried and
    refrigerated or frozen
3½ cups Basic Sea Stock (page 92) or Basic Vegetarian
    Stock (page 93)
¼ tablespoons Seasoned Soy Concentrate (page 96)
1 pound fresh soba noodles or 8 ounces dried soba
    noodles, freshly cooked (page 167) or reheated
    (page 168)
7 or 8 mitsuba stalks (page 26) or flat-leaf parsley sprigs,
    trimmed and coarsely chopped
¼ teaspoon shichimi tōgarashi (page 47)

To reheat previously made and refrigerated or frozen tempura pancakes, follow the directions in Kitchen Harmony notes included with the tempura pancakes recipe.

Meanwhile, pour the stock into a saucepan, add the soy concentrate, and stir to mix thoroughly. Place over medium-high heat, bring almost to a boil, and then adjust the heat to keep the stock at a gentle simmer. Warm the bowls in which you will be serving the noodles with boiling water (page 169).

Divide the noodles evenly among the warmed bowls. Pour the stock into the bowls, again dividing evenly. Lay 2 pieces of tempura pancakes over each portion. Finally, garnish each serving with an equal amount of the *mitusba* and sprinkle with an equal amount of the *shichimi tōgarashi*. Serve immediately.

Kitchen Harmony

If you do not have any Seasoned Soy Concentrate on hand, the stock can be seasoned in the following manner: In a saucepan, combine the stock with 2 tablespoons light-colored soy sauce, 1 tablespoon soy sauce, and 3 tablespoons mirin. Set the saucepan over low heat and cook, stirring occasionally, until the liquid is simmering. Remove from the heat and immediately add 3 tablespoons *katsuo-bushi* (page 18). After the flakes have sunk to the bottom of the pot, strain the stock into another pan and use it as directed in the recipe.

CHILLED CHINESE NOODLE SALAD

HIYASHI CHŪKA

Despite its name, this cold noodle salad, which calls for ramen, sometimes labeled chūka soba, *seems to be a Japanese invention, one that became popular in the postwar years and remains a favorite in many households today. When summer arrives, noodle shops throughout the country offer some variation on the* hiyashi chūka *theme. I prefer the more robust creamy-style dressing on all but the hottest, stickiest days of the year, when I find the lighter "clear" dressing is more to my liking.*

SERVES 4

Creamy-Style Dressing
2 tablespoons Basic Sea Stock (page 92) or water
$1/3$ cup Creamy Sesame-Miso Sauce (page 100)
$1/2$ teaspoon light-colored soy sauce

Clear-Style Dressing
$1/3$ cup rice vinegar, preferably junmai su (page 50)
1 tablespoon sugar
2 tablespoons soy sauce
1 tablespoon sesame oil

1 pound fresh or 8 ounces dried ramen
1 teaspoon sesame oil

Garnishes
2 Japanese or other cucumber with edible peel, total of about 6 ounces
4 slices baked ham, about 3 ounces total weight, cut into narrow strips $1^1/2$ inches long
4 Soy-Simmered Dried Shiitaké Mushrooms (page 188), thinly sliced
3 or 4 sheets Thin Omelet (page 290), cut into narrow strips $1^1/2$ inches long

1 ripe tomato, about 4 ounces, peeled and cut into
   8 wedges, or 1 ounce red pickled ginger, drained and
   shredded (optional)

1 tablespoon white sesame seeds, freshly dry-roasted
   (page 85) (optional)

1 teaspoon Japanese mustard (optional)

Prepare either or both dressings at least 2 to 3 hours, or up to a week, in advance so that they will be well chilled when serving. To make the creamy dressing, stir the stock into the thick sesame-miso mixture to thin it and then stir in the light-colored soy sauce. Transfer the dressing to an attractive pitcher that can come to table, cover, and refrigerate.

To make the clear dressing, combine the vinegar and sugar in a small saucepan and cook over low heat, stirring constantly, until the sugar has melted. Remove from the heat and stir in the soy sauce and sesame oil until well mixed. Transfer the dressing to a bottle or jar, cap tightly, and shake vigorously. Refrigerate the dressing and then transfer to an attractive pitcher to serve.

Cook the noodles according to package instructions or as directed on page 167. Drain, rinse in cold water, and drain again before tossing with the sesame oil. Divide the noodles among 4 plates. Ideally, the plates will be about 6 inches wide (to allow the noodles to be spread out properly) and have a flange or lip at the rim (to keep the dressing from overflowing). Or use shallow bowls.

The cucumbers will taste sweeter if you follow a procedure known as *aku nuki*, or "removing bitterness" (page 76). Next, cut the cucumbers in half lengthwise and place them, cut sides down, on the cutting board. Slice the halves crosswise on the diagonal into very thin, elongated half-moons.

Top each serving of noodles with clusters of cucumber half-moons, ham strips, mushroom slices, and omelet strips, arranged like the spokes of a wheel. Place 2 wedges of tomato or a cluster of shredded red pickled ginger at the center of each serving, if desired. To add textural interest to the dish, garnish each plate with an equal amount of the sesame seeds.

Serve with either or both dressings. Diners should pour their dressing of choice over the salad and toss to mix. If you want to add a fiery accent to the clear dressing, place a dab of mustard on the rim or edge of each bowl or dish, to be stirred, a bit at a time, into the noodles as they are eaten.

Kitchen Harmony

Another kind of Chinese noodle that the Japanese call *harusamé*, or "spring rain" (page 34), is delicious dressed with either the creamy or the clear dressing. Using 6 ounces of *harusamé*, first soften the noodles by placing them in a saucepan with just-boiled water. Let soak for 2 to 3 minutes. Place over high heat and cook for 2 minutes, or until the water returns to a boil. Drain and let cool. The noodles will clump together slightly but when tossed with sesame oil, they will separate.

Harmony at Table

With *washoku* principles of color, taste, and varied preparation methods in mind, this noodle salad plate becomes a light meal. Yellow egg, green cucumber, red tomato or pickled ginger, black mushrooms, and white sesame seeds provide a lively visual stimulant (and ensure nutritional balance) to a heat-wilted summer appetite. Sweet, sour, and salty flavors predominate, though the Chinese-style noodles, made with baking soda, have a slightly bitter edge and the pickled ginger and fiery mustard provide spicy accents. Using fresh and soy-simmered vegetables, boiled noodles, baked ham, and a skillet-seared omelet provide a variety of cooking methods.

THIN NOODLES ON ICE

SŌMEN

When the first steamy days of summer arrive, icy sōmen noodles appear on family tables throughout Japan. The early food memories of my husband, Atsunori, include eating nagashi sōmen with his family. Nagasu means "to flow," and this dish is named after the cascades of cooked and chilled noodles sent rushing through a tilted, bamboo trough into a large cedar tub. The idea is to capture the noodles as they flow by. With eight brothers and sisters, Atsunori became adept at strategically placing his chopsticks to trap large portions of the noodles before they reached the tub, or any of his siblings.

Nagashi sōmen used to be a popular summertime item on restaurant menus, especially in Atsunori's home region of Sanuki. Then, in the summer of 1996, a rash of food-poisoning incidents occurred throughout Japan. Although none of the outbreaks could be traced to sharing noodles from the same trough and tub, the government prohibited restaurants from serving nagashi sōmen and discouraged families from this kind of communal enjoyment in their homes.

Nowadays, sōmen noodles are commonly served "on the rocks," swirling in deep, glass bowls filled with glacierlike chunks of ice and water. A chilled, intensely seasoned soy-based dipping sauce accompanies the noodles. As the noodles are dipped, the sauce gets diluted with melted ice, so resist the temptation to thin it with water or stock.

SERVES 4

Dipping Sauce

$^1/_3$ cup light-colored soy sauce

$^1/_4$ cup mirin

2 teaspoons sugar

$^1/_2$ cup Basic Sea Stock (page 92)

$^1/_4$ cup katsuo-bushi (page 18)

6 bunches dried sōmen noodles, each about 1$^1/_2$ ounces

Ice cubes, if serving cold

Condiments

1 teaspoon peeled and grated fresh ginger

4 or 5 shiso leaves (page 26), stems trimmed and leaves finely shredded

2 tablespoons white sesame seeds, freshly toasted (page 85) and cracked or coarsely ground (optional)

Make the dipping sauce ahead of time so that it will be well chilled in advance of serving. Combine the soy sauce, mirin, sugar, and sea stock in a small saucepan and set it over low heat to cook, stirring occasionally. When the sugar is fully dissolved, add the *katsuo-bushi* and immediately remove the pan from the heat. Let cool to room temperature and then strain through a fine-mesh strainer into a small bowl or jar, pressing on the *katsuo-bushi* with the back of a spoon. (The soy-drenched *katsuo-bushi* can be recycled into a tasty filling for hand-pressed rice; see notes.) Cover and chill the sauce well before serving (it will keep, refrigerated, for 5 days to a week).

Cook the noodles using the *sashi mizu* technique (page 168) and drain. Rinse the noodles under running cold water to remove surface starch before draining them again.

To serve the *sōmen* "on the rocks," cook the noodles just before serving. They tend to stretch and go soggy if allowed to sit in water for too long. Fill deep, individual bowls with ice cubes. Lay the cooked and drained noodles over the ice cubes and then gently pour in cold water until the noodles barely float.

Divide the chilled sauce among 4 small, deep bowls. Divide the condiments among 4 small plates: a small mound of grated ginger, a tuft of *shiso*, and a small pile of sesame seeds, if desired.

Each diner seasons his or her dipping sauce with condiments to taste before lifting noodles from the ice water, dunking them briefly into the dipping sauce, and eating with gusto.

To serve the *sōmen* "dry," the noodles can be cooked, plated, and refrigerated (covered) 2 or 3 hours ahead of mealtime. When serving the noodles dry, the chilled dipping sauce is poured over the noodles, like a salad dressing. Since the noodles are not in water, you may want to add a small ice cube to the sauce just before serving to chill and dilute it.

As you drain the cooked noodles, divide them into 4 piles. Each of these will become a single serving. Now divide each of these single servings into 2, 3, or 5 clusters (the number 4 is avoided when plating food because of an unfortunate pun on the word for "death"). Swirl each cluster, much like you might twirl spaghetti with your fork in the bowl of a large spoon, and set the swirled clusters for each serving on an individual plate or shallow bowl. Garnish each plate or bowl with ginger and *shiso* to one side, and scatter sesame seeds, if desired, over the noodles. Divide the chilled sauce into 4 small bowls.

To eat, dress the noodles with the sauce and toss lightly, distributing the condiments throughout.

和食

Kitchen Harmony

The *katsuo-bushi* flakes used to make the sauce are intensely flavored and can be used to stuff hand-pressed rice balls (page 158). After making the sauce, mince the flakes with a sharp knife. Return the flakes to the saucepan and slowly heat them through, being careful not to scorch them. Stir in 1 to 2 tablespoons dry-roasted white sesame seeds. Allow the mixture to cool completely. Refrigerate for up to 2 weeks.

Harmony at Table

In Japan, *sōmen* noodles are associated with the midsummer festival Tanabata. Celebrated on July 7 in most parts of the country (a few regions keep to the old lunar calendar, which puts the festivities in August), the festival marks the time when celestial movements bring the stars Altair and Vega together across the Milky Way. The Japanese Tanabata legend, adapted from an even older traditional Chinese tale, has a cowherd, Kengyu, as the star Altair, and a weaving princess, Orihimé, as Vega. So enamored were they of each other that their work suffered, and the two lovers were banished to opposite ends of the firmament. After frequently beseeching the gods to reunite them, their wish was granted. A brief meeting would be permitted once a year.

Although white *sōmen* noodles are sold at supermarkets year-round, in the summertime you'll notice packages with an occasional noodle dyed a vivid pink (these are seasoned with *uméboshi*, page 38), bright yellow (made with egg and the color enhanced by the addition of *kuchinashi no mi*, or dried gardenia pods), or deep olive (from *matcha*, page 54). These colored noodles are meant to suggest the colored threads from which Orihimé weaves her cloth.

Sometimes *sōmen* noodles are tied into bundles at one end with kitchen string before cooking, so that they appear to flow like the Milky Way. If you would like to try your hand at this, follow the instructions in Buckwheat Noodle Roll (page 174).

To assemble a Tanabata menu, serve chilled *sōmen* noodles with an assortment of small dishes, keeping in mind the principles of five colors, five flavors, and five methods (or at least multiple methods). Yellow, salty-sweet, and seared-with-heat Rolled Omelet, Two Ways (page 287); nearly black, spicy Ginger-Stewed Eggplant (page 192); lightly blanched green beans or spinach dressed in Creamy Sesame-Miso Sauce (page 100); sweet-and-sour Red-and-White Pickled Radishes (page 221); and black-and-white, spicy-and-pungent Broiled Tōfu with Flavored Miso (page 281) would make a fine sampler plate.

CHINESE-STYLE NOODLES IN MISO-ENRICHED SOUP

MISO RAMEN

The ambivalence most Japanese exhibit regarding noodles is especially evident when ramen is the topic under discussion. Even though some people obsess over finding the best ramen and the elaborate rituals for eating it (some contend that the soup must be sipped first, others will insist that the noodles be given priority, still others claim that toppings must be variously stirred or not stirred), they still accord ramen, like other noodle dishes, lesser status than rice on menus. The essence of this culinary paradox was brilliantly captured in Itami Juzo's film Tampopo, a biting satire about a young widow who aspires to have the best ramen restaurant in all of Tokyo.

This recipe evolved over many years, as I prepared the noodle dish with whatever I had on hand at the time. Purists may find fault with my patching together of unlikely elements from so many different ramen styles. The use of iriko to enrich the stock shows signs of my culinary coming-of-age in Shikoku, where I first encountered a broth similar to this one (though without the miso) served at an udon shop. There, it was called shina soba, or "Chinese noodles." Readers looking for a satisfying bowl of noodles will, I hope, enjoy my eclectic rendition heaped with flash-seared vegetables and served in a piping-hot broth.

SERVES 4

4 or 5 iriko (page 17), trimmed (about $^1/_2$ ounce after trimming)

4 cups Smoky Chicken Stock (page 94)

2 cups cold water

2 or 3 scallions

8 or 9 ounces bean sprouts (about 4 cups)

1 teaspoon sesame oil

$^1/_4$ teaspoon salt

1 tablespoon saké

6 or 7 fresh shiitaké mushrooms, stems removed and sliced, or 4 ounces fresh maitaké mushrooms (page 33), trimmed and torn into bite-size pieces

1 pound fresh or 8 ounces dried ramen, freshly cooked (page 167) or reheated (page 168)

3 to 4 tablespoons mugi miso (page 32)

Place the iriko, stock, and water in a 3-quart pot. Set over low heat and leave to simmer for at least 30 minutes and up to 1 hour while you prepare the vegetable toppings. Check the stock every 5 or 10 minutes, adding water as needed to maintain a volume of at least $3^1/_2$ cups throughout the simmering time.

Trim away the root end of the scallions (these can also be added to the stock pot, to be removed later) and finely chop the green and white portions, separating them into 2 piles by their color. Rinse the bean sprouts in a basin of cold water, discarding any bean pods that float to the surface, and drain them.

Place a wok or large skillet over high heat. Add the bean sprouts and the white portion of the scallions. Dry-roast for a few seconds to throw off excess moisture from the vegetables before drizzling in $^1/_2$ teaspoon of the sesame oil. Sprinkle with the salt and stir-fry for another moment. Pour in the saké and stir-fry for yet another moment. Transfer the contents of the pan to a bowl and keep warm.

Add the mushrooms to the same pan over high heat and cook for about 15 seconds. Drizzle in the remaining $1/2$ teaspoon sesame oil and stir-fry for another 10 seconds or so. Pour the stock through a fine-mesh strainer held directly over the pan; discard the solids from the strainer. Adjust the heat to maintain a steady simmer while you assemble the bowls of noodles.

Warm the bowls in which you will be serving the noodles with boiling water (page 169). Place one-fourth of the noodles in each warmed bowl.

Place the miso in a *miso koshi* (page 77) and stir directly into the simmering liquid. Or place the miso in a bowl, ladle in some of the hot liquid from the pan, stir to mix it, and then add to the simmering liquid.

Ladle the piping-hot miso-thickened broth over the noodles and then top each bowl with a mound of the bean sprout mixture. Garnish the bowls with a shower of green scallion tops and serve immediately.

Noodle Folklore

Legend has it that Vice-Shogun Mito Mitsukuni (1628–c.1700), a prominent daimyo in the Mito domain who was known for his influence in politics of his era, was the first Japanese to sample ramen. As part of the school curriculum, every Japanese struggles through portions of *Dai Nihonshi,* the massive tome of Japanese history attributed to the learned Mito. But myth, enhanced by modern television dramas and comic books, teaches Japanese children that Mito was also a Robin Hood–like hero. Championing the cause of poor farmers claiming to be ill-treated by provincial magistrates, Mito, along with his two faithful retainers, traveled the countryside, convincing local villains to change their ways with just a flash of his Tokugawa crest.

But if he was so busy helping the poor, when did he have the chance to try ramen? Confucianism was part of the training of every samurai, and Mito is thought to have studied with a Chinese scholar by the name of Shu Shun Sui, a gentleman who also happened to have culinary skills. Mito sampled Shu's delicious noodles, and the rest, as they say, is history—or at least widely acknowledged folklore.

VEGETABLES

GROWING UP IN AMERICA in the 1940s and 1950s, I ate the usual vegetables of the day—carrots, peas, and corn. A decade later in Japan, I encountered the most incredible plant foods. Indeed, the sheer variety of marine and terrestrial vegetation that is consumed here continues to amaze, delight, and nourish me daily.

Wanting to share some of Japan's botanical bounty with you, I have selected a number of recipes that utilize, and celebrate, native Japanese vegetables, and others that enjoy a long history there. If some of these are new to you, I encourage you to read about them first in The *Washoku* Pantry. If you have never cooked with *wakamé* or *hijiki,* two of many appealing, calcium-rich aquatic plants; tender Japanese eggplants; daikon; *kabocha* squash; or burdock or lotus root, you will be surprised to discover how many dishes can be made with them. Spicy eggplant stewed with ginger is entirely different from roasted eggplant that nestles in dark miso-enriched broth—so different that they could be, and often are, presented at the same meal. Delightfully tart and refreshing, lemon-simmered *kabocha* squash is unlike soy-simmered *kabocha* richly sauced with minced chicken. So, consider starting with just one new vegetable and exploring its many possible flavors. A look at the index will help you identify recipes throughout the chapters that call for a particular ingredient.

For Japanese vegetables that may require some special effort to obtain, I have provided many suggestions on how to use them. Be assured, you will be properly rewarded for your efforts to find them. A list of resources, including where to find seeds for growing your own produce (even a small pot on a windowsill can yield an herb harvest), is included at the end of the book.

For both practical reasons (the likelihood of your being able to purchase or grow the lesser-known vegetables in your own community) and philosophic ones (transforming humble foodstuffs into magnificent meals is what the Japanese most admire), I have included many recipes for commonplace vegetables, too. Those same carrots, peas, and corn that I grew up eating in America, overcooked and buried under gobs of salty butter, are combined here instead with staples and seasonings from the *washoku* pantry—dried beans, rice, soy sauce, miso, and much more—to create a host of wholesome, nutritious dishes.

Many of the recipes in this chapter can become the centerpiece of a vegetarian meal. Others, in small quantities, are intended to accompany fish, meat, or egg dishes. Nature's glorious gifts from the mountains, forests, fields, and waterways of Japan are waiting to be savored.

SOY-BRAISED SUN-DRIED RADISH RIBBONS

KIRIBOSHI DAIKON

An inexpensive pantry item such as kiriboshi daikon *is just the sort of thing that frugal* washoku *households depend on to stretch the food budget and expand menus. Here, in its simplest form, dried daikon is simmered with strips of fried tōfu. If, however, you want to add greater volume and include other colors to fulfill the* washoku *five-colors guideline, try adding slivers of orange-red carrot and blanched green beans.*

SERVES 4 TO 6

1 generous cup (about 3 ounces) kiriboshi daikon
   (page 61)

2 fried tōfu slices, each about 6 by 3¹/₂ inches, blanched
   (page 75)

1¹/₄ cups Basic Sea Stock (page 92)

1¹/₂ tablespoons sugar

3 tablespoons soy sauce

¹/₂ teaspoon shichimi tōgarashi (page 47)

¹/₄ teaspoon black sesame seeds, freshly dry-roasted
   (page 85)

Soak the *kiriboshi daikon* in warm water to cover for 15 to 20 minutes. Then use rubbing motions (as though you were rinsing out stockings) to wash the strips well, making sure they are pliable and free from extraneous matter. Drain, gather up the strips in your hand, and squeeze out excess water.

Cut each slice of fried tōfu lengthwise into halves or thirds and then crosswise into narrow strips. Squeeze out excess moisture; you will have about 1 cup shredded fried tōfu.

Heat an 8- to 10-inch skillet, preferably nonstick, over high heat. Add the tōfu strips (you don't need extra oil; there will still be sufficient oil clinging to the tōfu) and cook for about 1 minute, or until the strips become aromatic and begin to brown around the edges.

Add the *kiriboshi daikon* and continue to dry-roast over high heat for another minute, stirring constantly to break up clumps. Add the stock and sugar and bring to a gentle boil, stirring to dissolve the sugar. Adjust the heat to maintain a steady, gentle simmer. If you have an *otoshi-buta* (page 84), place it on the vegetables. Or use a conventional lid slightly askew, swirling the pan occasionally in circular motions to ensure even cooking. Cook for 7 to 8 minutes, or until the liquid is reduced by half. Add the soy sauce and continue to simmer, stirring, until aromatic, well colored, and nearly all the liquid has been absorbed, about 5 minutes.

Remove the pan from the heat and let the daikon mixture cool in the skillet with the lid in place. It is during this cooling-down period that the flavors meld and enhance one another. Sprinkle with the *shichimi tōgarashi*, tossing to distribute well.

This dish is typically served at room temperature, but if you prefer to serve it hot, reheat it after it has cooled for 20 to 30 minutes. Just before serving, drain off the excess liquid and coax the mixture into small mounds in individual dishes. Garnish each portion with a few sesame seeds. The finished dish will keep, well covered, in the refrigerator for up to 5 days.

SOY-BRAISED HIJIKI AND CARROTS

HIJIKI NO NIMONO

All sea vegetables are rich in minerals, but hijiki *is an especially good source of calcium and iron. If you are eager to boost nutrition, I urge you to try this dish, a mixture of land and sea vegetables. Throughout Japan, it remains one of the most popular home-style dishes, appearing frequently in lunch boxes, on pub menus, and on family dinner tables.*

Illustrated on page 4

SERVES 4 TO 6

$^1/_4$ cup dried hijiki (page 41), preferably mé hijiki

1 teaspoon vegetable oil

1 carrot, peeled and cut into julienne strips
    (about $^3/_4$ cup)

1 tablespoon saké

1 cup Basic Sea Stock (page 92)

1 tablespoon sugar

2 to 3 tablespoons soy sauce

1 tablespoon white sesame seeds, freshly dry-roasted
    (page 85)

Soak the *hijiki* in warm water to cover for 15 to 20 minutes, or until soft. It will expand to many times its original volume, so choose a 2-quart bowl. Drain off the deep brown liquid. Rinse and drain again. Pat away the excess moisture with paper towels.

Heat the oil in a skillet, preferably nonstick, over high heat. Add the *hijiki* and quickly sauté, stirring constantly, for 1 to 2 minutes. When it becomes aromatic (pleasantly reminiscent of the seashore) and a bit glossy, add the carrot and continue to sauté for another minute.

Drizzle in the saké and toss the contents of the skillet until the saké evaporates. Add $^1/_2$ cup of the stock and lower the heat to maintain a steady, gentle simmer. If you have an *otoshi-buta* (page 84), place it on the vegetables. Or use a conventional lid slightly askew, swirling the pan occasionally in circular motions to ensure even cooking; check the level of liquid, adding stock or water to keep the food from scorching. Cook for 5 to 6 minutes, or until nearly all the liquid is gone.

Add the sugar and the remaining $^1/_2$ cup stock and continue to cook with the lid for 6 to 7 minutes, or until nearly all the liquid is gone. Test a piece of *hijiki*; it should give easily when pinched. If it does not, add a few spoonfuls of water and continue to simmer until tender. Do not add any soy sauce until the *hijiki* is tender.

Add 2 tablespoons of the soy sauce and cook for 1 to 2 minutes, or until the liquid is nearly gone. Taste and balance any unwanted sweetness by adding a few drops more soy sauce.

Remove the pan from the heat and let the *hijiki* mixture cool in the skillet with the lid in place. It is during this cooling-down period that the flavors meld and enhance one another.

This dish is typically served at room temperature, but if you prefer to serve it hot, reheat it after it has cooled for 20 to 30 minutes. Just before serving, drain off the excess liquid and coax the mixture into small mounds in individual serving dishes. Garnish each portion with the sesame seeds. The finished dish will keep, well covered, in the refrigerator for up to 5 days.

SOY-SIMMERED DRIED SHIITAKÉ MUSHROOMS

SHIITAKÉ NO UMANI

Dried mushrooms are not interchangeable with fresh ones. Each has its own place in the washoku *kitchen. Dried shiitaké have a depth of flavor that is desirable in slow-simmered dishes and as a garnish for cold noodle salads and scattered-style sushi. In the process of softening dried mushrooms, an intensely flavorful liquid results, and this broth is often used with, or in lieu of, classic dashi.*

This recipe yields about ¹/₂ cup sliced mushrooms, enough to garnish Five-Colored Foods with Sushi Rice (page 147) or Chilled Chinese Noodle Salad (page 178).

Illustrated on page 146

4 large dried shiitaké mushrooms, stems removed and
    caps softened in ³/₄ cup warm water (page 33)
³/₄ cup Basic Sea Stock (page 92)
1 tablespoon saké
1 tablespoon sugar
3 tablespoons soy sauce

Drain the mushrooms, reserving the soaking liquid. Combine ¹/₄ cup of the reserved soaking liquid and 6 to 8 tablespoons of the stock in a saucepan (use the larger amount of stock if you will be simmering without an *otoshi-buta*, page 84). Season with the saké and bring to a simmer.

Add the mushrooms. If you have an *otoshi-buta*, place it on the mushrooms to keep them submerged in the bubbling liquid, rather than bobbing on the surface. If you do not have a dropped lid, it is best to leave the pot uncovered (monitoring and adjusting the level of cooking liquid according to the suggestions below) because an ordinary lid askew will cause condensation to drip down into the pot, diluting the flavor. Cook for 6 to 8 minutes, or until the simmering liquid has been reduced by half.

Skim away any froth that appears, add the sugar, and cook for 7 or 8 minutes with the dropped lid in place, adding stock

or water if needed to keep the mushrooms from scorching. Add the soy sauce and cook for a final 2 to 3 minutes with the dropped lid in place, or until the simmering liquid is nearly gone and what is left is a bit syrupy.

Remove from the heat and let the mushrooms cool in the skillet with the dropped lid in place. During this cooling-down period, the flavors meld and enhance one another.

When completely cool, transfer the mushrooms to a glass jar and cover the top with plastic wrap to prevent interaction between the metal of the lid and the sweet soy-simmered food. Seal tightly with the lid. Refrigerate for up to 5 days. Serve chilled or at room temperature. The whole caps can be cut into thin strips or other shapes as needed.

Kitchen Harmony

In the *washoku* kitchen, dried shiitaké mushrooms also become part of a mélange known as *nishimé* (literally, "drenched" vegetables) that are soy-simmered successively in the same pot. The dried mushrooms usually go in the pot first, since they require extended cooking before soy sauce can be added. Daikon, carrots, and *konnyaku* (page 28) typically follow in that order, with a garnish of briefly blanched snow peas added just before bringing the dish to the table. If they are very large and thick, the soy-simmered dried shiitaké mushrooms can be sliced in half on the diagonal *sogi-giri* style (page 70), after they are cooked. *Nishimé* vegetables are served family style from a large bowl, with rice, or packed into an *obentō* for lunch.

SLOW-SIMMERED DAIZU WITH ASSORTED VEGETABLES

GOMOKU MAMÉ NI

The Japanese call dried soybeans daizu *(literally, the "important bean"). They are an excellent source of protein and delicious when slowly simmered with a variety of diced root and sea vegetables. This dish could be considered a vegetarian version of pork and beans.*

As with all dried bean preparations, cooking this dish is no culinary challenge, though you do need to plan ahead. The beans must be soaked for several hours (or overnight in the refrigerator) before cooking. And slow simmering, infusing one seasoning after the other, is what gives this dish its depth of flavor. Japanese will tell you that the order in which seasonings are added to slow-simmered dishes is "alphabetical." What they mean is that the words for saké, satō (sugar), shio (salt), shōyu (soy sauce), and su (rice vinegar) follow the order of hiragana, the Japanese cursive script writing system that is similar to an alphabet. But, since few non-Japanese are familiar with hiragana, most cooks will need to remember a seemingly arbitrary list. It is well worth the effort to memorize it!

SERVES 4 TO 6

$^1/_2$ cup dried soybeans

3 tablespoons saké

2 to 3 small dried shiitaké mushrooms, stems removed
    and caps softened in 1 cup warm water (page 33)

$1^1/_2$ cups Basic Sea Stock (page 92) or Basic Vegetarian
    Stock (page 93)

3 tablespoons sugar

1 small carrot, about 2 ounces, peeled and diced

About 10 square inches kombu (page 42), diced
    (leftovers from stock making are perfect)

1 ounce lotus root, peeled and diced (optional)

1 ounce burdock root, rinsed, lightly scraped
    (page 58), and diced (optional)

1 block konnyaku (page 28), about 5 ounces, diced,
    blanched (page 75), and drained (optional)

$^1/_4$ cup soy sauce

Rinse the dried soybeans, place them in a pot, and add cold water to cover by $^3/_4$ inch. Bring to a boil over medium-high heat and boil for about 5 minutes, or until the beans begin to float to the surface. Remove the pot from the heat, cover, and let the beans sit in the liquid for at least 3 hours. Or allow the beans to cool to room temperature, transfer them and any liquid in the pot to a glass jar with a tight-fitting lid, and refrigerate overnight. Either way, the beans should swell to nearly twice their original size.

Bring the beans to a boil over medium heat. Skim away any froth from the surface, lower the heat to maintain a gentle simmer, and add 1 tablespoon of the saké. Cook the beans uncovered, adding boiling water as needed to maintain a simmer while preventing the beans from sticking or burning, for 2 hours. Check the beans for tenderness: you should be able to spear them easily with a toothpick or find no resistance when you bite into one. Drain the beans and rinse them under running cold water to remove surface starchiness. Drain again.

Drain the mushrooms, reserving the soaking liquid, and cut into a dice. In a saucepan, combine $^1/_2$ cup of the reserved mushroom liquid, 1 cup of the stock, 2 tablespoons of the sugar, and the remaining 2 tablespoons saké. Stir over medium heat until the sugar has dissolved. Add the cooked beans; mushrooms; carrot; *kombu;* lotus and/or burdock root, if desired; and *konnyaku,* if desired, and bring to a simmer. If you have an *otoshi-buta* (page 84), place it on the beans and vegetables. If you do not have a dropped lid, it is best to leave the pot uncovered (monitoring and adjusting the level of cooking liquid according to the suggestions below) since an ordinary lid askew will cause condensation to drip down into the pot, diluting the flavor. Cook for 15 minutes, or until the simmering liquid has been reduced by half. Skim away froth that appears.

Add the remaining ¹/₂ cup stock and 1 tablespoon sugar. Continue to cook with the dropped lid in place for another 15 minutes, or until the vegetables, especially the lotus and/or burdock root if you are using them, are tender. Add more soaking liquid, stock, or water if needed to keep the vegetables and beans from scorching. There will be only a few tablespoons of liquid remaining in the pan. Add the soy sauce, stir, and cook for a final 5 to 6 minutes with the dropped lid in place, or until the simmering liquid is nearly gone and what is left is a bit syrupy.

Remove the pan from the heat and let the beans and vegetables cool in the pan with the dropped lid in place for superior flavor, or uncovered if you have been cooking without an *otoshi-buta*. It is during this cooling-down period that the flavors meld and enhance one another.

This dish is typically served at room temperature (it is packed into many *obentō* lunches), in small, deep individual dishes, about 3 tablespoons per portion. If you prefer to serve it hot, reheat it after it has cooled for 20 to 30 minutes. The finished dish will keep, well covered, in the refrigerator for up to 5 days.

Kitchen Harmony

If you want to reduce the total preparation time, use 1 cup canned soybeans (*daizu no mizu ni*). Drain the beans well and then combine them with the diced vegetables and 2 cups stock seasoned with 2 tablespoons each saké and sugar. Cook for 10 to 12 minutes, add the 3 tablespoons soy sauce, and cook for a final 5 to 6 minutes as in the main recipe.

SPINACH STEEPED IN BROTH

HORENSŌ NO OHITASHI

The word hitasu *means to "steep" or "moisten." In the* washoku *kitchen,* hitasu *is used as a method of preparing vegetables, most often leafy greens. The classic version of this dish is made with spinach that is first blanched and then marinated for a short time in a soy-tinged dashi.*

In Japan, bunches of fresh flat-leafed spinach with dirt still clinging to their rosy roots, and fat radishes and snowy white turnips with their leaves still attached, are for sale in every urban supermarket. At farmers' markets in many American communities, I have seen freshly uprooted leafy greens, such as kale and dandelion greens, and bunches of carrots and beets with greens intact that would make fine ohitashi.

Illustrated on page 279

SERVES 3 OR 4

¹/₂ cup Basic Sea Stock (page 92)

2 tablespoons Seasoned Soy Concentrate (page 96)

1 bunch spinach or other leafy greens, about 12 ounces, blanched (page 74)

Optional Garnishes

White sesame seeds, freshly dry-roasted (page 85)

Katsuo-bushi (page 18), preferably ito kezuri, freshly dry-roasted (page 85)

Shirasu-boshi (page 15)

Chirimen-jako (page 15)

Select a nonreactive container, such as a shallow glass baking dish, for marinating the greens and combine the stock and 1 tablespoon of the soy concentrate in it.

Lift the bundles of blanched greens from the icy water bath following their blanching and squeeze out the moisture. Remove the strings and place the bundles in the marinade. Let steep at room temperature for at least 30 minutes, or cover and refrigerate for up to 2 days.

When ready to serve, lift the greens from the marinade and gently press out excess moisture. Cut the bundles into 1-inch lengths and divide among individual serving dishes.

Drizzle a few drops of the remaining seasoned soy concentrate over each portion, and then garnish with one of the toppings.

Sesame seeds and curls of *katsuo-bushi* are at their nutty, smoky best when dry-roasted just before using. The small sardines, both fresh-blanched *shirasu-boshi* and semidried *chirimen-jako*, can be sprinkled over the moistened greens as is.

和食

Kitchen Harmony

Other leafy greens that lend themselves to the *ohitashi* method of preparation include *komatsuna* (page 63) and dandelion greens (page 61). When preparing either vegetable, use long cooking chopsticks or long-handled tongs that will allow you to hold the stem portion of the greens submerged in boiling water for 1 minute after the water returns to a boil and before releasing the leafy portion.

In addition, trimmed green beans and asparagus are good choices for *ohitashi.* These vegetables do not need to be tied together to align them, though the stem end of asparagus spears usually requires longer cooking than the tender top.

Ohitashi-style vegetables can be dressed in Creamy Tōfu Sauce (page 107) or Creamy Sesame-Miso Sauce (page 100) in lieu of the garnishes.

Harmony at Table

Ohitashi is plated either horizontally and sprinkled with garnishes, as described, or placed vertically and dipped into a garnish that clings to the top. To make a vertical arrangement that will not topple over, shape the greens into a neat, stubby, cylindrical bundle with a *sudaré* (page 87). Lay the *sudaré* on a cutting board with the slats running horizontal to it and the shorter ends at the top and bottom. Divide the blanched, marinated greens into 2 bunches. On the bottom third of the mat, place 1 bunch so that the roots face to the right, and place the second bunch so that the roots face to the left. This should make a pile of even thickness.

Grasp the mat, pinching both the right and left near corners with your thumbs underneath and index fingers on top. Lift up, coaxing the mat to encircle the bundle of greens. Pull toward you to tighten the top of the mat around the greens while tugging away on the bottom of the mat. Lift the top flap of the mat and finish rolling to make a snug cylinder. Place rubber bands around each end of the rolled mat to hold it in place. Stand the rolled mat on one end for 5 to 10 minutes; excess moisture will drain out, so place the mat over a dish or paper towel to absorb whatever liquid accumulates. Remove the rubber bands and unroll the mat. Cut the greens into 1-inch lengths.

Place 1 to 2 tablespoons freshly dry-roasted sesame seeds or crumbled *katsuo-boshi* in a small dish. With your fingertips, chopsticks, or tongs, gently lift the bundle of spinach and press the top of it into the seeds or flakes. Then invert the bundle of greens onto a serving plate or shallow dish, with the garnish clinging to the top.

GINGER-STEWED EGGPLANT

NASU NO SUZU NI

In Japan, eggplants reach their peak of flavor late in the summer and into the fall, a period of time referred to as zansho *(literally, "lingering heat") in the lunar calendar. Relentless days of high heat and humidity begin to take a toll on the appetite. That is when this gingery eggplant dish is especially appealing.*

I often make a double batch of this recipe in the relative cool of the evening and chill it for serving with cold noodles (Thin Noodles on Ice, page 180, or Buckwheat Noodle Roll, page 174) in the hot days ahead. If possible, use tender-skinned Japanese eggplants (considered "black" in the washoku *color scheme); not only does the deep-purple peel make an attractive presentation, but it is also packed with phytonutrients to boost overall nutrition.*

Illustrated on page 286

SERVES 4

    4 Japanese eggplants, about 3 ounces each
    1 teaspoon vegetable oil
    $^1/_3$ cup Basic Sea Stock (page 92)
    1 teaspoon saké
    1 scant teaspoon sugar
    $^1/_2$ teaspoon ginger juice (page 71), with peels reserved
    1 scant tablespoon soy sauce
    Dash of light-colored soy sauce, if needed
    Dash of mirin, if needed
    $^1/_2$ teaspoon white poppy seeds, freshly dry-roasted
       (page 85) (optional)

Trim away the stems from the eggplants and cut each eggplant in half lengthwise. With the cut surface to the board, make many fine, parallel slits on the diagonal into the skin side of each half. These slits should be very shallow, less than $^1/_8$ inch. Pat the eggplants dry.

In a skillet just large enough to hold the eggplant pieces in a single layer, heat the oil over high heat. Add the eggplant halves, skin side down, and sear them, pressing lightly to flatten to ensure that the entire surface comes in contact with the pan. Searing the skin side first will help keep the color vibrant.

Flip the eggplant halves over so that the skin side is facing up. Continue to sear for another minute before adding the stock, saké, sugar, and ginger peels. Lower the heat to maintain a gentle simmer. If you have an *otoshi-buta* (page 84), place it on the eggplants. If you do not have an *otoshi-buta*, you can improvise with a double thickness of parchment paper (cut in a circle, 1 inch smaller in diameter than your pan) weighted down with a small, flat lid from another pot. Cook for 2 to 3 minutes, or until the liquid is reduced by half. Add the soy sauce and discard the ginger peels. Simmer for another minute. Add the ginger juice and cook for another 30 seconds. Taste for seasoning: The eggplant will be fairly intense, but the flavors should be well balanced. Neither a salty (soy sauce), sweet (sugar), nor spicy (ginger) flavor should dominate the dish. If necessary, adjust with a little light-colored soy sauce or mirin.

Remove the pan from the heat and let the eggplant cool in the pan with the dropped lid or parchment paper in place for superior flavor. It is during this cooling-down period that the flavors meld and enhance one another and the color will brighten. Serve at room temperature or chilled. The finished dish will keep, well covered, in the refrigerator for up to 2 days.

When ready to serve, cut the halves into bite-size chunks and arrange them so that some show dark skin side up and others the pale center. For extra textural interest, garnish with white poppy seeds.

CHILLED ROASTED EGGPLANT

YAKI NASU

As fall approaches in Japan, the skins of eggplants in the market toughen a bit, and that is when this roasted eggplant dish is especially good. The eggplants are cooked whole, so the flesh remains moist and succulent and takes on a mild toasty flavor from the charred skin. Although this dish can be served hot from the grill, peeled and then drizzled with soy, I prefer it chilled—especially on an autumn evening when the temperatures still hover at summertime highs—and liberally garnished with aromatic herbs. Roasted eggplant also finds its way into miso-thickened soup (page 121).

SERVES 4

4 Japanese eggplants, about 3 ounces each

³/₄ cup Basic Sea Stock (page 92)

3 tablespoons Seasoned Soy Concentrate (page 96)

Optional Garnishes

1 or 2 shiso leaves (page 26), stems trimmed and leaves finely shredded

1 myōga bulb (page 26), finely shredded

2 or 3 tablespoons thin curls ito kezuri (page 20)

1 teaspoon grated fresh ginger

1 scallion, green tops only, finely chopped

Preheat a broiler or prepare a hot grill.

With the tip of a sharp knife, make 3 or 4 shallow lengthwise slits in each eggplant. If broiling the eggplants, place them on the rack on a broiler pan.

Place the eggplants under the broiler about 1 inch from the heat source or on the hottest part of the grill. Roast the eggplants, turning them occasionally with tongs, for 5 or 6 minutes, or until tender. To test, pinch the eggplants with tongs. They should yield easily. The skins may be slightly charred.

Remove the eggplants from the heat. When cool enough to handle, insert the tip of a toothpick or slender bamboo skewer just under the skin along the edge of one of the slits. Twirl the toothpick or skewer in place, and then, beginning at the stem end, draw it through the length of the eggplant. Peel back the released skin and repeat this action several times until the skin has been completely released. Trim away the stem and peeled-back skin.

Make a marinade for the grilled eggplants by combining all of the stock and half of the soy concentrate in a glass or ceramic loaf pan. Choose a size that will allow the eggplants to be totally covered by the marinade.

Sometimes Japanese cooks pull apart the whole eggplants, tearing them into ragged lengthwise strips to create more surface area that can better absorb the flavor of the marinade. If you will be cutting the eggplant into bite-sized chunks later, it is best to use this method. If, however, you want to serve the eggplants whole, allow a bit more time for them to soak up the flavor of the marinade. Transfer the eggplants to the marinade, cover with plastic wrap, and chill in the refrigerator for at least 1 hour and up to 24 hours.

When ready to serve, remove the eggplants from their marinade, allowing whatever liquid clings to remain. Either leave them whole or cut them into bite-sized pieces. Stack cut pieces in small, deep dishes, or arrange whole eggplants on narrow plates. Drizzle the remaining soy concentrate over each portion and garnish with some or all of the toppings.

EGGPLANT STUFFED WITH GROUND CHICKEN

HASAMI AGÉ

The classic version of this dish makes use of Japanese eggplants that are slit lengthwise and then stuffed with miso-seasoned ground chicken. The eggplants are then typically deep-fried.

Because Japanese eggplants are not always readily available outside of Japan, I offer an adaptation that makes use of circular slices of eggplant, rimmed with dark peel. And because not every home cook likes to deep-fry, I offer a pan-seared variation.

SERVES 4

Chicken Stuffing

3 ounces ground chicken meat

$^1/_2$ teaspoon dark miso, preferably Sendai miso

$1^1/_2$ teaspoons finely minced scallion (white and green parts), leek (white part only), or shallot

4 Japanese eggplants, about 3 ounces each, or 1 large round eggplant, about 1 pound

2 teaspoons cornstarch

Vegetable oil for deep-frying or pan searing

$^1/_2$ lemon, cut into 4 wedges

Soy sauce (optional)

To make the stuffing, in a small bowl, combine the chicken, miso, and scallion and mix well. If you will be using Japanese eggplants, divide the stuffing mixture into 8 equal portions. If you will be using a round European eggplant, divide the stuffing mixture into 4 equal portions.

If you are using Japanese eggplants, trim away the stems and cut each eggplant in half lengthwise. With the cut surface to the cutting board, and starting at the blossom end, make a single slit parallel to the board, stopping $^1/_2$ inch short of the stem end. This creates a flap in the eggplant half. Repeat to create a total of 8 eggplant halves, each with a flap. With a dry

pastry brush dipped into the cornstarch, lightly dust all cut surfaces of the eggplant.

Using a butter knife or small flexible spatula, spread a single portion of the chicken mixture on each of the 8 eggplant halves. Spread the mixture on the bottom surface of the slit, and press down lightly with the top surface (flap) to make a sandwich.

If you are using a round eggplant, trim away the stem and slice off a small piece from the opposite end to make a flat surface. Slice the eggplant crosswise into 8 rounds, each about $^1/_4$ inch thick. With the tip of a sharp knife, lightly score one side of each eggplant slice; choose the side with the greater surface area and make sure the scoring is very shallow. Keep the eggplant skin intact on the outer rim of each round. With a dry pastry brush dipped into the cornstarch, lightly dust all scored surfaces.

Using a butter knife or small flexible spatula, spread a single portion of the chicken mixture on the scored side of 4 round slices. Top each slice with a second slice, scored side down, to make a sandwich. Press lightly.

Deep-frying the stuffed eggplants will preserve the deep purple of the skins, and when fried at the proper temperature, the eggplants actually absorb less oil than when they are pan seared. To deep-fry the eggplants, pour oil to a depth of $1^1/_2$ to 2 inches into a wok or deep skillet and heat to 375°F on a deep-frying thermometer. Or test the oil temperature with trimmed scraps of eggplant. Ideally, the pieces will sink slightly, rise quickly, and then sizzle on the surface, coloring slowly. If the eggplant trimmings sink but do not surface immediately, the oil temperature is too low. If the eggplant trimmings never sink but sizzle immediately, the temperature is slightly high; gently stir the oil to cool it somewhat. If the eggplant trimmings sizzle and begin to color immediately, the oil is much too hot; lower the heat, stir, and wait for a moment before testing again. If you have no eggplant trimmings to use as a test, place the tip of an unvarnished, wooden chopstick in the oil. If small bubbles appear within a few seconds, the temperature is about 360°F. Wait an extra moment (to allow the oil to heat a bit more) before beginning to fry.

When the temperature is right, slowly lower the eggplant sandwiches, skin side first if using Japanese eggplants (this helps keep the purple color bright), into the hot oil. Work in batches to avoid crowding. Fry for 1½ minutes, undisturbed. Flip each sandwich and fry for another 45 seconds or so. Remove from the oil and let drain thoroughly on a rack covered with paper towels. If you are concerned about the meat filling being fully cooked, test by inserting a toothpick or thin, pointed skewer through the thickest part of the sandwich. It should meet with no resistance, and the meat juices should run clear.

To pan sear the eggplants, heat a skillet over high heat and drizzle in 1 or 2 tablespoons oil. When the oil is hot, working in batches to avoid crowding, add the eggplant sandwiches, skin side down if using Japanese eggplants (this helps keep the purple color bright), and cook for 2 to 2½ minutes. Flip the pieces (skin side is now facing up if using Japanese eggplants) and drizzle in an extra spoonful of oil, drawing an imaginary line around the cluster of cooking eggplant pieces. Continue to pan sear for another 1½ to 2 minutes. Remove from the skillet and let drain briefly on paper towels. If concerned about the meat filling being fully cooked, test by inserting a thin, sharp skewer through the thickest part of the sandwich. The skewer should meet with no resistance, and the meat juices should run clear.

Serve the stuffed eggplants piping hot or at room temperature with lemon wedges and soy sauce, if desired, on the side.

Kitchen Harmony

If you used Japanese eggplants, arrange them skin side up. Place 1 piece on the diagonal across the plate, with the narrow stem portion at the far right and the stuffed end on the left at the front. Prop up the second piece against the first one, draping it slightly with the stem end away.

If you used round eggplants, cut each sandwich in half to make half-moons. A single serving will be 2 half-moons. Stack them so that the straight edge on the bottom layer faces the person dining, and lean the other piece against it.

CARROTS AND KONNYAKU TOSSED IN CREAMY TŌFU SAUCE

KONNYAKU TO NINJIN NO SHIRA AÉ

This combination of vegetables, briefly braised in a soy-tinged broth and then folded into a creamy sauce, is typical of home-style cooking. Konnyaku is an inexpensive ingredient common in traditional Japanese kitchens. A modern-day concern with weight control also leads many Japanese to include konnyaku in their diet. It has no calories yet lends volume and a satisfying chewiness to a dish.

SERVES 4 TO 6

- 1 block konnyaku (page 28), about 6 ounces, drained
- 1/2 teaspoon sesame oil
- 2 or 3 slender carrots, about 6 ounces, peeled and cut into julienne
- 1/2 cup Basic Sea Stock (page 92)
- 1 tablespoon light-colored soy sauce
- 1 tablespoon mirin
- 1/2 cup Creamy Tōfu Sauce (page 107)
- 1 tablespoon white sesame seeds, freshly dry-roasted (page 85) (optional)

Cut the *konnyaku* into strips the same size as the carrot strips. Do not stack slices of *konnyaku* when cutting them, because they can easily slip away from you. Better to use the tip of your knife and pretend to draw lines as you cut through flat slices laid out, side by side, on your cutting board.

To eliminate excess liquid from the *konnyaku* so that it will absorb other flavors, you need to dry-roast it (page 85). Place a skillet over high heat, add the *konnyaku* strips, and cook, jiggling the pan until you hear a squeaking sound. Drizzle in the sesame oil and stir-fry over high heat for about 1 minute, or until fragrant. Add the carrots and cook for 1 minute, stirring constantly.

Add the stock and lower the heat to a bare simmer. If you have an *otoshi-buta* (page 84), cover the vegetables to keep them submerged in the liquid. Or use a conventional lid slightly askew, swirling the pan occasionally in circular motions to ensure even cooking. Cook for 3 to 4 minutes, or until the liquid is reduced by half. Season with the soy sauce and mirin and continue to cook for about 1 minute, or until the liquid is nearly gone and the vegetables look slightly glazed.

Remove the pan from the heat and let the *konnyaku* and vegetables cool in the skillet with the lid in place. It is during this cooling-down period that the flavors meld and enhance one another. When cool, fold the *konnyaku* and vegetables into the tōfu sauce.

Divide the sauced vegetables into 4 or 6 portions, gently molding each portion into a small mountain on a plate. If desired, garnish the peaks with a few sesame seeds to add textural contrast.

Kitchen Harmony

This dish can be made 2 days ahead. If you plan to make it in advance, store the vegetables and sauce separately, each in its own tightly lidded container. Pour off any accumulated liquid from the sauce and toss the carrots and *konnyaku* in it just before serving.

GREEN BEANS TOSSED IN CREAMY SESAME-MISO SAUCE

INGEN NO GOMA MISO AÉ

What Americans call green beans are known to the Japanese as ingen, *a vegetable that appears frequently on family and restaurant tables. Folklore credits Ingen (1592–1673), a Chinese Buddhist priest, with bringing the legume to Japan in the mid-seventeenth century. The beans are enjoyed in a variety of ways in washoku households, but I am particularly fond of them tossed in the thick, rich paste of sesame and miso known as* goma miso.

SERVES 4 TO 6

12 ounces young green beans

3 tablespoons Creamy Sesame-Miso Sauce (page 100)

1$^1/_2$ tablespoons white sesame seeds, freshly dry-roasted (page 85) (optional)

Choose the freshest, most tender green beans you can find, preferably those with fuzz still clinging to them. Snap off the stem end, pulling down along the length of the bean to remove any string that might be there. The Japanese keep the pointed (flowering) end intact, though most Americans tend to trim these away.

Bring a large pot of salted water to a rolling boil, add the beans, and blanch for 1 minute, or until bright green but still crisp. Drain the beans but do not refresh them under cold water. Instead, allow them to cool to room temperature naturally or cool them by fanning.

If you will be serving the green beans thinly sliced on the diagonal or cut into 1-inch lengths, now is the time to shape them. Toss the cut green beans in the sesame-miso sauce just before serving and divide into individual portions. Coax each portion into a mound. Garnish each serving with sesame seeds to add textural interest, if desired.

ASPARAGUS TOSSED WITH CRUSHED BLACK SESAME

ASPARA NO KURO GOMA AÉ

The classic version of this dish calls for using a suribachi *(page 73), the deeply grooved mortar found in nearly every traditional Japanese home kitchen. It is used for cracking and grinding the sesame seeds, for mixing the seeds with the soy and mirin, and then as a bowl for tossing the asparagus with the sauce. If you use a food processor to make the sauce, I recommend doubling the quantities of seeds, soy, and mirin.*

Illustrated on page 286

SERVES 4 TO 6

12 ounces asparagus, preferably pencil thin

2 tablespoons black sesame seeds, freshly dry-roasted (page 85)

2 teaspoons mirin

2 teaspoons light-colored soy sauce

1 to 2 teaspoons Basic Sea Stock (page 92) or water, if needed

Choose slender, tender young asparagus. Snap off the woody or fibrous ends of the spears. Slice the spears on the diagonal or straight across into 1- or 1$^1/_2$-inch lengths. Set aside the tip pieces.

Bring a large pot of salted water to a rolling boil and add all the asparagus pieces except the tips. When the water returns to a boil, add the tips and cook for another minute or so. When the water returns to a boil, check to see whether the asparagus pieces are done. They should be bright green but still crisp.

Drain the asparagus pieces but do not refresh them under cold water. Instead, allow them to cool to room temperature naturally (for softer asparagus) or cool them by fanning (for crisper asparagus).

To prepare the sauce in a *suribachi,* put the sesame seeds while they are still warm in the mortar and crush and grind, tapping the bowl as needed to concentrate the seeds in the center, until fully cracked. As the seeds become aromatic and slightly oily, add the mirin and soy sauce drop by drop, continuing to grind and crush the seeds. With a rubber spatula, follow the grain of the *suribachi* grooves, scraping in downward motions to concentrate the sauce in the bowl. If the sauce seems very thick, drizzle in a little stock and grind a bit more to blend. The final sauce should have the consistency of moist sand.

If you do not have a *suribachi,* double the quantities listed and transfer the sesame seeds while they are still warm into the bowl of a mini–food processor. Pulse to crush and crack them, stoppping the processor as needed to scrape down the sides of the bowl. Drizzle in the soy sauce and mirin through the feed tube, pulsing briefly once or twice to blend. If the sauce seems very thick, drizzle in a little stock and pulse to blend. The final sauce should be thick and moist with a coarse texture.

Toss the asparagus pieces in the sauce to coat well. Divide into individual portions, coaxing each into a mound, or stack the sauced vegetable either tepee style or pyramid style. Serve at room temperature.

Kitchen Harmony

If you have doubled the recipe to ensure enough volume to engage the blades of a food processor, transform the remaining thick sauce into an aromatic salad dressing by adding 2 tablespoons brown rice vinegar. Store in a sealed glass jar for up to 3 days in the refrigerator, adding $^1/_2$ teaspoon sesame oil just before serving for a richer sesame taste.

Harmony at Table

This recipe can be made with either black or white sesame seeds. The choice is usually an aesthetic one, rather than an issue of flavor or nutrition. The black seeds are typically paired with asparagus and green beans, while spinach, dandelion greens, and okra are more commonly dressed with a white sesame sauce.

Either the pine nut miso or the walnut miso sauce (page 106) can be used to dress asparagus in lieu of this black sesame mixture.

"SMASHED" BURDOCK ROOT TOSSED WITH CRUSHED WHITE SESAME

TATAKI GOBŌ

This dish takes its rather alarming name from the thwacking sound emitted when fiber-rich foods, such as burdock root, are tenderized with a blunt, heavy tool. In the traditional Japanese kitchen, this tool was a surikogi, the wooden pestle used in conjunction with a ceramic suribachi (page 73) to make the sesame sauce. In modern kitchens, in which food processors or plastic goma suri ki (hand grinders) crush the sesame, the back of a knife is commonly used, though a rolling pin would make a fine substitute.

Tataki gobō is often included in vegetarian menus, and in Kyoto, Osaka, and other parts of the Kansai area is served as part of osechi, a ceremonial assortment of New Year holiday foods. In addition to its ceremonial appearance on the New Year's table, this versatile dish is tucked into box lunches, served with omusubi (Hand-Pressed Rice, page 158), and appears as a small side dish to nibble with drinks. A chilled dry saké or crisp white wine will bring out the earthy flavor of the burdock dressed with sesame sauce.

If you use a food processor to make the sauce, I recommend doubling the quantities of seeds, soy, and mirin.

SERVES 4 TO 6

- 25 to 30 inches burdock root, preferably pencil thin, about 6 ounces, rinsed and lightly scraped, cut into 1¹/₂-inch lengths, and soaked (page 76)
- 2 tablespoons rice vinegar
- ¹/₃ cup white sesame seeds, freshly dry-roasted (page 85)
- 1¹/₂ teaspoons mirin
- 2 tablespoons soy sauce
- 1 to 1¹/₂ tablespoons Basic Sea Stock (page 92)

Have the burdock ready. Bring a 2- to 3-quart saucepan filled with water to a boil and add the vinegar. Add the drained burdock pieces and cook for 2 to 3 minutes, or until a toothpick or thin skewer inserted into a piece meets little resistance. Drain but do not refresh in cold water. Instead, allow the burdock root to cool naturally so that it retains its nutrients.

To prepare the sauce in a *suribachi,* put the sesame seeds while they are still warm in the mortar and crush and grind, tapping the bowl as needed to concentrate the seeds in the center, until fully cracked. As the seeds become aromatic and slightly oily, add the mirin and soy sauce drop by drop, continuing to grind and crush the seeds to a pastelike consistency. With a rubber spatula, follow the grain of the *suribachi* grooves, scraping in downward motions to concentrate the sauce in the bowl. Drizzle in the stock, a few drops at a time, as needed, grinding to blend thoroughly. The final sauce should have the consistency of a very thick, textured paste.

If you do not have a *suribachi,* double the quantities listed and transfer the sesame seeds while they are still warm to the bowl of a mini–food processor. Pulse to crush and crack them, stopping the processor as needed to scrape down the sides of the bowl. Drizzle in the mirin and soy sauce through the feed tube, pulsing briefly once or twice to blend. Drizzle in the stock, a few drops at a time, as needed, pulsing to blend. The final sauce should be the consistency of a very thick, textured paste.

Lay the drained, still-warm burdock root on a clean, dry cutting board and, with the wooden pestle used to grind the sesame, or the back of a knife or a rolling pin, lightly pound to break the fibers slightly. As you do so, some of the excess moisture will also splash out (wear an apron to protect your clothes). This action is called *tataki* and is the origin of the dish's name. Toss the smashed burdock root sticks in the sauce, coating them well.

To serve, stack the sauced vegetable either tepee style or pyramid style. Serve at room temperature.

Kitchen Harmony

This dish can be made 2 or 3 days ahead. If you plan to make it in advance, set aside half of the sauce in a tightly lidded container. Toss the burdock root in the remaining half of the sauce before storing in a separate, tightly lidded container. Just before serving, pour off any accumulated liquid from the sauced burdock root and toss in the sauce you set aside.

If you have doubled the recipe to ensure enough volume to engage the blades of a food processor, transform the remaining thick sauce into an aromatic salad dressing by adding 2 tablespoons brown rice vinegar. Store in a sealed glass jar for up to 3 days in the refrigerator, adding $^1/_2$ teaspoon sesame oil just before serving for a richer sesame taste.

Harmony at Table

Other *tataki* dishes you are likely to find on a Japanese restaurant menu include *aji tataki,* a tartar of horse mackerel and finely minced ginger, and *katsuo tataki,* slices of flash-seared bonito showered with "smashed" garlic and herbs.

GREEN SOYBEANS SERVED IN THE POD
ÉDAMAMÉ

An urban, summertime scene in Japan: on the rooftops of commercial buildings, in subterranean train station malls, and down alleys in neon-lit entertainment districts, jovial groups of office workers (some in the company of their bosses) have gathered in beer halls to quaff frosty mugs of draft beer and nibble piles of boiled édamamé *in their salty pods.*

SERVES 4 TO 6

    1 bunch fresh édamamé, about 1 pound, pods removed and treated (page 61), or 1 bag flash-frozen édamamé in the pod, 12 to 14 ounces
    1 teaspoon coarse salt

Bring a large pot filled with water to a rolling boil.

If cooking fresh *édamamé,* add the beans to the pot and cook for 8 or 9 minutes after the water returns to a boil. When about one-tenth of the pods look as though they are opening at the side seam, the entire batch should be tender. Test by taking an unopened pod from the pot and pressing out a bean. Bite and chew; the bean should be firm but tender, with no crunch.

If cooking frozen beans, toss them into the pot frozen and cook for no more than $2^1/_2$ minutes after the water returns to a boil. If cooking fully thawed beans, blanch them for only 45 seconds.

Drain the bean pods and cool them, fanning them rapidly to preserve their color. Do not cool by submerging them in ice water, because they will lose a great deal of their flavor in the water. As the bean pods cool, toss them in salt. Enjoy at room temperature, or chill in the refrigerator until ready to serve with icy beer. These beans are served in their pods, though only the beans are eaten. Press on the seam of pod to release the beans.

FRIED EGGPLANT WITH CRUSHED GREEN SOYBEANS

NASU NO ZUNDA AÉ

Crushing cooked édamamé *makes a thick, jade sauce that is popular in the Tohoku (northeast) region of Japan. There, the dish is called* zunda, *written with the calligraphy for "crushing" and "beans." Here is the savory version of* zunda aé, *most often used to dress fried or sautéed chunks of eggplant. Suggestions for making and using the sweet version of this nutritious sauce can be found in the accompanying notes. Traditionally,* zunda aé *was made by grinding the soybeans in a mortar. In the modern* washoku *kitchen, a food processor simplifies the process.*

Deep-frying the eggplant will preserve the dark-purple color of the skins, and when fried at the proper temperature, the eggplants actually absorb less oil than when they are pan seared. I provide directions for both deep-frying and pan searing.

SERVES 4

1 small bunch fresh édamamé, about 12 ounces,
    pods removed and treated (page 61), or 8 ounces
    flash-frozen édamamé in the pod

1 teaspoon mirin

1 teaspoon light-colored soy sauce

Vegetable oil for deep-frying or pan searing

3 or 4 Japanese eggplants, about 3 ounces each, trimmed
    but with skin intact and cut into $^3/_4$-inch chunks

Cook the *édamamé* as directed in Green Soybeans Served in the Pod (page 201). After the beans have cooled, shell them; you should have about $^1/_2$ cup. Remove the thin inner skin surrounding each bean before transferring the beans to a food processor. Pulse until well crushed. Between pulses, scrape down the sides of the bowl to make sure that all the beans are evenly mashed. Drizzle in the mirin and soy sauce and continue to pulse until well blended. The finished sauce should have small bits of bean evenly scattered throughout, and it should form a mass easily when pressed with a spoon.

To deep-fry the eggplants, pour oil to a depth of 2 inches into a wok or deep skillet and heat to 375°F on a deep-frying thermometer. Or test the oil temperature with trimmed scraps of eggplant. Ideally, the pieces will sink slightly, rise quickly, and then sizzle on the surface, coloring slowly. If the eggplant trimmings sink but do not surface immediately, the oil temperature is too low. If the eggplant trimmings never sink but sizzle immediately, the temperature is slightly high; gently stir the oil to cool it somewhat. If the eggplant trimmings sizzle and begin to color immediately, the oil is much too hot; lower the heat, stir, and wait for a moment before testing again. If you have no eggplant trimmings to use as a test, place the tip of an unvarnished, wooden chopstick in the oil. If small bubbles appear within a few seconds, the temperature is about 360°F. Wait an extra moment (to allow the oil to heat a bit more) before beginning to fry.

When the temperature is right, carefully lower the eggplant chunks, skin side first to preserve their color, into the oil. Fry for 1 minute, undisturbed, and then flip each chunk and fry for another 45 seconds or so, until tender. Either skewer a chunk with a toothpick (it should meet with no resistance) or gently squeeze with chopsticks or tongs (it should give easily). Using a fine-mesh strainer, transfer the eggplant pieces to a wire rack to drain, or transfer them to a tray or dish lined with paper towels ready to absorb excess oil. Let the eggplant pieces drain thoroughly.

To pan sear the eggplants, heat a skillet over medium-high heat. Drizzle 1 or 2 spoonfuls of oil into the pan. Working in batches to avoid crowding, place the eggplant pieces, skin side down, in the hot skillet (this helps keep the purple color bright). Cook for 2 minutes, undisturbed. Flip the pieces and drizzle in an extra spoonful of oil, drawing an imaginary line around the cluster of cooking eggplant chunks. Continue to pan sear for another minute, or until tender. Either skewer a chunk with a toothpick (it should meet with no resistance) or gently squeeze with chopsticks or tongs (it should give easily). Transfer the eggplant pieces to a rack lined with paper towels.

Whether frying or pan searing the eggplant chunks, blot them with paper towels to remove any excess oil. While the pieces are still warm, toss them with the crushed soybean sauce. The dish can be served either warm or chilled.

Kitchen Harmony

Zunda mochi, a snack-time variation on the theme, tops off *omochi* (page 39) with a sweetened version of the soybean sauce. If you would like to try this, add 2 tablespoons sugar to the savory sauce and cook over gentle heat for 3 to 4 minutes, or until the sugar is melted and well blended. Finish with a pinch of salt and let the sauce cool completely. Vanilla ice cream, in lieu of the *omochi,* is also yummy!

When favalike beans, called *sora mamé,* are used in lieu of the fresh green soybeans, the sauce is called *hibari aé,* or "skylark sauce."

LEMON-SIMMERED KABOCHA SQUASH

KABOCHA NO SAWAYAKA NI

Sawayaka means "refreshing," which describes this slightly tart, faintly sweet, and utterly restorative kabocha *squash dish perfectly. I crave this late in summer, when my body and spirit have been sapped by relentless days of heat and humidity. Serve it with any broiled fish, poultry, or meat dish.*

SERVES 4

- 1 cup Basic Sea Stock (page 92)
- 1 small lemon, zest removed in tiny strips and reserved, lemon juiced
- 2 tablespoons mirin
- 1/4 kabocha squash, about 10 ounces, cut into 8 beveled chunks (page 69) with seeds removed but skin intact
- 1 teaspoon light-colored soy sauce
- 1/2 teaspoon soy sauce
- Lemon or lime slices for garnish, if serving chilled (optional)

Combine the stock, lemon juice, and mirin in a pot wide enough to hold the squash pieces in a single layer. For a more assertive citrus flavor, add the spent lemon halves, too. Bring to a simmer over low heat and then skim away any froth that appears. Remove and discard the lemon halves and add the squash pieces, skin side down, in a snug single layer. Place an *otoshi-buta* (page 84) over the squash, or improvise one with a double thickness of cooking parchment, cut in a circle 1 inch smaller in diameter than your pan and weighted down with a small, flat lid from another pot. Adjust the heat to maintain a steady but not very vigorous simmer and cook for 3 to 4 minutes, or until barely tender. Test with a toothpick or bamboo skewer; it should pierce the squash but still meet with some resistance. Depending on the variety of *kabocha* squash and where it is grown, cooking time will vary widely.

Carefully flip the squash pieces over so that the skin faces up. Replace the lid or parchment and simmer for about 2 minutes. Test again with a toothpick; you should be able to pierce the skin without much difficulty, but the flesh should not be so soft that it crumbles. Add the light-colored soy sauce, swirl the pan to ensure even distribution, and continue to simmer for another minute or two. The toothpick should meet no resistance now. Add the soy sauce, swirl again, and simmer for a final 30 to 40 seconds.

Remove the pan from the heat and allow the squash to cool a bit in the pan with the lid or parchment in place. It is during this cooling-down period that the flavors meld and enhance one another. This dish is most often served at room temperature, though it is fine to serve it chilled, too. If you want to serve it warm, you can reheat it briefly.

When ready to serve, spoon whatever simmering liquid remains in the pan over the squash. Garnish portions with some of the zest. When serving this dish chilled, I like to add an extra garnish of citrus slices.

SOY-SIMMERED KABOCHA SQUASH WITH MINCED CHICKEN

KABOCHA NO TORI AN KAKÉ

Kabocha *squash, with its orangey-gold flesh and dark green, edible skin, appears often on Japanese family dinner tables. This particular dish, with the chicken sauce providing added volume and complexity of flavor, is standard home-style fare. When I make it, I usually pair a chunky chowder or miso-thickened soup and multigrain rice with it, and complete the menu with some sweet-and-sour condiment or Impatient Pickles (page 217).*

SERVES 4

- $^1/_4$ kabocha squash, about 10 ounces, cut into 12 beveled chunks (page 69) with seeds removed but skin intact
- $1^1/_2$ cups Basic Sea Stock (page 92)
- 1 tablespoon saké
- 2 teaspoons sugar
- $1^1/_2$ teaspoons soy sauce
- 1 tablespoon light-colored soy sauce
- 3 ounces ground chicken, preferably a mixture of breast and dark meat
- Pinch of salt (optional)
- 1 tablespoon cornstarch mixed with 1 tablespoon cold water to make a thin paste
- 1 scallion, green tops only, finely chopped, or 2 to 3 fresh chives, snipped (optional)

Arrange the squash pieces, skin side down, in a pot in a snug single layer. Add enough stock to cover the squash barely. Place an *otoshi-buta* (page 84) over the squash and bring the stock to a boil over high heat. Or, use a conventional lid slightly askew, swirling the pan occasionally in circular motions to ensure even cooking. Adjust the heat to maintain a steady but not very vigorous simmer. Cook for 3 to 4 minutes, or until barely tender. Test with a toothpick or bamboo skewer; it should pierce the squash but still meet with some resistance. Depending on the variety of *kabocha* squash and where it is grown, the firmness of the flesh and the cooking time will vary widely.

Add the saké and sugar and carefully flip the squash pieces over so that the skin faces up. Replace the lid and simmer for about 2 minutes. Test again with a toothpick; you should be able to pierce the skin without much difficulty, but the flesh should not be so soft that it crumbles.

Add the soy sauces and continue to simmer for another 2 minutes. The toothpick should meet no resistance now. Transfer the simmered squash, skin side down, to deep individual serving dishes.

Strain the liquid remaining in the pot if it looks very fibrous (some squashes "shed" fibers easily); otherwise, use the liquid as is. Add the remaining stock and bring to a simmer over medium heat. Add the chicken, stirring well to break up any lumps. At first the liquid will look cloudy, but as the chicken cooks, the liquid will clear and the chicken will turn white. If fat from the chicken is visible on the surface, skim it off. Taste a bit of the cooked chicken and adjust the seasonings with the salt, if necessary.

Pour the cornstarch paste into the simmering chicken, raise the heat to high, and cook, stirring constantly to keep the sauce lump free as it thickens. The sauce is ready when clear, glossy, and thickened. Top each squash portion with an equal amount of the sauce.

If you like, scatter the scallions over the top of each serving. This garnish dresses up the dish and adds another savory dimension to the overall flavor. Serve with chopsticks and spoons. In Japan, this dish typically comes to the table warm but not piping hot, though it is also sometimes served at room temperature.

SOY-SIMMERED KABOCHA SQUASH WITH RED BEANS

ITOKO NI

When I first encountered this preparation, I took the name literally (itoko is "cousin," in Japanese) and assumed it had something to do with relatives (perhaps the vague botanical relation between squashes and legumes?). I later learned that a slurring of okoto, or "important event," was the probable origin of the name of the dish, which had traditionally been served at the winter solstice.

The longstanding wisdom of washoku *foodways is at work here. In the past, nutritious squashes left from a late harvest were stored in farmhouses as winter settled in. Cooks knew that* kabocha, *rich in carotene and packed with vitamins A, C, and E, provided excellent nourishment, especially when it was combined with dried red beans, a year-round pantry staple bursting with iron, fiber, and vitamin B$_1$.*

SERVES 4

- $^1/_4$ cup dried adzuki beans, preferably sasagé mamé variety (page 14)
- 1 piece kombu (page 42), 1 inch square
- 3 tablespoons saké
- 1 tablespoon sugar
- 2 tablespoons soy sauce
- $^1/_4$ kabocha squash, about 10 ounces, cut into 12 chunks with seeds removed but skin intact (or partially peeled for a striped pattern)
- 1$^1/_4$ to 2 cups Basic Sea Stock (page 92)
- 1 teaspoon light-colored soy sauce

In this recipe, the beans are prepared—simmered with *kombu* and saké, then with sugar, and finally with soy—before the squash is cooked. Wash the beans carefully to remove straw, pebbles, or other unwanted matter; drain well; and place in small, heavy saucepan. Add cold water to cover and bring to a boil (the beans will begin to float to the surface). Remove the pan from the heat, cover, and, to achieve tender cooked beans, let the liquid cool to room temperature naturally. Transfer to a glass jar with a tight-fitting lid and let the beans sit at room temperature in cool weather for at least 3 hours or in warm weather in the refrigerator overnight. Either way, the beans will swell to nearly twice their original size. The liquid will be cloudy and dusty pink.

Return the beans and whatever liquid remains in the jar to the saucepan. If necessary, add cold water just to cover the beans completely. Add the *kombu* and 2 tablespoons of the saké and bring the mixture to a boil. Skim away any froth that appears (and discard any loose skins, if you prefer a tidy appearance to the final dish). Adjust the heat to maintain a steady simmer and cook for 30 minutes. Add more water as needed to keep the beans submerged in liquid throughout the cooking. Using an *otoshi-buta* (page 84) is an efficient way to keep the liquid from evaporating too rapidly. If you will be using a conventional lid instead, slightly askew, swirl the pan occasionally in circular motions to ensure even cooking, and check the level of the liquid; you may need to add water more often to keep the beans from scorching.

Add 2 teaspoons of the sugar and additional water if needed to keep the beans submerged and cook for 30 to 40 minutes longer. Test for tenderness: Squeeze a couple beans; they should give easily when pinched. If they do not, add water as needed to keep the beans submerged and continue to simmer until they are tender. Once the beans are tender, add the soy sauce and simmer for 8 to 10 minutes. Discard the *kombu*. Pour the contents of the pan through a fine-mesh strainer, reserving the liquid and beans separately.

Now that the beans have been prepared, you are ready to cook the *kabocha* squash. To encourage the bean sauce to cling to the squash, bevel the edges of the squash pieces (page 69).

(continued)

Arrange the squash pieces, skin side down, in a pot in a snug single layer. Add enough stock to cover the squash barely. Place an *otoshi-buta* (page 84) over the squash, or use a conventional lid slightly askew, swirling the pan occasionally in circular motions to ensure even cooking. Bring the stock to a boil over high heat. Adjust the heat to maintain a steady but not very vigorous simmer and cook for 3 to 4 minutes, or until barely tender. Test with a toothpick or bamboo skewer; it should pierce the squash but still meet with some resistance. Depending on the variety of *kabocha* squash and where it is grown, the cooking time and final texture will vary widely.

Add the remaining 1 tablespoon saké and 1 teaspoon sugar and carefully flip the squash pieces over so that the skin faces up. Replace the lid and simmer for about 2 minutes. Test again with a toothpick; you should be able to pierce the skin without

much difficulty, but the flesh should not be so soft that it crumbles. Add the light-colored soy sauce and 3 to 4 tablespoons reserved liquid from cooking the beans. Continue to simmer for another 2 minutes. The toothpick should meet no resistance now.

Transfer the simmered squash, skin side down, to deep individual serving dishes. Strain the cooking liquid to remove fibers and broken bits. If more than 2/3 cup of liquid remains, reduce it over high heat until 3 to 4 tablespoons remain. Taste the sauce and adjust the seasonings, if necessary, with either more light-colored soy sauce or sugar. Add the reserved beans to the liquid and heat briefly over medium-low heat, stirring constantly for 1 minute to allow the flavors to meld.

Top each squash portion with an equal amount of the sauce. Serve hot or at room temperature with chopsticks and spoons.

Kitchen Harmony

The red beans alone are yummy, or they can be served with sweet potatoes cooked in the same manner as the *kabocha*. The finished dish will keep well, covered and refrigerated, for 3 or 4 days. The flavors intensify with each reheating, which I like so much that I sometimes double the recipe just to be sure of having leftovers later in the week.

SWEET POTATO SIMMERED WITH KELP

SATSUMA IMO TO KOMBU NO UMA NI

Satsuma imo, *or "sweet potato," was probably first introduced to Japan by Portuguese missionaries and traders who came to Kyushu in the early part of the seventeenth century. Satsuma (the former name for Kagoshima on the island of Kyushu) was one of several locations where the red-skinned, golden-fleshed tuber was cultivated. It proved a hardy crop that helped stave off famine when rice and other grains failed, and it was, and still is, used in making confectionary.*

You may decide that this pleasantly sweet, slightly savory dish is a welcome alternative to candied yams for serving with fried or roast chicken or even turkey. Or, with washoku *considerations of colors, flavor palate, and cooking methods in mind, you may opt for pairing this dish with a green vegetable and salt-broiled or steamed fish.*

SERVES 4 TO 6

About 25 square inches kombu (page 42) (leftovers from stock making are perfect)

1 Japanese-style sweet potato, about 10 ounces, cut into 8 or 12 chunks with skin intact and soaked to hold color (page 76)

1^1/$_2$ cups Basic Sea Stock (page 92)

1^1/$_2$ tablespoons sugar

1 tablespoon light-colored soy sauce

1^1/$_2$ teaspoons mirin

1^1/$_2$ teaspoons soy sauce

If using softened *kombu* left over from stock making, cut it into many narrow strips with scissors. If using fresh (and still dried) *kombu*, soak it in cold water for 10 minutes (this liquid can be used instead of the stock, by the way) before cutting it into narrow strips.

Drain the potato chunks and place them with the *kombu* strips in a pot with the stock. If you have an *otoshi-buta* (page 84), cover and slowly bring to a simmer over low heat. Unwanted froth will float to the top and stick to the lid near the handle, making it easy to rinse away later. If you are not using a lid, skim away any froth as it appears while the potatoes and *kombu* are cooking.

Simmer for about 10 minutes, or until the potatoes and *kombu* are tender (a toothpick should meet no resistance when stuck into the thickest part of a potato chunk, and a piece of *kombu* should give easily when pinched). Add the sugar, light-colored soy sauce, and mirin, tilting and swirling the pan to distribute them all evenly. Simmer for 2 minutes and then add the soy sauce. Simmer for a final 2 minutes and remove the pot from the stove.

Allow the vegetables to cool to room temperature in whatever cooking liquid remains in the pot. It is during this cooling-down period that flavors meld, making for a better balance of savory and sweet.

When cool, remove the potatoes and *kombu* to individual serving dishes. Mound 2 or 3 potato chunks in each small dish so that both red peel and yellow flesh are visible. Gather a cluster of *kombu* strips and lean them against the potato pieces, placing them at a jaunty angle.

If a great deal of liquid remains in the pot, return it to the stove and reduce the liquid over high heat, stirring constantly. When only a few syrupy spoonfuls remain, drizzle this sauce over the potatoes and *kombu*. Serve at once, or at room temperature up to several hours later.

TEMPURA PANCAKES, TEMPLE VEGETARIAN STYLE

SHŌJIN KAKI AGÉ

The frugal washoku *household makes excellent use of kitchen scraps. One of the most delightful ways of using up slivers and chunks of root vegetables, sweet potatoes, and their peels is by making these crispy tempura pancakes. They can be served with a classic soy-based dipping sauce and condiments or they can be sprinkled with a flavored salt.*

If you have enough vegetable bits and pieces to make double or even three times the number of pancakes, go ahead and prepare extra ones and freeze them for use at a later date for topping noodles (Soba Noodles with Tempura in Soup, page 177) or a bowl of rice (Rice Topped with Tempura, page 154). Using self-rising flour (a mixture of low-gluten flour, with baking soda and salt added) for the batter yields excellent results.

MAKES 4 TO 6 PANCAKES

1-inch chunk Japanese-style sweet potato, or yam, about 1¹/₂ ounces, or 2-inch-wide by 3- or 4-inch-long strip sweet potato peel, soaked to hold color (page 76)

1-inch chunk burdock root, about 1 ounce, rinsed, lightly scraped (page 58), and cut into narrow julienne strips

1-inch chunk parsnip, about 1 ounce, scraped and cut into narrow julienne strips

1-inch chunk carrot and/or Kyoto red carrot, about 1 ounce each, scraped and cut into narrow julienne strips

1 scant tablespoon cornstarch

For the Dipping Sauce and Condiments (optional)

¹/₃ cup Basic Sea Stock (page 92)

1 teaspoon mirin

1 teaspoon light-colored soy sauce

1 teaspoon grated fresh ginger

2-inch chunk daikon, about 4 ounces, grated (page 59) to yield about ¹/₄ cup

Five Flavored Salts (page 112)

For the Batter

3 tablespoons ice water

2 tablespoons self-rising flour

For Frying

Vegetable oil for deep-frying

1 to 2 teaspoons sesame oil (optional)

Combine all the julienne-cut vegetables in a bowl. Blot up excessive moisture with paper towels. Sift the cornstarch over the vegetable strips and toss to ensure that all the vegetable surfaces are lightly dusted. Set aside.

The pancakes can be served with a dipping sauce and condiments or with a flavored salt. If you decide to serve the dipping sauce, combine the stock, mirin, and soy sauce in a small saucepan and place over low heat to keep warm. Have the grated ginger and daikon ready. If you decide to serve a flavored salt, select one from among the salts.

Prepare the batter just before frying. Pour the ice water into a small bowl and sift the flour over it. Stir to mix slightly. Lumps should be visible in the batter.

Pour the vegetable oil to a depth of 2 inches into a wok or deep skillet. Add the sesame oil (which lends nutty overtones to the finished dish) and heat to 370°F on a deep-frying thermometer. Or test the oil temperature with a few drops of batter. Ideally, the drops will sink slightly and then rise to the surface and puff quickly but not color immediately. At the same time, preheat the oven to 200°F.

When the oil is ready, place about one-fourth or one-sixth of the cornstarch-dusted vegetables in the bowl of a large soup ladle. Spoon ¹/₂ teaspoon of the batter over the vegetables and toss lightly to coat the vegetables with the batter. Carefully pour the contents of the ladle into the hot oil. The batter and cornstarch act as "glue" to hold the vegetable strips together.

If necessary, patch together the pancake once they are in the oil by adding a drop more batter or a few more vegetable strips. Repeat to make 1 or 2 more pancakes in this first batch.

Allow the pancakes to fry for about 1 minute, undisturbed. Flip them over and continue to fry for another minute, or until crisp. Using a fine-mesh strainer, transfer the pancakes to a wire rack on a tray to drain and slip into the warm oven. Use a fine-mesh strainer to clear the oil of batter bits before adding the next batch of pancakes.

Repeat to make 4 to 6 pancakes in all. Serve the pancakes hot with the sauce and condiments or the flavored salt (see notes).

和食

Kitchen Harmony

If you are making extra pancakes for serving at another time, place them on paper towels to cool when you remove them from the frying oil. Flip them once after they have drained for 2 or 3 minutes to make sure all excess oil is blotted away. Stack the cooled pancakes with a fresh piece of paper towel between the layers, place them in a zippered heavy-duty plastic bag, and gently press out the air before sealing the bag. Refrigerate for 1 or 2 days or freeze for up to 1 month.

To reheat frozen pancakes in a toaster oven, unwrap pancakes taken directly from the freezer and place them on a ridged foil pan that fits about 2 inches below the toaster coils. Toast for $1^1/_2$ minutes on medium-high heat, and then flip them over and repeat for 1 minute. Blot away any moisture with paper towels and let the pancakes sit for 3 or 4 minutes before toasting them for another minute on each side. To reheat refrigerated pancakes, toast them for 1 minute on each side. If the edges begin to scorch, cover the pancakes with foil after flipping them over.

To reheat frozen tempura pancakes in a conventional oven, preheat it to 250°F. Unwrap pancakes taken directly from the freezer and place them on a rack set over a foil-lined baking sheet. Bake them for 7 or 8 minutes, or until warm and dry. To reheat refrigerated pancakes, bake them for 4 or 5 minutes, or until warm and dry. If the edges begin to scorch, cover the pancakes with foil after 2 or 3 minutes.

Harmony at Table

The Japanese often serve tempura on a plate or in a shallow bamboo basket lined with folded rice paper. Paper doilies make an attractive alternative. If you are serving the tempura with flavored salt, put it in a separate small dish or crimped-edge foil liners (used to hold chocolates or candies).

If serving the tempura with the dipping sauce, serve the sauce in individual shallow bowls. Place a small mound of grated daikon topped with grated ginger next to the pancakes on the plate or in the basket, or on a separate small dish. Each person adds daikon and ginger to taste to their sauce before dipping each piece of tempura.

BURDOCK AND LOTUS ROOT CHIPS

YASAI CHIPPUSU

These crispy fried vegetable chips sprinkled with flavored salts are positively addictive. Served at many chic dining bars and upscale pubs in Japan nowadays, they are a modern approach to the traditional practice of making a little seem like a lot. A single stick of burdock or segment of lotus root makes a sizable pile of chips. The chips are a terrific beer snack, but I suggest you also try topping a green salad with them, in place of croutons.

SERVES 4 TO 6

> 1 segment lotus root, about 6 ounces (4 to 5 inches long)
> 1 burdock root, preferably 10 inches long and $^1/_2$ inch in
>   diameter, about 6 ounces, rinsed and lightly scraped
>   (page 58)
> Vegetable oil for deep-frying
> 1 to 2 teaspoons sesame oil (optional)
> Fragrant pepper salt and ocean herb salt (see Five
>   Flavored Salts, page 112)

Peel the lotus root and, using a very sharp knife or mandoline, cut it into tissue-thin slices. Place the slices on paper toweling and blot up excess moisture. The slices may discolor a bit and some may break. For this recipe, that's fine.

Cut the burdock root in half crosswise. Using a broad vegetable peeler, make tissue-thin strips about 5 inches long. Place the strips on paper toweling and blot up excess moisture. The strips may curl slightly, even snap, and discolor somewhat. Again, for this recipe, that's fine.

Pour the vegetable oil to a depth of $1^1/_2$ inches into a wok or deep skillet. Add the sesame oil (which lends nutty overtones to the finished dish) and heat to 350°F on a deep-frying thermometer. Or test the oil temperature with a slice of lotus root. Ideally, the slice will sink slightly and surface immediately to sizzle and slowly change to a golden color.

Fry the lotus root in 2 batches. At first the oil will be quite foamy. When the bubbles calm, stir to ensure that all surfaces are frying evenly. When the lotus chips have turned a golden color, use a slotted spoon to transfer them to a wire rack or a tray lined with paper towels. Repeat with the second batch of lotus root slices. Allow fried chips to drain until they are no longer oily in appearance but still warm. Divide the chips into 2 piles. Sprinkle a bit of each of the flavored salts onto each pile.

Now, fry the burdock strips in 2 batches the same way you fried the lotus root slices, but lower the temperature to 275 or 300°F. Burdock root tends to burn easily and needs to be watched closely. When the strips turn a pale champagne color, transfer them to a wire rack or a tray lined with paper towels. Divide into 2 piles and sprinkle a bit of each of the flavored salts onto each pile.

Serve the lotus root and burdock root chips warm or at room temperature, either in separate bowls or combined.

STEAMING RADISH SWATHED IN CITRUSY MISO SAUCE

FUROFUKI DAIKON

A fine example of Japanese-style comfort food, piping-hot radish swathed in fragrant miso sauce is particularly welcome on a blustery winter evening. Many renditions of this dish choose a pungent, dark miso sauce, but I offer a light, fruity sauce here.

SERVES 4

> 4 chunks daikon, each about 2 inches in diameter and
> 1 inch thick
> About 2 cups togi-jiru (page 39)
> 1 scant cup Basic Sea Stock (page 92) or Basic
> Vegetarian Stock (page 93)
> 1 teaspoon light-colored soy sauce
> 1 teaspoon mirin
> 1/4 cup Citrusy Miso (page 102)
> 1/4 teaspoon freeze-dried yuzu peel (page 28), crushed to
> a powder, or grated fresh lemon or lime zest

Peel the radish chunks, preferably in *katsura muki* (page 68) fashion so that you have 4 thin, broad pieces of peel you can use to make Fiery Parsnips (page 215). Bevel the edges of each chunk of daikon (page 69) to keep them from crumbling as they simmer in broth.

Place the radish slices in a single layer in a shallow pot or deep skillet. Add just enough of the *togi-jiru* to cover the radish completely. Slowly bring the water to a simmer over medium heat and cook for 5 to 6 minutes, or until the radish slices are barely tender (a toothpick should meet little resistance). Drain away the foamy rice residue and rinse the pieces of radish in fresh water. The starchy water will have given the radish slices a luminous appearance. Drain the radish slices well.

Combine the stock, soy sauce, and mirin in a pot, stir to mix, and add the radish slices. Place over medium heat, bring to a simmer, and cook for 8 to 9 minutes, or until tender (a toothpick should meet with no resistance).

While the radish is simmering, prepare the miso sauce or reheat previously made sauce. If you will be reheating sauce left from an earlier use or made in advance, thin it with a few drops of the seasoned stock in which the daikon simmered. Reheat slowly over low heat, stirring constantly until the mixture is bubbly, glossy, and the consistency of tomato ketchup.

To assemble the dish, spoon a bit of piping-hot sauce into the bottom of individual shallow bowls (preferably *nimono wan*, or lidded bowls). Place a hot radish slice on top of each pool of sauce and spoon the remaining sauce over the top. Garnish with the *yuzu* peel. Serve immediately.

———————— ————————

Kitchen Harmony

If you are looking to add color contrast to your menu, or if you prefer a more robustly flavored sauce, substitute 1/4 cup Pungent Red Miso Sauce (page 101) for the Citrusy Miso.

FIERY PARSNIPS

KIMPIRA

The classic version of kimpira *is made by stir-frying shredded burdock root until just tender. Often, carrot slivers are added, and sometimes julienned radish peels are used instead of the burdock root. A fiery blend of seven spices is always added at the end of cooking, and therein lies the origin of this dish's name,* kimpira.

A Paul Bunyan–like boy of legendary strength and bravery, Kimpira became the main character in an early-seventeenth-century jōruri opera. The popularity of this ballad style of theater was reflected in the culinary arena with Kimpira gobō *(burdock root) and other foods spiked with* tōgarashi *(page 47) that celebrated the folk hero's fiery determination.*

While in America, I made kimpira *with parsnips one day and discovered they were delicious. I have adjusted the balance of seasonings to accommodate their natural sweetness.*

SERVES 4

2 or 3 parsnips, about 7 ounces total weight

$^1/_2$ teaspoon sesame oil

1 teaspoon saké

$^1/_2$ teaspoon sugar

2 tablespoons soy sauce

Pinch of shichimi tōgarashi (page 47)

White sesame seeds, freshly dry-roasted (page 85) for garnish (optional)

To free the parsnips of dirt or other gritty material, scrub them with the rough side of a kitchen sponge or scrape them with the back of your knife. The peel, however, is nutritious and tasty and should not be stripped away. Slice the parsnips into narrow julienne strips about $1^1/_4$ inches long. You should have about $1^1/_2$ cups strips. Spread them out on a towel to dry.

In a nonstick skillet, heat the sesame oil over high heat. Add the parsnips and stir-fry for 1 minute, stirring constantly. Add the saké and stir fry for 1 minute. Add the sugar and cook, stirring occasionally, for 3 to 4 minutes more, or until the parsnips are lightly carmelized. Add the soy sauce and continue to cook and stir for 1 or 2 minutes, or until the liquid is nearly gone and the parsnips are just tender and well glazed.

Sprinkle with *shichimi tōgarashi* and toss to distribute well. Remove the pan from the heat and let the parsnips cool to room temperature.

Mound in small bowls as individual portions, or serve in a single bowl, family style, and garnish with the sesame seeds, if desired. Store leftovers in a glass jar in the refrigerator for up to 3 days.

Kitchen Harmony

If you buy some daikon to cook as a vegetable, grate as a condiment, shred for a salad, or pickle in brine, save the peels so you can make this splendid side dish. I first learned about vegetable-peel *kimpira* from a thrifty Japanese neighbor, and quite frankly I often buy the daikon now just to make this dish.

TOSA SEA SALAD

TOSA AÉ

The Bay of Tosa, on the Pacific coast of Shikoku Island, is famous for its katsuo *(bonito) catch, a great deal of which gets preserved as the smoky fish flakes known as* katsuo-bushi. *On Japanese menus, the presence of the word* Tosa *in the name of a dish alerts diners to the inclusion of* katsuo-bushi. *This appealing* wakamé *and cucumber salad is dressed with a vinaigrette that has been liberally infused with the smoky fish flakes.*

SERVES 4

- 4 Japanese or other cucumbers with edible peel, about 3 ounces each
- 1 teaspoon coarse salt
- 2 tablespoons dried bits wakamé (page 44), soaked and drained, or 3 ounces fresh-salted wakamé, rinsed, soaked, drained, and chopped
- 1 bunch radish sprouts, about 2 ounces, rinsed, trimmed, and cut into $^1/_8$-inch lengths
- $^1/_4$ cup Smoky Vinaigrette (page 99)

The cucumbers will taste sweeter if you follow a procedure known as *aku nuki,* or "removing bitterness" (page 76). Once you have completed that step, slice the cucumbers in half lengthwise. Place the halves, cut side down, on the cutting board, and thinly slice on the diagonal into elongated half-moons. Transfer the slices to a bowl and sprinkle with the salt. Toss lightly and let sit for 10 minutes, or until the slices "sweat," becoming pliable.

Place the cucumbers in a strainer and allow any accumulated liquid to drain off. Rinse the cucumbers under cold running water, drain, and squeeze lightly to press out excess liquid.

In a bowl, toss the cucumbers with the *wakamé.* Divide the mixture into 4 portions, coaxing each into a mound. Set the mounds in individual small, deep serving bowls. Garnish each portion with the radish sprouts. Just before serving, drizzle an equal amount of the vinaigrette over each salad.

———— ————

Kitchen Harmony

If you want to make this a more substantial salad, line a plate with mixed lettuces and cooked pasta, such as orzo or bow ties, and mound the salad in the center. Add sliced tomatoes and serve additional Smoky Vinaigrette on the side. For textural contrast, shower the salad with several spoonfuls of freshly dry-roasted sesame seeds (page 85).

IMPATIENT PICKLES

SOKUSEKI-ZUKÉ

The curious name refers to a quick method of brine-pickling veg-etables that speeds up the old-fashioned process. Traditionally, salted vegetables were snugly layered in large ceramic or wooden tubs with heavy stones placed on top to force liquid from them gradually. The weights would remain in place, sinking slowly as the vegetables wilted. Submerged in their own brine, the raw veg-etables slowly pickled.

Depending on the season and the water content of the partic-ular vegetable, the time required to produce a mature pickle varied. Even asa-zuké, or "lightly pickled" vegetables, could take as long as several days. In the countryside, most brine-pickling was rele-gated to a cool and relatively dry spot outside the house. It was never done in a busy kitchen, where the tubs would be in the way. Then, in the mid-1960s, a clever screw-top device, the shokutaku tsukémono ki, or "tabletop pickle pot," came on the scene and became an instant best-seller with homemakers in cramped urban kitchens. The small plastic pot sits on the kitchen counter, where it transforms bits and pieces of shredded cabbage or other leftover vegetables into a spirited side dish in only a few hours.

The texture and appearance of the pickled vegetables is simi-lar to coleslaw, but without mayonnaise or other cloying salad dressings. Impatient cooks, and others who may not have planned ahead, will especially appreciate this dish. My recipe guides you in the use of a shokutaku tsukémono ki. If you do not have one, you will find an alternative method on page 80.

Illustrated on page 79

SERVES 4

- ¹/₄ small, tightly packed head green or red cabbage, about 6 ounces
- 1¹/₂ teaspoons coarse salt
- 1 small Japanese or other cucumber with edible peel, about 3 ounces
- 1 or 2 myōga bulbs (page 26), finely shredded on the diagonal (optional)
- 1 piece kombu (page 42), preferably Rishiri kombu, Rausu kombu, or ma kombu, about 1 inch square
- ¹/₂ teaspoon soy sauce (optional)

With a sharp knife, cut the cabbage into very fine shreds, working against the grain (page 69). Use both dark outer and stiffer inner white leaves, as well as the core. Place the shred-ded cabbage in a glass or ceramic bowl and sprinkle 1 teaspoon of the salt over it. Toss lightly and let the cabbage sit while you slice the cucumbers.

The cucumbers will taste sweeter if you follow a procedure known as *aku nuki*, or "removing bitterness" (page 76). Once you have completed that step, cut the cucumber on the diago-nal into very thin slices and stack the slices. Cut them length-wise into long shreds, each tipped with dark green peel (page 70). Place the strips in a bowl and sprinkle with the remaining ¹/₂ teaspoon salt. Toss lightly and let sit for 10 minutes, or until the cucumber shreds are visibly moist and appear pliable.

Combine the cabbage and cucumbers in a bowl. To make a more complex-flavored pickle, include the *myōga*. Toss the mixture with your hands. Begin with a light touch, gradually exerting more pressure until you are able to squeeze a fair amount of liquid from the vegetables. Keep whatever liquid (brine) is exuded in the bowl.

The *kombu* goes in next. If you want to eat it with the pickles, cut it into threadlike slivers with scissors. Many home cooks prefer to use the *kombu* whole, however, discarding it after the pickle has matured. Note that its addition will cause the liquid to become slightly sticky. The *kombu* will become a bit slippery, especially at the edges. This is a good sign, because it is evidence that the natural glutamates in the kelp are doing their flavor-enhancing work.

Transfer the shredded vegetables, brine, and *kombu* to a *shokutaku tsukémono ki* (page 80). Screw the top in place under maximum pressure and marinate for at least 1 hour at room temperature or for up to 24 hours in the refrigerator. Or devise your own setup, allowing the weights to sit, undisturbed, for at least 3 hours at room temperature or for up to 36 hours in the refrigerator.

Just before serving, rinse the vegetables under cold running water and drain. Squeeze to make sure no water remains. Mound in a single bowl or in individual mounds on 4 plates. Drizzle the soy sauce over the mounded pickle, if desired.

Kitchen Harmony

In most big-city households, this sort of quick pickle is a way of using up vegetables a bit beyond their prime. Daikon, carrots, ruffle-leaved cabbages, and turnips are frequently pickled this way, sometimes pairing lemon zest and *tōgarashi* (page 42) with the *kombu* in lieu of the *myōga*. See Citron-Pickled Chinese Cabbage (right) for further ideas.

To transform these quick pickles into a salad, drizzle them with the clear-style dressing in Chilled Chinese Noodle Salad (page 178), Smoky Citrus-Soy Sauce (page 97), or Smoky Vinaigrette (page 99).

CITRON-PICKLED CHINESE CABBAGE

YUZU FUMI HAKUSAI

Cabbages of almost any sort lend themselves to brine-pickling, though hakusai, *known in the West as Chinese cabbage, is the most commonly used. Cabbage that is past its prime coleslaw days is perfect for making these citron-infused pickles.*

Fresh yuzu is hard to find outside of Japan, though increasingly the freeze-dried peel is sold in Asian grocery stores worldwide. It provides a subtle, almost floral tone to foods infused with it. Fresh lemon, lime, and/or grapefruit zest makes a fine substitute.

Illustrated on page 4

SERVES 8 TO 10

$^1/_4$ head Chinese cabbage, about 12 ounces

2 teaspoons coarse salt

1 tablespoon freeze-dried yuzu peel (page 28), crushed or cut with scissors into very small bits, or finely minced fresh lemon, lime, or grapefruit zest

1 piece kombu (page 42), preferably Rishiri kombu, Rausu kombu, or ma kombu, 2 to 3 inches square

1 tōgarashi (page 47), broken in half, seeds removed, and cut into thin strips

2 tablespoons rice vinegar

1 tablespoon fresh lemon, lime, and/or grapefruit juice

1 teaspoon mirin

1 teaspoon light-colored soy sauce

Soy sauce (optional)

If you are using very fresh cabbage, you will need to wilt it first: Cut the cabbage into 2 or 3 wedges through the core and spread them out on a tray on a sunny window ledge for a few hours. Or let the cabbage wedges sit out on a plate at room temperature overnight.

In a large bowl, stir together the salt and *yuzu* peel. Place the cabbage in the bowl and sprinkle half of the mixture over the cabbage, rubbing it into the thicker core and lifting layers of the leaves to sprinkle it between them. With sharp scissors, cut the *kombu* into a dozen strips. Lift the layers of cabbage leaves and distribute half of the *kombu* strips among them.

Allow the seasoned cabbage to sit in a bowl for 10 minutes, or until it begins to "sweat." The addition of the *kombu* will cause the brine to become slightly sticky. The *kombu*, too, will become slippery, which is a good sign, because it is evidence that the natural glutamates in the kelp are doing their flavor-enhancing work. Gently squeeze the cabbage, applying greater pressure as more liquid is exuded and it becomes very limp and pliable. Keep whatever liquid (brine) is exuded in the bowl.

The cabbage needs to be weighted down for a period of time in order to create brine in which it can pickle. Depending on your choice of equipment, the procedure will vary slightly.

If you are using a *shokutaku tsukémono ki* (page 80), sprinkle the remaining *yuzu*-salt mixture on the flat bottom of the device before laying the cabbage evenly on top. Pour in any accumulated brine from the bowl, and then scatter the remaining *kombu* strips over the cabbage. Add the *tōgarashi* strips, placing several between and among the cabbage leaves and allowing a few to float in the brine. Screw the top in place under maximum pressure and let sit for at least 8 hours at room temperature, or for up to 24 hours in the refrigerator. It is fine if liquid rises above the inner lid from the start, but if the brine does not rise above the inner lid after 2 or 3 hours, unscrew the top, flip the cabbage over, and add a few drops water. Replace the lid, again screwing it as tightly as possible.

If you are devising your own weights, scatter the remaining *kombu* strips on the inside of a glass bowl and lay the cabbage flat on top. Sprinkle the remaining *yuzu*-salt mixture over the cabbage. Pour in any accumulated brine, adding the *tōgarashi* strips to the pickling liquid. Lay a flat plate over all, and then place weights on top of the plate. See page 80 for more details on this method. Let sit, undisturbed, for at least 8 hours at room temperature, or for up to 24 hours in the refrigerator. It is fine if liquid rises above the plate from the start, but if the brine does not rise above the plate after 2 or 3 hours, remove the plate, flip the cabbage over, and add a few drops water. Replace the plate and place additional weight on top.

When ready, unscrew the jar's inner lid or remove the weights and plate from the bowl, and pour off any brine. Transfer the limp cabbage, including whatever strips of *kombu* or bits of citrus peel are clinging to it, to a 1-quart canning jar. It should be a snug fit, but use more than 1 jar, if necessary.

In a small bowl, stir together the rice vinegar, lemon juice, mirin, and light-colored soy sauce and pour the mixture over the cabbage to cover it, leaving ¼ inch of headroom in each jar. For a spicier pickle, keep the *tōgarashi* pieces in the liquid. For a milder pickle, discard them. Seal the jar(s) with clear plastic wrap and a tight-fitting lid, or use a Mason jar. Let the pickle mature at room temperature for at least 2 hours and up to 5 hours. Refrigerate until ready to serve; the cabbage will keep for up to 1 week.

Just before serving, remove the cabbage from its seasoned liquid and squeeze out any moisture. Chop coarsely. The *kombu* strips are edible, but if you find them tough, they can be removed. Pour a few drops of soy sauce over the pickle.

和食

Kitchen Harmony

When daikon, beet, or turnip tops have begun to wither, they can also be made into pickles. If you are pickling leafy greens, be sure to soak them first in cold water to remove any residual dirt. Spin them dry and then set them out to wilt on a tray in a sunny spot for several hours or at room temperature overnight. These citron-pickled greens as well as the cabbage are well suited to serving with braised, simmered, or stewed foods.

For a quicker version of brine-pickled vegetables, see Impatient Pickles (page 217).

NEW YEAR'S SALAD

KŌHAKU NAMASU

This "salad" of finely shredded daikon and carrot is accented with citrus and dried fruit and is dressed in a sweet-and-sour sauce. A red-and-white color scheme (the carrots are red, the radish is white) is often chosen for a celebratory menu in Japan. This particular dish typically graces holiday tables at the New Year.

SERVES 6 TO 8

- 3¹/₂-inch piece daikon, about 7 ounces, peeled and cut into thin strips (page 69)
- ¹/₂ teaspoon coarse salt
- 1-inch piece carrot, preferably Kyoto red carrot, about 2 ounces, peeled and cut into thin strips (page 69)
- ¹/₂ teaspoon freeze-dried yuzu peel (page 28), ground to a powder, or finely grated fresh lemon zest
- ¹/₂ small dried persimmon or 1 small dried apricot, finely shredded
- ¹/₂ cup Sweet-and-Sour Sauce (page 98), prepared with kombu piece

Place the daikon shreds in a bowl and sprinkle with ¹/₄ teaspoon of the salt. Allow the daikon shreds to sit undisturbed for about 2 minutes, or until they begin to "sweat." Gently toss, gradually increasing pressure with your fingertips, squeezing and pressing to wilt the daikon. Pour off any accumulated liquid and rinse the wilted daikon shreds briefly under running cold water to remove excess salt. Squeeze again. The daikon will be pliable at this point.

Place the carrot shreds in a bowl with the remaining ¹/₄ teaspoon salt and let sit undisturbed for about 3 minutes, or until they begin to "sweat." Gently toss, gradually increasing pressure with your fingertips, squeezing and pressing to wilt the carrot. Pour off the accumulated liquid and rinse the carrot shreds briefly under running cold water to remove excess salt. Squeeze again. The carrot will be pliable at this point.

Combine the carrots and radish in a bowl. Add the *yuzu* peel and dried fruit and toss well to distribute. Pour the Sweet-and-Sour Sauce over the vegetable-and-fruit mixture and toss lightly. Let stand for at least 1 hour at room temperature. Or, for longer storage (up to 3 days), transfer the mixture with its sweet-and-sour pickling liquid to a glass jar. With clean chopsticks or another kitchen tool, press down on the mixture, making sure it is submerged in the liquid. Place the *kombu* piece on top before capping. Cover the jar with plastic wrap (to keep the vinegar from reacting with the metal of the lid) and a tight-fitting lid, or use a Mason jar.

Just before serving, drain the daikon and carrot mixture and discard the *kombu*. Gently squeeze out excess moisture.

Kitchen Harmony

To garnish a platter of fish or meat, halve lemons crosswise, scoop out their pulp, and serve this salad gently mounded in the shells.

When peeling the radish and carrot, use the technique called *katsura muki* (page 68) to create long, thin continuous sheets. That way, you can use the leftovers to make Fiery Parsnips (page 215).

Harmony at Table

Toward the end of the year and through early February, a blood red carrot, known as *kintoki* or *Kyō ninjin* (literally, "the carrot from Kyoto"), comes to market in Tokyo as well as Kyoto. If you can find similar intensely red carrots at your market, this salad will be even more stunning.

RED-AND-WHITE PICKLED RADISHES

KŌHAKU SU-ZUKÉ

Bunches of small radishes, bright red with white necks and each the size and shape of my pinky finger, come to Tokyo markets with their leaves intact in the spring and summer. I usually trim off the leaves, reserving them for another use, before pickling the radishes in this sweet-and-sour style.

Illustrated on page 286

SERVES 4 TO 6

    10 to 12 small red radishes, trimmed (see notes)

    1 teaspoon coarse salt

    $^1/_2$ cup Sweet-and-Sour Sauce (page 98), prepared with kombu piece

If using slender, oblong radishes, typically red with white necks (the kind commonly available in Japan and many parts of Europe), slice each radish in half lengthwise, and then cut in half again to yield 4 baton-shaped pieces. If using a round all-red-on-the-outside, white-on-the inside variety (more commonly found throughout North America), slice each radish into quarters.

Place the radish pieces in a glass or ceramic bowl and sprinkle with the salt. Allow the radishes to sit undisturbed for about 5 minutes, or until they begin to "sweat" a bit. Gently toss, gradually increasing pressure with your fingertips, squeezing and pressing to wilt the radishes. Pour off any accumulated liquid and rinse the wilted radishes briefly under running cold water to remove excess salt. Squeeze again. The radishes will be pliable at this point.

Place the radishes in a glass jar and pour the Sweet-and-Sour Sauce over them, setting the *kombu* piece on top. Cover with plastic wrap (to keep the vinegar from reacting with the metal of the lid) and a tight-fitting lid, or use a Mason jar. Let the radishes stand for at least 30 minutes at room tempera-ture, or overnight. At first the radishes are mild and the colors, red and white, are bright and distinct. But the longer the radishes pickle, the more they "bleed," and the more intensely flavored they become. After 1 day, when the sweet-and-sour pickling liquid turns deep red and the radishes become rosy throughout, it is best to refrigerate them. The radishes will keep in a tightly covered jar in the refrigerator for up to 1 week. With clean chopsticks or another kitchen tool, press down on the radishes to make sure they are submerged in the sweet-and-sour pickling liquid.

Just before serving, discard the *kombu* piece and drain the radishes well, squeezing them lightly.

Kitchen Harmony

If you are pressed for time, the radishes can be cut into thin circles or half-moons instead of larger chunks. The thinner slices will pickle quickly—within 20 minutes.

Radish greens have a pleasantly spicy flavor and are packed with vitamin A and iron. Dip them briefly into boiling water, plunge them into cold water, and then drain them immediately to preserve their nutrients and improve their flavor. You can now use these blanched greens as you would any green leafy vegetable: add them to miso soup; dress them in Creamy Sesame-Miso Sauce (page 100) or Creamy Tōfu Sauce (page 107); or prepare them as you would Spinach Steeped in Broth (page 190) or Asparagus Tossed with Crushed Black Sesame (page 198).

SWEET-AND-SOUR LOTUS ROOT

SUBASU

Whenever I see fresh lotus root at the market (especially small, slender, straight segments that enable me to make lots of attractive slices), I double, or even triple, this recipe. Having subasu on hand in the refrigerator, I can easily dress up a salad, garnish a plate of broiled chicken or fish, or top a platter of scattered-style sushi.

Illustrated on page 146

MAKES ABOUT 30 TO 40 SLICES

    2 cups cold water
    2 tablespoons rice vinegar
    1 small segment lotus root, about 4 ounces, peeled, sliced
        as thinly as possible, and soaked (page 76)
    ¹/₂ cup Sweet-and-Sour Sauce (page 98), prepared with
        kombu piece

In a nonreactive saucepan, combine the water and vinegar and bring to a boil. Add the lotus root and blanch for less than a minute, or until barely tender and slightly translucent. Meanwhile, put the Sweet-and-Sour Sauce in a glass jar.

Drain the lotus root slices well but do not refresh under cold running water. Transfer them immediately to the jar holding the Sweet-and-Sour Sauce and arrange the *kombu* piece on top. With clean chopsticks or another kitchen tool, press down to make sure that the lotus root is submerged in the pickling liquid. Let cool to room temperature.

When completely cool, cover the top of the jar with plastic wrap (to keep the vinegar from reacting with the metal of the lid) and a tight-fitting lid, or use a Mason jar. Allow the pickled lotus root to "mature" in the refrigerator for at least 1 day. It will keep for up to several months.

Just before serving, discard the *kombu* piece, drain the slices, and blot them with paper towels.

Kitchen Harmony

To add color and flavor interest, lotus root is sometimes pickled with plum vinegar (page 49), the by-product of pickling *uméboshi*. If you would like to try making your own batch of naturally pink-tinted slices, refer to the notes in the Sweet-and-Sour Sauce recipe (page 98).

Harmony at Table

The Japanese often pair red (or pink) foods with white ones, a combination called *kōhaku* that signifies felicity. Make both the pink and the white pickled lotus root, and scatter them over a bed of soft lettuces for a festive salad. For a more traditional approach, use them to decorate Five-Colored Foods with Sushi Rice (page 147).

BLUSHING PINK GINGER

HAJIKAMI SU-ZUKÉ

This recipe will enable you to make your own pink pickled ginger, just like the kind served at your favorite sushi bar—even better, in fact, if you can source knobs of tender young shin shōga *(literally, "new ginger") that display a faint blush just beneath tissue-thin skin, a pigmentation that is enhanced by the pickling process. The lovely shade of pink that ginger turns when pickled is charmingly referred to as "embarrassing" or "blushing" in Japanese.*

Both knobs of new ginger and stalks of young stem ginger (yanaka shōga) *make embarrassingly vivid pickles.*

MAKES ABOUT ¹/₂ CUP THIN SLICES, OR 10 TO 12 GINGER STEMS

  2 knobs fresh new ginger, each about 2 ounces, or 3 or
      4 stalks young stem ginger
¹/₂ cup Sweet-and-Sour Sauce (page 98), prepared with
      kombu piece

With the back of your knife, scrape away the thin skin from the knobs of new ginger. Cut the ginger into tissue-thin slices with a very sharp knife or mandoline. Or, if using stem ginger, trim each stalk to about 2 inches in length and pull away any wayward or browning outer layers. Scrape away the thin skin from the knob portion. Halve each stem of ginger lengthwise.

Put the sauce in a glass jar. If pickling stem ginger, the jar should be tall enough to accommodate the stalks with ¹/₂ inch of headroom and just wide enough to allow for a snug fit. A jar with a lid is best. If the stem ginger is too tall, it can be covered with plastic wrap and secured with a rubber band.

Fill a 2-quart nonreactive pot with lightly salted water and bring to a rolling boil. If preparing new ginger, blanch the slices for 45 seconds after the water returns to a boil. If preparing stem ginger, holding the green stalk of stem ginger with long chopsticks or tongs, lower the knob portion into the pot of boiling water. Blanch for 1 minute. Then let the stalk slip into the water and blanch the whole shoot for an additional 30 seconds.

Drain the slices or stems and transfer them to the jar holding the sauce. With clean chopsticks or another kitchen tool, press down on the slices of new ginger to make sure that they are submerged in the liquid and place the *kombu* piece on top. Or, if using stem ginger, to maximize the color contrast between the yellow-and-pink knob and the green stalk, make sure that the knob portion of each piece is submerged in the liquid, but that the green stalk is not. Let cool to room temperature and then cover.

Allow the pickled ginger stems to "mature" in the refrigerator for at least 2 hours and up to 1 week. Sliced pickled ginger can be stored for several months. The ginger will turn blushing pink, naturally.

When ready to serve, remove the ginger from the pickling liquid and discard the *kombu*. Drain and blot away excess liquid. Slices are typically coaxed into a cluster or mound. The stem ginger is most often used as a garnish for broiled fish or chicken. Only the knob portion is eaten.

Kitchen Harmony

The pickling liquid that remains after eating a batch of pink ginger can be reused to make subsequent batches. Be sure to bring it to a full boil and cook for 2 minutes before straining it into a clean, dry glass jar. If necessary, increase the volume by combining this batch will freshly made Sweet-and-Sour Sauce. After making several batches of pickled ginger, the liquid is full of flavor and a charming shade of pink. Use it as a dressing for a salad or in place of the seasoned vinegar when making Sushi Rice (page 145).

FISH

LIVING IN TOKYO, I can buy high-quality fish at even the smallest food market in my neighborhood. Seasonality is evident, but on any given day, the mom-and-pop place near my train station has dozens of glisteningly fresh sea and stream species available—some still swimming in tanks and many others whole on ice, although most have been filleted. For anyone in a hurry, there are fish dressed and wrapped in plastic wrap in a refrigerated case near the cash register. And the supermarket down the street offers prepared fish and shellfish in addition to ready-to-cook items. Because I have such a wealth of resources close by, it is easy for me to pick and choose daily according to whim and budget.

Whether you have access to an abundant supply of fresh fish or need to make do with just a few species, understanding the flavor and texture characteristics of various fish will enable you to select and prepare them well. Being able to choose an appropriate cooking method for the fish at hand, and knowing how to substitute one species of fish for another, will rapidly increase your repertoire. Unfortunately, names can be confusing from region to region. Even from market to market within the same community, the same fish is often sold under a different label. Because of this, I urge you to refer to the descriptions of various fish included in the Washoku Pantry (page 10).

General information on purchase and storage can also be found there.

This chapter includes fifteen recipes for preparing fish by various methods, including grilling and broiling, pan searing, simmering, steaming and poaching, and frying. I have not included fresh, or raw, fish dishes, what most Americans know as sashimi, because the subject of selecting and handling fish to be consumed raw and the skill level needed to prepare such food successfully are beyond the scope of this book. (Incidentally, the word *sashimi* actually means "fresh slice," and in Japan can refer as easily to a slice of raw ripe tomato as it can to a slice of ruby red tuna. In classical cooking, *otsukuri* is the name given to the course that showcases the creative transformation of ingredients, most often sourced from the sea and nearly always untreated with heat.)

I have chosen, instead, to focus my energies on providing you with recipes and ideas that originated in home kitchens. Soy glazing, salt broiling, and poaching in packets are a few of the straightforward ways to prepare fresh fish. A dish such as Broth-Simmered Small Whole Flounders (page 234) may present a few kitchen challenges to anyone who has not cooked fish whole before, but if you are able to locate the ingredients, I urge you to expand your culinary skills. And while the notion of frying and then pickling and eating the whole body, including the head and tail, of small fish may be off-putting to some, the delicious Crisp Fried Smelts in Spicy Vinaigrette (page 245) made many converts among my volunteer recipe testers. Similarly, stronger-flavored fish such as mackerel and sardines may not seem immediately appealing, but Fish Simmered in Pungent Miso Sauce (page 233) is at its best when made with mackerel. And Simmered Snapper, Autumn Rain Style (page 236) actually tastes better prepared with full-flavored sardines than with mild snapper.

In Japan, fish is often the centerpiece of a menu, served as a main course accompanied by a few small vegetable selections. For a better understanding of how meals are assembled in general and how the recipes in this chapter can be incorporated into daily menus specifically, take a look at Putting Theory into Practice (page 3) and Washoku: The Five Principles (page 2).

Kitchen Harmony

On a Japanese menu, foods that have been seared with heat, either by broiling or grilling them, are called *yakimono*. The category also includes pan-seared or glazed dishes such as this one. When citrus juice is used, as in this recipe, I prefer pan searing because it does not dry out the fish the way grilling or broiling often does. I also think it is easier for home cooks to prepare fish in a skillet.

This recipe is best suited to thick fillets or steaks of oily fish, such as swordfish or kingfish. If you prefer a mild-flavored fish, try cod or sea bass; salmon works well, too. If you are cooking fish with the skin intact, sear the flesh side first and then flip to cook the skin side. When glazing, begin and end with the flesh side.

CITRUS-AND-SOY-GLAZED SWORDFISH

KAJIKI MAGURO NO YŪAN YAKI

There are several stories offered on the origin of the name yūan yaki, which is a citrus-infused variation on glaze grilling. One explanation is that an eighteenth-century tea master by the name of Yūan Kitamura created the dish for a kaiseki menu he was preparing. Another explanation suggests that the inclusion of yuzu, a variety of citron prized for its fragrant skin, provided the sound yu and therefore the name. The calligraphy chosen to write yūan yaki on a menu alerts Japanese diners as to which interpretation that chef, or restaurant, favors. Most commonly seen today is the combination of "profound" and "hermitage," offering yet another, more philosophic twist to this succulent preparation.

In Japan, where fresh yuzu can be purchased at any market from November through March, the entire fruit would be used in preparing this dish. The fragrant yellow zest, which is the part of the fruit that is usually consumed, would be set aside to dust the glazed fish just before bringing it to table. The astringent juice, which is not often used, would be added to the marinade to tone down the oiliness of the fish.

Outside Japan, where fresh yuzu is difficult to find, I suggest its complex flavor by combining lime, grapefruit, and lemon, using each citrus fruit in a slightly different way. I take juice from lime and grapefruit to replicate the citron's refreshingly acerbic quality, and I take zest from lemon peel to approximate its sweet, floral tones.

SERVES 4 TO 6

1 tablespoon fresh lime or grapefruit juice
2 tablespoons saké
1 pound swordfish or other meaty fish steaks or fillets, cut into 4 to 6 pieces
2 tablespoons soy sauce
3 tablespoons mirin
1 teaspoon vegetable oil

Glaze

1 tablespoon fresh lime or grapefruit juice
1 tablespoon soy sauce
2 teaspoons sugar
1 to 2 tablespoons Basic Sea Stock (page 92) or water, if needed
1 tablespoon grated lemon zest

Stir together the citrus juice and saké in a glass or other nonreactive dish just large enough to hold the fish in a single layer. Rinse the fish under cold water and pat dry. Add the fish to the dish and marinate for 5 to 10 minutes. Add the soy sauce and mirin and marinate the fish for another 5 minutes at room temperature, or covered in the refrigerator for no longer than 1 hour. Extended marinating will toughen the fish and make the soy and citrus flavors too intense.

Remove the fish from the marinade and blot away excess moisture with paper towels. Heat a nonstick skillet just large enough to hold the fish in a single layer over high heat. Drizzle in the oil, add the fish, and sear for 2 minutes, or until lightly browned and fragrant. Flip and sear the second side for about 1 minute, or until it begins to brown. (If the pieces are more than $3/4$ inch thick, you may need to lower the heat and cover the pan for a minute to allow the heat to penetrate the fish.) To test for doneness, press the fish lightly; it should feel fairly firm.

To make the glaze, combine the lime juice, soy sauce, and sugar in a small bowl and stir to mix. Pour this mixture around the edge of the pan and stir or shake the pan vigorously until the sugar is dissolved. If the sauce looks in danger of scorching, add the stock. Flip the fish and continue to braise over high heat for about $1^{1}/_{2}$ minutes, or until the fish feels firm and the sauce is very foamy and reduced by half.

To serve, drizzle the glaze over the fish and sprinkle with the lemon zest.

SANSHŌ PEPPER–CRUSTED GROUPER

KUÉ NO ARIMA YAKI

Arima, an area not far from Kyoto famous for its crop of sanshō *pepper berries, lends its name to dishes made with them. For example, a fish pan seared with a* sanshō *crust appears as Arima* yaki *on menus. The classic version of the dish is made by crushing the pepper berries and mixing them with light, sweet miso to create an intense sauce. Plain fish is grilled over hot coals and then slathered with the miso mixture and briefly grilled again.*

Much of the sanshō *harvested in the area is preserved in soy sauce, Tsukuda ni* style, *or dried and then either coarsely cracked or crushed to a powder. Partially cracked, fully dried pepper berries sold in refillable mills are increasingly available in Asian grocery stores outside Japan, and it is worth the trouble to track down a source for them to make this recipe. The freshly ground dried berries have both fire and aroma, resulting in an especially tasty coating.*

SERVES 4

    1 pound grouper fillet with skin intact, cut into 4 pieces
    2 teaspoons dried sanshō berries (page 47), freshly
      ground
    $^1/_4$ teaspoon coarse salt
    1 teaspoon cornstarch
    1 to 1$^1/_2$ tablespoons vegetable oil
    1 tablespoon saké
    4 lemon wedges

Rinse the fish pieces under cold running water and pat dry with paper towels. If the pieces are more than $^1/_2$ inch thick, make shallow slits on the skin side to ensure even cooking.

In a shallow, flat-bottomed container such as a baking dish, mix the *sanshō*, salt, and $^1/_2$ teaspoon of the cornstarch. Dredge each piece of fish, flesh side only, in the mixture, pressing the pieces lightly to make sure the surface is fully coated and the mixture adheres. Flip the fish and lightly dust

the skin side with the remaining $^1/_2$ teaspoon cornstarch. Using a pastry brush will make this easier.

Select a skillet large enough to hold the fish in a single layer and place over medium-high heat. When the pan is hot, drizzle in 1 tablespoon of the oil, add the fish, flesh side down, and sear for about 2 minutes, or until crusty brown and fragrant. If necessary, press each piece with a spatula to ensure that the entire surface comes in contact with the skillet.

Flip the fish with the spatula and sear the skin side for about 1 minute, or until slightly blistered, drizzling more oil around the fish as needed. As the skin shrinks a bit, the flesh side will plump up. Flip again, returning the flesh side to the skillet. Press each piece with the spatula to flatten a bit.

Pour the saké around the fish slices and jiggle the skillet to deglaze it. Lower the heat to low and place a tight-fitting lid on the pan. Continue to cook for 2$^1/_2$ to 3 minutes, allowing the heat to penetrate the fish. To test for doneness, press the fish lightly with a spatula, fingertips, or chopsticks; it should feel firm.

Transfer the fish pieces, flesh side up, to individual serving dishes. Garnish each plate with a lemon wedge.

Kitchen Harmony

This recipe works well with many varieties of fish. If you cannot find grouper, try cod or sea bass. Salmon is appropriate, too, though the fillets are typically thinner and take less time to cook through. Ideally, the fish fillet should have the skin intact, which helps keep the flesh moist.

MISO-MARINATED BROILED FISH

SAIKYŌ YAKI

Before refrigeration, the Japanese preserved freshly caught fish in various ways. One of the most popular was putting it in a marinade of mellow bean paste. Even though refrigeration is readily available nowadays, the Japanese still like the rich flavor of miso-marinated fish. Fresh salmon, saberfish (tachiuo), kingfish (sawara), and black cod (gindara) are especially delicious prepared this way. The fillets can be marinated for a few days in the refrigerator. If you follow the guidelines provided here, the marinade can be reused (see notes, page 230).

For anyone who is impatient, or who does not wish to devote shelf space in the refrigerator to this endeavor, I have provided a fast-acting variation that approximates the slower, more traditional method. In either case, you will need to wrap the fish in cloth or gauze to produce the most flavorful, attractive result.

Illustrated on page 4

SERVES 4 TO 6

1$\frac{1}{2}$ pounds fish fillet with skin intact, cut into 4 to 6 pieces

Traditional Marinade

2$\frac{1}{2}$ to 3 cups sweet, light miso, preferably Saikyō miso

$\frac{1}{4}$ cup mirin

1 tablespoon bits of freeze-dried yuzu peel (page 28) or
    grated fresh lemon or orange zest (optional)

Impatient Marinade

1 teaspoon coarse salt

$\frac{1}{3}$ cup sweet, light miso, preferably Saikyō miso

2 tablespoons mirin

1 tablespoon saké

1 tablespoon freeze-dried yuzu peel (page 28), crushed to a
    powder, or grated fresh lemon or orange zest (optional)

Lemon or lime wedges (optional)
Blushing Pink Ginger (page 223) (optional)

If preparing fish by the traditional method, rinse the fish pieces under cold running water and pat them dry. To make the marinade, combine the miso, mirin, and *yuzu* peel, if desired, in a nonreactive container and stir to mix well. Adding the *yuzu* will make any oily fish, such as kingfish, more delicate in flavor.

Depending on the size of your container, you will marinate the fish in a single layer (a wide, shallow gratin dish or other baking dish) or in 2 layers (a deep, narrow glass loaf pan). Using a flexible spatula or the back of a large spoon, push aside half of the marinade if making 1 layer, and about two-thirds of the marinade if making 2 layers.

Lay a single thickness of *sarashi* cloth (page 77) or a double thickness of cheesecloth or surgical gauze over the marinade. Arrange the cloth so that about half of it is used to cover the marinade (press it lightly in place) and you have enough extra material to enclose the fish. Lay pieces of the fish on the marinade-moistened cloth, being careful not to overlap the slices. Fold the extra cloth over the fish pieces to enclose them. Spread the remaining marinade over the cloth if you are making a single layer. If you are making 2 layers, repeat to make a second layer in the same manner, using half of the remaining marinade between layers and half on top. Place a sheet of plastic wrap over the top of the marinating "sandwich" of sliced fish, pressing lightly to ensure even distribution of the marinade.

Allow the fish to marinate at cool room temperature (no warmer than 75°F) for at least 6 hours or in the refrigerator for up to 2 or 3 days. The fish will develop a heady, fermented aroma; turn a golden, translucent color; and become a bit slippery and sticky to the touch. The longer the fish marinates, the firmer and the more intensely salty sweet it will become.

If preparing the fish by the impatient method, rinse the fish pieces under cold running water and pat dry with paper towels. Place the fish on paper towels and sprinkle both sides with the salt. Let stand for 5 minutes, or until it "sweats." Blot away excess moisture with paper towels.

Lay a single thickness of *sarashi* cloth (page 77) or a double thickness of cheesecloth or surgical gauze over a baking sheet. Arrange the fish slices on the cloth, being careful not to overlap them. Cover the fish with more cloth.

To make the marinade, combine the miso, mirin, saké, and *yuzu* peel, if desired, in a bowl and stir to mix well. Adding the *yuzu* will make any oily fish, such as kingfish, more delicate in flavor. Using a pastry brush, paint the cloth-wrapped fish with the marinade. Flip the fish pieces over and paint the other side. Allow the fish to marinate at cool room temperature (no warmer than 75°F) for at least 20 minutes or in the refrigerator for up to 1 hour. The fish will become a bit slippery to the touch.

Preheat a broiler or prepare a medium-hot grill. Scrape away the miso marinade and remove the fish from its cloth wrapping. If you wish to reuse the marinade, consult the accompanying notes.

If broiling, place the fish pieces skin side up on a shallow disposable aluminum pan or on the tray of a broiler pan and place in the broiler about 3 inches from the heat source. If grilling, because the marinated fish scorches easily, it is best to place it skin side down on the grill. Broil or grill for 3 to 4 minutes, or until the skin begins to bubble and even chars a bit in places, and then flip the pieces. Broil or grill for another 2 to 3 minutes. Ideally, the fish will be slightly crusty and golden on the surface and white (or pink, if you are using salmon) and succulent inside.

Arrange the fish on individual serving plates. To enhance the citrus overtones of this dish, accompany the fish with lemon wedges. Or, for a spicier accent, garnish each plate with Blushing Pink Ginger, either a cluster of slices or a stalk of stem ginger.

Kitchen Harmony

To reuse the miso marinade, carefully scrape the miso off the cloth that was used to wrap the fish. Transfer the marinade to a clean glass jar, cover with plastic wrap (to prevent interaction with the cap and create a tighter fit) and a tight-fitting lid, or use a Mason jar. Label the jar with the date and the fact that fish had been marinated in the mixture. This marinade should never be tasted, nor should this miso be used in any other recipe. As a marinade, though, it can be reused several times within a 4- to 6-week period, if refrigerated when not in use. The cloth can also be saved and reused. Rinse it well in warm water, squeeze, and set out to dry. Store in a zippered plastic bag, refrigerated with the jar of marinade.

SALT-BROILED KINGFISH

SAWARA NO SHIO YAKI

Shio yaki, or salt broiling, is a standard Japanese cooking method, especially for fish. Historically, fish was either skewered and placed vertically around a hearth or laid flat on mesh screens and suspended over hot charcoal embers. Today's Japanese home kitchens are equipped with small, below-the-countertop broiler units (the Japanese call them "grills," even though the source of heat is above the food).

In the early fall, slender, silvery fish call sanma *are salt broiled whole. In the spring, delicate* ayu *trout get similar treatment. Because many Americans are reluctant to serve fish whole, this recipe calls for fillets. I have chosen kingfish because it is a fairly mild-flavored fish with relatively few bones that are easily removed after cooking. Fillets of bass, snapper, grouper, porgy, or salmon can also be cooked in this manner as long as part of their flesh is protected by skin.*

SERVES 4

4 kingfish fillets with skin intact, about $^1/_2$-inch-thick fillets or steaks, 3 ounces each

1 teaspoon coarse salt

2 tablespoons saké

3-to 4-inch chunk daikon, 6 to 8 ounces, peeled and grated (page 59) to yield about $^1/_2$ cup

1 lime or lemon, cut into 4 wedges

2 teaspoons soy sauce

Blushing Pink Ginger (page 223) (optional)

Preheat a broiler or prepare a medium-hot grill.

Rinse the fish under cold running water and pat dry with paper towels. Arrange the fish pieces, skin side up, on paper towels. Sprinkle half of the salt over the fish and lightly rub the salt into the skin. Flip the fish over and sprinkle the remaining salt over the flesh, but do not rub. Let stand at cool room tem-

perature for 5 to 6 minutes, or until it "sweats." Blot away excess moisture with paper towels. Sprinkle the fish, flesh side up, with the saké.

If broiling, place the fish pieces skin side up on a shallow disposable aluminum pan or on the tray of a broiler pan and place in the broiler about $1^1/_2$ inches below the heat source. If grilling, place skin side down on the grill. Grill or broil the kingfish for 6 to 7 minutes, or until the skin begins to brown and bubble and even char in places. Wedge a flat, heat-proof spatula between the fish and the grill to see if the surface has crusted slightly and will release easily. If not, wait another minute and try again. Flip the fish and cook for another 2 to 3 minutes, until the flesh is opaque and firm (press the fish lightly with a spatula, fingertips, or chopsticks to verify).

Arrange the fish on individual serving plates. Coax the grated daikon into 4 small mounds. Place 1 radish mound and 1 lime wedge on each plate. Serve the soy sauce for drizzling over the daikon. Or, for a spicier accent, garnish each plate with Blushing Pink Ginger, either a cluster of slices or a stalk of stem ginger.

Harmony at Table

The Japanese typically present small whole fish such as trout with the head to the left, tail to the right, and the belly facing forward on the plate. This is referred to as the "correct" position. Even when plating fillets or steaks, the thicker portion (the part nearer the head when the fish was alive) is set to the left, with the belly forward.

BROILED AIR-DRIED FISH

ICHIYA-BOSHI

Traditionally, bountiful catches of fish were gutted, salted, and set out to dry to extend their shelf life. The generic term for these sorts of fish is himono *(literally, "the dried thing"), though these air-dried fish are actually quite moist to the touch and wonderfully succulent when broiled or grilled.*

These same fish are also known as ichiya-boshi *(literally, "dried overnight"), especially when they appear on the menus of pub-style restaurants or on breakfast trays at small family-style* minshuku *(modest lodgings similar to bed-and-breakfasts in America and Europe). The Japanese typically broil or grill these fish (skin side to the flame until bubbly and slightly charred, then flipped and cooked until opaque) and serve them with grated daikon drizzled with soy sauce or with lemon wedges. They make a quick meal on a busy day.*

SERVES 4

2 to 4 ichiya-boshi (page 15), about 1$^1/_2$ pounds total, thawed if frozen

2 tablespoons saké

3- to 4-inch chunk daikon, 6 to 8 ounces, peeled and grated (page 59)

1 lemon or lime, cut into 4 wedges

Preheat a broiler or prepare a medium-hot grill.

Rinse the fish under cold running water and pat dry with paper towels. Place the fish in a shallow baking dish and sprinkle all the surfaces evenly with saké to moisten.

If broiling, place the fish pieces skin side up on a shallow disposable aluminum pan or on the tray of a broiler pan and place in the broiler about 1 inch below the heat source. If grilling, place skin side down on the grill.

Watch carefully, because air-dried fish scorches easily. Cooking times vary with the size and variety of fish, and with the type of broiler or grill you are using. Most air-dried fish will take 3 to 4 minutes for the skin to brown and bubble and even char in places. At that point, you should flip the fish. Another 2 minutes should suffice to complete cooking most air-dried fish. The fish is done when the flesh is opaque, rather than translucent. Another way to check progress is to try gently lifting the tail; if the backbone easily separates from the flesh, the fish is ready.

Arrange the fish on individual serving plates with the head to the left, tail to the right, and the belly facing forward on the plate. Coax the grated daikon into 4 small mounds. Place 1 radish mound and 1 lemon wedge just in front of the tail on each plate, or in separate small dishes.

FISH SIMMERED IN PUNGENT MISO SAUCE

AO-ZAKANA NO MISO NI

A classic technique employed in the Japanese home kitchen, miso simmering is particularly well suited to preparing oilier fish, a category called ao-zakana *(literally, "blue" fish) that is made up of fish rich in omega-3 fatty acids. By adding this technique to your kitchen repertoire, particularly this version accented with fresh ginger, I hope you'll enjoy eating pompano, mackerel, and other* ao-zakana *more often.*

SERVES 4

1 piece kombu (page 42), about 10 inches square

$^1/_3$ to $^1/_2$ cup water

1 small knob fresh ginger, about $^1/_2$ inch

2 whole pompanos, about 12 ounces each, cleaned, head and tail removed, and cut in half on the diagonal, or 4 mackerel or kingfish steaks with skin and center bone intact, about 4 ounces each

1 teaspoon coarse salt

Boiling water

3 to 4 tablespoons Pungent Red Miso Sauce (page 101)

Place the *kombu* and $^1/_3$ cup water in a shallow pan just wide enough to hold the fish in a single layer. Peel the ginger, adding the peels to the pan.

Cut the peeled ginger into tissue-thin slices, stack the slices, and cut the slices into very fine threads. Soak the ginger threads in cold water for 2 to 3 minutes to mellow their sharpness and make them crisp. Drain and gently but firmly press away all the liquid. Coax the ginger threads into 4 haystacks; set aside to use as a garnish.

Rinse the fish under cold running water and pat dry with paper towels. If you are preparing pompano, with a sharp knife, make decorative slashes on the skin (*kazari-bōchō*, page 68) to keep it from shriveling in an unattractive manner. If you are using fish steaks, there will not be a large enough area of skin to warrant this technique. Sprinkle the fish pieces with the salt, turning to cover all surfaces evenly. Let the pieces stand for a few minutes, or until they "sweat."

To keep unwelcome odors at bay, and to prevent the final sauce from becoming marred with unattractive scum, you need to treat the fish to a procedure called *shimo furi,* or "frost falling" (page 74), using boiling water. Once that step is complete, bring the water, kombu, and ginger peels to a boil over high heat. Lower the heat to maintain a steady but not too vigorous simmer. Add the "frosted" fish, piece by piece, swirling the pan to keep the fish from sticking to the bottom or sides. It is fine to place the fish on the *kombu.*

Stir in the miso sauce, lower the heat to a gentle simmer, and poach the fish for 2 to 3 minutes, preferably with an *otoshi-buta* (page 84) in place. Or improvise one with a double thickness of cooking parchment, cut in a circle 1 inch smaller in diameter than your pan and weighted down with a small, flat lid from another pot. This will help control splattering and ensure more even distribution of heat. If the fish looks in danger of scorching, add water as needed.

When the sauce has reduced by about half, remove and discard the ginger peels. (The *kombu* can be removed and discarded or it can remain and be eaten with the fish.) Remove the dropped lid, raise the heat to medium high, and further reduce the sauce to the consistency of tomato paste. To keep the fish from losing its shape, gently swirl the pan, rather than stirring, as the sauce reduces.

Serve the fish hot or allow it to cool in the pan to room temperature (cooling will intensify the flavor of the miso sauce). With a broad spatula, transfer the fish to individual serving plates and spoon the thick sauce from the pan over the fish. Garnish each plate with a haystack of ginger threads.

BROTH-SIMMERED SMALL WHOLE FLOUNDERS

KOKAREI NO SUGATA NI

Braising small fish whole, called sugata ni, *is a moderately advanced kitchen skill, requiring dexterity and patience with detail work. If you have access to fresh small flounders or other small flatfish, such as sole, I encourage you to try preparing them this way. You will be rewarded for your effort because cooked on the bone, these soy-braised whole fish are far more flavorful than fillets. And when prepared with care, the presentation is spectacular.*

I will guide you through the tricky spots, beginning with instructions for scaling and gutting the fish (so that you can do this yourself, or ask your fishmonger to do it the way it is described here). For anyone without access to small whole fish, I have included directions for fish steaks in the accompanying notes.

SERVES 2

> 2 whole small flounder or sole, 6 to 8 ounces each
> 2 pieces kombu (page 42), preferably ma kombu, each the same dimension as a single portion of fish
> $^1/_2$ cup water
> $^1/_2$ cup saké
> 1 burdock root, 10 to 12 inches long, rinsed and lightly scraped (page 58) (optional)
> 2 cups togi-jiru (page 39) or water
> 1 very small knob fresh ginger, about $^1/_4$ inch long
> 1$^1/_2$ tablespoons soy sauce
> 1$^1/_2$ tablespoons mirin
> 1 teaspoon sugar

The scales of small flounder are very small and can be easily removed with the tip or the back of your knife. Lay the head flat on your work counter, top side (with the eyes) facing down, and hold the tail with paper towels to ensure a secure grip. Working from the tail toward the head, use light scraping motions to remove the scales, then flip the fish over and repeat the procedure on the top side. An odorless, slightly sticky,

grayish film will come off with the scales; this is entirely normal. Rinse your knife and both sides of the fish under running cold water and pat the fish dry with paper towels.

With the top side of the fish facing you, lift up the edge of the gill cavity (it will look like a jawbone) near the small breast fin and remove the gills by tugging on them lightly with your fingertips. If the gills do not easily come away, use the tip of your knife to sever them from the head.

Next, locate the intestinal cavity on the underside of the fish. It is the small, semicircular area just behind the gill cavity; sometimes it appears to bulge (when filled with roe), and at other times it seems indented. With the tip of your knife, make a diagonal slit through the middle of this area just deep enough to allow you to remove the internal organs, but not so deep that it pierces the other side of the fish. With your fingertips, scoop out the contents of this cavity (the Japanese prize fish roe, however, and will leave them intact), then rinse and dry the fish again.

Finally, to ensure even and thorough cooking, make decorative slashes, or *kazari-bōchō* (page 68).

To assemble the braising liquid, place the 2 *kombu* pieces in a shallow pan or skillet large enough to hold both fish in a single layer. Add the water and saké and soak the *kombu* for 10 to 15 minutes, or until pliable.

The burdock root will add greater complexity of flavor and additional volume to this dish. If you decide to include it, now is a good time to parboil it. If you have *togi-jiru* on hand, use it; it makes the burdock root sweeter and enhances its woodsy aroma. If you do not have it, use plain tap water. Cut the burdock root into 1$^1/_2$-inch lengths. If the pieces are much thicker than a pencil, cut them lengthwise into $^1/_4$-inch-thick strips. Bring the water to a boil over medium-high heat, add the burdock root, and cook for 5 to 6 minutes, or until barely tender (a toothpick should meet with little resistance). Drain and rinse lightly under cold water.

Peel the ginger and add the peels to the braising liquid. Then grate the peeled ginger and squeeze to extract about 1 teaspoon juice (page 71). Set the ginger juice aside.

Bring the braising liquid to a boil over medium heat. Add the soy sauce, mirin, and sugar and stir to mix. When bubbles appear again at the edges of the pan, remove and discard the ginger peels and carefully arrange both fish, top side facing up, each on its own piece of *kombu*.

With a ladle, spoon some of the braising liquid over the fish until the decorative slashes are clearly defined (the skin shrinks, exposing the flesh) and the fins behind the gills have stiffened a bit. Add the parboiled burdock pieces around the edges of the pan and adjust the heat to maintain a steady but gentle simmer. Place an *otoshi-buta* (page 84) over the fish and burdock root. Or improvise a dropped lid with a double thickness of cooking parchment, cut in a circle 1 inch smaller in diameter than your pan and weighted down with a small, flat lid from another pot. This will keep the fish moist and ensure even coloration. Simmer for about 8 minutes, or until cooked. To test for doneness, press the fish lightly with fingertips or a spatula at the spot where the flesh is thickest; it should feel fairly firm. Add the reserved ginger juice and swirl the pan to blend it well. Ideally, you will be left with 2 to 3 tablespoons slightly thickened liquid and the burdock root will be tender and deeply colored.

One at a time, carefully slip a broad spatula under a fish, bringing along a base of *kombu* (the kelp is entirely edible) with it, and place each fish on an individual plate, belly facing forward on the plate. Lean several sticks of braised burdock root at a jaunty angle against each fish. Serve the fish piping hot or at room temperature, with the sauce spooned over it. If more than 1/2 cup of liquid remains in the pan after transferring the fish to serving plates, reduce it to a saucelike consistency over medium-high heat.

Kitchen Harmony

If you cannot find, or prefer not to use, small whole flatfish, a version of this soy-braised fish can be made with halibut or flounder steaks about 3/4 inch thick. Make sure that pieces are sized for individual portions, and that each piece can be set on its own sheet of softened *kombu*.

Harmony at Table

As I have pointed out, when the Japanese present whole fish at table, they position them with the head facing left, the tail to the right, the belly forward, and the back away from the diner. Certain flatfishes that live on the ocean floor, however, may be reversed. Unlike round fish, which have one eye on each side of their head, flatfish have both eyes on the top of their head. Depending on the species, the eyes could be facing right or left when the belly is forward and the back is away. When placing flatfish on a plate to serve, arrange the fish with the top side (with the eyes) facing up, the belly forward, and the head pointing to either the right or the left.

When choosing plates for individual servings of whole fish, practical considerations include the size and depth of the vessel and its ability to hold sauce spooned over the fish. Aesthetically, you may choose to create a dramatic contrast of dark against light, or you might prefer a playful camouflage effect. (Depending on the home environment in which the fish had camouflaged itself, the top side could be dark, light, or speckled.)

SIMMERED SNAPPER, AUTUMN RAIN STYLE

KINMEDAI NO SHIGURÉ NI

In general, fair weather prevails throughout Japan in the fall, although there are occasional days of chilly drizzle when the leaves start to turn. This stop-and-start autumnal rain is called shiguré, *a word that in the world of culinary endeavors conjures up ginger-laced, soy-stewed seafood, as in these richly colored, intensely seasoned red snapper fillets.*

SERVES 4 TO 6

4 or 6 pieces red snapper, rockfish, or perch fillet with
    skin intact, 3 to 4 ounces each

1 small knob fresh ginger, about 1 inch long

Poaching Liquid

4 or 6 pieces kombu (page 42), preferably Rausu kombu,
    each the same dimension as a single portion of fish

2 tablespoons saké

1/2 cup water

Simmering Liquid

1/4 cup soy sauce

3 tablespoons mirin

1 tablespoon sugar

1 tablespoon saké or water

1 teaspoon cornstarch mixed with 1 teaspoon cold water
    to make a thin paste, if needed

Rinse the fish pieces under cold running water and pat dry with paper towels. With a sharp knife, make several shallow decorative slashes (*kazari-bōcho*, page 68) in the skin side of each piece. This will ensure even and thorough cooking and prevent the fish skin from tearing and shrinking in an unattractive manner.

Peel the ginger and reserve the peels. Cut the peeled ginger into thin slices, stack the slices, and cut into fine threads. Soak the ginger threads in cold water for a few minutes to mellow their sharpness and make them crisp. Drain and gently squeeze out excess moisture. Set aside the peels and the threads separately.

To make the poaching liquid, lay the *kombu* in a shallow pan or skillet large enough to hold the fish pieces in a single layer. The *kombu* will enhance and meld flavors and prevent the fish from sticking to the pan. Add the saké, water, and the reserved ginger peels and bring to a boil over high heat. Lower the heat to a steady but gentle simmer.

Lay the fish pieces, skin side up, in the pan, each on its own piece of *kombu*. Poach, spooning liquid over the fish frequently, for 2 minutes, or until the decorative slashes are clearly defined (the skin shrinks, exposing the flesh) and the edges turn opaque. Skim away any froth and remove and discard the ginger peels.

Add the simmering liquid ingredients—the soy sauce, mirin, and sugar—and top with an *otoshi-buta* (page 84). Or improvise a dropped lid with a double thickness of cooking parchment, cut in a circle 1 inch smaller in diameter than your pan and weighted down with a small, flat lid from another pot. This will keep the fish moist and ensure even coloration. Simmer the fish for 6 to 7 minutes. If the fish looks in danger of scorching during the simmering, add a few drops of either saké or water, or a mixture of the two. To test for doneness,

press the fish lightly with fingertips or a spatula at the spot where the flesh is thickest; it should feel fairly firm. Ideally, you will be left with about 3 tablespoons glossy liquid and the fish will have become richly colored.

Carefully slip a broad spatula under a piece of fish one at a time, bringing along a base of *kombu* (the kelp is entirely edible) with it. Place the fish on an individual plate with the thicker portion (the part nearer the head when the fish was alive) set to the left, with the belly forward. If the sauce in the pan seems loose and you would prefer a sauce that clings a bit to the fish, add the cornstarch paste to it and cook over high heat, stirring constantly, until it thickens. Serve the fish piping hot or at room temperature, with the sauce spooned over it. Garnish with the ginger threads.

Kitchen Harmony

Because ginger helps tone down assertive odors while enhancing the richness of oily fish, it is often used when preparing shad and other members of the herring family (*nisshin*) and sardines (*iwashi*). In America, shad is a springtime delicacy that can be prepared, with or without the roe, in the same manner as the snapper fillets in this recipe.

COLD POACHED SALMON IN BAMBOO LEAVES

SHAKÉ NO TAKÉ-ZUTSUMI MUSHI

Aki-jaké (literally, "autumnal salmon"), a mild-flavored, rosy-fleshed fish similar to Coho salmon, is most plentiful (and quite inexpensive) in early fall. This same time period, known as zan-sho (lingering heat) on the Japanese lunar calendar, is when energy levels and appetites typically wane. In America, a slightly different phenomenon—a spell of exceedingly warm weather after the first autumnal frost—is called Indian summer, and might also make a fine time to serve this dish. Such matching of seasonal abundance with prime eating pleasure is what the Japanese notion of shun is all about.

SERVES 4 TO 6

 1 pound salmon fillet, skin intact

 4 or 6 dried bamboo leaves (optional)

 4 or 6 pieces kombu (page 42), preferably Rausu kombu, Rishiri kombu, or ma kombu, each the same dimension as a single portion of fish

 8 or 12 thin lemon slices

 $^1/_3$ cup saké

 $^1/_4$ cup water

 1 to 2 teaspoons wasabi paste

 2 tablespoons soy sauce

Rinse the salmon under cold running water and pat dry with paper towels. Cut the salmon into 4 or 6 equal portions of 3 or 4 ounces each. Ideally, each piece will be 2 to 3 inches long, $^3/_4$ inch thick, and $1^1/_2$ inches wide.

Ideally, the salmon pieces are wrapped in bamboo leaves, but you can use cooking parchment if you cannot find the leaves. I do not recommend the use of aluminum foil, because it often imparts a metallic aftertaste.

If using dried bamboo leaves, lay the leaves speckled side down and shiny side up on a flat work surface and clean as directed on page 84. Place a piece of *kombu,* aligning it horizontally, at the center of each leaf to prevent the fish from sticking to it and to lend a pleasant seashore aroma to the finished dish. Put a piece of salmon, skin side down, on each piece of *kombu,* and then top each piece of salmon with a lemon slice. Starting at the broad end, fold over the bamboo leaf. Then fold over the narrower, slightly triangular end, to enclose the fish loosely. Pinch the sides of each packet and tuck in the edges a bit to ensure the fish is protected. Secure each bundle with its own self-tie (a thin strip of dried bamboo) or with kitchen string.

If using cooking parchment, cut 4 or 6 pieces each about 6 inches square and place on a flat work surface. Place a piece of *kombu,* aligning it horizontally, at the center of each piece of parchment to prevent the fish from sticking to it and to lend a pleasant seashore aroma to the finished dish. Put a piece of salmon, skin side down, on each piece of *kombu,* and then top each piece of salmon with a lemon slice. Bring the top and bottom edges of the parchment paper up to meet and then fold over together several times to lie flat across the top of the fish. Close the right and left sides of the paper packet by folding them down and turning them under. Secure each packet with kitchen string.

Select a shallow, wide pan in which the fish packets will fit in a single layer. (If necessary, double the amount of poaching liquid and split the packets between 2 pans.) Arrange the packets in the pan and add the saké and water. Bring to a boil over medium heat and adjust the heat to maintain a steady simmer. Poach the fish for 3 to 5 minutes. To test for doneness, gently press or pinch the packets with tongs or long cooking chopsticks. The fish should feel fairly firm. If necessary, peek inside a packet to see whether the fish is opaque. When it is ready, remove the pan from the heat and let the fish cool in the poaching liquid until no longer hot to the touch.

Remove the packets from the pan and open them. Keep the fish on the kelp, but discard the wilted lemon slice and replace it with a fresh slice. (The *kombu* is entirely edible.) Using a broad spatula, transfer each piece of fish directly to an individual plate for serving. Or wrap in plastic wrap and chill in the refrigerator for at least 1 hour and up to 3 days.

Garnish each serving with a dab of wasabi at the center of each lemon slice. Serve the soy sauce on the side for dipping.

Kitchen Harmony

Do not hesitate to double this recipe, since the dish will keep for up to 3 days in the refrigerator. For a truly refreshing and restorative menu, I serve the salmon with Ginger-Stewed Eggplant (page 192) and Green Beans Tossed in Creamy Sesame-Miso Sauce (page 198).

SOLE STEAMED WITH SOUR PLUM AND HERBS

HIRAMÉ NO UMÉ SHISO MUSHI

This steamed fish, redolent with tangy plum sauce and herbs, can be served piping hot and sauced with a delicate sea broth, or it can be enjoyed chilled with a bracing dip of wasabi-infused soy sauce. Either way, the fragile fish is wrapped to protect it during steaming. Although cooking parchment can be used, it is worth the trouble to track down bamboo leaves (také no kawa) because of the subtle, woodsy aroma they impart to the fish.

SERVES 4

1 pound sole fillet

4 dried bamboo leaves (optional)

4 pieces kombu (page 42), preferably Rausu kombu, Rishiri kombu, or ma kombu, each the same dimension as a single portion of fish

1 tablespoon bainiku or 1 uméboshi (page 38), pit removed and flesh mashed

3 or 4 shiso leaves (page 26), stems trimmed and leaves finely shredded

5 or 6 mitsuba stalks (page 26), trimmed and minced

$1/4$ teaspoon cornstarch

Sauce if Serving Hot

1 cup Basic Sea Stock (page 92)

2 teaspoons Seasoned Soy Concentrate (page 96)

$1/2$ teaspoon cornstarch mixed with $1/2$ teaspoon water to make a thin paste

Sauce if Serving Chilled

$1/2$ teaspoon wasabi paste

1 to 2 tablespoons light-colored soy sauce

Rinse the fish under cold running water and pat dry with paper towels. Cut the fish into 8 broad, thin pieces using the slicing technique known as *sogi-giri* (page 70). Each piece should be about $2^{1}/_{2}$ inches wide, 4 inches long, and no more than $^{1}/_{2}$ inch thick at the center (though slightly thinner at the edges).

Ideally, the sole pieces are wrapped in bamboo leaves, but you can use cooking parchment if you don't have the leaves. I do not recommend the use of aluminum foil, because it often imparts a metallic aftertaste.

If using dried bamboo leaves, lay the leaves speckled side down and shiny side up on a flat work surface and clean as directed on page 84. Place a piece of *kombu*, aligning it horizontally, at the center of each leaf to prevent the fish from sticking to it and to lend a pleasant seashore aroma to the finished dish. Arrange a piece of sole on each piece of *kombu*, aligning the fish horizontally so that it does not extend beyond the width of the bamboo leaf. With a butter knife or small spatula, spread one-fourth of the plum paste over each piece of fish.

In a small bowl, toss together the *shiso* and the *mitsuba* and then set aside half of the mixture to use later as a garnish. Toss the remaining herbs with the cornstarch, and divide this mixture among the 4 fish pieces. Top each portion with a second piece of fish. Press lightly to seal the "sandwich" of fish and herbs.

Starting at the broad end, fold over the bamboo leaf. Then fold over the narrower, slightly triangular end, to enclose the fish loosely. Pinch the sides of each packet and tuck in the edges a bit to ensure the fish is protected. Secure each bundle with its own self-tie (a thin strip of dried bamboo) or with kitchen string.

If using cooking parchment, cut 4 pieces each about 20 inches long and 6 inches wide. Fold each of these pieces in half to create 4 parchment wrappers of double thickness, 10 by 6 inches. (When steaming this fish, a sturdy wrapper is needed to seal in moisture and aroma.) Place a piece of *kombu*, aligning it horizontally, at the center of each piece of parchment to prevent the fish from sticking to it and to lend a pleasant seashore aroma to the finished dish. Put a piece of fish on each piece of *kombu*, aligning the fish horizontally so that a border of at least 1½ inches of parchment remains on the right and left. With a butter knife or small spatula, spread one-fourth of the plum paste over each piece of fish.

In a small bowl, toss together the *shiso* and the *mitsuba* and then set aside half of this mixture to use later as a garnish. Toss the remaining herbs with the cornstarch, and divide this mixture among the 4 fish pieces. Top each portion with a second piece of fish. Press lightly to seal the "sandwich" of fish and herbs.

Bring the top and bottom edges of the parchment paper up to meet and then fold over together several times to lie flat across the top of the fish. Close the right and left sides of the paper packet by folding them down and turning them under. Secure each packet with kitchen string.

Bring the water in the bottom of a steamer to a boil. Adjust the heat to maintain a steady but gentle flow of steam and place the packets on the steamer rack. Cover and steam the fish for 5 minutes. Remove the steamer from the stove. Carefully remove the lid, lifting it away from you to avoid being burned by the steam. To test for doneness, gently press or pinch the packets with tongs or long cooking chopsticks. The fish should feel fairly firm. If it does not, replace the lid, move the steamer back onto the stove, and steam for another minute.

Remove the steamer from the stove and allow the fish to self-steam *(murasu)* for another 2 minutes.

To enjoy the fish hot, heat serving plates in the steamer or a preheated oven set to 200°F and make the sauce while the fish is self-steaming. In a small saucepan, combine the stock and soy concentrate over high heat until bubbles appear at the edge of the pan. Add the cornstarch mixture and stir until thickened.

Remove the packets from the steamer and open them. Some liquid will have been trapped in the packets; carefully drain off. Using a broad spatula, carefully transfer each fish sandwich, kelp side down, to a warmed plate. Spoon some of the sauce over the fish, and then garnish with the reserved *shiso-mitsuba* mixture. The kelp may be eaten along with the fish, although it will be a bit chewy.

To enjoy the fish chilled, let each steamed fish sandwich, still in its packet, cool sufficiently to handle it comfortably. Some liquid will have been trapped in the packets; open one side of the packet to drain off, and then rewrap each packet in plastic wrap. Refrigerate the wrapped packets for at least 2 hours and up to 24 hours. When ready to serve, remove the fish sandwiches from their packets, kelp side down, and place on chilled plates. Shower the fish with the reserved *shiso-mitsuba* mixture. In small individual dip dishes, place a dab of wasabi and a drizzle of soy sauce. The kelp may be eaten along with the fish, although it will be a bit chewy.

CLOUD-STEAMED BASS

SUZUKI NO KASUMI AN KAKÉ

The poetic name of this dish refers to the fluffy mound of grated root vegetables that tops the bass. Other mild-flavored but meaty fish, such as red snapper, grouper, or cod, can be prepared in the same manner.

SERVES 4

Cloud Topping

2-inch chunk daikon or rutabaga, about 4 ounces

1 small potato, preferably red- or white-skinned new potato, or small piece lotus root, about 2 ounces

$^1/_2$ egg white from large egg

Pinch of salt

4 slices sea bass fillet, with skin intact, or bass steaks, 3 to 4 ounces each

4 dried bamboo leaves (optional)

4 pieces kombu (page 42), preferably Rausu kombu, Rishiri kombu, or ma kombu, each the same dimension as a single portion of fish

Sauce

$^1/_3$ cup Basic Sea Stock (page 92)

1 teaspoon light-colored soy sauce

2 teaspoons saké

1 teaspoon mirin

$^1/_2$ teaspoon cornstarch mixed with $^1/_2$ teaspoon water to make a thin paste

1 teaspoon wasabi paste

To make the cloud topping, peel and grate the daikon and potato, combine them, and then drain off excess moisture as directed for daikon on page 59. You should have about $^1/_2$ cup.

In a bowl, combine the egg white and salt and beat with a whisk or several pairs of chopsticks until soft peaks form. Add the grated vegetable and fold in gently but thoroughly.

Ideally, the bass pieces are wrapped in bamboo leaves, but you can use cooking parchment if you don't have the leaves. I do not recommend the use of aluminum foil, because it often imparts a metallic aftertaste.

If using dried bamboo leaves, lay the leaves speckled side down and shiny side up on a flat work surface and clean as directed on page 84. Place a piece of *kombu*, aligning it horizontally, at the center of each leaf to prevent the fish from sticking to it and to lend a pleasant seashore aroma to the finished dish. Put a piece of fish, skin side down if using fillet, on each piece of *kombu*. Top each piece of fish with one-fourth of the cloud mixture. Starting at the broad end, fold the bamboo leaf loosely over the cloud mixture. Then fold over the narrower, slightly triangular end, to enclose the fish loosely. Pinch the sides of each packet and tuck in the edges a bit to ensure the fish is protected. Secure each bundle with its own self-tie (a thin strip of dried bamboo) or with kitchen string if necessary, taking care not to mash the cloud mixture.

If using cooking parchment, cut 4 pieces each about 8 inches square and place on a flat work surface. Place a piece of *kombu*, aligning it horizontally, at the center of each piece of parchment to prevent the fish from sticking to it and to lend a pleasant seashore aroma to the finished dish. Put a piece of fish, skin side down, on each piece of *kombu*. Top each piece with one-fourth of the cloud mixture. Bring the top and bottom edges of the parchment paper up to meet loosely over the cloud mixture and then fold over together several times to secure shut. Close the right and left sides of the paper by folding them down loosely and turning them under the packet. Secure each packet with kitchen string, taking care not to mash the cloud mixture.

Bring the water in the bottom of a steamer to a boil. Adjust the heat to maintain a steady but gentle flow of steam and place the packets on the steamer rack. Cover and steam the fish for 5 minutes. Remove the steamer from the stove. Carefully remove the lid, lifting it away from you to avoid being burned by the steam. To test for doneness, gently press or pinch the sides of the fish at the bottom of each packet with tongs or long cooking chopsticks. The fish should feel fairly firm. If it does not, replace the lid, move the steamer back onto the stove, and steam for another minute.

Remove the steamer from the stove and allow the fish to self-steam (*murasu*) for another 2 minutes.

While the fish is self-steaming, heat shallow serving bowls in the steamer or a preheated oven set to 200°F and make the sauce. In a small saucepan, combine the stock, soy sauce, saké, and mirin over high heat until bubbles appear at the edge of the pan. Add the cornstarch mixture and stir until thickened.

Open the packets of fish. Some liquid will have been trapped in the packets; carefully drain. Using a broad spatula, carefully transfer each portion, kelp side down, to a warmed bowl. Spoon some of the thickened sauce over the cloud topping and around the fish. Garnish the top of each portion with a small dab of wasabi. Diners dissolve the wasabi in the surrounding sauce as they eat. Serve piping hot. The kelp may be eaten along with the fish, although it will be a bit chewy.

Harmony at Table

The Japanese have special lidded bowls called *nimono wan* that simplify the service of this sort of steamed and sauced food. Warmed shallow soup bowls or plates that have a lip or flanged edge can also be used. In Japan, the flavorful broth can be sipped directly from the bowl, though often a spoon is supplied.

CRISP FRIED SMELTS IN SPICY VINAIGRETTE
WAKASAGI NO NANBAN-ZUKÉ

This dish appears frequently on izakaya *(pub-style restaurant) menus and is also enjoyed in many homes in Japan. In Japanese restaurants in America, however,* wakasagi no nanban-zuké *(literally, "crisp fried smelts, southern barbarian style") rarely shows up on the English side of the menu. The curious name of this dish refers to the Portuguese (the aforementioned "barbarians") who settled in the southern port of Nagasaki, on Kyushu, late in the sixteenth century. They brought with them* escabeche, *a fried and pickled seafood delicacy popular in their homeland that the Japanese adapted to their own taste.*

SERVES 4 TO 6 AS AN APPETIZER

6 to 7 ounces smelts, preferably 2 inches or smaller (about 40 fish)

Salted water for rinsing fish (should taste briny, like the ocean)

Cornstarch for dusting

Vegetable oil for deep-frying

1 to 2 teaspoons sesame oil (optional)

Marinade

$^2/_3$ cup Basic Sea Stock (page 92)

$^1/_2$ cup rice vinegar, preferably brown rice vinegar

2 tablespoons light-colored soy sauce

2 tablespoons mirin

1 teaspoon saké

1 tōgarashi (page 47)

2 tablespoons snipped fresh chives or finely chopped scallions

The Japanese usually keep the heads and tails of smelts intact, just gutting the belly cavity, but you may be happier removing the heads and tails along with the guts. If you prefer to use filleted fish, refer to the Kitchen Harmony notes (page 246).

Rinse the cleaned fish thoroughly in the salted water. Gently pat the fish dry, inside and out, with paper towels, and then dust them lightly with cornstarch.

You will need oil to a depth of at least 2$^1/_2$ inches in the pan. I find that a wok, narrow at the base and wider at the top, is the best implement for this. Add the vegetable oil (and for a nuttier flavor, the sesame oil) and heat to 350°F on a deep-frying thermometer. Or test the oil by dropping a pinch of cornstarch into it. It should sink ever so slightly, surface, and disperse immediately, sizzling but not coloring. If the cornstarch does not surface right away, the oil is not hot enough; if it colors right away, the oil is too hot.

Working in batches to avoid crowding, fry the fish for 2 to 3 minutes, or until the bodies are firm when lifted from the oil and the eyes have clouded over. (Smelts with heads and tails intact require the longer time.) Transfer the fish to paper towels to drain. When all of the fish have been fried once, refry them, again in batches, at a slightly higher temperature (about 375°F) for 1 minute to make them crispy. Drain on fresh paper towels.

To make the marinade, combine the stock, vinegar, soy sauce, mirin, and saké in a glass or other nonreactive container just large enough to allow the fish to lie submerged in the marinade. Break the *tōgarashi* in half and discard the seeds if you wish to keep the fish just pleasantly spicy. If your taste runs toward the incendiary, keep the seeds as well. Break the pod into several small pieces and stir them into the sauce. Transfer the freshly fried fish to the marinade; you will hear a hissing sound if the fish are still hot.

Once steam is no longer rising, cover the container snugly with plastic wrap. Let the fish pickle at cool room temperature for at least 6 hours or in the refrigerator for up to 3 days. The extended pickling time will "melt" the bones of the fish, allowing you to consume them whole, thereby greatly enhancing their nutritional value. Extended pickling time will, however, markedly sharpen the piquant taste.

Have ready individual serving plates. A typical single serving is 7 or 8 fish. Lift the fish from the marinade and stack them with the heads pointing to the left, tails to the right, bellies facing forward and backs away from the diner (the proper position for serving whole fish). Just before serving, sprinkle the chives liberally over the fish.

Kitchen Harmony

Several types of fish are suitable for frying and marinating in this manner. Smelts are probably the most common. In Japan, miniature *mamé aji* (literally, "bean-sized mackerel") are also popular. These, too, are gutted, rinsed in salted water, dusted in cornstarch, and fried whole before they are marinated in the same spicy sweet-and-sour sauce used for the smelts. After pickling, the heads, tails, and entire skeletal structure are soft enough to consume whole.

Fillet of flounder or sole, sliced into narrow strips about ¹/₂ inch wide and 2 inches long, can be similarly prepared. After rinsing the strips in fresh (not salted) water, pat them dry with paper towels. Dredge them in a combination of flour and cornstarch and fry for 1 minute, or until crisp and barely colored. Drain and marinate them in the same sauce you use for the smelts. Because there are no bones, marinating time is short: only 3 to 4 hours at room temperature or at most overnight in the refrigerator. Garnish with snipped fresh chives or finely minced red onion.

SEASONED SALMON FLAKES
SHAKÉ NO OBORO

Semipreserved fish, such as salt-cured salmon, were a mainstay of the old-fashioned washoku *kitchen. Typically, they were simply broiled and served with grated daikon for breakfast, lunch, or dinner. Today, lightly cured ama-jio shaké (literally, "sweet-salted salmon") is sold in every supermarket in Japan and still enjoyed for its vibrant taste.*

When I first came to Japan, I marveled at the way frugal households recycled leftover chunks of salt-cured fish. Salmon was especially tasty, and the flakes could be kept on hand for another week or so to stuff into omusubi *(rice "sandwiches") or to top* ocha-zuké *(bowls of rice in tea broth). Commercially prepared seasoned salmon flakes are sold in glass jars or vacuum-sealed pouches in most Japanese food markets. Nearly all of these products are loaded with preservatives, however, so it is best to make your own, either from traditionally salt-cured salmon steaks or from fresh fish. I provide instructions for both here.*

Illustrated on page 163

MAKES ABOUT 1 CUP

Traditional Salmon Flakes

1 small slice mild salt-cured red salmon with bones and skin intact, about 3 ounces

1 piece kombu (page 42), about 2 inches square (leftover from stock making is perfect)

1 tablespoon saké

¹/₂ teaspoon sugar

1 teaspoon light-colored soy sauce

Fresh Salmon Flakes

1 small slice fresh salmon fillet with skin intact, about
  3 ounces

1/2 teaspoon coarse salt

1 piece kombu (page 42), about 2 inches square (leftover
  from stock making is perfect)

2 tablespoons saké

1 teaspoon mirin

1 teaspoon light-colored soy sauce

To make traditional salmon flakes, rinse the salt-cured fish under cold running water and pat dry with paper towels. To make fresh salmon flakes, rinse the fish under cold running water and pat dry with paper towels. Rub ¼ teaspoon of salt into the skin of the salmon, and then sprinkle the remaining ¼ teaspoon over the flesh. Place the salted salmon, skin side up, on a rack set over a plate or tray to catch the drippings. Let the fish "sweat" at cool room temperature for 25 to 30 minutes or in the refrigerator for 2 to 3 hours. Blot away excess moisture with paper towels.

Whether making traditional or fresh salmon flakes, place the salmon and *kombu* in a small saucepan and add cold water just to cover the fish. Bring the water to a rolling boil and blanch the salmon for 2 minutes, or until it is just cooked through. The color will change from red to pink and the flesh will become opaque. Drain and discard the water and the kelp. Rinse the fish under cold running water and pat dry with paper towels.

Separate the pink meat from the skin, bones, and dark (fatty) meat, keeping the pink meat and discarding the balance. Flake the pink meat as finely as possible by rubbing it between your fingertips or forcing it through a wide-mesh strainer. Place the flaked meat in a nonstick skillet. Add the saké and sugar if you are making traditional flakes from salt cured salmon, or add the saké and mirin if you are making flakes from fresh salmon. Toss and stir to distribute evenly.

Slowly cook the salmon flakes over low heat, stirring the fish flakes constantly with a broad, wooden spatula to keep them from scorching. As the salmon begins to dry, after 4 to 5 minutes, dribble in the soy sauce, stirring vigorously to distribute evenly. Continue to stir. After 3 to 4 minutes longer, the salmon will become slightly fluffy and quite aromatic and may even caramelize a bit.

Remove the pan from the heat and let the flaky fish cool completely. If large lumps still exist, rub them between your fingertips to separate. Refrigerate whatever you do not use right away in a tightly lidded jar. It will keep for up to 1 week.

Kitchen Harmony

Use these fish flakes to make Rice Tossed with Salmon Flakes (page 144) and Toasted Rice in Green Tea Broth (page 162) and as a filling for Hand-Pressed Rice (page 158). You can mix the salmon flakes with snipped fresh chives or finely minced fresh parsley and a spoonful of mayonnaise to make a wonderful spread for crackers or toast.

PANKO-BREADED FRIED COD

OHYŌ NO FURAI

This lunch-box favorite calls for breading mild-flavored fish with coarse shards of panko *and then deep-frying it. Even hours after frying, the coating remains crunchy.*

SERVES 3 OR 4

12 ounces cod, flounder, or other mild-flavored
  white fish fillet

$^1/_8$ teaspoon salt

$^1/_4$ cup all-purpose flour

1 egg beaten with 2 tablespoons cold water

$1^1/_2$ cups panko (page 14)

Vegetable oil for deep-frying

Lemon wedges

Tonkatsu sōsu (page 51) (optional)

Rinse the fish under cold running water and pat dry with paper towels. Cut the fish into 12 thin pieces using the slicing technique known as *sogi-giri* (page 70). Each piece should be about 2 inches wide, $2^1/_2$ inches long, and no more than $^1/_4$ inch thick at the center (though slightly thinner at the edges).

Transfer the fish pieces to a plate and sprinkle with the salt. Let stand for 5 minutes, or until they "sweat." Blot away excess moisture with paper towels.

Have the flour in a shallow bowl, the egg mixture in a second shallow bowl, and the *panko* on a plate. One at a time, dust the fish pieces lightly with the flour, dip them into the egg mixture, and then coat them with the *panko.* To make sure each piece is fully coated, lay the egg-dipped fish on a pile of the crumbs and, using scooping or shoveling motions with a spoon, cover the top of the fish with crumbs. Lightly press the top layer with the back of the spoon or dry fingertips. Set the breaded fish aside on a dry paper towel.

You will need oil to a depth of at least $2^1/_2$ inches in the pan. I find that a wok, narrow at the base and wider at the top, is the best implement for this. Add the oil and heat to about 375°F on a deep-frying thermometer. Or test the oil with a pinch of bread crumbs to which some of the egg wash still clings. The crumbs should sizzle gently on the surface, coloring very slowly. If the crumbs sink, the oil is not hot enough. If the crumbs sizzle on the surface and begin to color rapidly, the oil is too hot.

Working in batches of 3 or 4 pieces, fry the fish, turning once, for about 1 minute on each side, or until golden brown. Transfer the fish to paper towels to drain.

If you want to serve the fish hot, serve immediately or hold for up to 10 minutes in a preheated 200°F oven. If you want to serve the fish at room temperature, let the pieces cool on a towel paper–lined rack away from drafts.

When ready to serve, provide lemon wedges, and if you want to add a spicier accent, *tonkatsu sōsu,* too.

———— ————

Kitchen Harmony

Harusamé noodles (page 34) can be used in place of *panko* as a coating in this recipe. Using 2 to 3 ounces *harusamé,* first break the noodles into bits using a food processor fitted with the metal blade. Pulse until the pieces are about $^1/_3$ inch in length. When fried, *harusamé* puffs up, so the bits should not be densely packed onto the surface of the fish.

OCTOPUS SALAD

TAKO NO KARASHI SU MISO AÉ

Octopus is a meaty sea creature with a mildly briny flavor. When properly prepared, it is tender with a satisfying bite. I have seen rosy boiled octopus in many American fish markets, especially those that cater to customers of Mediterranean heritage. And when octopus is not available, boiled shrimp, fresh-cooked lobster or crabmeat, or cleaned squid, cut into rings and briefly blanched, makes a good substitute.

In Japan, saladlike dishes dressed with tangy mustard sauce are typically served in small portions. In a home setting or at a pub or other casual eatery, this piquant tidbit might accompany a chilled beer or a flask of saké, rather than be served as part of a meal. Similarly, on formal occasions, several chunks of dressed octopus are sometimes landscaped along with other assertively seasoned morsels to create a zensai, or appetizer course.

See the notes for a suggestion on transforming the octopus into a main-course salad.

SERVES 6 AS AN APPETIZER, 2 OR 3 AS A MAIN COURSE

- 3 or 4 meaty legs boiled octopus, about 8 ounces total weight
- 1 tablespoon fresh lemon or lime juice
- 3 tablespoons Tart Miso-Mustard Sauce (page 99)
- 1 bunch radish sprouts, about 2 ounces, rinsed, trimmed, and divided into 6 clusters

Rinse the octopus legs and pat them dry. To create multiple surfaces that will catch and hold the piquant sauce, cut the legs into thin slices across the grain using the slicing technique known as *sogi-giri* (page 70). Or, if you prefer, cut the legs into ¹/₂-inch dice. Toss the octopus pieces in the lemon juice and let stand for about 10 minutes.

If you have sliced the octopus, drain and gently squeeze away excess lemon juice. Coax this mass into 6 small mounds and arrange each in a small bowl or on a tiny plate. If you have diced the octopus, divide into 6 portions and stack each portion pyramid style in a small dish.

Spoon some of the miso-mustard sauce over each octopus serving and lean a cluster of radish sprouts against it. Serve at once.

————  ————

Harmony at Table

To serve as a substantial salad, arrange the octopus on a bed of assorted lettuces, endive, and radicchio. Turn the thick, creamy mustard sauce into a salad dressing by either thinning it with a spoonful or two of Basic Sea Stock (page 92) or mixing it with 1 tablespoon each vegetable oil and rice vinegar. Garnish the salad with thinly sliced, briny pitted black olives and small red and yellow grape tomatoes. For additional punch, add minced radish sprouts.

Though now more of a Mediterranean dish than a Japanese one, the salad still retains a welcome *washoku* air.

MEAT AND POULTRY

Born in 1907, my mother-in-law was a vegetarian in the way that many women of her generation were: they cooked daily with fish-enriched stocks and ate eggs, integrating them with Buddhist vegetarian cooking, or *shōjin ryōri,* that eschews all flesh. And, of course, she cooked meat for others, though she never ate any herself.

The "traditional" diet in which rice was consumed with relish and reverence, and soy products and fish were the protein mainstay of the meal, has undergone major shifts in the past few decades. In particular, the consumption of animal fats in the form of red meat (and dairy products) has noticeably increased. Whereas recipes appearing in magazines that I bought twenty-five years ago called for one hundred grams of meat (a little under a quarter of a pound) to feed a family of four or five, today the same one hundred grams would serve only two or three. Some of the dishes in the vegetable and tōfu chapters of this book, such as Soy-Simmered Kabocha Squash with Minced Chicken (page 205), Eggplants Stuffed with

Ground Chicken (page 194), and Bitter Melon, Tōfu, and Pork Scramble (page 282), are of this old-fashioned sort. In those days, monthly menu plans meant to help newlyweds manage a household budget would suggest meat as the centerpiece of a meal only once or twice a week. Special occasions on which family would gather might feature *nabémono* (one-pot dishes), such as sukiyaki or *mizutaki* (made with chicken), to be shared by all. But this was food for celebration, not everyday fare.

In thinking about meat recipes to include in this book, I decided to share with you some of the classics of the modern *washoku* home kitchen as I first encountered them several decades ago. Here, then, are my "top ten" meat recipes, culled from nostalgia—dishes that I know will be immediately appealing while suggesting to you new ways of cooking with familiar ingredients. I have taken a middle-of-the-road approach to portion size; you may find the amounts I list to be a bit modest, though older generations in Japan would find them generous.

TENDER-STEWED CURRIED CHICKEN

TORI NIKU NO YAWARAKA NI, KARÉ FŪMI

During my first year living and working in Tokyo, I splurged and bought a television set. It was true then (1967), and remains true today, that everyone who owns a TV in Japan must pay a fee to the national broadcasting organization. With the bill came a programming guide. In it I spotted a short blurb about a cooking show called Kyō no Ryōri (Today's Cooking).

The twenty-minute segment, broadcast live every weekday, featured no-fuss, low-cost home-style fare. Not only was I trying to make ends meet on a limited budget, but I was also trying to fathom the unfamiliar products on store shelves, and make sense of the puzzling shopping habits of Japanese homemakers. The program, and its companion monthly magazine, became my primer as I taught myself to read product ads, food labels, cooking instructions, and other printed matter that turned the necessities of daily living into a grand adventure.

And, thanks to Kyō no Ryōri, I was introduced to the wondrous ways of tender stewing tough, sinewy chicken. The most challenging part of this technique is resisting the temptation to stir and flip the poultry constantly as it cooks. Indeed, enryō (reticence) and gaman (restraint) are words you often hear in Japan—to describe not only proper kitchen procedure, but laudable social behavior, too.

The version of tender-stewed chicken I offer here is curry flavored. Cooked and seasoned this way, the chicken becomes the cornerstone of an enormously popular dish, karei raisu, or rice curry. It is also paired with udon on noodle shop menus. Or you can transform tender-stewed chicken into a five-color salad platter by following the suggestions in the accompanying notes.

MAKES ABOUT 3 CUPS; SERVES 4 AS RICE CURRY
(PAGE 155) OR 6 AS A SALAD

- 12 to 14 ounces boneless chicken thigh meats with skin intact
- 3 tablespoons saké
- 2 tablespoons cornstarch
- 1 tablespoon vegetable oil
- 1 large yellow onion, about 8 ounces, chopped
- 2 teaspoons Japanese curry powder
- Pinch of coarse salt
- $^1/_2$ to $^3/_4$ cup Basic Sea Stock (page 92)
- 2 teaspoons soy sauce
- About 1 teaspoon mirin, if needed

Cut the chicken into pieces about 1 inch square, trimming away any gristle or large pieces of fat but keeping the skin attached. Do not worry about the sinews; this style of cooking tenderizes cuts of meat such as this.

In a bowl, stir together the saké and cornstarch to make a thin paste. Add the chicken, toss to coat evenly, and marinate for at least 10 minutes at room temperature or for up to 4 hours in the refrigerator.

Heat the oil in a nonstick skillet over high heat. Place the chicken, with whatever cornstarch paste clings to it, skin side down in the pan. Spread out the pieces to cover the entire surface. Sear the chicken, undisturbed, for 1$^1/_2$ minutes (*gaman, gaman . . .* just leave it alone). The edges of the meat will begin to turn white.

With the tips of long cooking chopsticks or the flat edge of a flexible spatula, lift a piece of chicken to see whether a crust has formed. Do not worry if you need to scrape a bit to achieve this. If, however, you find too much resistance, lower the heat a bit and continue to let the chicken cook undisturbed for another minute before trying again. Flip the pieces of chicken (skin side up) and let them brown, undisturbed (more *gaman*) for another minute on the meat side.

Shake the pan, pushing the chicken to one side, and add the onion. Lower the heat a bit and sauté the onion for about 3 minutes, or until aromatic and wilted. It is fine if the onion caramelizes slightly. Shake the pan again to mix the chicken and onion together. Sprinkle with the curry powder and salt, stirring to distribute evenly.

Add $^1/_2$ cup of the stock, stirring up any crusty bits that may be clinging to the bottom or sides of the pan. Adjust the heat to maintain a steady but not vigorous simmer and cook for 2 minutes, adding more stock as needed to keep the chicken from scorching. The onion pieces will gradually lose their shape, becoming part of the thickening sauce.

Add the soy sauce and continue to simmer until the liquid is reduced and quite thick. This will take about 5 minutes. Taste and, if necessary, adjust the sweetness by adding the mirin a few drops at a time (Japanese curry powder is quite sweet compared to American and European brands).

Remove from the heat. You can serve the dish hot over rice as a full meal (see Rice Curry, page 155). Or let the curried chicken cool in the pan, cover, and refrigerate to serve as a salad (see notes) with crusty bread or as a sandwich filling stuffed into a pita pocket. It will keep for up to 3 days.

Harmony at Table

To transform this curried chicken into a five-color salad, arrange an assortment of lettuces on individual plates. A combination of soft lettuces, such as red leaf and Boston or Bibb, and crunchy ones, such as romaine or even iceberg, is a good choice. The slight bitterness of endive or radicchio highlights the sweeter elements of the curry. Nestle several spoonfuls of the curried chicken in the center of the lettuces. Decorate the platter with cherry tomatoes or strips of sweet red pepper and some black olives. Blanched cauliflower or pickled pearl onions could serve as the white element.

SOY-STEWED CHICKEN WITH VEGETABLES

CHIKUZEN NI

Chikuzen is the one-time name for the part of Kyushu now known as Fukuoka. Historically, this simple braised dish was made with suppon (snapping tortoise), but today poultry is the norm. The Japanese prefer dark-meat chicken for its richer flavor and greater succulence. If you can find fresh lotus root or fresh burdock root in your market, either, or both, provides a nice textural contrast to the other ingredients in this mélange.

SERVES 4

2 tablespoons saké

1 tablespoon cornstarch

1 pound boneless chicken thighs with skin intact, trimmed of gristle and fat, and cut into $1/2$-inch cubes

1 block konnyaku (page 28), 10 to 12 ounces, drained

3 small dried shiitaké mushrooms, stems removed and caps softened in 1 cup warm water (page 33)

1 tablespoon canola or other mild vegetable oil

1 small carrot, about 2 ounces, peeled and cut with rolled cut (page 69)

2-inch piece lotus root, about 1 ounce, peeled and cut with rolled cut (page 69) (optional)

2-inch piece burdock root, about 1 ounce, rinsed and lightly scraped (page 58) and cut with rolled cut (page 69) (optional)

$3/4$ cup Basic Sea Stock (page 92)

2 teaspoons sugar

$1 1/2$ tablespoons soy sauce

2 tablespoons fresh or thawed, frozen shelled green peas, blanched

In a bowl, stir together 1 tablespoon of the saké and the cornstarch to make a thin paste. Add the chicken, toss to coat evenly, and marinate for at least 30 minutes at room tempera-

ture or for up to 2 hours in the refrigerator. This marinade will help tenderize the dark meat.

Lightly score the surface of the *konnyaku* block with finely spaced, shallow cuts. Flip the loaf over and repeat the scoring on the other side. This design permits the *konnyaku* to absorb more of the flavorful braising liquid as it cooks. Slice the loaf lengthwise into 5 equal strips. Cut the strips crosswise 4 times to make a total of 20 cubes.

Drain the mushrooms, reserving the soaking liquid, and cut into quarters.

Place a large skillet or wok, preferably nonstick, over high heat. Toss in the *konnyaku* and dry-roast it (page 85), jiggling the pan to throw off any residual moisture. When the *konnyaku* cubes begin to make squeaking sounds, drizzle the oil into the pan in a spiral motion, working from the outer edge toward the center. Stir-fry the cubes for 30 seconds and then push them to one side of the pan to make room for the chicken.

Add the chicken, with whatever cornstarch paste clings to it, skin side down. Allow the chicken to cook, undisturbed, for about 1 minute, or until it browns slightly and a crust forms on the bottom. Shake the pan vigorously to release the chicken and then add the mushrooms, carrot, and the lotus and/or burdock root, if using. Stir-fry for 30 seconds and then add $1/2$ cup of the stock and all the reserved mushroom liquid, the remaining 1 tablespoon of saké, and the sugar. Lower the heat to maintain a steady, gentle simmer. If you have an *otoshi-buta* (page 84), place it on the chicken and vegetables. Or use a conventional lid slightly askew, swirling the pan occasionally in circular motions to ensure even cooking; check the level of liquid, adding stock or water to keep the food from scorching. Cook for 10 to 12 minutes, or until the liquid is nearly gone and the vegetables are tender (a toothpick should meet little resistance).

(continued)

Remove the lid and drizzle the soy sauce into the pan in a spiral pattern, working from the outer edge toward the center. Lightly toss the chicken and vegetables with a spatula to ensure even distribution. Replace the lid and continue to cook for 1 minute, or until the liquid has been reduced to only a spoonful. Let the chicken and vegetables cool in the pot with the lid in place. It is during this cooling-down period that the flavors meld and enhance one another.

This dish is often served at room temperature. If you want to serve it hot, reheat it briefly. It can be covered and refrigerated for up to 3 days. To preserve their color, add the peas just before serving.

Kitchen Harmony

A purely vegetarian version of this dish can be made with cubes of fried tōfu, called *atsu agé* (page 56), in lieu of the chicken. Replace the sea stock with water or Basic Vegetarian Stock (page 93). The fried tōfu does not require the cornstarch-saké marinade, and you may not need to add oil to the pan either, since the surface of the tōfu is often sufficiently oily to prevent sticking.

Harmony at Table

Serve this dish family style, mounded in a shallow bowl with a serving spoon, or divide it into 3 or 4 individual portions, being sure to have an equal number of pieces of each vegetable in every portion. Arrange the chicken and vegetables in a seemingly random manner so that the colors are nicely balanced.

TANGY SEARED CHICKEN WINGS

TORI TÉBA SAKI NO SU ITAMÉ

When asked, most Japanese will say they prefer dark-meat chicken to light. Indeed, legs, thighs, and wings are typically sold at a higher unit price in Japan than breast meat is. Over the years, my own tastes have shifted, and I have come to appreciate the richer, more complex flavor of dark-meat poultry.

In this recipe I call for whole wings or whole thighs. However, this recipe works well using only the short, plump wing drumsticks, too. (In that case, reduce the simmering time by 3 to 5 minutes.) White meat will toughen and dry out and is not recommended.

When you cook chicken wings or thighs in this vinegar-spiked braising liquid, calcium is leached from the bones. This enriches the sauce, making it delightfully tangy. The natural gelatin can be enhanced by the addition of unflavored gelatin powder to make a nutritious aspic from the cooking juices (see notes).

SERVES 4 TO 6

12 chicken wings or 6 chicken thighs

2 Japanese leeks or small Western leeks, or 1 yellow onion (optional)

1 teaspoon canola or other mild vegetable oil, if needed

$^3/_4$ cup Basic Sea Stock (page 92)

$^1/_4$ cup saké

$^1/_4$ cup rice vinegar

2 teaspoons sugar

3 tablespoons soy sauce

Depending on how the chicken was cut, you may find flaps of skin or shards of bone and cartilage clinging to the meat. Do not remove the skin, but do trim away any excess skin, if necessary, and then rinse the chicken pieces under cold running water. Pat the pieces dry with paper towels.

If you are planning on serving the chicken at the table, rather than as finger food at a buffet or picnic, adding seared leeks or onion makes the sauce even better. Slice the white portion of the leeks lengthwise and then cut crosswise into $^1/_2$-inch pieces. Rinse briefly under cold water to remove any grit and drain well. Or cut the onion into 8 to 12 wedges.

Choose a skillet or saucepan that will be wide enough to hold the chicken pieces in a single layer; it does not need to be deeper than $1^1/_2$ inches. If you want to make this dish as lean as possible, use a nonstick skillet. The amount of oil required, if any at all, to brown the chicken pieces will depend on the fat content of the poultry. Try searing the chicken without any oil to start. It is likely that its natural fat will melt and provide sufficient lubrication. But if the chicken looks in danger of scorching, drizzle the oil into the pan in a spiral pattern, working from the outer edge toward the center.

Brown the chicken pieces well on one side, and then flip them and brown the other side, too. After flipping them, add the leeks or onion and allow them to brown a bit in the chicken fat or oil. When the browned leeks or onions become very aromatic, after about $1^1/_2$ minutes, remove them and set aside.

Add the stock, saké, vinegar, and sugar and jiggle the pan lightly to make sure the sugar dissolves. If you have an *otoshi-buta* (page 84), place it on the chicken pieces. Or use a conventional lid slightly askew, swirling the pan occasionally in circular motions to ensure even cooking. Lower the heat to maintain a steady, gentle simmer and cook for about 18 minutes for wings and about 25 minutes for thighs. Check the amount of liquid every 5 minutes or so. If it is reducing too rapidly, adjust the heat and add a few spoonfuls of water or stock. When the chicken is fall-off-the-bone tender, add the soy sauce and cook for 1 minute. There should be $^1/_4$ to $^1/_2$ cup liquid remaining in the pan.

Remove the pan from the heat and allow the chicken to cool in the braising liquid. It is during this cooling-down period that the flavors meld and enhance one another. If you will be serving this as a picnic food, discard the leek or onion and serve the chicken at room temperature. If you want to enjoy this dish warm, reheat briefly just before serving. Arrange the chicken pieces on a platter or on individual plates. Return the leeks or onion to the skillet over high heat and cook until the liquid is reduced by half. Spoon this sauce over the chicken.

Kitchen Harmony

If you want to make aspic from the cooking juices, dissolve 1 teaspoon unflavored gelatin powder in an equal amount of cold water and stir to dissolve. Allow the gelatin to swell before adding it to the pan juices. Over low heat, slowly stir to dissolve completely. Pour the gelatin into a small, shallow baking dish. Cover with plastic wrap (to avoid transfer of aromas) before chilling in the refrigerator. When gelled, flip it out onto a cutting board and dice or cut into decorative shapes.

Harmony at Table

Although a bit messy to eat with fingers, these chicken wings make fine picnic food. Have plenty of paper napkins or moist travel tissues on hand. When serving at table, you may want to set out warm wet towels, what the Japanese call *oshibori* (literally, "the wrung out cloth").

GINGERY GROUND CHICKEN

TORI SOBORO

This gingery soy-simmered chicken is a popular topping for rice (Rice Bowl with Three-Colored Topping, page 153) and stuffing for omusubi (Hand-Pressed Rice, page 158). Less soupy than a Sloppy Joe, the texture is similar to a dry curry or stiff chili con carne. It freezes well, so do not hesitate to double the recipe.

MAKES ABOUT 2 CUPS, ENOUGH FOR 3 OR 4 PORTIONS
SERVED AS A TOPPING OR 10 TO 12 PORTIONS AS
A STUFFING

12 ounces ground chicken, preferably a combination of
    dark and light meat
2 tablespoons saké
2 teaspoons sugar
2 tablespoons soy sauce
1 teaspoon ginger juice (page 71)

Place the chicken in a skillet. Add the saké and sugar and stir to separate the bits of meat before starting to cook. Place the pan over low heat and cook, continuing to break up the meat into crumblike clusters. At first the liquid will look cloudy, but within a few minutes it will become clear and the meat will turn white.

Skim the liquid to remove excess fat and then add the soy sauce. Continue to simmer for another 2 to 3 minutes and then add the ginger juice. Turn up the heat to reduce the excess liquid in the pan. Ideally, about 1 teaspoon will remain. Remove from the heat, let cool to room temperature, cover, and refrigerate for up to 3 days or freeze for up to 1 month. Reheat over low heat, adding a few drops of water, if necessary, and stirring to break up clusters.

GINGERY SEARED PORK

SHŌGA YAKI

Featured on many daily-special menus at diners and other casual eateries, slices of intensely seasoned gingery pork make a satisfying meal, especially when garnished with vegetables and accompanied by miso soup and a large bowl of steaming rice. If you are looking for ways of incorporating gingery pork into a Western menu, try it as a sandwich filling with crisp lettuce on a crusty roll.

SERVES 4

12 to 14 ounces boneless lean pork butt or boneless loin,
    in a single piece
2 teaspoons ginger juice (page 71)
2 tablespoons saké
1½ tablespoons soy sauce
3 bell peppers, preferably 1 each green, red, and yellow,
    quartered lengthwise and stem, seeds, and ribs
    discarded
2 tablespoons canola or other mild vegetable oil

Partially freeze the pork to make it easier to slice, then cut into paper-thin slices across the grain. From a piece this size, I usually get 12 to 15 large slices and some shreds. (I use any scraps to make Miso-Thickened Pork and Vegetable Soup, page 119, the next day.) If you are having trouble getting broad slices, do not worry. Shredded or torn pieces are fine.

In a shallow glass container, stir together the ginger juice and saké to make a marinade. One at a time, dip the pork slices into the mixture, turning each slice to make sure that all surfaces of the meat come in contact with the liquid. When all of the slices have been dipped, arrange them in the container in the remaining liquid, stacking them as needed if the container is small. Cover and refrigerate for at least 20 minutes and up to 1 day. Add the soy sauce 10 to 15 minutes before cooking (do not add it sooner, or the meat will toughen).

The pork and peppers will be cooked in two consecutive stages: an initial searing over high heat, and then a second glazing over medium heat. Using a heavy cast-iron skillet will yield the best results. Place it over high heat, add 1 tablespoon of the oil, and tilt and rotate the skillet to coat the entire surface well. When the oil is hot (to test, flick a drop of the marinade into the pan; it should sizzle loudly and be instantly aromatic), place the pork slices in batches, being careful not to crowd the skillet. Sear the meat until it begins to buckle and the edges change color, about 30 seconds. Flip the slices over and sear the other side, flattening them with the back of a spatula to avoid excessive curling. Remove the slices from the skillet as they change color. Set them aside on a plate.

Lower the heat and add the peppers, skin side down. Sear for about 45 seconds, letting them brown and blister slightly and become aromatic. Turn them over and continue to sear for another minute. They should still be crisp-tender and very aromatic. Add a drop more oil to the skillet, if necessary, to keep the peppers from scorching. Remove the peppers and set them aside on a plate.

Return the pork, all at once, to the skillet with whatever juices remain from the first searing that have collected on the plate. Sauté over high heat, turning the slices several times, for about 2 minutes, or until all the surfaces are well glazed and slightly browned. Return the peppers to the skillet for the final 30 seconds. Cover the skillet with a lid just before removing it from the heat. This allows the pork and peppers to continue to cook by retained heat for an extra few moments. Serve immediately.

Kitchen Harmony

The skillet may look discouragingly encrusted with marinade after cooking. Soak it in warm, sudsy water immediately after using for at least 10 minutes. The crust will lift.

Harmony at Table

The gingery pork and peppers can be placed directly on steaming rice in a deep *domburi* bowl, with the pan juices drizzled over the rice. It will look most attractive if you spread the slices of meat to cover two-thirds of the rice, and cluster the peppers in the remaining section. Because the meat is thinly sliced, it should be easy to grasp and eat with chopsticks. If you prefer to use a knife and fork, it might be better to arrange the gingery pork on a plate with the peppers as a garnish and serve the rice—or rolls—on the side.

PORK AND WAKAMÉ DUMPLINGS

WAFŪ GYŌZA

Active culinary exchange between the Asian mainland and Japan has more than a thousand years of documented history. But the Japanese first credited with eating the Chinese-style pan-seared dumplings known as gyōza was the relatively modern (seventeenth century) statesman Mito Mitsukuni. Although Mito was best known for his Robin Hood–like good deeds, he was also reputed to be a sophisticated gastronome, fond of Chinese dumplings, ramen, and even cheese.

The widespread appeal of gyōza today, however, can be traced to Japanese soldiers returning from duty in Manchuria after World War II. In post-war Japan, plump and tasty dumplings that could stretch small quantities of precious meat became immediately popular. Gyōza have been a dinnertime favorite in Japanese homes since those days, and also are commonly found on menus at ramen shops and neighborhood pubs.

In the 1970s, when Atsunori and I were raising our daughter in Tokyo, programs at hōikuen facilities (childcare for toddlers of working mothers) included lunch and snacks prepared by the kitchen staff. The policy was to insist that every child eat every food regardless of his or her likes and dislikes. Rather than engage in pitched battle over abhorred food, the institutional approach was culinary sleight-of-hand, hiding the problem food in some clever way, thereby getting the child to eat despised items. Providing full nutrition was part of the curriculum, as was the teaching of table manners that included a "no waste" rule.

At the time, Rena hated carrots, leeklike negi, and cabbage, yet according to her hōikuen teacher, she ate these foods joyfully (without knowing, of course) when they were hidden in gyōza. When I was given the recipe, I realized that the dumplings served at the Baby Lee hōikuen also included a visibly large amount of wakamé, a nutritious sea vegetable that she adored! I feel certain you will like these dumplings as much as she did.

MAKES 20 TO 24 DUMPLINGS

Dumplings

2-inch piece small leek, minced

1 large cabbage leaf, including thick stem portion, minced

1 tablespoon dried bits wakamé (page 44)

6 ounces ground pork

1 tablespoon grated carrot

1 tablespoon saké

1 teaspoon dark miso

2 teaspoons sesame oil

1 package dumpling wrappers (page 14), 20 to 24 wrappers

$1/4$ cup water

Dipping Sauce

3 tablespoons soy sauce

$1^1/_2$ tablespoons rice vinegar, preferably brown rice vinegar

To make the filling, place the leek, cabbage, and wakamé in a food processor and pulse until the mixture is finely minced. The dried wakamé will pick up moisture from contact with the other vegetables and begin to soften.

Transfer the vegetable mixture to a deep bowl and add the pork, carrot, saké, miso, and $1/2$ teaspoon of the sesame oil. Knead the mixture with your hands to ensure even distribution. Gather the meat mixture into a ball, lift it, and then throw it back with force into the bowl. Repeat this action 4 or 5 times—a bit like baseball practice. This pitching tenderizes the meat and ensures the mass will hold together.

Divide the meat mixture into quarters and then divide each portion 5 or 6 times (1 small portion will become the filling for a single dumpling). Nearby, have a small dish of cold water ready, and a flat plate on which to line up the stuffed dumplings.

Lay a dumpling wrapper on a dry surface, and place 1 small portion of the meat in the center of it. With a fingertip moistened with water, trace a line along half of the edge of the round wrapper. Fold the wrapper over to enclose the filling, and pinch in the center to seal the edges together at that spot. Holding the filled half-circle in one hand, pleat the closer edge of the wrapper, to both the right and left of the center sealed point, pressing it to the flat edge of the wrapper at the back. Set aside the stuffed dumpling, with the plump meat-filled side down and the pleated-wrapper edge up. Repeat to make 20 to 24 dumplings in all.

In a skillet large enough to cook all the dumplings at once, heat 1 teaspoon of the remaining sesame oil over medium-high heat. Carefully line up the dumplings, side by side, in the pan in clusters of 5 or 6 each. Arrange them so that the meat-filled portion is in contact with the skillet. Cook the dumplings for 3 minutes, or until nicely browned on the bottom. Check the progress by lifting 1 or 2 dumplings by their pleated edge.

Pour in the water. When the hissing and splattering die down, drizzle in the remaining 1/2 teaspoon sesame oil around the edge of the skillet. At the same time, lower the heat to keep the liquid at a bare simmer, and immediately place a lid on the skillet to trap the moisture. This type of cooking is called *mushi yaki,* or "steam searing," and ensures that the pork will be thoroughly cooked, yet moist and succulent.

Check the progress after 2 minutes. When the wrappers appear translucent and the meat is firm (check by pressing lightly with a spoon or gently pinching with chopsticks), remove the lid and raise the heat slightly. Continue to cook until all the water has evaporated and only the oil remains, about 2 minutes. Once you hear a sizzling sound, shake the skillet. The dumplings should slide about, most likely in clusters. If they seem to stick to the skillet, move the skillet away from the stove and replace the lid for a moment.

While the dumplings are cooking, make the dipping sauce: In a small bowl, stir together the soy sauce and rice vinegar. Pour into a serving pitcher or distribute among individual dipping dishes.

Remove the dumplings, a cluster at a time, with a broad, flexible spatula. Flip them so that the seared surface faces up and serve hot. For an appetizer, serve 5 or 6 dumplings for a single serving; serve twice that many for a main course in a family-style meal. Accompany with the dipping sauce.

Kitchen Harmony

In English-language cookbooks, Chinese dumplings similar to these are often called pot stickers. I suspect the name is a result of the difficulty in removing the dumplings from the skillet after cooking. The Japanese keep their *gyōza* from sticking, and tearing, by the addition of sesame oil to the steaming liquid. The oil remains in the pan after the liquid has evaporated.

BITE-SIZED PORK CUTLETS

HITO KUCHI TONKATSU

The prototype for these bite-sized cutlets is tonkatsu, *deep-fried breaded pork, a hybrid dish inspired by Dutch and Prussian food that evolved during the Meiji period (late-nineteenth-century Japan). Today,* tonkatsu *is standard fare appearing on restaurant menus and family dinner tables throughout Japan.*

These mini-versions are often included in obentō *boxes because the crust remains crunchy and the meat juicy even hours later at room temperature. The cutlets are stuffed with a flavorful filling, so there is no need to serve the usual* tonkatsu sōsu, *a thick Worcestershire-like sauce, with them.*

MAKES 8 ROLLS TO SERVE 2 OR 3 AS A MAIN COURSE,
4 TO 6 AS AN APPETIZER

> 10 to 12 ounces lean pork butt or boneless loin, in a
> single piece
> 4 or 5 shiso leaves
> 1 tablespoon bainiku or 1 uméboshi (page 38),
> pit removed and flesh mashed
> $^1/_2$ sheet toasted nori
> 1 tablespoon Leek Miso (page 103)
> $^1/_4$ cup all-purpose flour
> $^1/_2$ small egg beaten with 2 tablespoons cold water
> 1 cup panko (page 14)
> Vegetable oil for deep-frying

Cut paper-thin slices against the grain from the block of meat (partially freezing the pork will make it easier to slice). You should get 8 to 10 slices each measuring about $2^1/_2$ inches wide, 4 inches long, and $^1/_8$ inch thick. If you are having trouble getting broad, even slices, do not worry. Pieces can be patched together. (Inevitably, I produce some shreds, too, and I use these scraps to make Miso-Thickened Pork and Vegetable Soup, page 119.)

Separate and spread out the large slices on a cutting board, shorter sides at the top and bottom. (If you are patching pieces together, be sure to overlap them, keeping the larger slice on the bottom and closer to you.) Each slice will become a roll, half of them filled with *bainiku* and *shiso* leaves, and the other half filled with toasted nori and miso.

Trim away the stem from each *shiso* leaf, and cut the leaves in half lengthwise. Place the straight, cut edges of each half leaf flush, right and left, with the longer sides of the meat, overlapping the leaf halves in the center if necessary. Take a small portion of the plum paste and, using a butter knife or small spatula, spread it thinly over the leaves. Starting from one of the shorter ends of the meat, roll away from you jelly-roll fashion. Repeat to make a total of 4 or 5 rolls filled with *shiso* and plum. Set aside the rolls, seam side down.

Cut the nori into 4 or 5 strips, 1 strip for each slice of meat remaining. Lay the nori in the center of a pork slice so the edges are flush, right and left, with the longer sides of the meat. With a butter knife or small spatula, spread a bit of the miso on the nori. Starting from one of the shorter ends of the meat, roll away from you jelly-roll fashion. Repeat to make a total of 4 or 5 rolls filled with nori and miso. Set aside the rolls, seam side down.

One at a time, dust the rolls with the flour. Pay special attention to the seam, keeping it sealed and dusting over it. Using a pastry brush makes this easy. Then, one at time, dip the flour-dusted rolls into the egg mixture. To make sure each roll is fully coated, lay the egg-dipped roll on a pile of the *panko* crumbs and, using scooping or shoveling motions with a spoon, cover the top of the roll with crumbs. Lightly press the top layer with the back of the spoon. Set the breaded rolls aside on a dry paper towel. Or you can coat the rolls 1 to 2 hours in advance of frying, cover them lightly with paper towels, seal them with plastic wrap, and then refrigerate them until time to cook them.

You will need oil to a depth of at least $2^1/_2$ inches in the pan. I find that a wok, narrow at the base and wider at the top, is the best implement for this. Add the oil and heat to 375°F on a deep-frying thermometer. Or test the oil with a pinch of bread crumbs to which some of the egg wash still clings. The crumbs should sizzle gently on the surface, coloring very slowly. If the crumbs sink, the oil is not hot enough. If the crumbs sizzle on the surface and begin to color rapidly, the oil is too hot.

Working in batches, add the breaded rolls a few at a time and fry undisturbed for about 2¹/₂ minutes, turning them only once at the midway point. They should be golden brown and firm. To test for doneness, lift out a roll and insert a toothpick through the center of it. If liquid appears around the tiny hole, it should be clear. If it is tinged with pink, fry the rolls for another 20 to 30 seconds. Transfer the rolls to paper towels to drain.

If you wish to eat the rolls hot as a featured dish, cut each roll in half and serve immediately. If you wish to serve them at room temperature packed into a lunch box or as an appetizer, let them cool completely on a paper towel–lined rack away from drafts. For appetizers or a lunch box, insert decorative toothpicks into the rolls, then cut each in half or thirds.

Harmony at Table

Tonkatsu is typically made with boneless loin, which is cut into ¹/₄-inch-thick slabs, breaded, and fried. The cooked slices are then cut into strips, to make them easier to eat with chopsticks, and the strips are reassembled into slices and set at a jaunty angle against a mound of finely shredded cabbage (page 69). A tuft of parsley, a wedge of tomato, and perhaps a small mound of creamy potato salad clustered at the border where cabbage and cutlet meet complete the plate. *Tonkatsu sōsu* drizzled over the cabbage and cutlets is the usual accompaniment, except in and around the Nagoya region, where a dark sauce made from Hatchō miso, thinned with a bit of mirin and dashi, is the norm.

SOY-GLAZED BEEF BURGER

TERIYAKI BAAGA

American hamburgers, served on round buns with french fries and cola drinks on the side, have been a popular menu item in Japan for several decades. Long before the current fast-food version appeared, though, soy-glazed beef patties, garnished with bevel-cut carrots and a green vegetable and served with a side of plain boiled rice, found favor among trendsetting Japanese of the day.

This old-fashioned version is part of what the Japanese call yōshoku (literally, "Western-style food"). When I first arrived in Japan, I was often served hamburgers like these, prepared in a skillet and glazed with a demi-glace–like sweetened soy gravy, by well-meaning friends who thought I might be suffering from culinary homesickness. For me, it was a brand new approach to a familiar food.

MAKES 4 PATTIES

    2 teaspoons canola or other mild vegetable oil

    1 small yellow onion, finely minced

    2 tablespoons saké

    1¹/₄ pounds ground round

    ¹/₂ cup panko (page 14) or 2 slices day-old white bread, lightly toasted and crumbled

    2 tablespoons beaten egg

    2 teaspoons dark miso, preferably Sendai miso

    2 tablespoons sugar

    1 tablespoon hot water

    3 tablespoons soy sauce

Heat 1 teaspoon of the oil in a skillet over medium-low heat. Add the onion and sauté for about 2 minutes, or until wilted and slightly aromatic but not browned. Add 1 tablespoon of the saké and deglaze the pan, scraping up any browned bits.

Remove the pan from the heat and allow the onion to cool to room temperature.

In a bowl, combine the beef, *panko,* and egg. Add the miso and the cooled onion and knead with your hands to ensure even distribution. The Japanese will often gather the meat mixture, lift it, and throw it back with force into the bowl, repeating this action 4 or 5 times—a bit like baseball practice. Although the mixture will be fairly soft, this pitching ensures the meat mass will hold together. Divide the meat mixture into 4 equal portions, and shape each portion into an oval patty about 4 inches long, $2^1/_2$ inches wide, and $3/_4$ inch thick.

Add the remaining 1 teaspoon oil to the same skillet you used to sauté the onion and place over medium heat. When hot, add the patties and sear on the first side until browned, about 1 minute. Flip and sear the second side, pressing to flatten. The surface may crack a bit, but this is of no concern. Lower the heat, add the remaining 1 tablespoon saké, cover, and cook for 5 to 6 minutes for medium-rare. To check for doneness, press the meat with your fingertip or the back of a spoon. It should feel fairly firm. Then, poke a patty with a toothpick. The juices should run slightly pink. For a well-done burger, cook, covered, for 8 to 10 minutes. When pressed, the meat will feel very firm and juices will run clear.

In a small bowl, combine the sugar and hot water and stir to dissolve the sugar. Add the soy sauce and stir again to mix thoroughly. Return the skillet to high heat and pour the soy mixture into it, scraping the bowl with a rubber spatula to make sure all the sugar is added. Shake the skillet to coat the beef patties, and flip them once after a minute to make sure they are evenly glazed.

Serve the burgers hot, spooning any extra sauce on top.

Kitchen Harmony

If you want to serve this dish in its old-fashioned manner, blanch carrot sticks (Japanese carrots are thick, so that a bevel-cut $1^1/_2$-inch chunk makes a single portion) and a green vegetable. Although the Japanese favor neat bundles of leafy greens, such as Spinach Steeped in Broth (page 190), you may prefer to serve a few snow peas, green beans, or asparagus spears instead. Typically, the vegetables are arranged leaning against the burger, which is placed at the center of a white, round plate. Plain white rice is served on a flat plate (that is what makes it Western to Japanese eyes) on the side.

SOY-STEWED BITS OF BEEF

GYŪNIKU NO TŌZA NI

The style of stewing known as tōza ni is one of many techniques employed in the washoku *kitchen to extend shelf life of otherwise perishable foodstuffs. More commonly applied to clams and other seafood, soy stewing is a tasty way of preparing meat, too. Soy-stewed beef can be frozen for longer storage, though the* shirataki *noodles should be left out, because they toughen and become rubbery when frozen.*

In Japan, cuts of meat such as kiri otoshi *(bits and pieces) make this an affordable dish. Many beleaguered moms and harried housewives make this intensely seasoned beef when their local supermarket has a sale on thinly sliced cheaper cuts, and they find a moment to set this to simmer on a back burner. Once made, it can be packed into a child's lunch box, served in a pinch for dinner* dom-buri *style on reheated rice, or nibbled as an appetizer with drinks.*

SERVES 4

- 8 to 10 ounces boneless stewing beef
- 1 small package shirataki noodles (page 28), about 6 ounces, drained and chopped into 2-inch-long pieces
- $1/2$ teaspoon vegetable oil
- $2/3$ cup Basic Sea Stock (page 92)
- 1 tablespoon sugar
- 2 tablespoons saké
- 3 tablespoons soy sauce

Partially freeze the beef to make it easier to slice, then cut into paper-thin slices across the grain. Do not worry about the slices shredding and losing their shape. Tissue-thin slices ensure that the final dish will be tender, and since it is served mounded as clusters, irregular pieces are just fine. Blot up any extra moisture from the chilled meat with paper towels.

Place a small nonstick skillet over high heat, add the *shirataki* noodles, and dry-roast them (page 85), jiggling the pan to throw off any residual moisture. Drizzle the oil into the pan in a spiral motion, stir-fry for 30 seconds, and then push the noodles aside to make room for the beef. Add the beef, sear for 1 minute, and then stir the beef and noodles together. Add $1/3$ cup of the stock and lower the heat to maintain a steady simmer. If you have an *otoshi-buta* (page 84), place it on the beef and noodles. Or use a conventional lid slightly askew, swirling the pan occasionally in circular motions to ensure even cooking. Cook for 5 to 6 minutes, adding more water or stock if needed to prevent scorching. If froth floats to the surface, remove it with a spoon.

Add the sugar, saké, and the remaining $1/3$ cup stock, re-cover, and continue to cook for 7 to 8 minutes, or until the beef is tender. As with most simmered foods in the *washoku* kitchen, the soy sauce is added last. Add it now, stir, and simmer for another 5 to 6 minutes covered by an *otoshi-buta*, or 3 to 4 minutes if using a conventional lid set slightly askew. In either case, the sauce should be reduced to less than a spoonful. Remove from the heat and allow the meat to cool down with the lid in place so that the flavors can meld.

If you want a more intense flavor, reheat the mixture over medium heat after it has thoroughly cooled (add a few drops of water or stock to prevent scorching), and then simmer with the *otoshi-buta* in place until the sauce is reduced almost to a glaze. This stop-and-start method of stewing concentrates the soy seasoning. Serve the beef warm or at room temperature.

Kitchen Harmony

Use this soy-stewed beef to make a colorful, nutritious meal-in-a-bowl by following the example of Rice Bowl with Three-Colored Topping (page 153) made with gingery ground chicken.

FLASH-SEARED STEAK WITH TWO SAUCES

GYŪ SUTEKI, OROSHI PONZU, GOMA MISO SOÉ

A limited number of pampered Japanese steers (yes, they do guzzle beer and receive daily massages) are raised to make wa gyū, *premium Japanese beef. Several areas of Japan are famous for their* wa gyū, *particularly Kobe, a port city not far from Osaka, and Yonezawa, a landlocked city in the southern part of Yamagata Prefecture. These Kobe-style beef cattle, famed for their richly marbled and meltingly tender meat, are also being raised in America.*

This recipe for flash-seared steak is a good way to enjoy tender, high-quality meat. Served with two dipping sauces, smoky, sour, and sharp oroshi ponzu *and creamy, nutty, and mild Creamy Sesame-Miso Sauce, you can alternate flavors with each mouthful. I usually start with the smooth, rich sesame sauce and finish with the zippy, citrus-and-radish-infused soy sauce.*

SERVES 4

$^1/_3$ cup Creamy Sesame-Miso Sauce (page 100)

1 tablespoon Basic Sea Stock (page 92) or water,
  if needed

6 ounces daikon

$^1/_3$ cup Smoky Citrus-Soy Sauce (page 97)

1 piece beef suet, about 1 inch square, or
  1$^1/_2$ tablespoons vegetable oil

4 filets mignons or other tender cut of premium beef,
  each about 3 ounces and 1 inch thick

Prepare your sauces just before you cook the meat. If your sesame sauce seems too thick, adjust with stock or water. To make *oroshi ponzu*, peel the daikon (save the peels and make a side dish following instructions in Fiery Parsnips, page 215) and then grate and drain it (page 59). Add to the Smoky Citrus-Soy Sauce and stir to mix.

In a heavy skillet, melt the suet or heat the oil over high heat. Add the meat and sear for 1 minute, or until the bottom is well browned and the top edges begin to color. Flip the meat and sear the other side for another minute. For medium-rare meat, cover and cook for 1 minute longer.

To eat with chopsticks, thinly slice the seared steak before plating. However, if you will be placing a knife and fork at the table, this is not necessary. Serve the steak with the dipping sauces, each in its own small dish.

TŌFU AND EGGS

ENCOURAGED BY THE RECENT INTEREST outside Japan for the health benefits of eating soy products, I gathered together many of my favorite tōfu recipes and sent them out to my enthusiastic recipe testers around the world. As their replies came back, it became apparent that purchasing high-quality tōfu products was difficult, if not impossible, in many locations. I considered including a recipe for homemade tōfu, but making it from scratch was more of a commitment than most of my testers were willing to make for such a highly perishable item.

Instead, I narrowed my criteria and selected only those tōfu dishes that could be made successfully with the products available. If any dish calls for an ingredient that demands considerable effort to obtain or requires a special skill to make it, I have made sure that the recipe is versatile and keeps well, either refrigerated for several days or frozen for several weeks. Interestingly, many of these tōfu dishes have turned out to be ones with deep culinary history—the wisdom, and tastes, of the ancients prevailed!

I decided to group these tōfu recipes with recipes in which eggs play a prominent role. This pairing offers an alternative for anyone who wants to avoid meat and fish as the main protein component of the meal. Of course, not all tōfu recipes are vegetarian. In fact, in Japan, tōfu is often combined with meat, poultry, or seafood in cooking. However, since many Americans like to prepare tōfu as an alternative to meat, I offer instructions for making most of the tōfu dishes in a vegetarian manner.

All egg recipes in this book call for chicken eggs, the most common type of egg consumed in Japan (quail eggs are also popular and sold in supermarkets throughout the country). Because chickens in Japan are usually feed a diet rich in sea vegetables, the yolks are bright orange, rather than yellow, and lower in cholesterol than most American eggs. My far-flung recipe testers reassured me that these recipes worked well with their locally available product.

SILKEN TŌFU TOPPED WITH MUSHROOMS

TŌFU NO KINOKO AN KAKÉ

This dish is standard fare in many vegetarian households. Depending on the variety and combination of mushrooms used in the sauce, the dish can be quite delicate (slender, pale enoki with a floral scent) or quite robust (dark, full-bodied shiitaké and maitaké with their woodsy aroma).

SERVES 2

1 block tōfu, preferably silken tōfu, about 14 ounces, drained and pressed (page 77)

2 teaspoons vegetable oil

8 to 10 ounces fresh mushrooms (page 32), such as shiitaké, enoki, maitaké, shiméji, or hon shiméji, stems discarded or trimmed depending on type

$^1/_4$ teaspoon coarse salt

2 tablespoons saké

$^2/_3$ cup Basic Sea Stock (page 92) or Basic Vegetarian Stock (page 93)

1 teaspoon light-colored soy sauce

$^1/_4$ teaspoon soy sauce

1 teaspoon mirin

$1^1/_2$ teaspoons cornstarch mixed with $1^1/_2$ teaspoons cold water to make a thin paste

2 scallions, trimmed, white and green parts minced

Cut the tōfu in half vertically to make 2 large blocks. Each will become a serving.

If you have 2 fairly deep, microwave-safe attractive serving dishes, you can use them both to heat and serve the tōfu, eliminating the need to transfer the tōfu and risk crumbling it. If not, use a glass baking dish in which the tōfu can be heated in the microwave. Place the tōfu in the dishes or dish.

Heat the oil in a heavy skillet over high heat. Add the mushrooms and cook, stirring, for about 1 minute, or until lightly browned and fragrant. Sprinkle with the salt, and then add the saké and deglaze the pan, scraping up any browned bits. The mushrooms will wilt slightly. Add the stock, the soy sauces, and the mirin and cook, stirring, for 2 minutes.

While the mushrooms are cooking, heat the tōfu in a microwave oven on the highest setting for $1^1/_2$ to 2 minutes. This timing will ensure that the tōfu is heated through. A fair amount of milky liquid will be exuded; carefully pour it off or blot it up with paper towels.

When the tōfu is piping hot, add the cornstarch paste to the mushroom mixture over high heat and stir for about 1 minute, or until lightly thickened.

If the tōfu has been heated in a single dish, transfer to 2 individual plates. Pour the hot mushroom sauce evenly over the tōfu and garnish with the scallions. Serve immediately with spoons.

TŌFU-STUFFED FRESH SHIITAKÉ MUSHROOMS

NAMA SHIITAKÉ NO GISEI TSUTSUMI

The word gisei is written with calligraphy for "imitate" and "man-ufacture," suggesting that the names of dishes that include this word are intended as meat substitutes, especially in Buddhist veg-etarian meals. Inspired by several dishes that appear in an eighteenth-century cookbook called Tōfu Hyaku Chin (One-Hundred Delicacies Made with Tōfu), I have updated gisei-dōfu, using it as a filling to stuff shiitaké mushrooms.

Traditionally, mountain yam (page 64) is used to bind the mashed tōfu into a firm mass, making the dish strictly vegetarian. But because only a small quantity is used and the fresh tuber is often difficult to find outside Japan, I have substituted egg and cornstarch for the sticky yam in this recipe. If you have a couple ounces of fresh mountain yam on hand from making Handmade Deep-fried Tōfu Dumplings (page 276), you can use a teaspoon or so of ground or grated yam in place of the egg-cornstarch mixture.

SERVES 4

- $^{1}/_{2}$ block firm tōfu, about 6 $^{1}/_{2}$ ounces, drained and pressed (page 77)
- $^{1}/_{4}$ teaspoon sweet, light miso
- 1 $^{1}/_{2}$ tablespoons beaten egg
- 2 $^{1}/_{2}$ tablespoons cornstarch
- 12 plump, uniform fresh shiitaké mushrooms, about 3 ounces total weight
- 1 tablespoon vegetable oil
- 2 teaspoons mirin
- 2 teaspoons light-colored soy sauce
- $^{1}/_{3}$ cup Basic Sea Stock (page 92)
- $^{1}/_{2}$ teaspoon fragrant pepper salt (see Five Flavored Salts, page 112)
- $^{1}/_{2}$ teaspoon ocean herb salt (see Five Flavored Salts, page 112)

Place the tōfu, miso, and egg in a food processor and pulse until creamy and smooth, about 10 seconds. Transfer the tōfu mixture to a small bowl. Sprinkle 1 $^{1}/_{2}$ tablespoons of the corn-starch over the tōfu and, using a spatula and cutting and fold-ing motions, mix thoroughly.

Remove the stems from the mushrooms (save them for enhancing a soup stock or for making Seasoned Soy Concen-trate, page 96) and wipe the caps clean. If the underside of the cap appears to be trapping grit, brush it clean with a cotton-tipped stick (the kind used for cosmetics or medication). Dust the underside of the caps with the remaining 1 tablespoon cornstarch; a pastry brush will simplify the task.

Stuff the mushroom caps with the tōfu mixture, dividing it evenly. Use a butter knife or spatula to press out any air that might be trapped between the mushroom and the filling, and to smooth the surface, mounding the mixture in the center ever so slightly.

Use a skillet large enough to hold the mushrooms in a single layer. Place the skillet over medium heat and drizzle in the oil, swirling it to coat the surface evenly. Place the mush-rooms, filling down, in the skillet. Press down on the mush-rooms ever so slightly with an *otoshi-buta* (page 84) or a broad, flat spatula. Hold for a few seconds to ensure the filling adheres to the mushroom caps, then sear the mushrooms for 1 minute undisturbed, or until the filling is very lightly crusted over.

Flip the mushrooms so that the filling faces up. Again, press lightly on the mushrooms and hold for a few seconds. Lower the heat ever so slightly and add the mirin, soy sauce, and stock. When the liquid begins to bubble, flip the mush-rooms again, so the filling is face down. Raise the heat to medium-high and simmer for a few minutes until the skillet juices have reduced and thickened.

(continued)

Remove the mushrooms from the skillet and arrange them on individual plates or on a single platter. Turn some mushrooms so that the light filling is visible, and others so that the dark caps show. Pour any skillet juices over the mushrooms. Serve warm or at room temperature with the seasoned salts on the side. If your menu has no other spicy accent, the peppery *sanshō* salt is a good choice. If your menu is lacking in foods from the sea, the *ao nori* sea herb salt provides a briny touch.

Kitchen Harmony

The same *gisei-dōfu* mixture used to stuff these mushrooms makes a fine filling, with the addition of *hijiki* (page 41), shredded carrot, and fresh green peas, for stuffed cabbage, kale, or other sturdy leaves. Trim away the hard core from large leaves (these tough pieces can be used in Pork and Wakamé Dumplings, page 260, or Impatient Pickles, page 217), and then blanch briefly to make them pliable. I usually figure on ¹/₄ cup of filling for every leaf measuring 4 to 5 inches in width.

Place a spoonful of the tōfu-and-vegetable mixture in the center of each leaf, fold the right and left edges over to enclose the filling, and then roll up to make a log-shaped packet. Close with a toothpick or tie with ribbons of *kampyō* (page 63) and simmer in the same manner as the fried tōfu pouches in Treasure Boats (page 278).

SESAME-CRUSTED TŌFU
TŌFU NO PIRI KARA GOMA AGÉ

Tōfu is dismissed as bland and uninteresting by some Americans. I prefer, instead, to think of it as a fine backdrop against which spicy flavors and interesting textures can be showcased. In this recipe, smooth chunks of tōfu are coated with crunchy, nutty sesame seeds and then deep-fried. Sauced with a ginger-laced, chili-spiked soy broth, this dish is far from dull!

Illustrated on page 175

SERVES 4

1 block silken tōfu, 12 to 14 ounces, drained and pressed (page 77)

Coating

1 tablespoon cornstarch

1 egg white beaten with 1 tablespoon cold water

¹/₄ cup black sesame seeds, freshly dry-roasted (page 85) or unroasted

¹/₄ cup white sesame seeds, freshly dry-roasted (page 85) or unroasted

Vegetable oil for deep-frying

Sauce

2 tablespoons Basic Sea Stock (page 92)

1 tablespoon soy sauce

1 tablespoon mirin

2 teaspoons ginger juice (page 71)

1 bunch radish sprouts, about 2 ounces, trimmed (page 26)

¹/₄ teaspoon shichimi tōgarashi (page 47)

Slice the tōfu into 8 equal pieces, each about 1¹/₂ inches square and ³/₄ inch thick. Gently pat dry all newly exposed surfaces. Ready the ingredients for coating the tōfu by putting the egg white wash in a small bowl and the cornstarch, white, and black sesame seeds each in its own wide, shallow container.

Begin by dusting each chunk of tōfu lightly with cornstarch. A pastry brush simplifies the task. Dip half of the chunks first into the egg white wash and then into the black sesame seeds. To be sure each piece is fully coated, lay the piece of egg-dipped tōfu on a pile of sesame seeds and, using scooping or shoveling motions with a spoon, cover the top with seeds, flipping the chunk when necessary. Set aside the tōfu chunk on a dry paper towel. Repeat to coat the remaining tōfu chunks in the same manner with the white sesame seeds.

To deep-fry the chunks, pour oil to a depth of at least $2^{1}/_{2}$ inches into a pan. I find that a small Chinese wok, narrow at the base and wider at the top, is the best pan to use. Heat the oil to 350°F on a deep-frying thermometer. Or test with a few sesame seeds, preferably seeds to which some of the egg wash has clung. The seeds should sink ever so slightly, rise immediately, and then sizzle on the surface, coloring slowly. If the seeds sink but do not rise to the surface immediately, the oil temperature is too low. If the seeds never sink but sizzle immediately, the temperature is slightly high; gently stir the oil to cool it somewhat. If the seeds begin to color immediately, the oil is much too hot; lower the heat, stir, and wait for a moment before testing again.

Fry the coated tōfu 2 or 3 chunks at a time, turning them once after about 1 minute. To prevent the tōfu from becoming greasy, do not flip the chunks back and forth as you fry. Fry those chunks coated with the white seeds first, since it will be easier to judge how quickly they are coloring. Tōfu is a precooked food, so you don't have to be concerned with "cooking" it, only with crisping it. Ideally, the white seeds will turn a lovely golden color (the black seeds will not change color) and become slightly aromatic. Skim your oil between batches to clear away wayward seeds.

Transfer the fried tōfu to paper towels to drain, turning them once after 30 seconds or so to blot up excess oil from all the surfaces.

To make the sauce, in a small, attractive pitcher (if you plan to bring it to table) or bowl (if you plan to spoon it into individual dipping dishes), combine the stock, soy sauce, mirin, and ginger juice. Stir to mix.

To assemble the dish, place 2 chunks of tōfu, one crusted with white seeds, the other with black seeds, in each of 4 shallow bowls or deeply flanged plates. Garnish each serving with a few stalks of radish sprouts. Either provide each diner with an individual dish of sauce, or place a pitcher of the sauce on the table so that each diner can drizzle some of it over his or her serving. Set the table, or individual servings, with a small mound of *shichimi tōgarashi.* Serve the tōfu hot or let cool to room temperature. The sesame crust remains crunchy and nutty even when cool.

Kitchen Harmony

This method of sesame-crusting works well with thin slices of boneless, skinless chicken, fish, or meat.

SOY-SIMMERED DEEP-FRIED TŌFU DUMPLINGS

GANMODOKI NO NIMONO

With the introduction of Buddhism to Japan in the late eighth century, the consumption of animal flesh was shunned. Dishes such as this one, which features tōfu dumplings known as ganmo or gan-modoki (literally, "wild goose remembered," a poetic expression alluding to a taste memory of wild game), became common fare. Here, the dumplings are braised with earthy dried mushrooms, chunks of root vegetables, and a low-calorie, high-fiber tuber aspic known as konnyaku, to create a hearty vegetarian stew.

The ready availability of inexpensive, commercially prepared dumplings throughout Japan today makes this dish a popular choice among modern home cooks. When available at Asian groceries outside Japan, ganmo are usually found in the freezer section. Or you can try your hand at making them a home. Once assembled, this dish keeps well in the refrigerator for several days. It can be reheated as needed, though each time it is warmed up, the flavors intensify.

SERVES 4

3 large dried shiitaké mushrooms, stems removed and caps softened in $^3/_4$ cup warm water (page 33)

$1^1/_2$ cups Basic Sea Stock (page 92) or Basic Vegetarian Stock (page 93)

2 tablespoons saké

$1^1/_2$ tablespoons sugar

1 block konnyaku (page 28), 10 to 12 ounces, drained

1 large carrot, about 5 ounces, peeled and cut with rolled cut (page 69)

1 segment lotus root, about 3 ounces, peeled and cut with rolled cut (page 69), or 6-inch piece burdock root, rinsed, lightly scraped (page 58), and cut with rolled cut (page 69)

8 small fried tōfu dumplings, each about 2 ounces, either homemade (page 276) or purchased

$3^1/_2$ tablespoons soy sauce

1 teaspoon light-colored soy sauce, if needed

12 sugar snap or snow peas, stem end and string removed

Drain the mushrooms, reserving the soaking liquid, and cut into quarters. Combine $^1/_4$ cup of the mushroom liquid, $^3/_4$ cup of the stock, and the saké in a small saucepan, set over medium-high heat, and bring to a simmer. Add the mushrooms and adjust the heat to maintain a steady, gentle simmer. Skim away any froth that appears and then add the sugar. If you have an *otoshi-buta* (page 84), place it on the mushroom pieces to keep them submerged in the bubbling liquid, rather than bobbing on the surface. Or use a conventional lid slightly askew. Continue to simmer for 10 minutes.

Score the top and bottom surfaces of the *konnyaku* block with many shallow, horizontal strokes of a knife to create a more textured surface (this allows the *konnyaku* to absorb more of the deeply flavored simmering liquid). Cut the block into 12 pieces; triangles are fun. Bring water to a rolling boil in a saucepan. Add the *konnyaku* pieces and, after the water returns to a boil, blanch them for just under 1 minute (page 75). Drain but do not refresh under cold water.

Add the carrot, lotus or burdock root, and *konnyaku* chunks to the pan of simmering mushrooms. Add another $^1/_4$ cup mushroom liquid and the remaining $^3/_4$ cup stock and continue to cook for about 5 minutes, preferably with an *otoshi-buta* on top, until the root vegetables are barely tender.

Move the vegetables aside and add the dumplings so they lie flat on the bottom of the pan. Cook for another 3 to 4 minutes, adding water or more stock only if the dumplings look in danger of scorching. If you are not using an *otoshi-buta*, turn the dumplings after 2 minutes to ensure even cooking and coloration.

Add the soy sauce and simmer for a final 3 or 4 minutes, or until the liquid is reduced to just a few spoonfuls and the dumplings and vegetables become saturated and even slightly glazed with the sauce. Taste the sauce; if it seems too sweet, adjust with light-colored soy sauce; begin with just a drop, adding up to 1 teaspoon, if necessary.

If you are making this dish ahead to serve at another time, allow the mushrooms, carrots, lotus root, *konnyaku*, and fried tōfu dumplings to cool naturally in the pot in which they were cooked, with the *otoshi-buta* in place. During this cooling-down stage the flavors meld and intensify. Refrigerate for up to 5 days, reheating as needed to serve hot.

To assemble the dish, place 2 fried tōfu dumplings with several chunks each of carrot, lotus or burdock root, and *konnyaku* in each of 4 shallow bowls. Spoon whatever liquid remains over the dumplings and garnish each portion with 3 sugar snap peas. Serve warm or at room temperature.

Kitchen Harmony

If using frozen homemade fried tōfu dumplings, thaw them as directed in the dumplings recipe.

HANDMADE DEEP-FRIED TŌFU DUMPLINGS

TEZUKURI GANMODOKI

Deep-fried tōfu dumplings, made with mashed tōfu and minced vegetables, have appeared on temple vegetarian menus for more than a thousand years. Although nowadays commercially pre-pared dumplings are available in supermarkets and tōfu specialty shops throughout Japan, I have included this recipe for homemade dumplings for anyone who appreciates artisanal foods. Freshly fried, these tōfu dumplings are best enjoyed piping hot with a bit of grated ginger and a drizzle of soy sauce. If you decide to make sev-eral batches and freeze the extras, you can enjoy them later in Soy-Simmered Deep-fried Tōfu Dumplings (page 274).

A prerequisite for making these handmade dumplings is access to fresh mountain yam, or yama imo. Peeled and ground raw, this glutinous yam becomes a sticky mild-flavored paste, forming the "glue" that holds the mashed tōfu together in dumpling or patty form. A single tablespoon of the ground raw yam (about 1 ounce) will be enough to bind 10 ounces of densely pressed tōfu. Since you will need to buy more than 1 ounce, consult the notes for sugges-tions on using leftovers.

MAKES 8 DUMPLINGS

    1 block firm tōfu, 14 to 16 ounces, drained and pressed
       (page 77)
    1 ounce mountain yam, peeled (page 64)
    2 teaspoons black sesame seeds
    Vegetable oil for deep-frying
    $^{1}/_{2}$ ounce fresh ginger, peeled and grated (optional)
    1 tablespoon soy sauce (optional)

In the traditional Japanese kitchen, a *suribachi* (page 73) was, and still is, used to make these dumplings. Using a *suribachi* will yield the best texture with the least effort, though the dumpling mixture can be mashed by hand, too. The use of a blender, food processor, or other automated grinding and mashing equipment is not recommended, however, because such tools incorporate air into the tōfu mixture.

To make the dumpling mixture in a *suribachi*, begin by pounding and then mashing the tōfu with circular motions of the *surikogi* (pestle), stopping to scrape down the sides as needed. Mash and grind for about 2 minutes, or until the tōfu is smooth. Tap the *suribachi* on the countertop to concentrate the mashed tōfu in the center, scraping down any tōfu that remains clinging to the sides. If using a flexible spatula in addition to the pestle, avoid shredding it by scraping down the tōfu mixture in the same direction as the grooves in the *suribachi*.

Grind the yam by rubbing it in circular motions against the grooves near the top edges of the *suribachi* containing the mashed tōfu. Or use a grater, preferably a ceramic one (page 71), to grate the yam. When the yam is ground, it should be a sticky, thick, smooth, glutinous mass that peels away easily from the surface of the *suribachi* or grater.

Scrape the yam down into the bowl and gradually combine it with the tōfu by squeezing the mixture, forcing it between your fingers, and then gathering it into a mass, pressing it with the palm of your hand against the sides of the bowl. Repeat this squeeze, gather, and press procedure until there are no more lumps and the tōfu mixture is fairly smooth. Add the sesame seeds, folding them into the mixture.

To make the dumplings, begin by gathering the tōfu mix-ture in your hands. Lift, and throw it back with force into the bowl, repeating this action 4 or 5 times, a bit like throwing a baseball from hand to mitt. Although the mixture will be fairly soft, this procedure ensures the tōfu mass will hold together and that excess air will be forced out, making the mixture very dense.

With lightly oiled hands, gather up the tōfu mixture and divide it into 8 equal portions. Shape each portion into a dumpling by pitching it back and forth between your hands. Pat and coax each into an oval about 1¹/₂ inches long, 1 inch wide, and ³/₄ inch thick.

To deep-fry the dumplings, pour oil to a depth of at least 2¹/₂ inches into a pan. I find that a small Chinese wok, narrow at the base and wider at the top, is the best pan to use. Unlike many fried foods, this recipe requires low oil temperatures at the start. Begin by bringing your oil to a temperature of about 250°F on a deep-frying thermometer. Carefully slide the dumplings, one at a time, into the hot oil. They should sink, but not stick, to the bottom of the pan. Few, if any, bubbles will appear at first. The dumplings will rise very slowly, sizzling and bubbling only slightly. After 3 or 4 minutes, they should float on the surface and be just barely colored.

When all the dumplings have risen to the surface, raise the heat under the pan so that the oil temperature rises to 350°F. This will cause the dumplings to color nicely. Fry for 4 or 5 minutes, flipping the dumplings occasionally to ensure even coloration. As they fry, they will appear puffy. When they have turned a burnished brown (what the Japanese call *kitsuné iro,* or "fox colored"), transfer the dumplings to paper towels to drain, turning them once after 30 seconds or so to blot up the excess oil from all surfaces. As they cool and drain, they deflate.

If your pan is small, you will need to fry the dumplings in 2 batches. If this is the case, complete the low-temperature cooking for both batches first, transferring the first batch to paper towels while frying the second batch. Skim the oil between batches to clear away any wayward sesame seeds that are littering the oil.

Serve the freshly fried dumplings hot in individual bowls or plates. Mound the ginger on top and drizzle the soy sauce over all, if desired.

Or let the dumplings cool completely, blot up any excess oil with fresh paper towels, and then use towels to wrap the dumplings individually (or at least separate them one from another) before placing them in a freezer-strength zippered plastic bag. Press out as much air as possible, seal the bag, and freeze for up to 1 month. When thawing, keep the dumplings wrapped and allow 4 or 5 hours in the refrigerator or about 1 hour at room temperature. Use within 12 hours of thawing.

Kitchen Harmony

If you have yam left over, you can use it to make seafood fritters: Mix equal parts all-purpose flour and ground or grated yam and thin beaten egg. The final mixture should be the consistency of thick pancake batter. Toss in chunks of squid, octopus, shrimp, clams, or oysters. Carefully drop the mixture by spoonfuls into deep vegetable oil heated to 325°F. The fritters will puff and color slightly, cooking through in about 2 minutes. Drain on paper towels and serve hot with flavored salt (see Five Flavored Salts, page 112).

Although mountain yam has been used as a binder in the *washoku* kitchen for making tōfu dumplings, fish sausages, and soba noodles for centuries, it is increasingly difficult to find it in neighborhood markets, even in Japan. Other similar glutinous yams, such as *naga imo* and *yamato imo,* are sometimes easier to find, though they will not be as thick and sticky when grated. They can be used with the addition of an equal amount of cornstarch.

TREASURE BOATS

TAKARA-BUNÉ

At the Japanese table, foods resembling ships laden with treasure conjure up images of prosperity. These plump fried tōfu pouches, stuffed with shredded vegetables and folded and tied with edible gourd ribbons, are configured as treasure boats brimming with abundance set upon a shallow sea of soy-flavored broth. One or two make an interesting vegetable side dish to serve with fish, meat, or poultry. Or several, served with bundles of leafy greens, can become a main course in a vegetarian meal.

MAKES 10 OR 12 POUCHES

- 2 ribbons kampyō (page 63), each about 2 yards long, soaked in warm water for 5 minutes
- $^1/_4$ teaspoon coarse salt
- 1 small package shirataki noodles (page 28), about 6 ounces, drained and coarsely chopped
- 5 or 6 fried tōfu slices, each about 6 by $3^1/_2$ inches
- 1 tablespoon hijiki (page 41), soaked in warm water for 15 minutes
- 2 or 3 small fresh shiitaké mushrooms, stems removed and caps thinly sliced, or 2 ounces fresh wild mushrooms, stems trimmed or removed and caps thinly sliced, depending on type
- 1 small chunk carrot, about $^1/_2$ ounce, peeled and finely shredded
- 2 tablespoons fresh or thawed, frozen shelled green peas
- $^3/_4$ to 1 cup Basic Sea Stock (page 92)
- 1 tablespoon saké
- 2 teaspoons sugar
- $1^1/_2$ tablespoons soy sauce
- $^3/_4$ pound leafy greens, prepared as Spinach Steeped in Broth (page 190) (optional)

Remove the *kampyō* from its soaking water, and squeeze out the excess liquid. Rub with salt, kneading the gourd ribbons until soft and velvety, about 30 seconds. Rinse under cold water. Bring a small pot of water to a rolling boil, add the *kampyō*, and blanch for about 30 seconds. Remove the *kampyō* from the pot and let cool to room temperature.

Return the water in the pot to a boil. Add the *shirataki* noodles and, after the water retuns to a boil, blanch them for just under 1 minute (page 75). Remove the noodles with a fine-mesh skimmer or a small-hole slotted spoon and let cool to room temperature.

Again return the water to a boil and blanch the fried tōfu slices (page 75) until they puff up. Drain the slices and, when cool enough to handle comfortably, wrap in paper towels and press out as much moisture as possible. Cut each slice across in half and pry open each half to make a square pouch (page 56). You will have 10 or 12 pouches total.

In a small bowl, combine the softened *hijiki, shirataki* noodles, mushrooms, carrot, and peas. Mix well and divide into 10 or 12 portions. Stuff each pouch with a portion of the vegetable mixture. Close by pressing down on one open edge, tucking it in slightly to enclose the filling. Fold in the right and left sides (it will look somewhat like an envelope flap), and roll the stuffed bean curd over so the "seam" is on the bottom.

Lay an uncut *kampyō* ribbon on a flat surface. Place a stuffed pouch, folded edge facing down, on top near one end. Tie the ribbon, making a knot on top. Snip the ribbon with scissors, or cut with a knife. Repeat with the remaining pouches, using the second ribbon for tying half of them.

In a wide, shallow pot or flameproof earthenware casserole, combine the $^3/_4$ cup stock, saké, and sugar and bring to a rolling boil over high heat. Adjust the heat to maintain a steady simmer and add the pouches, knots facing down. If you have

an *otoshi-buta* (page 84), place it over the pouches. It will simplify your work and produce superior results. If you do not have one, you will need to flip the pouches every few minutes to ensure even cooking. When you do, check the level of the simmering liquid. Ideally, there will be at least several spoonfuls at all times. When necessary, add more stock to prevent scorching. Simmer the pouches, skimming away any froth that appears, for a total of 8 to 10 minutes, or until the vegetables and the *kampyō* ties are tender. Then add the soy sauce and simmer for a final 2 minutes.

To assemble and serve, divide the greens among 4 or 5 small bowls or use deep plates that can hold a bit of broth. The greens can be arranged as a mound at the back, against which the pouches will rest, or as bundles set to the side. Place 2 or 3 stuffed pouches in each bowl or plate. Spoon the broth from the pot over all to moisten. Serve immediately.

Kitchen Harmony

A similar dish, called *fuku-bukuro,* is made by gathering the edges of each pouch to resemble a plump gift-filled sack and tying the top closed with the *kampyō.* This is a bit trickier to assemble than the boat-shaped pouch, but with some practice you should be able to make these attractive edible grab bags. In place of the vegetables, you can fill the pouches with ground meat (chicken is most common), *omochi* (page 39), or a raw egg that poaches in the pouch as it simmers in the broth.

The *fuku-bukuro* obsession is not just culinary. The Japanese love grab bags filled with unknown merchandise, and you can find them for sale at department stores and specialty shops throughout Japan during the first week of the New Year. *Fuku-bukuro* and *takara-bune* often appear on menus early in the year, too.

BROILED TŌFU WITH FLAVORED MISO

TŌFU DENGAKU

In 1782, Tōfu Hyaku Chin (One-Hundred Delicacies Made with Bean Curd) was published in Edo (the former name of Tokyo) and became a best-seller among the local literati and merchants. Although the recipes themselves were neither new nor original, the idea of compiling so many dishes made from tōfu into a single volume was revolutionary.

Of the one hundred recipes, a dozen were dengaku *preparations, tōfu slathered with flavored miso pastes before broiling. Strictly speaking, the term* dengaku *applies to the sticks on which the tōfu is skewered (alluding to an ancient ritual dance performed on stilts during rice planting). In gastronomic circles today, however, it usually refers to the sweet-and-salty miso paste that is spread on vegetables, seafood, and tōfu. Tōfu dengaku is as appealing a dish now as it was centuries ago.*

MAKES 12 SMALL PIECES

- 1 block tōfu, preferably grilled tōfu, 12 to 14 ounces, drained and pressed (page 77)
- 1 tablespoon Leek Miso (page 103)
- 1 tablespoon Citrusy Miso (page 102)
- 1 tablespoon Pungent Red Miso Sauce (page 101)
- $^1/_2$ teaspoon black sesame seeds, freshly dry-roasted (page 85)
- $^1/_4$ teaspoon Japanese mustard

Slice the tōfu in half horizontally. Carefully flip the top piece over to expose the inner ungrilled surface (grill marks on both pieces should lay against the cutting board; if using regular tōfu, both outer sides of the block should be against the board). With the tip of a sharp knife, slice each half into 6 small pieces.

Line the rack of a broiler tray that will fit in your broiler or toaster oven with aluminum foil, and transfer the tōfu pieces, grilled sides down, to it. Slip the tray under the broiler about 2 inches from the heat source, or in the lowest position in the toaster oven. Heat the tōfu for about 2 minutes, or until the surface develops a very light crust. With pot holders, remove the pan and place it on a trivet or other heat-resistant surface.

With a butter knife or small spatula, spread the Leek Miso on the top (ungrilled) surface of 4 of the tōfu pieces, using $^3/_4$ teaspoon for each piece. Repeat with the Citrusy Miso on 4 more tōfu pieces, and finally the Pungent Red Miso Sauce on the final 4 tōfu pieces.

Return the tōfu to the broiler or toaster oven and cook for 1 to 2 minutes, or until the bean paste is bubbly, aromatic, and slightly browned. Light miso pastes, such as the citrus-infused one and the leek-flavored one, will scorch easily, so monitor these carefully.

Remove the tōfu from the rack with a spatula. If you want to serve the tōfu true to its Japanese name, use special double-pronged bamboo skewers known as *dengaku kushi*. Or substitute 2 round wooden toothpicks, placing them parallel to each other. Since wood burns easily under a broiler, I recommend that you insert the skewers after you remove the tōfu from the foil-lined rack just before serving.

To garnish the tōfu, sprinkle a few black sesame seeds in the center of each piece topped with citrus-infused miso, and place a small dab of mustard in the center of each piece topped with the pungent red miso. The tōfu topped with Leek Miso is not garnished.

Serve hot or at room temperature in sets of three, one of each flavor.

BITTER MELON, TŌFU, AND PORK SCRAMBLE

GOYA CHAMPURU

Just as the name Hawaii is used for both a state and an island, Okinawa is both a Japanese prefecture and an island in the Ryukyu archipelago that stretches from Kyushu, in Japan's southwest, to Taiwan. And like Hawaii, the food culture of Okinawa is a mixture of indigenous habits, other Asian cuisines, and Polynesian elements. In Okinawa, vestiges of the post-war American occupation can also be seen in the use of canned luncheon meat in many dishes. Champuru, a stir-fried hodgepodge of firm or extra-firm tōfu, meat, and vegetables (most often knobby-textured goya, or bitter melon), is recognized throughout Japan as the signature dish of Okinawa.

The version that I offer here makes use of ground pork, instead of luncheon meat or bacon. And, thanks to a Japanese colleague of mine, a native of Okinawa who passed on her "tip," I add a healthy dose of brown rice vinegar at the very end of cooking. Rather than add a sour note, the rich whole-grain vinegar mellows the intense astringency of the bitter melon and aids in its digestion.

SERVES 4

  1 bitter melon, about 8 ounces

  $^{1}/_{2}$ teaspoon salt

  1 teaspoon sesame oil

  2 to 3 ounces ground pork

  2 teaspoons saké

  1 block firm or extra-firm tōfu, 14 to 16 ounces, drained
    and pressed (page 77) and cut into 12 to 16 pieces

  1 tablespoon Basic Sea Stock (page 92)

  $1^{1}/_{2}$ tablespoons brown rice vinegar

  1 scallion, trimmed, white and green parts finely chopped

Cut the bitter melon in half lengthwise. With a spoon, scoop out and discard the seeds and spongy material down the center of each half. Place the halves, cut side down, on a cutting board and thinly slice into half-moons. Place the slices in a bowl and sprinkle them with $^{1}/_{4}$ teaspoon of the salt. Toss to coat evenly and set aside for at least 10 minutes and up to several hours to reduce the astringency of the bitter melon. Pour off any accumulated liquid and then rinse, drain, and pat dry the slices. This step, known as *aku nuki* (page 74), or "removing bitterness," is important to the flavor and texture of the finished dish. Because the salt is rinsed away, it does not add significantly to the sodium level of the dish.

Heat a large skillet or wok over high heat and drizzle in $^{1}/_{2}$ teaspoon of the sesame oil. Add the ground pork and sear it undisturbed for a few seconds. When lightly crusted, begin to stir-fry the meat, breaking up the lumps, for about 1 minute, or until the meat is no longer pink. Sprinkle with the remaining $^{1}/_{4}$ teaspoon salt and continue to stir-fry. As the meat juices clear, add the saké and then the bitter melon. Continue to stir-fry over high heat for 1 minute.

Add the tōfu and continue to stir-fry over high heat, crumbling the tōfu a bit as you do, for about 1 minute. Add the remaining $^{1}/_{2}$ teaspoon sesame oil and stir-fry for another minute to meld the flavors. In the final moments of cooking, drizzle in the stock and vinegar, tossing to distribute the seasonings.

Just before serving, shower the scallion over all. Serve at once.

SOY-SIMMERED FRIED TŌFU

ABURA AGÉ NO NIMONO

This recipe takes slices of plain fried tōfu, called abura agé, *and transforms them into intensely flavored pockets that can then be stuffed with sushi rice (Sushi Pillows, page 152), shredded and tossed into a pilaflike chirashi-zushi (Five-Colored Foods with Sushi Rice, page 147), or used to top bowls of steaming-hot soup noodles (Foxy Soup Noodles, page 172).*

MAKES 6 OR 8 SQUARES OR TRIANGLES

   3 or 4 fried tōfu slices, each about 6 by 3¹/₂ inches

   ¹/₃ cup Basic Sea Stock (page 92)

   1¹/₂ tablespoons Seasoned Soy Concentrate (page 96)
     or 2 teaspoons saké, 1 scant tablespoon sugar, and
     1¹/₂ tablespoons soy sauce

Bring a pot of water to a rolling boil and blanch the tōfu slices (page 75). Drain the slices and, when cool enough to handle comfortably, press out as much moisture as possible. Cut each slice in half, either on the diagonal to make triangles or across the center to make squares. If you will be stuffing the tōfu with sushi rice later, it is best to pry the pouches open (page 56) before simmering them in the broth.

Heat a skillet, preferably nonstick, over medium-high heat. Arrange the tōfu pieces in a single layer and press on them with a spatula or *otoshi-buta* (page 84) until they sizzle (ample oil will still be clinging to the surface of the slices even after blanching them). Flip the slices and sear briefly on the other side. The slices may color slightly.

Pour in the stock and lower the heat to maintain a steady simmer. Season with the soy concentrate and cook for about 3 minutes, or until nearly all the liquid has been absorbed. To ensure even coloration, use an *otoshi-buta* while cooking. Or turn the slices once, about halfway through cooking. Allow the fried tōfu to cool in the pan with the lid in place (the flavors are absorbed and intensified during this cooling-off stage).

The simmered slices will keep, tightly covered, in the refrigerator for up to 4 days.

TŌFU CHEESE

TŌFU NO MISO-ZUKÉ

Although the English name might suggest new wave or fusion fare, this classic preparation was included in the eighteenth-century all-tōfu cookbook Tōfu Hyaku Chin. By marinating pressed tōfu in miso, mild-flavored tōfu is transformed into a heady, fermented loaf with a rich, creamy texture reminiscent of a soft, ripe cheese. For a more delicate texture, use silken tōfu; for a more substantial and robust version, use firm tōfu.

At a multicourse feast, small cubes or thin slices of this miso-marinated tōfu are served as an appetizer. The tōfu marries well with dry saké or sparkling wine.

MAKES ABOUT 20 THIN SLICES

   3 tablespoons mugi miso (page 32)

   2 tablespoons saké

   1 tablespoon mirin

   1 small block silken or firm tōfu, 10 to 12 ounces,
      drained and pressed (page 77)

   1 teaspoon ao nori (page 41)

Put the miso, saké, and mirin in a small saucepan and stir to combine. Place over medium-low heat and cook, stirring, for about 2 minutes, or until small bubbles appear on the surface. Remove from the heat and allow the marinade to cool, uncovered and undisturbed, to room temperature.

If you used *sarashi* cloth (page 77) or several layers of cheesecloth to drain and press your tōfu, you can reuse the cloth for marinating. Carefully unwrap the pressed tōfu and set it aside on a plate while you rinse the cloth in running cold water and squeeze out all the excess moisture. Rewrap the tōfu snugly in a single layer of *sarashi* or a double layer of cheesecloth.

If you used paper towels and the microwave to drain and press your tōfu, discard this initial wrapping and carefully rewrap the pressed tōfu in a single layer of *sarashi* cloth or a double layer of cheesecloth.

Select a small, shallow glass baking dish, enamel-lined container, or plastic container. (The aroma of the marinade cannot be easily washed away from a synthetic material, so be prepared to dedicate whatever plastic container you choose to this task.) Spread one-half of the miso marinade over the bottom of the container, covering a 6-inch square area. Place the wrapped tōfu on top of the marinade and cover it with the remaining miso marinade. Make sure that the marinade is evenly distributed over the surface of the tōfu. Cover the container tightly and refrigerate for at least 12 hours and up to 2 days. Or set out at cool room temperature for at least 8 hours and up to 18 hours.

Check on the progress after 2 or 3 hours. If liquid has accumulated in the container, pour it off. The longer the tōfu marinates, the more intense it becomes. To keep the tōfu from becoming too heady, remove it from the marinade, wrap it in a fresh cloth or paper towel, and refrigerate it. It will keep for up to 2 days.

To serve, unwrap the tōfu and cut into ¼-inch-thick slices or small cubes. Take a pinch of *ao nori*, rub it between your thumb and index finger to release its seashore aroma, and then lightly dust the tōfu with the herb.

Harmony at Table

In the spring, you might try pairing the tōfu with Asparagus Tossed with Crushed Black Sesame (page 198), while in the autumn, Burdock and Lotus Root Chips (page 213) would be a better choice. At any time of year, the "cheese" can also be spread on crackers or toast points.

CHILLED EGG CUSTARD

TAMAGO-DÕFU

Custards are found in both Asian and Western cuisines. Though many are sweet, this Japanese custard is savory. Served chilled and spiked with fiery wasabi, this silky, slightly spicy custard is particularly welcome on a muggy summer day. Prepare it in the cool of an evening and refrigerate to serve up to 2 days later.

SERVES 4

3 large eggs

$^2/_3$ to $^3/_4$ cup Basic Sea Stock (page 92)

1 teaspoon mirin

Pinch of salt

Pinch of sugar

Dash of light-colored soy sauce

2 teaspoons wasabi paste

1 tablespoon Seasoned Soy Concentrate (page 96)

1 teaspoon cold water

Break the eggs into a glass measuring pitcher. Beat them well to blend together the whites and yolks. Let the foam settle a bit before reading the measurement. You should have $^2/_3$ to $^3/_4$ cup beaten eggs. Add an equal amount of stock. If your stock is freshly made, make sure it has cooled to room temperature before mixing it with the eggs; if it has been made ahead, it can be used straight from the refrigerator. Stir the eggs and stock together and then season with the mirin, salt, sugar, and soy sauce. Stir again to mix well. Strain the egg mixture through a fine-mesh strainer into another bowl to ensure a smooth, foamless liquid.

In professional kitchens, the custard is steamed in a special metal mold called a *nagashi-bako* and the finished custard is sliced into small squares. However, using individual heat-proof ramekins will simplify your work. Slowly pour the seasoned egg mixture into the ramekins. Remove any bubbles from the surface by dragging them with the tip of a toothpick up the sides of the container.

Fill the bottom of your steamer with water and set it over medium-high heat. Place the filled containers in the steamer and replace the lid. When a strong, steady flow of steam begins, steam for 2 minutes. Then lower the heat and steam for about 8 minutes longer. (After the initial stage of high heat, the lower the temperature you can manage without interrupting the flow of moist heat, the silkier the final custards will be.) Test for doneness by slipping the point of a toothpick into the center of a custard and then remove it. If no liquid fills the puncture point, the custard is cooked.

Remove the containers from the steamer and let them cool on a rack for 5 minutes, or until steam is no longer rising from them. Cover with plastic wrap and refrigerate until well chilled or for up to 48 hours.

When ready to serve, remove the plastic wrap. If condensation has formed on the surface of the custards, carefully pour it off. Place a small dab of wasabi in the center of each custard. Mix the soy concentrate with the water in a small bowl and spoon it over the custards. Or bring the sauce to table in an attractive pitcher, so that each person can drizzle a bit around the edge of his or her custard. The custards are eaten with a spoon.

ROLLED OMELET, TWO WAYS

A classic in the washoku *kitchen, thick rolled omelets are made by cooking a seasoned egg mixture, layer by layer, in a pan, preferably a square or rectangular Japanese omelet pan (page 81). The resulting omelet block or log is a favorite in* obentō *lunches. Slices of rolled omelet also appear at the sushi bar, where they are nicknamed* gyoku, *or "jewel" (an alternative reading of the first calligraphy in the pair* tama *and* go, *which together mean "egg").*

Rolled Omelet, Tokyo Style

ATSU TAMAGO YAKI

The Tokyo thick rolled omelet is robustly flavored, though rather sweet. Some cooks finish it with a caramelized outer surface. When it is served as part of a larger meal, in lieu of a grilled fish or a piece of meat, a mound of grated daikon, drizzled with soy sauce, helps tone down the sweetness.

MAKES 1 ROLL OR 8 TO 10 PIECES

- 3 jumbo or 4 extra-large eggs
- 3 tablespoons Basic Sea Stock (page 92)
- 1 tablespoon saké
- 2 teaspoons sugar
- $1/4$ teaspoon salt
- Vegetable oil for seasoning pan
- 1- or 2-inch chunk daikon, about 2 ounces, peeled and grated (page 59) to yield about $1/4$ cup (optional)
- 1 teaspoon soy sauce (optional)

Break the eggs into a bowl and remove the white squiggly clumps (called *chalazae*) that often cling to the yolk; if these are left intact, they make unattractive white streaks in an otherwise

A warm-weather obentō *meal, comprised of (from top left) Rolled Omelet, Asparagus Tossed with Crushed Black Sesame (page 198), Ginger-Stewed Eggplant (page 192), Red-and-White Pickled Radishes (page 221), and Hand-Pressed Rice (page 158)*

smooth, yellow sheet. Season the eggs with the stock, saké, sugar, and salt. Stir to mix thoroughly, but try not to incorporate air as you do so. Strain the mixture through a fine-mesh strainer. You should have a generous cup of the egg mixture.

A rectangular or square Japanese omelet pan (page 81) will make it easier for you to produce thick rolled omelets than a small, round pan (5 or 6 inches in diameter) will, but I have provided instructions for the latter as well. With either shape, a pan with a nonstick surface will help you control the degree to which the omelet caramelizes.

Heat the pan over medium heat, and then season it with a thin film of oil: Use long cooking chopsticks to grasp an oiled wad of paper towel and brush the entire surface of the pan with it. Pay special attention to the corners. Alternatively, use a pastry brush to apply the oil.

Test the temperature of the pan by dipping the point of a cooking chopstick or the tines of a fork into the egg mixture and then touching the surface of the pan. Ideally, as the egg-dipped tip touches the hot pan, the egg will jump up and stick to the chopstick or fork, coming cleanly away from the pan. If the egg sticks to the pan, you need to heat the pan longer; if the egg browns, the pan is too hot and you need to remove it from the heat and let it cool slightly.

When the pan is ready, gently pour in a scant $1/4$ cup of the egg mixture for the first layer, adding it in a steady flow. With smooth wrist motions, swirl the egg mixture to coat the surface of the pan evenly. Keep the egg mixture in motion, using repeated gentle wrist action, until it no longer flows. Cook the egg for about 45 seconds, or until the edges dry a bit. Remove the pan from the heat and let the egg sheet continue to cook by retained heat for another 20 to 30 seconds before beginning to roll it up.

If you are using a rectangular or square pan, start at the back of the pan, flipping and rolling the egg mass forward. The Japanese use chopsticks to accomplish this, but a heat-resistant or flexible metal spatula also works well. After rolling the mass forward, swab or brush the back of the pan lightly with oil and then push the rolled egg to the back of your pan. Swab or brush the front of the pan lightly with oil.

To make the second layer, pour a scant $^1/_4$ cup of the egg mixture into the pan, adding it gently but all at once. Lift the rolled egg at the back of the pan to allow the fresh egg mixture to flow under it. Swirl this freshly poured egg mixture to cover the front surface of the pan evenly. Keep the pan over medium heat until the edges dry a bit. Remove the pan from the heat, roll the egg mass to the front of the pan, and let it cook by retained heat for another 20 to 30 seconds. After rolling the mass forward, swab or brush the back of the pan lightly with oil and then push the rolled egg to the back of your pan. Swab or brush the front of the pan lightly with oil. Repeat, making 3 or 4 more layers, until the egg mixture is used up.

If you are using a round pan, begin to make the roll by flipping in the sides of the first layer of egg, both right and left, toward the center to create straight edges; the side flaps should be about $^1/_4$ to $^1/_2$ inch wide. Using chopsticks or a spatula, roll the egg mass forward over these flaps. Swab or brush the back of the pan lightly with oil before pushing the rolled egg to the back of your pan. Swab or brush the front of the pan lightly with oil.

Continue to make several more layers, each using a scant $^1/_4$ cup of the egg mixture added gently but all at once to the pan. After each addition, lift the rolled egg mass to allow the fresh egg mixture to flow under it. With each layer, fold the sides, both right and left, toward the center to create straight side edges. If the egg mixture in the center of the pan seems very loose, remove the pan from the heat and let the omelet cook by retained heat for another 20 to 30 seconds.

Whether using a square or round pan, carefully shape the final layer to make an even roll. If your omelet pan has a sloped edge on the far side, hold the rolled omelet against it for several moments to finish off the edge. In Tokyo, this outer sur-face is intentionally caramelized in spots. Flip the finished omelet out onto your cutting board or a flat plate.

If you want to create ridges on the surface of your omelet, as pictured on page 286, transfer it while still warm to a *sudaré* mat (page 87). Place the omelet across the mat, parallel to the slats, and at the center. Fold the edges of the mat over the omelet to enclose it. Flip, so that the seam of the mat now lies flat on your board. Place a small cutting board or plate on top of the mat to exert gentle pressure until the omelet has cooled. When you peel back the mat, ridges will have formed on the omelet.

If you are slicing the omelet without shaping it further, let it cool slightly before slicing it to avoid tearing. If you have made a roll or block that is more than 2 inches wide, slice it in half lengthwise before cutting crosswise 3 or 4 times to create 8 or 10 slices. If you have made a roll or block less than 2 inches wide, cut it crosswise into 8 or 10 slices.

Kitchen Harmony

It is possible to add fillings to these rolled omelets in two ways: scattered throughout the egg mixture to create the effect of confetti, or laid flat over the second or third layer of poured egg mixture to create a swirl pattern when rolled up. If a confetti effect is what you want, a combination of Gingery Ground Chicken (page 258), Seasoned Salmon Flakes (page 246), or shredded cooked crabmeat with finely minced dill and/or chives or other herbs is a good choice. If you prefer a swirl pattern, a half sheet of toasted nori or a slice of boiled ham works nicely.

In Japan, omelets such as these are typically served at room temperature, though you may prefer to serve them piping hot or chilled. A single portion is typically 2 pieces, unless the omelet is served as a main course, in which case it makes 2 servings of 5 pieces each. When the omelet is served as a main course, a mound of grated daikon, drizzled with soy sauce, is placed to the right of the omelet. Spread a bit of the grated radish on each slice as you eat.

To store the omelets, cover tightly and refrigerate for up to 4 days.

Rolled Omelet, Kansai Style

DASHI MAKI TAMAGO

Kansai refers to the area embracing Osaka and Kyoto, and the thick rolled omelet enjoyed there is pale yellow and quite savory. Because this version is softer and more pliable than the Tokyo style, it can be coaxed into various shapes while still warm. Slices of these decoratively configured omelets are often included in elegant boxed obentō lunches. Flower shapes are especially popular.

Seasoning the egg mixture, selecting and preparing your pan, and cooking the Kansai rolled omelet are essentially the same as for the Tokyo omelet. The difference lies in the balance of flavors in the egg mixture, and in maintaining a lower pan temperature.

MAKES 1 ROLL OR 8 TO 10 PIECES

- 3 jumbo or 4 extra-large eggs
- 3 tablespoons Basic Sea Stock (page 92)
- 1 tablespoon saké
- 1 teaspoon mirin
- 1/4 teaspoon light-colored soy sauce
- 1/4 teaspoon salt
- Vegetable oil for seasoning pan

Break the eggs into a bowl and remove the white squiggly clumps (called *chalazae*) that often cling to the yolk; if these are left intact, they make unattractive white streaks in an other-

wise smooth, yellow sheet. Season the eggs with the stock, saké, mirin, light-colored soy sauce, and salt. Stir to mix thoroughly, but try not to incorporate air as you do so. Strain the mixture through a fine-mesh strainer. You should have a generous cup of the egg mixture.

To cook the omelet, follow the instructions for Rolled Omelet, Tokyo Style (page 287). The difference lies primarily in maintaining a slightly lower pan temperature throughout cooking. As with the Tokyo-style omelet, though, it will be easier to shape the omelet if you use a rectangular or square Japanese omelet pan.

Let the omelet cool slightly before slicing it to avoid tearing. If you have made a roll or block that is more than 2 inches wide, slice it in half lengthwise before cutting crosswise 3 or 4 times to create 8 or 10 slices. If you have made a roll or block less than 2 inches wide, cut it crosswise into 8 or 10 slices.

In Japan, omelets such as these are typically served at room temperature, though you may prefer to serve them piping hot or chilled. A single portion is typically 2 pieces, unless the omelet is served as a main course, in which case it makes 2 servings of 5 pieces each. To store the omelets, cover tightly and refrigerate for up to 4 days.

Harmony at Table

Rolled omelets can be shaped to resemble flowers to add visual interest and textural fun. To shape omelets: Lay the *sudaré* mat, preferably an *oni sudaré*, or "monster" mat (page 87), on a flat surface with the jagged points facing up. The slats should be horizontal to you. Place the rolled egg, still warm, across the mat, parallel to the slats, not far from the edge nearest you. Grasp the mat, pinching both the right and the left near corners with your thumbs underneath and your index fingers on top. Lift up, coaxing the mat to encircle the warm omelet. After resting the top portion of the mat over the omelet, press the far edge down to lie on the bottom portion of the mat. Gently tug back on the top of the mat while pulling away on the bottom to tighten the mat around the egg mass. Lift the top portion of the mat and finish rolling to make a cylinder. This is the same motion you see chefs at the sushi bar use to make plump rolled sushi. Place rubber bands around each end of the rolled mat to hold it in place. If you are using a regular mat (without the deep ridges), insert 5 round chopsticks, parallel to the slats, between the mat and rubber bands; these will exert pressure on the omelet so that indentations will form as it cools, making it look more like a flower. Cover with plastic wrap and refrigerate for at least 30 minutes or up to several hours. Unwrap, remove the rubber bands, and unfurl the mat. Slice crosswise to make 8 to 10 "flowers."

THIN OMELET

USU TAMAGO YAKI

These thin omelets are flipped with a single chopstick, a skill that admittedly takes a bit of practice to master. But once you learn the technique, you will find it useful in making crepes and blini, too. In the washoku *kitchen, thin egg sheets such as these are typically sliced into narrow ribbons and scattered over sushi rice. They can also be used to wrap or enclose other foods. In this book, I have called for them in Five-Colored Foods with Sushi Rice (page 147) and Chilled Chinese Noodle Salad (page 178).*

Illustrated on page 146

MAKES 6 OR 7 SMALL CIRCLES, OR 4 OR 5 RECTANGULAR OR SQUARE SHEETS

> 3 extra-large or jumbo eggs
> 2 tablespoons saké
> 3 tablespoons Basic Sea Stock (page 92)
> $^1/_2$ teaspoon sugar
> $^1/_4$ teaspoon salt
> 1 teaspoon cornstarch mixed with 1 tablespoon cold
>   water to make a thin paste (optional)
> Vegetable oil for seasoning pan

Break the eggs into a bowl and remove the white squiggly clumps (called *chalazae*) that often cling to the yolk; if these are left intact, they make unattractive white streaks in an otherwise smooth, yellow sheet. Season the eggs with the saké, stock, sugar, and salt. Stir to mix thoroughly, but try not to incorporate air as you do so. Strain the mixture through a fine-mesh strainer. You should have a generous cup of the egg mixture.

If you will be using the omelet sheets to wrap or enclose other foods, stir in the thin cornstarch paste to "strengthen" the egg mixture.

A rectangular Japanese omelet pan (page 81), preferably nonstick, will make it easier for you to produce a thin omelet than a small round pan (5 or 6 inches in diameter) will—the rectangular shape is easier to flip—but I have provided instructions for a round pan as well.

Heat the pan over medium heat, and then season it with a thin film of oil: Use long cooking chopsticks to grasp an oiled wad of paper towel and brush the entire surface of the pan with it. Pay special attention to the corners. Alternatively, use a pastry brush to apply the oil.

Test the temperature of the pan by dipping the point of a cooking chopstick or the tines of a fork into the egg mixture and then touching the surface of the pan. Ideally, as the egg-dipped tip touches the hot pan, the egg will jump up and stick to the chopstick or fork, coming cleanly away from the pan. If the egg sticks to the pan, you need to heat the pan longer; if the egg browns, the pan is too hot and you need to remove it from the heat and let it cool slightly.

When the pan is ready, pour in a measured amount of the egg mixture. If using a standard rectangular pan, 4 by 7 inches, pour in a full $1/4$ cup of the egg mixture. If you are using a small round pan, 5 or 6 inches in diameter, pour in a scant $1/4$ cup of the egg mixture. Using smooth, swirling motions, tilt and rotate the pan to cover the surface evenly. Cook over medium heat for about 45 seconds, or until the edges of the omelet shrink a bit from the sides of the pan. Remove the pan from the heat and let the egg sheet continue to cook by retained heat for another 30 to 40 seconds before flipping it over. Try flipping it the Japanese way: Trace around the edge of the omelet with the tip of a single chopstick to make sure it is not sticking to the sides of the pan. Using a combination of twirling and twisting strokes, work the chopstick under the egg sheet across its width and then lift up (the omelet is now draped across the chopstick) and invert the omelet.

Allow the other side to dry off—this will take at most 30 seconds additional exposure to heat—before flipping it out of the skillet. Continue to make the omelets in the same manner with the remaining egg mixture, re-oiling the pan each time and stacking the omelets as you go (they will not stick to each other).

Let the egg sheets cool to room temperature. They will keep, well covered, in the refrigerator for up to 5 days.

Kitchen Harmony

Once you master the art of thin-omelet making, you can use the egg sheets in various ways: in place of nori to make rolled sushi (page 149) or for draping *omusubi* (Hand-Pressed Rice, page 158). Or use the egg sheets instead of thin sliced bread or tortillas to make wraps: layer smoked salmon, ham, or turkey on an omelet sheet, scatter with sprouts or top with soft lettuce leaves, and roll up.

IMPATIENT CODDLED EGGS

SOKUSEKI ONSEN TAMAGO

Japan's many natural hot springs, or onsen, attract travelers seeking a respite from the pressures of daily life. Resort facilities, both Western-style hotels and more traditional inns, or ryōkan, pamper their guests with sumptuous banquets and leisurely bathing in mineral-rich waters. Guests typically check in late in the day and take a long soak in one of the deep hot tubs before feasting on local delicacies. After a restful night's sleep on a fluffy futon, breakfast is served. And onsen tamago, eggs set to soak in the mineral baths until the whites are softly set but the yolks still runny, are often featured at the morning meal.

The recipe I offer here, its name a seeming oxymoron, is suitable for city dwellers with no access to natural hot springs and for impatient cooks who hope to be finished in the kitchen in less than ten minutes. True onsen tamago are left to bathe for hours in lukewarm, mineral-rich water before they are swaddled in towels, like babies, to keep them warm. That is why I have called my version of this dish coddled eggs.

SERVES 4

4 large eggs, at room temperature

6 cups cold water

1 cup Basic Sea Stock (page 92)

2 tablespoons mirin

1¹/₂ tablespoons light-colored soy sauce

1 scant teaspoon wasabi paste

4 or 5 fresh chives, snipped, or 1 scallion, green tops only, finely minced

It is best to start with eggs at room temperature, rather than taken directly from the refrigerator. I set my eggs on a cool kitchen counter for about an hour.

Pour 5 cups of the water into a 2- or 3-quart saucepan with a tight-fitting lid and bring to a rolling boil. Remove the pan from the heat as soon as the water boils and immediately add the remaining 1 cup cold water. This will cool the boiling water to about 160°F, the temperature at which egg whites begin to solidify (yolks "cook" at slightly lower temperatures).

Using a ladle or long-handled spoon, carefully lower the eggs into the hot water. As the eggs sink below the surface of the water, you may see small bubbles rise to the top. Cover the pan immediately and set a kitchen timer for 7 minutes.

If you will be serving the eggs warm, combine the stock, mirin, and soy sauce in a small saucepan and heat the mixture over medium heat while you wait for the timer to signal that the eggs are ready. When the timer goes off, remove the eggs promptly with a slotted spoon and transfer them to a bowl of cold water. When you can handle them comfortably (after 2 or 3 minutes), remove the eggs from the water and pat the shells dry with a kitchen towel. They are now ready to eat.

If you will be serving the eggs cold, prepare the sauce ahead of time and chill it. Or pour the freshly made warm sauce into a lidded plastic container and place in the freezer for 10 to 15 minutes. When the timer (set for 7 minutes to cook the eggs) goes off, remove the eggs promptly from the pot with a slotted spoon and transfer them to a bowl of cold water. If you want to cool the eggs quickly, run cold water over them for several minutes, or add ice cubes to the bowl of water. Reset the timer for 10 minutes, to remind you of the sauce chilling in the freezer and to signal you to remove the eggs from the cold water. Pat the shells dry.

Just before serving the eggs, whether warm or cold, crack the shell at the larger end (this is where air is trapped as the egg cooks, making this end easier to peel), lightly tapping it on a hard surface. Carefully peel the shell away; some of the white may cling to it. If necessary, use a small spoon to scoop the egg from the shell, being careful not to pierce the yolk, and set each egg in its own small, shallow cup or small, deep dish. Pour some of the sauce over each egg and top with a dab of wasabi and a sprinkle of chives. Diners mix the wasabi in the sauce as they break the egg. Eat with a spoon.

If you will not be serving the eggs right away, label the shells with the date and some other mark to indicate that they are cooked. Place in the refrigerator for up to 3 days. The sauce can be kept chilled for up to 1 week.

Kitchen Harmony

Softly set eggs such as these can be served as you would any poached eggs, on toast or with hashed meat and fried or roasted potatoes. Another *washoku* way to serve them is atop *udon* noodles (Moon-Viewing Noodles in Broth, page 171).

DESSERTS

IN AMERICA, DESSERT—nearly always something sweet and of questionable nutritional value—is served at the conclusion of a meal. Typical American breakfast foods, such as sugar-frosted cereals, doughnuts, muffins, scones, and toast spread with jam, are really desserts in disguise. From childhood, many Americans think of dessert as a reward for finishing "healthy" foods first—a fitting compensation for eating vegetables. Indeed, when diet menus deny dessert, Americans feel somehow deprived of a basic right.

In contrast, the classic Japanese meal concludes on a savory note of miso-enriched broth, rice, and pickles, though fruit, often listed on formal menus as *mizugashi* (literally, "water sweets"), may be presented after the final soup-and-rice tray is cleared from the table. Sugar and other sweeteners such as honey, barley malt, and mirin are used in cooking throughout the meal to balance such salty seasonings as miso and soy sauce and to bring the tangy, tart flavors imparted by vinegar, citrus, and astringent plum into harmony with the rest of the meal.

Yet the Japanese adore confectionary of all sorts and consume pastries, cakes, cookies, taffy, and other candies with great pleasure. These sweet foods have traditionally been enjoyed apart from mealtime, however, either in conjunction with ceremonial tea or as *oyattsu* (literally, the "eighth seg-

ment," a reference to the section of the ancient sundial that corresponds to about four o'clock in the afternoon). This habit of eating dessert as a separate, late-afternoon meal persists and seems not to interfere with appetite at dinnertime, despite the fact that dinner tends to be early (six o'clock for dinner reservations and eight-thirty for last orders are common at many restaurants).

Today, Japanese distinguish between *yōgashi*, or Western-style confectionary that typically use dairy products and wheat flour, and *wagashi*, or indigenous confections made from fruits, certain tubers, beans, nuts and seeds, sea vegetables, and rice flour. Both *yō* (west) and *wa* (east) sweets, along with many hybrid creations, are commonly enjoyed late in the day as *oyattsu*, when they are almost always accompanied by refreshingly bitter green tea, strongly brewed English-style tea, or coffee.

Because the notion of dessert, and the role played by sweets in general, is so different in Japan than it is in America, choosing recipes to include in this chapter was especially challenging. I decided to accommodate the expectations of my fellow Americans by selecting dishes that would provide both a sense of reward and be deemed a fitting conclusion to a full meal. But in doing so, I have been careful to utilize many ingredients from the traditional *washoku* pantry.

GREEN TEA ICE CREAM

MATCHA AISU

Creamy, cold, and sweet with a hint of bitterness, green tea ice cream has become the classic conclusion to dining at Japanese restaurants throughout America. The recipe that I offer here is essentially the same as the one that appeared in An American Taste of Japan, *the cookbook I wrote in 1985. Twenty years later, it is still the best green tea ice cream I know.*

MAKES 1 PINT

1/3 cup sugar

1/3 cup cold water

1/2 teaspoon mirin

2 teaspoons matcha (page 54)

1/2 cup whole milk

1/2 cup half-and-half

In a small saucepan, combine the sugar and water. Stir the mixture over low heat to melt the sugar and then continue to simmer for about 5 minutes, or until a bit syrupy. Add the mirin, stir, and remove the pan from the heat.

In a small bowl, combine 1 tablespoon of the warm syrup and the *matcha* and stir until dissolved. Return this sweet tea concentrate to the saucepan and stir until completely blended. To retain optimal aroma and ensure an intense jade color, do not reheat the mixture. Stir in the milk and half-and-half and mix thoroughly.

If you are using an ice-cream maker, pour the tea-and-milk mixture into the machine and follow the manufacturer's instructions for making a soft-set ice cream. For most models, about 10 minutes of chilling and churning should suffice. Pour the semifrozen mixture into a 3-cup freezer-safe container with a snug-fitting lid. Tap the container gently on a countertop to force out any air bubbles that might be trapped below the surface. Cover and freeze for at least 2 hours, or until firm throughout.

If you are using a blender, electric mixer, or whisk and freezer trays, pour the tea-and-milk mixture into a flat, shallow freezer-safe container, filling it no more than two-thirds full (the mixture will expand). Tap the container gently on a countertop to force out any air bubbles that might be trapped below the surface. Cover and freeze for 1 1/2 hours, or until nearly firm. Transfer the semifrozen mixture to a blender and pulse in a few short spurts. Or, with a handheld electric mixer or a whisk, whip the mixture vigorously in a deep bowl. Return the mixture to the same container, re-cover, and freeze again for another 45 minutes, or until firm (but not rock-hard) throughout. Repeat the blend or whip step one more time to achieve a silkier texture.

The final ice cream should be smooth but not too hard. When ready to serve, transfer one or two scoops to pre-chilled bowls. The jade color of the ice cream makes for a dramatic presentation against black tableware.

RAINBOW ICE

NIJI AISU

Here are five fruit-flavored ices made with ama-zaké, *each vividly flavored and naturally hued. Serving a small portion of each can bring a harmonious close to a full meal or provide a refreshing snack on a hot day. In keeping with the color and flavor principles of* washoku, *I offer yellow (banana-ginger and Golden Delicious apple), red (strawberry and Ruby grapefruit), and green (honeydew melon). Sweet and tart flavors predominate, although spicy (ginger) and bitter (grapefruit) provide welcome accents. A pinch of salt or light-colored soy sauce in each frozen dessert helps brighten the fruit flavors.*

If you like, complete the color spectrum by adding a black-and-white cookie (dark chocolate and vanilla) or chocolate-dipped macaroon (coconut or almond) to the dessert menu. Doing so will also add another cooking method, namely baking, to the fresh category (various fruits).

Because the water content and sweetness of fruits vary, amounts in the ingredients list should be considered a guideline, not absolute measurements. The total volume in each case is 1 to 1¹/₄ cups puréed fruit and ama-zaké.

MAKES 2 OR 3 ICE POPS, OR 8 TO 10 SMALL ICE CUBES, IN EACH OF 5 FLAVORS

Ruby Grapefruit

¹/₃ cup ama-zaké (page 51)

1 large Ruby grapefruit, about 14 ounces, peeled, seeded, and cut into membrane-free sections

Pinch of coarse salt

Strawberry

¹/₃ cup ama-zaké (page 51)

2¹/₂ to 3 cups strawberries, 10 to 12 ounces, hulled and sliced

¹/₄ teaspoon fresh lemon juice

Pinch of coarse salt

Banana-Ginger

¹/₃ cup ama-zaké (page 51)

1 small banana, about 5 ounces, peeled and sliced

¹/₄ teaspoon fresh lemon juice

¹/₄ teaspoon ginger juice (page 71)

Drop of light-colored soy sauce

Apple

¹/₃ cup ama-zaké (page 51)

1 Golden Delicious apple, about 9 ounces, cored, peeled, and diced

¹/₂ teaspoon fresh lemon juice

¹/₂ teaspoon brandy (optional)

Pinch of coarse salt

Honeydew Melon

¹/₃ cup ama-zaké (page 51)

2¹/₄ cups peeled, seeded, and diced lushly ripe honeydew melon, about 8 ounces

1 teaspoon fresh lime juice

¹/₂ teaspoon Midori (melon liquor) (optional)

Drop of light-colored soy sauce

Each of the fruit-flavored ices is made in the same manner: A blender or food processor is used to combine the *ama-zaké* and the fruit to make a creamy purée. Have 5 measuring cups ready to receive each flavor as it is processed. You will need to wash and dry your blender or food processor carefully before you make each new flavor.

To begin making each flavor, place the *ama-zaké* in the blender or food processor and pulse until creamy and smooth. Then add the fruit and pulse until smooth.

Some flavors require lemon or lime juice to balance acidity and to hold color. Add it to the puréed fruit mixture and pulse to mix. Add the ginger juice for the banana-ginger ice at the same time. You can add a little brandy to the apple ice or Midori to the melon ice at the same time to add depth and complexity of flavor and to make it taste more "grown-up."

Taste each mixture before adding the salt or soy sauce. Adjust the amount as needed to balance and brighten the flavors. Pulse to distribute evenly.

If you have a traditional Popsicle maker, fill and freeze according to the manufacturer's instructions. You will be able to make 2 or 3 full-sized ice pops from each flavor.

To fashion a rainbow assortment of mini-ices, pour the fruit mixtures into mini-cube ice trays (about 1 1/2 teaspoons per cube). Cover and freeze for about 3 hours, or until fully set. Release from the trays just before serving.

Or transfer each flavor to a separate shallow, flat-bottomed plastic container. Cover and freeze for about 3 hours, or until fully set. Cut into 1/2-inch cubes.

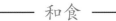

Kitchen Harmony

Other flavors you may wish to try include mango (use the melon recipe as your guide, substituting rum for the Midori), fresh peaches and/or apricots (use the apple recipe as your guide, substituting plum wine for the brandy), or persimmons and pears (use the strawberry recipe as your guide).

If you want a silky-textured ice that can be scooped out and you have an ice-cream maker, double or triple the recipe as needed to produce sufficient volume to engage the mechanism of your machine.

BLACK SESAME ICE

KURO GOMA AISU

In her Tokyo restaurant, Sen, chef Yumiko Kano serves na kaiseki, an elegant and thoroughly imaginative approach to macrobiotic cuisine. She often concludes her multicourse feasts with a silky-textured ice. Utilizing ingredients from the traditional washoku pantry, Ms. Kano updates them inventively. One such foodstuff, ama-zaké, a fermented sweet rice mash traditionally consumed as a health drink and sipped on certain ceremonial occasions, makes a fabulous nondairy "ice cream."

Asian cultures have a long history of using black sesame, both medicinally and to make sweet snacks. Currently, black sesame ice cream is wildly popular in Japan. In this recipe, ama-zaké transforms black sesame paste into a silky smooth, intensely nutty ebony ice. Warning: This creamy, decadent dessert is addictive!

SERVES 4

1 cup ama-zaké (page 51)
1/4 cup black sesame paste (page 46), stirred to blend oil thoroughly
1/4 teaspoon soy sauce

Most packages of *ama-zaké* contain about 250 grams (sometimes subdivided into five packets of 50 grams each), which measures just short of a standard American dry measuring cup. Add cold water to total 1 cup.

Place the *ama-zaké* in a blender or food processor and pulse until creamy and smooth. Add the sesame paste and continue to pulse until fully blended.

Drizzle in the soy sauce. It will mellow the intense sweetness of the *ama-zaké* and heighten the nuttiness of the sesame. Pulse again to make sure the mixture is smooth, lustrous, and the consistency of very thick cream.

Pour the sesame mixture into a freezer-safe pint container with a snug-fitting lid. Tap the container gently on a counter-top to force out any air bubbles that might be trapped below the surface. Cover tightly and freeze for at least 4 hours.

The final sorbet is soft, creamy, and easy to scoop out smoothly. To keep scoops perfectly round, you can shape them ahead and refreeze them in a waxed paper–lined container. When ready to serve, place in well-chilled dishes.

Kitchen Harmony

Less costly than the paste, and probably easier to obtain in North American markets, black sesame seeds can be dry-roasted and crushed to make a similar frozen treat. The texture will not be as creamy, but the flavor is still intensely nutty, and the slight crunchi-ness is not unlike praline. If you want to make the black sesame ice from whole seeds, use $1/3$ cup and dry-roast them (page 85). Transfer the still-warm seeds to the clean, dry bowl of a food processor and pulse until crushed to the consistency of moist sand. Scrape down the sides of the bowl occasionally to make sure the seeds are evenly crushed. Add the *ama-zaké* and continue to pulse until well blended. Drizzle in the soy sauce, and pulse again to mix well. Transfer the mixture to a freezer-safe container and tap gently on a countertop to force out any air bubbles that might be trapped below the surface. Cover tightly and freeze until completely firm, about 4 hours.

Harmony at Table

Because this frozen dessert is jet black, some diners mistakenly imagine it will taste of anise because it looks like licorice.

For an especially dramatic presentation, nestle a scoop of the ice in a milky-glazed, rough-hewn ceramic bowl. Add a bright yellow whole chestnut in syrup (page 46) and place a red lacquered spoon, in readiness, nearby. Unlike the rude shock of metal, the satiny sur-face of lacquered wood feels luxurious against the lips when eating frozen foods.

Or serve the dark sesame ice in brightly colored glass or pottery dishes garnished with Green Tea Chocolate-Almond Clusters (page 300) or shredded coconut.

GREEN TEA CHOCOLATE-ALMOND CLUSTERS

MATCHA-CHOKKO

Blending white chocolate with green tea is a winning combination, one that tones down the cloying sweetness of white chocolate with the fresh, grassy bitterness of green tea. I first tasted this appealing mix a few years ago on the occasion of White Day, March 14, when men give gifts of white chocolate to all the women who gave them dark chocolate on February 14. Reciprocity is an important aspect of gift giving and has been incorporated into Valentine's Day rituals in Japan.

Although the history of chocolate in Japan goes back several hundred years, the consumption of it at today's levels is definitely a postwar phenomenon. In general, the Japanese believe that all women have a sweet tooth, while men prefer salty foods. And, until the mid-1970s, the commercial market for chocolate in Japan was almost exclusively female. Then came the introduction of Valentine's Day, but with a twist. In the Japanese version, women give to men. Women are expected to buy small gifts of chocolate for the "important" men in their lives—father, teacher, boss, husband, or boyfriend. Because pressure is put on women to conform to this ritual, it is called giri chokko, *or "obligatory chocolate." (Giri is one of those guilt-laden words for which the Japanese have a fondness, and* chokko *is short for chocolate.)*

These nut clusters, made of slivered almonds and white chocolate infused with jade-colored matcha, *are a fitting reward for having fulfilled Valentine duties. For superior flavor, check the label on the white chocolate to make sure it contains cocoa butter.*

MAKES A DOZEN CLUSTERS

3 ounces white chocolate, finely chopped (about $1/4$ cup)

2 teaspoons matcha (page 54)

2 ounces unsalted, slivered almonds (about $1/4$ cup)

To melt the chocolate, place it in a double boiler. Care needs to be taken to avoid moisture when melting it (any moisture, even a thin film of steam, can make the chocolate seize, or develop lumps). Ideally, the water in the bottom of the boiler will be between 110° F and 120° F. Stir with a spoon until it melts completely. When you lift up the spoon, the molten chocolate should flow easily in ribbons back into the pan.

In a small bowl, combine the *matcha* with a small spoonful of the molten white chocolate and stir well to mix thoroughly. Gradually add the remaining chocolate, stirring constantly until well mixed.

Spread cooking parchment on a flat work surface. Toss the slivered almonds into the melted green tea chocolate. With a spatula, scrape this mixture out onto parchment paper in a dozen mounds and allow them to dry and set. In a dry, cool room, this will take about 2 hours. When dry, peel the clusters off of the parchment. For extended storage, transfer to a closed container and place on a cool, dark shelf for up to 3 weeks.

Serve with strong brewed coffee or tea (either green or English-style black tea).

ZENSAI PARFAIT

Nearly every traditional tea parlor in Japan will offer some varia-tion on the warm, sweet adzuki bean concoction known as zensai. My updated version of this washoku classic is a multitextured, multilayered affair I pile into tall glasses and call a parfait. I top a scoop of green tea ice cream with a shower of crunchy corn flakes (trust me on this—it works) and a spoonful of warm, chunky bean jam (think hot fudge sauce), repeat the order, and then top the whole thing off with a dollop of whipped cream and a bright yellow chestnut.

SERVES 4

- ¹/₂ cup heavy whipping cream, icy cold
- 1¹/₂ tablespoons powdered sugar
- ¹/₂ teaspoon vanilla extract
- 4 kuri no kanrō ni (page 46)
- 1 cup Chunky Red Bean Jam (page 108)
- 1 pint Green Tea Ice Cream (page 296)
- 1 cup unsweetened corn flakes or other whole-grain cereal

In a bowl, using a handheld electric mixer or a whisk, whip the cream until soft peaks form. Sprinkle in the powdered sugar and continue to beat until the cream stiffens. Drizzle in the vanilla extract and beat until well mixed and stiff peaks hold their shape. Fit a pastry bag with a star tip and fill the bag with the whipped cream. Chill until ready to use.

Drain the chestnuts, returning any excess syrup to the glass jar in which they were packed.

Place the red bean jam in a small pan or in the top pan of a double boiler. Add 1 tablespoon of the chestnut syrup, place the pan over low heat, and heat, stirring to prevent scorching. When the sauce is glossy, thick, and slightly aromatic, after about 2 minutes, remove from the heat and let cool to room temperature, or chill in the refrigerator.

In each of 4 tall glasses, assemble the parfaits. Begin with a small scoop of ice cream. Next add some corn flakes, and then spoon in some of the bean jam. Repeat to make another layer each of ice cream, corn flakes, and bean jam.

To finish each parfait, pipe out a swirling mound of whipped cream on top, and then set a single chestnut at a jaunty angle on the peak. Serve immediately with long-handled spoons.

WAFŪ WAFFLE

Japan's genteel tea-parlor culture thrives in tandem with the frantic pace of modern urban life. Although many classy confectionery-shops-cum-cafés inspired by French pâtisseries *prosper in Tokyo, I prefer to seek out* kanmi-dokoro, *or "places to consume traditional sweets," when I want a late-afternoon pick-me-up. Sometimes my taste runs toward classic preparations, such as abé kawa mochi, a type of warm and gooey rice taffy dusted with toasted soy flour that is particularly welcome on a chilly winter day, or Uji kintoki, shaved ice mounded over red bean jam and topped with jade-colored tea syrup that refreshes on a sticky summer day. More often, I order cross-cultural creations such as these Japanese-style waffles.*

Somewhat like pie à la mode (only far better, I think), the contrast of warm and crisp waffle with creamy, cold ice cream is delightful. And the deeply ridged waffle anchors the ice cream (it can't slide away as it begins to soften), trapping the syrup, and the bean jam, too. You will need self-rising flour, a low-gluten wheat flour that comes already mixed with baking soda and salt, to make the waffle batter.

SERVES 4

Waffle Batter
1 small egg
³/₄ cup whole milk
1 cup self-rising flour

¹/₂ teaspoon vegetable oil
1 cup Chunky Red Bean Jam (page 108)
1 pint vanilla ice cream
2 tablespoons kinako (page 14)
¹/₂ teaspoon ground cinnamon
¹/₂ cup Brown Sugar Syrup (page 110)

To make the waffle batter, in a bowl, combine the egg, milk, and flour and stir to mix thoroughly. Set the batter aside for a few minutes to let the baking soda do its work (bubbles will appear and break on the surface). This "rising" step ensures that you will end up with waffles that are light and airy and have a crisp crust.

I find that even waffle irons coated with a nonstick surface benefit from a swabbing with vegetable oil. Before you preheat a waffle iron, moisten a swab of sturdy paper towel with the oil and use it to wipe all the surfaces that will come in contact with the batter.

Preheat the waffle iron. When it indicates that it is ready (most models have a lamp feature that alerts you; follow the directions that came with your iron), pour in the batter. Make 4 smaller waffles each about 3 inches across, and halve them on the diagonal. Or make 1 very large waffle, about 10 inches in diameter, and use wedges or squares for individual servings. You can keep the first waffles warm in a preheated 200°F oven while you make subsequent ones.

For each serving, place a single waffle wedge or square in a shallow bowl or on a plate that has a flange or deep rim. Top with ¹/₄ cup of the bean jam and nestle a scoop of vanilla ice cream alongside. In a small bowl or cup, stir together the *kinako* and cinnamon. Then, using a sifter or fine-mesh strainer, dust the ice cream with the mixture. Set another waffle wedge or square on top of the jam and drizzle a little of the sugar syrup on top and around the bowl or plate. Put out additional syrup on the table and serve immediately.

FALL FRUITS WITH FLAVORED MISO SAUCE

AKI NO MIKAKU

In Japan, autumn announces its arrival at markets with Aki no Mikaku, the "Delicacies of Fall." Among the many eating pleasures that the cool days bring are firm, honey-sweet persimmons; plump, rosy-fleshed figs; and crisp, juicy pears and apples. These fruits are best just peeled and sliced and served with a flavored miso dip. The salty-sweet miso complements the fruit in much the same way that a sharp cheese marries well with certain fruits.

Almost any variety of apple or pear will do, but Asian pears and firm, yet juicy Japanese apples pair particularly well with miso dips. And try to find Japanese persimmons that are fully ripe long before they turn soft. Their crunchy texture adds to the enjoyment of this dish.

SERVES 4

    1 persimmon, preferably Jiro (page 27), 8 to 10 ounces
    1 Asian pear, preferably kosui nashi or shinsui nashi
       (page 27), 8 to 10 ounces
    1 apple, preferably Mutsu or Fuji, 8 to 10 ounces
    Fresh lemon juice (optional)
    4 large figs, 2 to 3 ounces each
    2 tablespoons Citrusy Miso (page 102)
    2 tablespoons Pungent Red Miso Sauce (page 101)

Rinse all the fruits under cold running water and pat them dry. Trim off the stem end from each fruit. If you are adept at making a continuous circular peel, known as *katsura muki* (page 68), peel the persimmon, pear, and apple using this technique. It is desirable because it creates slight ridges that help the miso dip cling to the cut fruit later.

If you have peeled the persimmon, place it, stem end down, on a cutting board and cut it into 8 wedges. Or you can place the unpeeled persimmon, stem end down, on the board and cut it into quarters. Then, cut each quarter in half to make 8 wedges in all. Peel each wedge in a single, lengthwise stroke, cutting from the blossom end to the stem end.

Use the tip of your knife to dislodge the visible black seeds in the wedges. Other seeds, embedded deeper in the wedges, can be removed as the wedges are being eaten.

The pear can be peeled and cut in the same manner as the persimmon, using either technique. Trim its core away once the fruit is in wedges.

The apple can be peeled and cut in the same manner as the persimmon, using either technique. Trim its core away once the fruit is in wedges. Or you can leave the rosy peel intact, but slice the fruit into thinner wedges because the peels on Japanese apple varieties can be tough.

If you are concerned about the pear and apple wedges turning brown (from contact with the air), brush the pieces with a bit of lemon juice diluted with a few drops of water.

Japanese figs are large and have maroon skins often striped with green. The flesh is fairly firm and creamy white near the skin and rosy at the center. To peel, pull back the skin, much like peeling a banana, working from the pointed stem end to the bulbous flowering end. Cut each fig lengthwise into quarters.

Arrange the cut fruits on a platter or on individual plates. Place a small spoonful of each of the miso sauces beside the fruits. The caramel overtones of the light miso sauce are particularly good with the apple and figs, while I prefer the fudge-like dark miso sauce with the persimmon and pear.

COMPOTE OF EARLY SUMMER FRUITS WITH CITRUSY MISO SAUCE

SHOKA NO SACHI

Japan's orchards produce magnificent summer fruits, each variety basking in the kitchen limelight for just a few weeks before yielding to the next in succession. The Japanese call this Shoka no Sachi *(literally, the "Bounty of Early Summer").*

I know I must bear the oppressive rains that begin late in May to enjoy my beloved biwa *(loquats) and apricots in June and July. I reward myself by making this early summer fruit compote. Any number of fruits, individually or in combination, can be used (see notes for suggestions on American berries, nectarines, and melons) to make compotes, but if you can find a source for Japanese loquats, you are in for a special treat.*

SERVES 4

8 apricots, about 2$^1/_2$ ounces each

8 loquats, preferably a Japanese variety, about
    1$^1/_2$ ounces each

Grated zest and juice of $^1/_2$ lemon

$^1/_2$ cup cold water

$^1/_3$ cup sugar

2 tablespoons saké

1 acorn-size knob fresh ginger, preferably new ginger,
    about $^1/_4$ ounce

2 tablespoons Citrusy Miso (page 102)

You need to divide the fruits into neat, easy-to-eat segments before poaching. Apricots and Japanese loquats are freestone, rather than cling, making this fairly simple to do. Apricots are eaten with their skin intact, and the loquats peel easily.

To prepare the apricots, rinse the fruits under running cold water and then pat dry, being careful not to bruise them. Using the tip of a very sharp knife, draw a shallow line around 1 apricot, following the natural indentation of the fruit and

beginning and finishing at the stem end. You should hear a light scraping noise as the tip of the knife touches the pit. Pull the halves apart and then pry the pit loose with your fingertips. Leave the skins intact. Repeat with the remaining apricots to yield 16 halves in all.

To prepare the loquats, rinse the fruits under running cold water and then pat dry, exerting just enough pressure to rub away fuzz without bruising the fruit. This loosens the skins, making them easier to peel. To peel, starting at the stem end of 1 fruit, pull back the skin, much like peeling a banana. Trim off the flowering (puckered) end. Cut the fruit in half and scoop out the seeds, pulling away as much membrane as possible without bruising the fruit. Repeat with the other loquats to yield 16 halves in all.

In a bowl, toss the apricot and loquat halves with the lemon juice to coat evenly, and then arrange the fruits in a snug single layer in a skillet or shallow saucepan about 7 inches in diameter. Set the pan aside.

To make the poaching liquid, in a saucepan, combine the water, sugar, and saké and bring to a simmer over medium-high heat, stirring to dissolve the sugar. Cook the poaching liquid for about 1 minute, or until small bubbles begin to appear.

Meanwhile, peel the ginger and add the peels to the poaching liquid. Grate the ginger and squeeze to extract about 1 teaspoon juice (page 71) and set it aside. Continue to simmer the poaching liquid for about 3 minutes, or until it thickens slightly and the bubbles become larger and foamy.

Pour the poaching liquid over the fruit; it will reach barely half its depth. If you have an *otoshi-buta* (page 84) that is not stained with soy sauce from soy-simmered preparations, it can be placed directly on the fruit. If you do not have one, top the fruit with a sheet of cooking parchment cut $^1/_2$ inch smaller in diameter than the pan and lay a small, flat lid from another pan on top of the parchment. The lid should apply just enough light pressure to keep the parchment in contact with the fruit. Place the pan over medium heat, bring to a simmer, and poach the fruit for 2 minutes, or until the fruits turn translucent.

Remove the pan from the heat and let the fruits cool to room temperature with the dropped lid in place. It is during this cooling-down period that the flavors develop and enhance one another. The skins of the apricots will have loosened and wrinkled, but they are flavorful and should remain part of the presentation.

When the fruits are cool, remove and discard the ginger peels and, using a slotted spoon, transfer the fruits to a glass jar or other nonreactive container, cover, and chill in the refrigerator for at least 20 minutes and up to several days.

Add the miso sauce and ginger juice to the poaching liquid remaining in the pan and stir to mix. This sauce can be served at room temperature or chilled.

When ready to serve, spoon a pool of the miso sauce onto each of 4 chilled plates or shallow bowls. Arrange the fruits— 4 pieces each of apricot and loquat—over the sauce. Garnish with the lemon zest and serve at once.

Kitchen Harmony

You can vary this recipe depending on which fruits you find at the market. Nectarines and plums (especially Greengage plums) can be poached in the same manner as the apricots, with their skins intact. If you want to use berries and melon, do not poach them. Instead, make a lemon-infused syrup for berries or a ginger-infused syrup for melons and add it to the miso sauce. Serve the sauce with the berries or melon.

POACHED PEACHES IN LEMON-GINGER MISO SAUCE
HAKUTŌ NO DENGAKU

Delicate white peaches and pungent dark miso may seem like an unlikely combination, but just as savory cheeses complement the natural sweetness of fruit, so, too, does the salty-spicy sweetness of the miso sauce.

SERVES 4

> 4 very ripe white peaches, preferably a Japanese variety, 6 to 8 ounces each
> Grated zest and juice of $^1/_2$ lemon
> $^1/_2$ cup cold water
> $^1/_3$ cup sugar
> 2 tablespoons saké
> 1 walnut-sized knob fresh ginger, preferably new ginger, about $^1/_2$ ounce
> 2 tablespoons Pungent Red Miso Sauce (page 101)

All white peaches need to be peeled before poaching. Rinse the fruits under running cold water and then pat dry, exerting just enough pressure to rub away fuzz without bruising the fruit. This loosens the skins, making them easier to peel later.

Some peach varieties are freestone, while others are cling. The latter are more challenging to halve or quarter, which is why I suggest here that you make 6 to 8 wedgelike sections, removing each in turn from the pit. Using the tip of a very sharp knife, draw a shallow line around 1 peach, following the natural indentation of the fruit and beginning and finishing at the stem end. You should hear a light scraping noise as the tip of the knife touches the pit. Try twisting to pull half of the fruit away from the pit. If you sense resistance, assume the peach is a cling type and proceed to slice into either 6 or 8 wedges. Try removing the peel with your fingertips, beginning at the stem end. If you feel resistance, use a knife. Repeat with the remaining peaches.

With a pastry brush, paint the peeled peach wedges with the lemon juice. Arrange the wedges in a snug single layer, slightly overlapping them, in a shallow saucepan about 7 inches in diameter.

To make the poaching liquid, in a saucepan, combine the water, sugar, and saké and bring to a simmer over medium-high heat, stirring to dissolve the sugar. Cook the poaching liquid for about 1 minute, or until small bubbles begin to appear.

Meanwhile, peel the ginger and add the peels to the poaching liquid. Grate the ginger and squeeze to extract about 2 teaspoons juice (page 71). Set the juice aside.

Pour the poaching liquid over the fruit; it will barely cover the wedges. If you have an *otoshi-buta* (page 84) that is not stained with soy sauce from soy-simmered preparations, it can be placed directly on the fruit. If you do not have one, top the fruit with a sheet of cooking parchment cut 1/2 inch smaller in diameter than the pan and lay a small, flat lid from another pan on top of the parchment. The lid should apply just enough light pressure to keep the parchment in contact with the peaches. Place the pan over medium heat, bring to a gentle simmer, and poach the peaches for 4 minutes. If the fruit looks in danger of scorching, add a few drops of water. The peaches may still be quite firm, depending on the variety, which is fine. When cooking some white peach varieties, the poaching liquid becomes tinted with pink.

Add half of the ginger juice (about 1 teaspoon) to the pan and swirl to distribute. Remove the pan from the heat and let the peaches cool to room temperature with both the inner lid and a lid that fits the saucepan snugly, trapping in moisture. It is during this cooling-down period that the flavors develop and enhance one another.

When the peaches are cool, remove and discard the ginger peels and, using a slotted spoon, carefully transfer the peaches to individual serving dishes. Cover the dishes with plastic wrap and chill in the refrigerator for at least 30 minutes and up to 24 hours.

Add the miso sauce and the remaining ginger juice (about 1 teaspoon) to the poaching liquid remaining in the pan and stir to mix. This sauce can be served at room temperature or chilled.

When ready to serve, spoon the miso sauce over the peaches. Garnish with the lemon zest and serve at once.

COFFEE ZELI

This recipe for coffee-flavored gelatin is fun to serve in demitasse cups, garnished with a dollop of sweet whipped cream. Using kan-ten, which is extracted from aquatic plants, makes this dessert firmer than aspics made with ordinary gelatin.

SERVES 4 TO 6

1 packet (4 grams) powdered kanten (page 41),
    or 1 stick kanten, about 7 inches long by 1 inch thick
    and 1 inch wide

$^1/_4$ cup water

$1^3/_4$ cups strong freshly brewed coffee or 2 tablespoons
    instant coffee dissolved in $1^3/_4$ cups boiling water

2 tablespoons sugar

$^1/_2$ cup heavy whipping cream, icy cold

$1^1/_2$ tablespoons powdered sugar

If using powdered *kanten,* dissolve the contents of the packet in the water. Stir to dissolve completely; the grains will swell slightly. Add the coffee, stirring to combine well. Transfer the mixture to a 2-quart nonreactive saucepan.

If using stick *kanten,* break it into 2 or 3 pieces and place them in a bowl with cold water to cover. If you have an *otoshi-buta* (page 84) that is not stained with soy sauce, use it to sub-merge the *kanten,* or use a small plate. Allow the *kanten* to soak for 5 or 6 minutes, or until softened. When the *kanten* is pli-able, squeeze out and discard all the liquid. Shred into small pieces and place them in a 2-quart nonreactive saucepan. Add the water and $^1/_2$ cup of the coffee, place over medium heat, and cook, stirring constantly, until the *kanten* dissolves. Add the remaining $1^1/_4$ cups coffee in a steady stream, stirring to combine.

Whether you have used stick or powdered gelatin, add the sugar to the coffee mixture and stir to dissolve completely. Bring the mixture to a boil over medium heat and then adjust the heat to maintain a gentle simmer. Cook for 2 to 3 minutes, stirring. The mixture will reduce and thicken ever so slightly.

Divide the mixture among 4 to 6 demitasse cups. If bubbles form as you pour, lance them or drag them with the point of a toothpick to the edge of the cup. Pull the bubbles up the sides of the cup to remove them. Let the coffee mixture set (and cool down) before covering with plastic wrap. Although the gelatin will set without refrigeration, chilling it (for at least 30 min-utes or up to 2 days) will improve its flavor.

In a bowl, using a handheld electric mixer or a whisk, whip the cream until soft peaks form. Sprinkle in the pow-dered sugar and continue to beat until stiff peaks form. Cover and refrigerate until serving.

When ready to serve, top each portion with a small dollop of whipped cream. Serve with a spoon.

Kitchen Harmony

More traditional aspics, such as sweet bean paste–based *yōkan* and savory stock-based *nikogori,* are sometimes molded in a special con-tainer called a *nagashi-bako.* If you do not have demitasse cups or other small, attractive containers or a *nagashi-bako* in which to make the gel-atin, pour the coffee into a small chilled glass loaf pan (about 6 by 2 by $2^1/_2$ inches). Let the coffee mixture set (and cool down) before covering with plastic wrap, and then chill to improve its flavor.

To unmold the gelatin for serving, dip a butter knife into cold water and then run it around the inner edges of the loaf pan. Invert the pan onto a cutting board and lift off the pan. Cut the block of coffee gel-atin into $^1/_4$-inch cubes. Divide the diced gelatin among 4 dessert bowls. Top each portion with a small dollop of whipped cream.

RESOURCES

Most retail operations outside of Japan that stock Japanese food-stuffs and equipment cater to a wide range of customers, from homesick Japanese college kids (who crave junk food, instant ramen, and prepared food ready for takeout) to avid fans of local Japanese restaurants (who often want do-it-yourself sushi kits). You will be most successful in obtaining quality products if you first familiarize yourself with the items you want to purchase (consult the corresponding entries in The *Washoku* Pantry and In the *Washoku* Kitchen).

The businesses described below are mostly online enterprises, though I also include a few actual stores where I, or some of my recipe-testing volunteers, have shopped. Most fresh foods, especially tōfu, vegetables, and fish, will need to be purchased in your own community. I close this section with a brief market tour of a few of my favorite places in and around Tokyo.

For those readers who would like to know more about A Taste of Culture, the culinary arts program I offer in Tokyo, I invite you to visit my website at: www.tasteofculture.com

Katagiri
www.katagiri.com
Phone: (212) 755-3566

Their New York store is in midtown Manhattan. Foodstuffs are in the main store, equipment is in a small annex a few doors down the block. They stock (or can order) *otoshi-buta* (dropped lids), *shokutaku tsukémono ki* (they call them "pickle presses"), and many kinds of graters and *suribachi*. Online you can order many of the basic pantry items: rice vinegar; soy sauce; *Hidaka kombu; hijiki; iriko; kanten* sticks; Saikyō and Hatchō misos; California-grown, Japanese-style rice; multigrain mixtures to cook with rice; *konnyaku* (they list it as "yam cake"); *kampyō;* and *kiriboshi daikon.*

Also in New York City, catering largely to a young, college crowd are **JAS Mart** (3 locations: 35 St. Marks Pl., between 2nd and 3rd Aves., phone: 212-420-6370; 2847 Broadway, between 110th and 111th Sts., phone: 212-866-4780; and 34 E. 23rd St., phone: 212-387-8882) and **Sunrise Mart** (4 Stuyvesant St., between E. 9th St. and 3rd Ave., phone: 212-598-3040).

Kitazawa Seed Company
www.kitazawaseed.com
Phone: (510) 595-1188; fax:(510) 595-1860

If you have a small garden, or can manage several deep pots on a windowsill, I urge you to grow some Japanese vegetables and herbs for yourself. Kitazawa has seeds (with helpful instructions for the novice on planting, pruning, and harvesting your crop) for most of the fresh vegetables I call for in my recipes. Wondering where to start? Try some of the turnips (the *hinona* make incredible pickles, as do the *hidabeni* varieties); *shiso* plants will provide you with lots of herbaceous leaves, edible flowers, and seed pods; Yasakanaga (a hybrid) eggplants have tender skins and are easy to grow; *komatsuna* is a bit challenging to grow, but definitely worth the effort.

Korin
www.korin.com, www.korin.com/knives/knife_jp.php
Phone: (800) 626-2172, (212) 587-7021

Korin supplies many Japanese restaurants with equipment and tableware, but the company does not limit its business to the trade. They carry difficult-to-find items such as *otoshi-buta* (dropped lids), rice molds, and a dizzying array of knives and other cutting implements. Their informative website includes a minitutorial on the subject of knives. Purchases can be made online or at their showroom, located at 57 Warren Street, in the Tribeca section of Manhattan.

Maruwa
www.maruwa.com/index_e.html

Maruwa has several stores in the San Francisco Bay Area and an extensive line of products, primarily shelf-stable pantry items, that can be ordered online. Their website includes full-color photos of most of their product line. This site can be a one-stop shopping trip for most of the basics: miso (Saikyō shiro miso, Hatchō miso, Sendai miso, *mugi* miso), soy sauce, rice vinegar, *kombu* (their *yama dashi kombu* is equivalent to my *ma kombu;* their *dashi kombu* is equivalent to my *Hidaka kombu*), and Shirakiku brand *niboshi iriko* that they translate as "dried whole anchovy."

Maruwa carries respected Japanese brands such as Riken (known for their *wakamé* and other sea vegetables) and Ninben and Marutomo (known for their *katsuo-bushi*), Shinsei (known for their sesame seeds and sesame paste), both S&B and House brands for seasonings such as wasabi, mustard, *ichimi*, and *shichimi*. In addition, quality *kuro-zatō*, many kinds of dried noodles (soba, *sōmen, udon, kishimen, harusamé*), *kiriboshi daikon, kampyō*, and a wide selection of green teas are also available. Refrigerated items include various kinds of tōfu and *konnyaku*.

Three other California-based operations are **Marukai Market, Mitsuwa Marketplace,** and **Tokyo Fish Market**. Although Mitsuwa and Marukai have websites that provide directions to their actual stores (Mitsuwa also has stores in New Jersey and Illinois; Marukai's outlets are all in southern California) their products are not available for order online. Tokyo Fish Market, just around the corner from my publisher's offices in Berkeley, California, sells fresh herbs and Japanese vegetables, fresh fish, and an array of noodles and other shelf-stable pantry items, as well as a small selection of cooking equipment and tableware. Mitsuwa Marketplace: www.mitsuwa.com; phone in Los Angeles, CA: (213) 687-6699 or (877) 648-7892 (mail order). Marukai Market: www.marukai.com; phone in Los Angeles, CA: (213) 893-7200. Tokyo Fish Market: 1220 San Pablo Ave., Berkeley, CA; phone: (510) 524-7243.

Miyamoto Foods, Inc.
www.sushilinks.com
Phone in Montreal, Quebec: (514) 481-1952

Their website is almost exclusively devoted to sushi; their store in Montreal, however, is well stocked with basic pantry items.

Quality Natural Foods
www.qualitynaturalfoods.com
Toll-free phone: (888) 392-9237

The health-promoting potential of foods such as *uméboshi* plums and various sea vegetables has led companies, such as this one, that specialize in natural foods to stock many items imported from Japan. (I do not recommend using marine plants harvested from American coastal areas, since they are often seasoned to appeal to American tastes in much the same way that tōfu and other soy products are flavored in nontraditional ways.) This website also offers equipment such as *suribachi*, pickle presses, knives, and graters.

South River Miso
www.southrivermiso.com
Phone in Conway, MA: (413) 369-4057; fax: (413) 369-4299
Email: mail@southrivermiso.com

I first met Christian Elwell, proprietor of South River Miso, many years ago at a health food trade show. I have been a fan of his products ever since, especially his golden millet (rather sweet and highly textured, but utterly wonderful in many of the miso-based sauces in this book) and mellow barley (it has a rich, heady aroma) miso pastes. South River Miso also makes unusual varieties of miso from chickpeas and adzuki beans. Their website provides detailed information on how miso is made.

Uwajimaya
www.uwajimaya.com
Phone in Seattle: (206) 624-6248;
Phone in Oregon: (503) 643-4512

Their stores in the Seattle area and in Oregon are well stocked with a wide range of products that cater to second- and third-generation Asian Americans and to adventurous locals who like to cook with authentic products. Their website has an interesting and informative "dictionary" of items, but no pictures or label information.

• • •

I conclude this resource section with a few highlights from my adopted hometown, Tokyo. These are old-fashioned, mom-and-pop–style establishments that I have patronized for decades. These stores have no email addresses or websites. In order to verify their (often quirky) business hours, I provide local (Japan) phone numbers; once you are in Tokyo, I suggest you have someone call for you (perhaps a smattering of English will be spoken by the person who answers the phone, but don't count on it).

In Tsukiji's outer market, **Tsukiji Jōgai Ichiba**, most shops are open from 6 AM until about 1 PM:

Kawabé Shōten
4-7-5 Tsukiji KY Bldg. 1st floor
Chuo-ku, Tokyo
Phone: 03-3541-3019

Purveyors of superior *katsuo-bushi* fish flakes, their top-of-the-line *tokujō* is exquisite stuff—rich and smoky, gossamer-thin shavings. Their fresh-dried *iriko* sardines pack a flavor wallop. The best of Kawabé's goods are sold loose, by weight, but they also carry some sealed, prepackaged versions of many of their products.

Suita Shōten
4-11-1 Tsukiji, Chuo-ku, Tokyo
Phone: 03-3541-6931

Their fabulous *kombu* is pictured on page 43. In addition to numerous varieties of kelp, they carry *kombu amé*, a chewy, caramel-like candy made from kelp and barley malt (individually wrapped, they keep for months; the inner wrapping is edible rice paper).

Yabu Kita En
4-7-5 Tsukiji KY Bldg. 1st floor
Chuo-ku, Tokyo
Phone: 03-3542-2041

Terrific teas, mostly from Shizuoka, southwest of Tokyo. *Matcha iri genmaicha*, a mixture of toasted brown rice and green tea dusted with ceremonial *matcha*, is their most popular item. Freshly brewed samples are often available. Teas can be vacuum-sealed when you buy them, for simple transport home. In addition to teas, Yabu Kita En sells the highest grade of toasted nori.

In **Kitchijoji**, a bustling modern community on the western outskirts of Tokyo, you can still buy food and supplies in a warren of cramped alleys across the street from the train station shopping mall. The retro-looking covered arcade, known as Harmonica Yōko-chō, houses several of my favorite shops:

Tsuchiya Shōten
1-8-3 Honcho, Kitchijoji
Musashino-shi, Tokyo
Phone: 0422-22-2905

Many of the items pictured in this book were purchased at Tsuchiya, a pleasantly cluttered shop specializing in *kambutsu* (literally, "dried things"). Top quality pantry staples such as *kombu, katsuo-bushi , kiriboshi daikon, hijiki, iriko, kampyō,* and dried shiitaké mushrooms are sold here. Tsuchiya also sells their own tasty version of *kombu amé* (kelp caramels).

Tsukada Suisan
1-1-8 Honcho, Kitchijoji
Musashino-shi, Tokyo
phone: 0422-22-4829

Delicious fish sausages (especially the *chikuwa*); if you don't have a local kitchen in which to cook, you can nibble the fully cooked sausage right there.

Yamariya
1-2-5 Honcho, Kitchijoji
Musashino-shi, Tokyo
Phone: 0422-21-4188; fax 0422-22-2043

The aroma of roasting *hōjicha* that emanates from this purveyor fills the marketplace, beckoning shoppers. The display case at the sales counter shows samples of the dozens of teas they carry. Freshly brewed samples of their Inokashira house tea (a mildly grassy, pale green infusion) are often available. This and the roasted *hōjicha* tea can be purchased in vacuum-sealed packages that travel well.

The old market in **Ogikubo**, where I lived and operated a cooking school in the 1970s, was torn down about twenty years ago. Many of the displaced vendors gathered under one roof, in an extension to the train station's Lumine vertical mall. Three of my favorites there are:

Inageya
Ogikubo Town Seven, Kami Ogi
Suginami-ku, Tokyo
Phone: 03-3391-6581

Incredible chicken; several prepared items (chicken meatballs, skewers of yakitori) for immediate gratification.

Momii
Ogikubo Town Seven, Kami Ogi
Suginami-ku, Tokyo
Phone: 03-3398-3661

Although soy-stewed sea vegetables and fish prepared in the *tsukudani* style will keep well for several days if refrigerated, unless you live in Tokyo, Momii's scrumptious tidbits are best enjoyed on the spot.

Nomichi
Ogikubo Town Seven, Kami Ogi
Suginami-ku, Tokyo
Phone: 03-3392-3315

They carry the best quality adzuki beans (including *sasage mamé* that "bleed" a gorgeous scarlet shade) and *daizu* (including black *kuro mamé* and pale green "nightingale" *uguisu mamé*) in addition to other *kambutsu* staples.

INDEX